Modification

Modifiers and modification have been a major focus of inquiry for as long as the formal study of semantics has existed, and remain at the heart of major theoretical debates in the field. Modification offers comprehensive coverage of a wide range of topics, including vagueness and gradability, comparatives and degree constructions, the lexical semantics of adjectives and adverbs, crosscategorial regularities, and the relation between meaning and syntactic category. Morzycki guides the reader through the varied and sometimes mysterious phenomena surrounding modification and the ideas that have been proposed to account for them. Presenting disparate approaches in a consistent analytical framework, this accessibly written work, which includes an extensive glossary of technical terms, is essential reading for researchers and students of all levels in linguistics, the philosophy of language, and psycholinguistics.

- Uses an accessible, pedagogical style for greater understanding of the empirical phenomena, theoretical proposals, and analytical tools
- Provides detailed, worked-out examples of technical computations
- Includes a glossary of technical terminology

MARCIN MORZYCKI is Associate Professor of Linguistics at Michigan State University.

KEY TOPICS IN SEMANTICS AND PRAGMATICS

'Key Topics in Semantics and Pragmatics' focuses on the main topics of study in semantics and pragmatics today. It consists of accessible yet challenging accounts of the most important issues, concepts and phenomena to consider when examining meaning in language. Some topics have been the subject of semantic and pragmatic study for many years, and are re-examined in this series in light of new developments in the field; others are issues of growing importance that have not so far been given a sustained treatment. Written by leading experts and designed to bridge the gap between textbooks and primary literature, the books in this series can either be used on courses and seminars, or as one-stop, succinct guides to a particular topic for individual students and researchers. Each book includes useful suggestions for further reading, discussion questions, and a helpful glossary.

Already published in the series:

Meaning and Humour by Andrew Goatly

Metaphor by L. David Ritchie

Imperatives by Mark Jary and Mikhail Kissine

Modification by Marcin Morzycki

Forthcoming titles:

The Semantics of Counting by Susan Rothstein

Game-Theoretic Pragmatics by Anton Benz

Pragmatics and the Philosophy of Language by Mitchell Green

Distributivity by George Tsoulas and Eytan Zweig

Implicature by Jacques Moeschler and Sandrine Zufferey

Experimental Pragmatics by Ira Noveck

Irony by Joana Garmendia

Semantics and Pragmatics in Sign Languages by Kathryn Davidson

Propositional Logic by Allen Hazen and Jeffrey Pelletier

Modification

MARCIN MORZYCKI

CAMBRIDGE
UNIVERSITY PRESS

CAMBRIDGE
UNIVERSITY PRESS

University Printing House, Cambridge CB2 8BS, United Kingdom

One Liberty Plaza, 20th Floor, New York, NY 10006, USA

477 Williamstown Road, Port Melbourne, VIC 3207, Australia

314-321, 3rd Floor, Plot 3, Splendor Forum, Jasola District Centre, New Delhi - 110025, India

79 Anson Road, #06-04/06, Singapore 079906

Cambridge University Press is part of the University of Cambridge.

It furthers the University's mission by disseminating knowledge in the pursuit of education, learning and research at the highest international levels of excellence.

www.cambridge.org
Information on this title: www.cambridge.org/9780521264167

© Marcin Morzycki 2016

This publication is in copyright. Subject to statutory exception and to the provisions of relevant collective licensing agreements, no reproduction of any part may take place without the written permission of Cambridge University Press.

First published 2016
First paperback edition 2019

A catalogue record for this publication is available from the British Library

Library of Congress Cataloging in Publication data
Morzycki, Marcin, author.
Modification / Marcin Morzycki.
  pages cm.
Includes bibliographical references and index.
ISBN 978-1-107-00975-2 (Hardback : alk. paper)
1. Grammar, Comparative and general–Adverbials. 2. Semantics.
3. Semantics (Philosophy)   I. Title.
P284.M67 2016
415–dc23   2015020026

ISBN 978-1-107-00975-2 Hardback
ISBN 978-0-521-26416-7 Paperback

Cambridge University Press has no responsibility for the persistence or accuracy of URLs for external or third-party internet websites referred to in this publication, and does not guarantee that any content on such websites is, or will remain, accurate or appropriate.

Contents

Acknowledgments   page x

1. Preliminaries   1
   1.1 Two problems   1
   1.2 What this book is and isn't   2
   1.3 Background assumptions   3
       1.3.1 Glossing logical notation   3
       1.3.2 Theoretical framework   4
       1.3.3 Notational and typographical conventions   7
   1.4 What, if anything, is modification?   8
   1.5 Roadmap   12
2. The lexical semantics of adjectives: more than just scales   13
   2.1 Introduction   13
   2.2 How adjectives and nouns combine: a typology   14
       2.2.1 Intersective interpretations   14
       2.2.2 Subsective interpretations   16
       2.2.3 Apparently subsective intersective interpretations   20
       2.2.4 Ordinary non-subsective adjectives   22
       2.2.5 Privative adjectives, which may not exist   24
   2.3 The type of adjectives and the nature of subsectivity   26
       2.3.1 How powerful are adjectives?   26
       2.3.2 Siegel: the Doublet Theory   30
       2.3.3 Larson: events inside the nominal extended projection   34
       2.3.4 The implicit-argument approach   41
       2.3.5 How much power is too much? Impossible adjectives   42
   2.4 The menagerie of adjectives   44
       2.4.1 A word about adjective classification   44
       2.4.2 Temporal-ordering adjectives   45

v

                2.4.3 Classificatory/relational adjectives 48
                2.4.4 The trouble with stone lions 53
                2.4.5 The attributive-with-infinitive construction 55
                2.4.6 Adnominal degree modifiers 57
        2.5 Adjectives where they have no right to be: adverbial readings 59
                2.5.1 A scope puzzle 59
                2.5.2 Frequency adjectives: the facts 60
                2.5.3 The adverbial reading of frequency adjectives 63
                2.5.4 The internal reading of frequency adjectives 67
                2.5.5 Average Americans and parasitic scope 68
                2.5.6 Sameness and difference 74
                2.5.7 Other adverbial readings and the bigger picture 77
        2.6 Adjective position and syntactic issues 79
                2.6.1 Attributive vs. predicative, prenominal vs. postnominal 79
                2.6.2 Indirect modification 81
                2.6.3 Stage-level/individual-level contrasts 82
                2.6.4 A focus position? 84
        2.7 What is it to be an adjective? 85
        2.8 Questions for further reflection and discussion 86
        2.9 Suggestions for further reading 87
3 Vagueness, degrees, and gradable predicates 88
        3.1 Introduction 88
        3.2 Vagueness 89
                3.2.1 Identifying vagueness 89
                3.2.2 Vagueness vs. ambiguity 91
                3.2.3 Vagueness vs. imprecision 93
                3.2.4 Some foundational questions 96
        3.3 Theories of vagueness and gradability: a false start 97
                3.3.1 Three approaches 97
                3.3.2 Fuzzy logic 98
        3.4 The inherent vagueness approach 100
                3.4.1 Extension gaps 100
                3.4.2 Precisification and supertruth 102
                3.4.3 Comparatives 104
                3.4.4 Degree words 107
                3.4.5 Degree functions and comparatives revisited 108
        3.5 The degree-based approach 109
                3.5.1 Degrees 109

Contents

        3.5.2 Gradable predicates   112
        3.5.3 Borderline cases and context-dependence   115
        3.5.4 The tautology and contradiction issue   117
        3.5.5 Comparatives   118
        3.5.6 Degree words   119
        3.5.7 Varieties of degrees   119
  3.6 Degree or not degree? That is the question   121
  3.7 Scales and the lexical semantics of adjectives   124
        3.7.1 Antonyms   124
        3.7.2 Open and closed scales   131
        3.7.3 Dimensional and non-dimensional adjectives   138
        3.7.4 Extreme adjectives   140
        3.7.5 Gradable modal adjectives   144
        3.7.6 On scales and categories   145
  3.8 Questions for further reflection and discussion   147
  3.9 Suggestions for further reading   148

4 Comparatives and their kin   149
  4.1 Introduction   149
  4.2 The syntax and semantics of the extended AP   150
        4.2.1 Getting terminology out of the way   150
        4.2.2 The unpronounced in comparative clauses   150
        4.2.3 First steps   152
        4.2.4 The big DegP view   157
        4.2.5 The small DegP view   159
        4.2.6 Scope and degree operators   163
        4.2.7 The Russell ambiguity   168
        4.2.8 Quantification and comparative clauses   169
  4.3 Other degree constructions   171
        4.3.1 Differential comparatives and measure phrases   171
        4.3.2 Equatives   173
        4.3.3 Superlatives   174
        4.3.4 Sufficiency and excess   176
        4.3.5 Degree exclamatives and degree questions   177
        4.3.6 Metalinguistic comparatives   178
        4.3.7 Comparison of deviation   180
        4.3.8 Indirect comparison   181
  4.4 Neutralization and positive-entailingness   183
  4.5 The crosslinguistic picture   186
        4.5.1 Measure phrases   186

- 4.5.2 Comparison strategies 187
- 4.5.3 How much degree is there in your degree constructions? 188
- 4.6 Questions for further reflection and discussion 191
- 4.7 Suggestions for further reading 191

5 Adverbs 193
- 5.1 Introduction 193
- 5.2 Classifying adverbials 194
- 5.3 The compositional puzzle 197
  - 5.3.1 Modifiers of propositions? 197
  - 5.3.2 Subject-oriented adverbs and the predicate-modifier approach 199
  - 5.3.3 Problems for the intersective approach 201
  - 5.3.4 Davidsonian events: the intersective approach redeemed 204
- 5.4 Manner and subject orientation 208
  - 5.4.1 Augmentation and passive-sensitivity 208
  - 5.4.2 The Neo-Davidsonian strategy and thematic roles 212
  - 5.4.3 Comparison classes and related tools 215
  - 5.4.4 The bottom-up analytical strategy 221
  - 5.4.5 Topic-orientation 223
  - 5.4.6 Is there such a thing as a manner? 226
- 5.5 Speaker-oriented adverbials 228
  - 5.5.1 Speech-act adverbials 228
  - 5.5.2 Evaluative adverbs 233
  - 5.5.3 Modal adverbs 235
  - 5.5.4 Polarity 236
- 5.6 Locative adverbials 237
  - 5.6.1 Types and positions of locative adverbials 237
  - 5.6.2 Vector Space Semantics 238
- 5.7 Adverbs as modifiers of adjectives 240
- 5.8 Phenomena we will mostly set aside 243
  - 5.8.1 Temporal adverbials 243
  - 5.8.2 Adverbs of quantification 245
- 5.9 Adverb order revisited 246
- 5.10 Questions for further reflection and discussion 248
- 5.11 Suggestions for further reading 249

6 Crosscategorial concerns 250
- 6.1 Introduction 250
- 6.2 Amounts and cardinality scales 251

        6.2.1 Quantity adjectives and number words   *251*
        6.2.2 Amount comparatives   *255*
  6.3 Gradability and non-adjectival predicates   *257*
        6.3.1 Verbal gradability   *257*
        6.3.2 Nominal gradability   *260*
  6.4 Hedging and reinforcing across categories   *262*
  6.5 Nonrestrictive modifiers   *267*
  6.6 Predicates of personal taste   *271*
  6.7 Questions for further reflection and discussion   *273*
  6.8 Suggestions for further reading   *274*
7 Taking stock   *276*
  7.1 Back to the beginning   *276*
  7.2 Where to from here?   *279*

Glossary   *284*
References   *298*
Index   *330*

Acknowledgments

A few years ago, I ran into a Polish expression: *nie mój cyrk, nie moje małpy* ('not my circus, not my monkeys'). It means 'ain't my problem'. Of course, with any published piece of work, it's **always** your monkey. You're responsible, no matter how big a mess it has made or how incompletely it discussed measure phrases in Chapter 6. And the thing about a book is that it's a ridiculously huge monkey, so there's no telling what calamities it might have caused that will remain unnoticed until the monkey is in print. For that reason, I am indebted to the people below, who have helped keep it from running amok entirely.

I received particularly extensive and detailed line-by-line comments about the entire book from Alan Bale and Tom Ernst. Alexis Wellwood and Martin Schäfer likewise heroically tackled the full manuscript. I benefited a great deal from all of their efforts. Many others provided helpful feedback on various smaller scales. Among them were (alphabetically) Claudia Maienborn, Dan Lassiter, Galit Sassoon, Jason Merchant, Jessica Rett, Joost Zwarts, Luca Sbordone, Muffy Siegel, Pasha Koval, Peter Klecha, Rajesh Bhatt, Ryan Bochnak, Sebastian Löbner, Taehoon Kim, and Vladislav Poritski. I'm grateful to them all. Their comments shaped how I thought about a number of things, influenced the presentation, set me straight about where I erred, and saved me some embarrassment. Many parts of the book would have taken a very different form or omitted important elements had it not been for conversations over the years with Angelika Kratzer, Barbara Partee, Chris Kennedy, Lisa Matthewson, and Roger Schwarzschild among others. The whole enterprise would have seemed less worthwhile had it not been for the encouragement of a surprising number of people who I won't attempt to name individually, but I'm grateful to them all.

Among my principal influences in shaping this book have been current and former students at Michigan State University. They shaped my thinking on many issues and provided theoretical insights, empirical observations, pointers to literature, and new ways of looking at things. And of course they provided a proving ground for modes of

Acknowledgments

explanation and pedagogical strategies. These include especially the semanticists – Adam Gobeski, Ai Matsui Kubota, Ai Taniguchi, Alex Clarke, Chris O'Brien, Curt Anderson, David Bogojevich, E. Matthew Husband, Gabriel Roisenberg Rodrigues, Karl DeVries, Kay Ann Schlang, Olga Eremina, Peter Klecha, and Taehoon Kim – and others working in syntax, semantics, and acquisition, including Adam Liter, Adina Williams, Greg Johnson, Hannah Forsythe, Joe Jalbert, Kyle Grove, Marisa Boston, Ni La Lê, and Phil Pellino. More generally, our local syntax–semantics community has provided an entertaining and intellectually fulfilling environment, and writing this would have been far more painful without them. My faculty colleagues, particularly Alan Munn and Cristina Schmitt, warrant special mention in this regard.

Helen Barton at Cambridge University Press was a pleasure to work with, and far more tolerant of me than I had any right to expect. In a book with pedagogical aspirations, it doesn't seem inappropriate to acknowledge the influence of my own teachers, including Angelika Kratzer, Barbara Partee, Kyle Johnson, Lisa Matthewson, Sandy Chung, Jim McCloskey, Donka Farkas, and Bill Ladusaw among others. It was a 1999 seminar of Lisa's on modification that most oriented me in that direction.

Finally, none of this would have been possible without the unfailing support, encouragement, feedback, and advice of Anne-Michelle Tessier and my dog, Hildy. Hildy's advice and feedback largely focused on the importance and pressing urgency of belly rubs. I regret that I was unable to incorporate that more fully into the text. It nevertheless bears directly on keeping one's priorities in order. Anne-Michelle's assistance was more intellectually wide-ranging and involved less shedding. I couldn't hope to adequately express my debt to either of them.

1 Preliminaries

1.1 TWO PROBLEMS

There are at least two significant problems with writing a book about the semantics of modification. The first is that it's not at all clear what modification is, precisely. The second is that it's not at all clear **whether** it is – that is, whether it exists as a single coherent grammatical phenomenon.

'Modification' and 'modifier' are the sorts of terms that we routinely use as though they had agreed-upon theoretical content. Yet they're useful in part precisely because, as McNally (forthcoming) observes, they lack a generally accepted, formally explicit theoretical definition. In the absence of a theoretical definition, it wouldn't be unreasonable to expect a clear descriptive one. Even here, though, we may need to set aside the 'clear' and, for that matter, the 'one'. In most contexts, to say that something is a modifier, or that it modifies something else, is not to make a falsifiable claim. Of course, that doesn't mean such claims are inherently suspect, but it's best not to have any illusions about how much weight they can bear.

That's the first problem, the terminological one. The second problem is more profound: to solve the first problem and provide a solid definition of modification, it would really help if it were a single phenomenon or natural class of phenomena. But it may be that 'modification' is merely a cover term for a motley assortment of constructions, facts, and puzzles that may, in various combinations, have some features in common.

Of course, it's not necessary to solve these problems in order to talk about them. Perhaps it's only in talking about them at some length that one can begin to address them. It might be an interesting journey, even if it turns out that modification isn't really a useful notion semantically. Nevertheless, the term appeals to us for some reason. Surely we should ask whether it does so because there is, in fact, a genuine grammatical insight behind it, something in the real world to which it refers?

Before we can address this, there is some practical business to attend to.

1.2 WHAT THIS BOOK IS AND ISN'T

This book is about formal linguistic semantics. That said, I really hope it might prove useful to people approaching it from other theoretical and methodological perspectives as well – if nothing else, in its characterization of the facts and of various particular puzzles. It has two primary target audiences. One is graduate students and advanced undergraduates who have undergone the initial rites of passage into formal semantics and have (at least) survived with their will to continue intact. Another is researchers in related fields, who sometimes find themselves in a distinct though not entirely dissimilar situation. They may have a longstanding familiarity with work in semantics, but a passive one, as spectators but not practitioners. If they would like to play a more active role, neither general introductory texts nor handbook articles are ideally suited to their needs.

This is intended as something between an advanced textbook and a topical survey of research in a broad area, a bridge between the basic orderly framework-building of textbooks and the sophisticated, cacophonous, and often formally challenging to-and-fro of the primary literature. The aim is to present some analytical tools and concepts that can serve as a starting point for the reader's own research. It's to provide a way of thinking about a particular set of problems and a sense of where to look to find out more.

A number of things follow from that. First, I have tried to emphasize problems over particular solutions and analytical strategies over particular instances of them. That said, the most interesting problems often emerge only against the background of some theoretical assumptions. It's impossible to be surprised if you have no expectations.

Second, there is no attempt here to be comprehensive. 'Modification' is a topic so broad that it could encompass virtually all of semantics. There may be no area of the field in which some class of modifiers hasn't been a major concern. So, in the interests of keeping the book a reasonable length – in fact, finite – there are many interesting topics of potential discussion that I will forgo. Discussion of adverbials other than adverbs in the strict sense will be conspicuously absent, as will discussion of relevant work in psycholinguistics and language acquisition. The focus will be on the grammar of adjectives, adverbs, and degrees.

Third, I have tried to maintain a consistent theoretical framework throughout. When encountering the literature for the first time, people

1.3 Background assumptions

are sometimes struck with a kind of intellectual vertigo. They have a few hard-won analytical tools in hand, but soon discover that work in semantics varies widely in formalism, style of analysis, and theoretical assumptions. It's as though they had just learned Italian only to find, upon visiting Italy, that people freely switch between Italian, French, Portuguese, Latin, and for some reason Japanese – and a handful of people seem to be saying really interesting things in Klingon. There is no solution to this in the long term other than to learn to deal with it. Nevertheless, I have enforced an artificial consistency on the discussion, translating various ideas into a single analytical and representational language. (Italian, one is tempted to say, taking the analogy too far.) This, of course, entails making many small adjustments to the original proposals, and a few larger ones. I call attention to the latter.

The book presupposes familiarity with the essential tools of formal semantics. I've tried to keep things relatively accessible, but engaging most of the content fully will require some previous background. Having absorbed the first few chapters of Heim and Kratzer (1998), Chierchia and McConnell-Ginet (1990) – or the relevant parts of volume two of Gamut (1991) or certain other semantics textbooks – should be sufficient. That should include a general understanding of quantification, lambda abstraction, and semantic types.

I have attempted to make the chapters of the book as independent of each other as possible. There are some dependencies that are difficult to avoid, though – you will get more out of Chapter 4 (on comparatives) if you have first read Chapter 3 (on vagueness, degrees, and the lexical semantics of gradable predicates). Chapter 6 (on crosscategorial phenomena) is best read in light of all preceding ones. But, on the other hand, if you wanted to skip past further preliminaries now and dive right into Chapter 2, you would not suffer unduly for having done so.

1.3 BACKGROUND ASSUMPTIONS

1.3.1 Glossing logical notation

Some introductory courses and textbooks develop a sophisticated semantics without recourse to logical notation other than lambdas, so I should briefly gloss the symbols I'll rely on. Many readers will want to skip this section. Obviously, one shouldn't mistake it for the shortest introduction to logic ever written. It just provides a way of mapping symbols onto familiar concepts or natural-language paraphrases.

First, some connectives, which make new propositions out of old ones:

(1) $\neg p$ 'it's not the case that p' or 'p is false'
$p \land q$ 'p and q'
$p \lor q$ 'p or q (or both)'
$p \to q$ 'if p, then q' or 'p is false or q is true'

Only the last of these is tricky. It's customary to paraphrase it as a conditional, but the second, more unwieldy paraphrase is more accurate. For our purposes, remembering the intuitive version will suffice.

Next, quantifiers:

(2) $\exists x[\ldots]$ 'there is an x such that ...'
$\forall x[\ldots]$ 'for every x, ...'
$\forall x \in S[\ldots]$ 'for every x in the set S, ...'

Combining these elements, an existentially quantified sentence like (3) can be represented with conjunction:

(3) a. A dog is furry.
b. $\exists x[\mathbf{dog}(x) \land \mathbf{furry}(x)]$
'there is an x such that x is a dog and x is furry'

But for universal quantification, the conjunction strategy won't fly. *Every dog is furry* doesn't mean that for every x, x is a dog and furry – that would require that everything be a dog. So we need another connective:

(4) a. Every dog is furry.
b. $\forall x[\mathbf{dog}(x) \to \mathbf{furry}(x)]$
'for every x, if x is a dog, then x is furry'

This correctly restricts our attention to dogs.

1.3.2 Theoretical framework

The question 'what theoretical framework are you using?' has two answers, one short and the other long. The short one is 'Heim and Kratzer (1998), more or less, with variations'. For many readers, this will be sufficient, and they need not bother with the rest of section 1.3.2. For the rest, here's the long answer.

As stated, the book adopts the Heim and Kratzer framework in most things. One departure is that it will use less English and more logic as a metalanguage in stating denotations. Even so, although most of the denotations will be well-formed logical expressions of an appropriate logic, I will follow Heim and Kratzer in treating them as

1.3 Background assumptions

components of a metalanguage that might at times include bits of English as well. I won't adopt an indirect interpretation system of the classically Montagovian sort, in which much of the semantics resides chiefly in how expressions of natural language are translated into expressions of a logic. One additional peculiarity is that I've systematically curried/schönfinkeled all logical predicates for consistency – that is, I will write **eat**(y)(x) rather than **eat**(x, y).

As for the syntactic assumptions, they are conventionally generative but with a minimum of theoretical commitments. For the most part, only the shape of trees – the constituency, not syntactic category – will matter, and I'll often omit syntactic category labels entirely. Where a neutral term like 'nominal' becomes inappropriate, I assume DP is the category of, for example, *the monkey from Cleveland* (Abney 1987), and NP as the category of the next maximal projection down (*monkey from Cleveland*).

I assume that the syntax has movement, and that quantified nominals usually take scope by undergoing Quantifier Raising (QR). The way I'll represent movement will diverge in a notational way from Heim and Kratzer's. In their standard treatment, a moved expression such as a generalized quantifier leaves behind an individual-denoting trace in the position it previously occupied. This trace receives a numerical index. By moving, the quantifier creates next to its landing site a binder for this index. This is represented as a number that occupies a node in the tree, which branches from the node to which the displaced quantifier is attached. Thus, for them, QR looks like this:

(5)   a.   Floyd deloused every monkey.

         b.

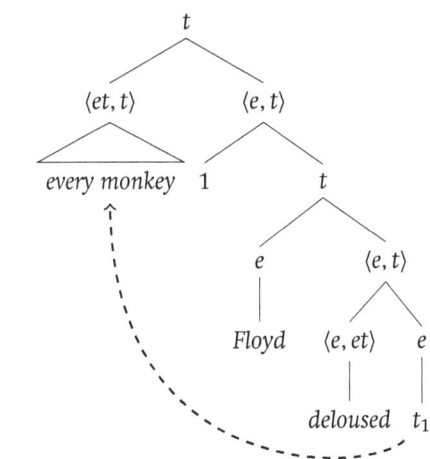

The trace is then interpreted as a variable, over which the binding node triggers lambda abstraction. In contrast, I'll represent movement in this way:

(6)
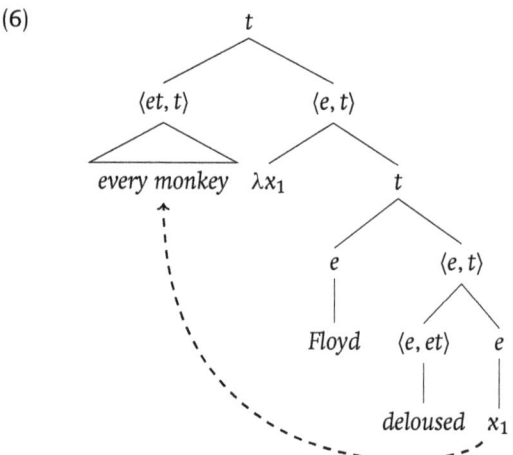

This simply replaces the trace with the corresponding variable and the binder with the corresponding lambda. (It's a little easier to read than the original when there are both individual- and degree-denoting expressions moving.) In a somewhat more unusual move, I will use variables with numerical indexes whenever they are associated with movement, as a subtle reminder of the more standard indexed-trace representation and of their connection to movement. The purist is free to disregard the non-subscripted material, which will render the representation virtually identical to the original.

As (6) reflects, I will occasionally place variables directly into the object language – that is, hang them from trees or from expressions in trees – in, again, a relatively standard fashion. Variables introduced this way and left free are assumed to get their value from the context(ually supplied assignment function).

Here is an example of how a computation might run (I'll generally skip more steps than I do here):

(7) a. $[\![every]\!] = \lambda P_{\langle e, t \rangle} \lambda Q_{\langle e, t \rangle} . \forall x [P(x) \rightarrow Q(x)]$

  b. $[\![every\ monkey]\!] = [\![every]\!] ([\![monkey]\!])$
  $= \lambda Q_{\langle e, t \rangle} . \forall x [[\![monkey]\!] (x) \rightarrow Q(x)]$
  $= \lambda Q_{\langle e, t \rangle} . \forall x [\mathbf{monkey}(x) \rightarrow Q(x)]$

  c. $[\![deloused]\!] = \lambda x \lambda y . \mathbf{deloused}(x)(y)$

1.3 Background assumptions

    d. $[\![\text{Floyd deloused } x_1]\!] = [\![\text{deloused}]\!]([\![x_1]\!])([\![\text{Floyd}]\!])$
        $= [\lambda x \lambda y \,.\, \textbf{deloused}(x)(y)](x_1)(\textbf{Floyd})$
        $= \textbf{deloused}(x_1)(\textbf{Floyd})$

    e. $[\![\lambda x_1 \text{ Floyd deloused } x_1]\!] = \lambda x_1 \,.\, \textbf{deloused}(x_1)(\textbf{Floyd})$

    f. $[\![\text{every monkey}]\!]([\![\lambda x_1 \text{ Floyd deloused } x_1]\!])$

$$= \left[\lambda Q_{\langle e,t \rangle} \,.\, \forall x \begin{bmatrix} \textbf{monkey}(x) \to \\ Q(x) \end{bmatrix} \right] \left([\![\begin{smallmatrix} \lambda x_1 \text{ Floyd} \\ \text{deloused } x_1 \end{smallmatrix}]\!] \right)$$

$$= \forall x \begin{bmatrix} \textbf{monkey}(x) \to \\ [\![\lambda x_1 \text{ Floyd deloused } x_1]\!] (x) \end{bmatrix}$$

$$= \forall x [\textbf{monkey}(x) \to [\lambda x_1 \,.\, \textbf{deloused}(x_1)(\textbf{Floyd})](x)]$$

$$= \forall x [\textbf{monkey}(x) \to \textbf{deloused}(x)(\textbf{Floyd})]$$

I have not represented the assignment function explicitly. Again, the purist can reconstruct how things would look if I had.[1]

The type system I assume is standard except where otherwise noted. On occasion, I will switch into an intensional system with overt quantification over possible worlds.

1.3.3 Notational and typographical conventions

The conventions I'll observe, notational and typographic, are relatively self-explanatory, but for the sake of explicitness, I'll list them:

- I will omit '1 iff' in, e.g., '$[\![\text{Floyd exploded.}]\!] = 1$ iff $\textbf{exploded}(\textbf{Floyd})$' and write, e.g., $f(x)$ in place of $f(x) = 1$
- constants will be in **boldface**, variables in *italics*
- the types of variables for functions will be indicated as subscripts next to the lambdas that introduce them
- words used in a technical sense for the first time will be in SMALL CAPS (I'll adhere to this practice consistently even at the cost of making a few pages look like comments on a blog post, full of DERANGED ANGRY YELLING)
- emphasis is indicated with **boldface**
- outside of examples, the object language is in *italics*
- 'iff' abbreviates 'if and only if'

---

[1] The relevant steps are the move from the denotation of a pronoun-like unpronounced element in the syntactic tree, $[\![x_1]\!]$, to the logical variable x_1 (really, there should be an assignment function that maps from one to the other); and the application of a Predicate Abstraction Rule like Heim and Kratzer's to interpret the floating object-language lambda.

The conventions about variable names are as follows:

- P, Q for properties of individuals or events
- R for relations
- G for gradable degree predicates, any type with both a d and an e in it: $\langle e, d \rangle$, $\langle e, dt \rangle$, $\langle d, et \rangle$
- D for properties of degrees, type $\langle d, t \rangle$
- p, q for propositions, type $\langle s, t \rangle$
- $f, g, \ldots$ for other functional types
- $e, e', \ldots$ for events, type v (not s, as is common; I'll reserve that for worlds)
- $d, d', \ldots$ for degrees, type d
- $w, w', \ldots$ for possible worlds, type s

1.4 WHAT, IF ANYTHING, IS MODIFICATION?

With that out of the way, we can return to the substantive question at hand: what precisely is modification? Does it constitute a single grammatical phenomenon?

The easiest answer to give – and, after some reflection, simultaneously the more obvious and more surprising one – is no. We think of the grammar largely in terms of predicates and their arguments. 'Modifier' is simply a term for linguistic expressions that don't fit neatly into either conceptual box. If this is right, construing modification as a unified phenomenon is doubly mistaken. First, it's uselessly broad. Writing a book about modification would be like writing a book about arguments: essentially an impossibility. One can talk coherently of argument **structure**, of course, but this isn't evidence that all expressions that happen to be arguments have something essential in common. Second, on this understanding, modifiers would be the complement of a natural class – that is, a meaningless set defined in reverse, like non-Bolivian non-dermatologists. If you had encountered a class like this in a phonology problem set, you would be justified in suspecting you had taken a wrong turn somewhere.

But there is another way of looking at the question, even if it's harder to perceive. One place to start is consulting one's intuitions about the use of the term, however inconsistent or precarious they may be. An adjective is a modifier, except for when it isn't. An adverb is almost always a modifier, though adverbs might really be just glorified adjectives in any case. A prepositional phrase is sometimes a modifier and sometimes it isn't, depending perhaps on whether it's an adjunct.

1.4 What, if anything, is modification?

A noun or noun phrase isn't a modifier, but what about in, say, *died last night*? Functional elements like tense morphemes, modal auxiliaries, and most determiners clearly aren't modifiers. Clauses are modifiers in various adjoined positions, but not elsewhere.

In this meandering litany, one can discern something about the nature of the conceptual struggle. The categories most readily at hand are syntactic, but we seem to be groping for something semantic. The references to syntactic category seem to be a clumsy proxy for an adequate language to talk about the lexical semantics of expressions, one that might ultimately express an intuition about their distribution too. Clearly, all this will need to be firmed up to make progress on the broader question.

In one respect, that can be done immediately. There is behind the whole thing a kind of equivocation that needs to be corrected. It's between two ways of characterizing a phrase. There is a difference between labels for the **internal** characteristics of phrases and for the **external** role they play in the constructions they enter into. Terms like 'subject', 'complement', 'adjunct', 'resultative', or 'purpose clause' all unambiguously characterize constituents by the role they play as part of larger ones, their external role. Terms like 'noun' unambiguously name lexical categories, and no one is inclined to use them to mean, say, 'complement to a verb' (setting aside sloppy talk of 'acting as a noun' in first-semester undergraduate assignments and prescriptivist harangues). They're characterizations of an internal property of a word and of the phrases it heads, not of their relation to larger expressions. The term 'modifier' is uncomfortably perched astride this fence. It characterizes both a family of (internal) lexical semantic characteristics and a family of (external) distributional ones. That, I think, may account for some of the conceptual muddle.

The internal sense of 'modifier', then, to a very crude first approximation, may amount to just this: you're a modifier if you're an adjective or an adverb. That probably makes you pretty good at gradability. The external sense of 'modifier' has to do with crosscategorial parallels in the role an expression plays. You're a modifier if you're adjoined to something that you're not a semantic argument to. You very well might have a semantics that can be expressed with *and*: a *red dinosaur* is red and a dinosaur.

Obviously, the distinction doesn't instantly cut through the haze. However, it is useful because, for the external sense, it's possible to provide a straightforward and rigorous (if imperfect) definition of modification in terms of semantic type. As we'll see in subsequent chapters, on one classical way of thinking, a modifier is any expression that maps a type to the same type: that is, anything whose denotation is type ⟨τ, τ⟩, where τ is a type. When τ is a predicate type, anything with this kind of meaning is called a PREDICATE MODIFIER. An example:

(8)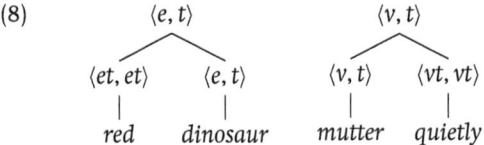

The meaning of *red* is a function that maps dinosaurs to red dinosaurs, the meaning of *quietly* is a function from mutterings to quiet mutterings:

(9)   a. ⟦ *red dinosaur* ⟧ = ⟦ *red* ⟧ (⟦ *dinosaur* ⟧)
    b. ⟦ *mutter quietly* ⟧ = ⟦ *quietly* ⟧ (⟦ *mutter* ⟧)

All the elements combine by function application.

Much of the time, there's an even simpler option – indeed, one that is often preferable, as we'll see. That's INTERSECTIVE MODIFICATION, in which an element denotes a property (of individuals or events or anything, in principle) and combines with something else that denotes the same kind of property:

(10)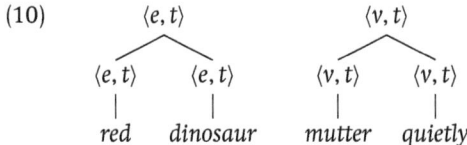

The idea here is that *red dinosaur* should denote a property of individuals that are red and dinosaurs, and *mutter quietly* a property of events that are mutterings and quiet. This is 'intersective' in the sense that, in set-theoretic terms, it involves intersecting the set of red things with the set of dinosaurs (or the set of muttering events with the set of quiet events). Function application can't achieve this for (10), of course. The types don't fit. But a rule of intersective interpretation such as Heim and Kratzer (1998)'s Predicate Modification (suitably generalized to events) can. It allows the modifiers in (9) to combine as in (11):

(11)   a. ⟦ *red dinosaur* ⟧ = λx . ⟦ *red* ⟧ (x) ∧ ⟦ *dinosaur* ⟧ (x)
    b. ⟦ *mutter quietly* ⟧ = λe . ⟦ *quietly* ⟧ (e) ∧ ⟦ *mutter* ⟧ (e)

1.4 What, if anything, is modification?

This is the desired result, but it comes at the price of introducing into the grammar a specialized rule to achieve it.

McNally (forthcoming), who wrestles with the same conceptual problem we face, adopts a working definition of 'modifier' based on a feature the two approaches share: a modifier is 'an expression which combines with another expression to produce a result with the same semantic type'. We will explore all these ideas in much greater depth in subsequent chapters. The important point for the moment is that they establish that providing a semantic definition of 'modifier' on the basis of certain external properties of an expression is possible.[2] They certainly **don't** establish that there is an interesting natural class here beyond the types, though.

Whatever the answers to these questions might be, something about this purely type-based characterization doesn't seem fully satisfying. Shouldn't there be more to modification than mere combinatorics? Here, we might need to turn to the other, internal sense of modification. And here, it's not so clear whether types alone will help. They may, as we'll see in Chapter 3, but it's not obvious. Syntactic category helps, too – 'adjectives and adverbs' seems straightforward enough – but again, it doesn't get at an essentially semantic internal notion of modification. So this will have to remain a bit murky. Still, having the question hanging in the air as we proceed will be useful, if only because it frames the discussion. We've now taken a few tentative, incremental steps toward a clearer way of thinking about it. But the question remains: what, if anything, is modification?

In light of all this big-picture rumination, the question suggests some topics we will need to confront. We will need to talk about compositional principles. That's crucial to the external sense of modification. But we'll also need to talk about syntactic category, adjectives and adverbs in particular, and something deeper: what kind of lexical semantics is especially associated with them. In the combinatorial principles briefly glimpsed above, there was a perfect symmetry between the adjectival and the adverbial case. That's distinctively modifier-like. If the notion of modification is to be useful, it may well be in characterizing regularity in crosscategorial behavior – a crucial element of being a modifier may be behaving consistently irrespective of the syntactic neighborhood you're in. As we proceed, I'll occasionally

---

[2] This definition isn't bullet-proof, as we'll see when we return to the issue in the final chapter.

draw attention to such crosscategorial connections, and I'll address some remaining ones in Chapter 6.

1.5 ROADMAP

Chapter 2 is concerned with what adjectives mean, both as a matter of their lexical semantics and in the context of particular constructions. It also examines the occasionally quirky way they combine semantically with their neighbors. Chapter 3 turns to the semantics of vagueness, an age-old philosophical puzzle, and its grammatical cousin, gradability. It considers two major analytical approaches to the problem, and then deploys one of them to probe into how scalar notions are represented in the semantics of gradable predicates and what variation there is in this respect. Comparatives and other degree constructions (equatives, superlatives, etc.), have long been one the major topics of semantic inquiry, and the principal proving ground for theories of gradability. They are the focus of Chapter 4. Chapter 5 takes up a less well understood topic, the semantics of adverbs. One of the great challenges in that area, which adjectives don't present in the same way, is providing an account of the different interpretations they receive in different syntactic positions. By Chapter 6, the essential background will be in place to confront some remaining phenomena that cut across more than one category, or indeed across virtually all of them. Finally, Chapter 7 concludes with a brief return to some of the questions raised in this chapter.

2 The lexical semantics of adjectives: more than just scales

2.1 INTRODUCTION

If, at virtually any point in the last decade or two, one formed one's impressions about linguistic theory entirely on the basis of cursory glances at conference announcements – a terrible, terrible idea – one might have concluded that the semantics of adjectives is, above all, the semantics of scales. From a certain perspective, what makes an adjective special, what distinguishes it from a noun or verb, is that it is associated with a scale: *tall* is about the height scale, *ugly* is about the ugliness scale, and so on.

Well, of course, there's more than a little truth in this. It's certainly true that scales are a major part of what makes adjectives interesting, and for that reason they have been the object of a great deal of study – and for that reason, too, they will be a major concern throughout the rest of this book. But to suppose that an adjective has nothing more to offer us than its scale is to do it a grave injustice.

This chapter will strive to vindicate this claim. It's about the lexical semantics of adjectives, but it is **not** about scales. Section 2.2 presents a typology of adjectives according to their effect on the modified noun. Section 2.3 sketches various theoretical approaches that shed light on that typology. Section 2.4 begins the exploration of particular analytically tractable classes of adjectives, focusing on adjectives that interact in interesting ways with their nouns. Section 2.5 continues the exploration of adjective classes, but shifts the focus to adjectives with surprising scope properties. Finally, section 2.6 considers additional issues closely linked to the syntax of adjectives, including their relative order and the positions they can occupy.

Two terminological notes. First, throughout this chapter I will, for convenience, use the terms 'adjective' and 'noun' when what I actually mean is 'the maximal projection of an adjective' (AP or DegP, depending on one's syntactic preferences) and 'an appropriate projection of a noun' (NP or perhaps N′, depending on one's syntactic preferences).

The second point is standard, but needs glossing: I will use ATTRIBUTIVE ADJECTIVE to refer to noun-modifying adjectives (ones attached to a projection of a noun) and PREDICATIVE to refer to the others.

2.2 HOW ADJECTIVES AND NOUNS COMBINE: A TYPOLOGY

2.2.1 Intersective interpretations

Not all relationships between an adjective and a noun it modifies are the same. One respect in which they vary is in how much influence the adjective has in the relationship. In some cases, the relationship is fairly equal. In others, the adjective is the dominant – indeed, for some cases one is tempted to say 'abusive' – partner. It will therefore be useful to lay out a basic typology of adjective–noun relationships, one that has become more or less standard. It has its roots early in formal semantics, the evolution beginning roughly with Montague (1970), Parsons (1972), and Kamp (1975) and continuing through Kamp and Partee (1995) and much subsequent work. Many of the empirical observations that underlie it can be found outside of formal semantics, including notably in Bolinger (1967b, 1972).

The simplest, most ordinary kind of adjective–noun relationship is a symmetric one. We will linger on this for a moment, because it is only in comparison with these symmetric relationships that the peculiarity of the others stands out. (The discussion in this subsection elaborates the discussion of intersective modification generally in Chapter 1.) One such straightforward case is in (1), in which the adjective and the noun each give rise to straightforward entailments:

(1)   Floyd is a Canadian surgeon.
       a. *entails:* Floyd is Canadian.
       b. *entails:* Floyd is a surgeon.

Importantly, neither of these entailments depends on the other. Each is an independent fact about Floyd.

Indeed, these entailments together are sufficient to characterize the meaning of the sentence. If (and only if) both of them are true, the sentence itself is true:

(2)   Floyd is Canadian.
       Floyd is a surgeon.
       ⎯⎯⎯⎯⎯⎯⎯⎯⎯⎯⎯⎯⎯⎯⎯⎯⎯⎯⎯⎯⎯⎯
       therefore: Floyd is a Canadian surgeon.

2.2 How adjectives and nouns combine: a typology

A natural way to think about this is in terms of sets. For Floyd to be a Canadian surgeon, he must be a member of two sets: the set of Canadians and the set of surgeons. Equivalently, he must be a member of the intersection of these sets.

So this, the simplest form of adjectival modification, is intersective. If we think of the denotation of an adjective as simply a set of individuals, this can be represented as in (3):

(3)　　⟦ Canadian surgeon ⟧ = ⟦ Canadian ⟧ ∩ ⟦ surgeon ⟧

The set talk is customary in this context but dispensable. One could just as well speak of 'conjunctive interpretation' and write something like (4):

(4)　　⟦ Canadian surgeon ⟧ = λx . ⟦ Canadian ⟧ (x) ∧ ⟦ surgeon ⟧ (x)

In (4), the adjective and noun are treated as denoting a simple property (in the extensional sense; type $\langle e, t \rangle$).

All of this follows from a principle of intersective interpretation such as the Predicate Modification Rule of Heim and Kratzer (1998), which interprets modifiers in precisely this intersective way (I have taken minor liberties with the formulation):

(5)　　PREDICATE MODIFICATION
　　　　If a branching node α has as its daughters β and γ, and ⟦ β ⟧ and ⟦ γ ⟧ are both of type $\langle e, t \rangle$, then ⟦ α ⟧ = λx . ⟦ β ⟧ (x) ∧ ⟦ γ ⟧ (x).

That is, the properties denoted by β and γ are combined to yield the property an individual has iff it satisfies them both. Switching back from function-talk to set-talk, the rule would be as in (6):

(6)　　PREDICATE MODIFICATION (in terms of sets)
　　　　If a branching node α has as its daughters β and γ, and ⟦ β ⟧ and ⟦ γ ⟧ are both sets of individuals, then ⟦ α ⟧ = ⟦ β ⟧ ∩ ⟦ γ ⟧.

The similarity between (6) and (3) is presumably apparent, as is the similarity between (5) and (4).

The careful reader will have discerned that nothing interesting has taken place so far in this section. Ideally, this will have lulled her into a false sense of security. Before we move on, though, it's worth perturbing that security at least slightly. An important property of intersective interpretations is that they create flat semantic representations in

16 THE LEXICAL SEMANTICS OF ADJECTIVES: MORE THAN JUST SCALES

which adjectives aren't scope-bearing, including with respect to other adjectives, as (7) reflects:

(7)   a. $[\![\text{famous Canadian surgeon}]\!] = \lambda x\,.\,\textbf{famous}(x) \wedge \textbf{Canadian}(x) \wedge \textbf{surgeon}(x)$
       b. $[\![\text{Canadian famous surgeon}]\!] = \lambda x\,.\,\textbf{Canadian}(x) \wedge \textbf{famous}(x) \wedge \textbf{surgeon}(x)$
       c. $[\![\text{famous Canadian surgeon}]\!] = [\![\text{Canadian famous surgeon}]\!]$

Without further refinements, the prediction is that the relative order of intersective adjectives should never matter semantically. This doesn't seem to be the case (see section 2.6). Nor does it accord with most people's intuitions about these adjectives. The expressions in (7c) **feel** like they don't actually mean precisely the same thing, somehow, though the difference is hard to articulate. The feeling that adjacent intersective adjectives take scope over each other is so persistent and widespread that one occasionally encounters linguists talking in a way that presupposes that they do. Perhaps this should worry us.

2.2.2 Subsective interpretations

When an adjective and noun combine intersectively, the adjective maintains a kind of truth-conditional independence. It makes its contributions to the truth conditions without regard to what the noun is doing. This means it is possible (that is, valid) to reason as in (8):

(8)   Floyd is a Canadian surgeon.
       Floyd is an arsonist.
       ─────────────────────────────────
       therefore: Floyd is an Canadian arsonist.   (valid)

One can freely replace *surgeon* with an arbitrary other noun that also characterizes Floyd and arrive at a true sentence. This is precisely what an intersective interpretation predicts. It allows us to conclude that he is in the set of Canadians because he is a Canadian surgeon, and that if he is also in the set of arsonists, he is a Canadian arsonist (because he is in the intersection of the sets of Canadians and arsonists).

This tidy state of affairs, however, is not the only empirical possibility. Changing the adjective can upend this kind of reasoning:

(9)   Floyd is a $\begin{Bmatrix}\text{skillful}\\\text{lousy}\\\text{experienced}\\\text{typical}\end{Bmatrix}$ surgeon.

2.2 How adjectives and nouns combine: a typology

If this were true and interpreted intersectively, it should allow us to reason as in (10):

(10) Floyd is a skillful surgeon.
Floyd is an arsonist.
———————————————————
therefore: Floyd is a skillful arsonist. (invalid!)

But of course this does not actually follow. To be a skillful surgeon, one must be skillful at surgery. To be a skillful arsonist, one must be skillful at arson. For the most part, surgery and arson require different skill sets.

Trying to analyze the situation in intersective terms makes the problem even clearer. To arrive at an intersective interpretation of *skillful surgeon*, we would first have to identify the set of skillful individuals. This is the essence of the problem. It's unclear how to go about this, at least in general. The best one could do would be to identify a set of individuals that are skillful at anything at all – that is, that aren't unskilled at absolutely everything. But that's not what *skillful* actually means. We are only comfortable evaluating it with respect to some particular kind of activity. For similar reasons, we wouldn't be comfortable identifying once and for all the set of the lousy, the experienced, or the typical. In all these cases, more information is required, and – in attributive uses – that information comes from the noun.

So how to make sense of this? There doesn't seem to be a single straightforward answer, or even a consensus about what is going on, so I will for the most part postpone this question until section 2.3. It would be nice, however, to cling to a simple set-theoretic way of understanding the situation. We still can. On these readings, the meaning of the adjective and noun together is not the intersection of their meanings, but it is still a **subset** of the meaning of the noun. For example, the set of skillful surgeons is a subset of the set of surgeons, and likewise for lousy or experienced arsonists (and so on):

(11) 〚 *skillful surgeon* 〛 ⊆ 〚 *surgeon* 〛
〚 *lousy arsonist* 〛 ⊆ 〚 *arsonist* 〛
〚 *experienced arsonist* 〛 ⊆ 〚 *arsonist* 〛

For this reason, these are usually called SUBSECTIVE readings.[1]

---

[1] If one were inclined to be difficult, one might challenge even the relatively weaker claim that subsective adjectives are really subsective. Roger Higgins (in personal

The term 'subsective' is descriptively convenient, but it's important to emphasize that it doesn't lead to an analysis in the way that 'intersective' does. Behind the term 'intersective' is a single, testable hypothesis about what adjective–noun combinations mean. But there is no such clarity behind the term 'subsective'. There are many conceivable hypotheses about how adjectives and nouns combine that are consistent with having the combination denote a subset of the noun meaning. Indeed, the intersective interpretation hypothesis is among them, because the intersection of two sets is a subset of both of them. (So all intersective modification is subsective as well, though I will use 'subsective' to mean 'subsective but not intersective'.)

The examples of subsective adjectives so far have been unambiguously subsective. That's not always the case. Probably the best-known example of such an ambiguity is (12):

(12)   Olga is a beautiful dancer.

Related kinds of subsective adjectives that aren't always discussed explicitly under the rubric of subsectivity include those in (13):

(13)   a. Floyd is an old friend.
       b. Floyd is a big idiot.
       c. Floyd is a religious official.

These differ from e.g. *skillful* in that they give rise to an easily perceptible ambiguity between two readings, one intersective and the other subsective:

(14)   Olga is a beautiful dancer.
       a. *intersective:* Olga is beautiful and a dancer.
       b. *subsective:* Olga dances beautifully.

(15)   Floyd is an old friend.
       a. *intersective:* Floyd is old and a friend.
       b. *subsective:* Floyd has been a friend for a long time.

communication to Karina Wilkinson cited in von Fintel and Heim 1999) points out examples such as *My chisel is a good screwdriver*, which would superficially seem to suggest that the set of good screwdrivers includes some non-screwdrivers. Another way of understanding this fact is available, though: the adjective might prompt us to widen the extension of *screwdrivers* to include things it otherwise wouldn't have. Such a coercion operation is precisely what Partee (2007) proposes for, e.g., *fake gun*, discussed in section 2.2.5.

2.2 How adjectives and nouns combine: a typology

(16) Floyd is a big idiot.
  a. *intersective:* Floyd is (physically) big and an idiot.
  b. *subsective:* Floyd is very idiotic.

(17) Floyd is a religious official.
  a. *intersective:* Floyd is religious and he is an official (e.g. president of the USA).
  b. *subsective:* Floyd holds a religious office (e.g. the papacy).

As a consequence, it is possible to deny the content of the adjective on one reading while asserting it on the other without contradiction:

(18) a. That beautiful dancer isn't beautiful.
  b. That big idiot isn't big.
  c. Your old friend isn't old.
  d. That religious official isn't religious. (He's an Anglican bishop. He's only in it for the music and costumes.)

This is impossible for purely intersective adjectives, as in (19a), and – at least without just the right discourse context – for subsective adjectives of the *skillful* class:

(19) a. ??That Canadian surgeon isn't Canadian.
  b. ??That skillful surgeon isn't skillful.

The class of subsective adjectives that also have intersective readings is useful as well in that they reveal that the particular choice of noun can be crucial to achieving the subsective reading:

(20) a. ??That beautiful sunset isn't beautiful.
  b. ??That big ferret isn't big.
  c. ??Your old father isn't old.
  d. ??That religious person isn't religious.

In (20), simply changing the noun eliminated the subsective reading, and thereby rendered the sentences contradictory.

All that said, the term 'subsective reading' almost certainly groups together a number of distinct phenomena, which it may be wise not to tie together too closely. Each of the kinds of examples considered in this section – *skillful surgeon*, *beautiful dancer*, *old friend*, *religious official* and *big idiot* – raise different analytical issues. We will confront them individually in section 2.3.

2.2.3 Apparently subsective intersective interpretations

There is an important caveat to be issued here. One might think that examples such as (21) (an old chestnut) and (22) (a version of an example in Kennedy 2007) are like the subsective adjectives discussed above:

(21) a. a small elephant
 b. a big mouse

(22) a. an expensive Honda
 b. a cheap BMW

In (21), the puzzle is, essentially, that small things are smaller than big things, but a small elephant is bigger than a big mouse. An intersective semantics superficially seems incompatible with this fact. On such an interpretation, all we'd have to work with are sets of mice, elephants, small things, and big things. If something is in the small-thing set, everything smaller than it must be, too. Suppose Dumbo is an elephant in the small-thing set and Mickey is a mouse in the big-thing set. Mickey is smaller than Dumbo, so Mickey must be in the small-thing set as well. Mickey is therefore both small and big. That's odd enough, but the reasoning works equally well the other way: Dumbo has to be both small and big too, for similar reasons (he's bigger than a big thing, namely Mickey). If both animals are members of both sets, we should equally well be able to describe Dumbo as a big elephant and Mickey as a small mouse. But of course, that's not at all how things work. The problem in (22) is perfectly parallel.

Although a simple intersective interpretation seems to yield the wrong result, the actual interpretation is still subsective:

(23) $[\![\text{small elephant}]\!] \subseteq [\![\text{elephant}]\!]$
 $[\![\text{expensive Honda}]\!] \subseteq [\![\text{Honda}]\!]$

So one might conclude that these are simply non-intersective subsective adjectives. One would be in excellent company, including Montague (1970) and Wheeler (1972). But, on the prevailing view, things aren't as they seem. With some additional theoretical refinements, these turn out to be intersective after all.

What's really going on (Kamp 1975; Siegel 1976a,b; Chierchia and McConnell-Ginet 1990; Kamp and Partee 1995; Heim and Kratzer 1998; Larson 1999; Landman 2000; Kennedy 2007) actually has to do with vagueness and how we go about resolving it. In *big mouse*, for example, speakers assume a standard of bigness that is appropriate to the objects

2.2 How adjectives and nouns combine: a typology

being compared: mice. With respect to that comparison class, the standard of bigness might be quite low, and we take *big* to means something like 'big for a mouse'. In *big elephant*, speakers assume a standard appropriate to elephants, one that is much higher, and we take *big* to mean something like 'big for an elephant'. The other examples work similarly. Of course, vagueness is not limited to attributive adjectives. Precisely the same issue arises in predicative positions:

(24)   a. Dumbo is small.
       b. Mickey is big.

Even in attributive positions, vagueness resolution isn't always determined by the choice of head noun. Other factors can be more consequential:

(25)   a. That $\left\{\begin{array}{l}\text{toddler}\\\text{fraternity}\end{array}\right\}$ built a big snowman.
                                                 (based on Kamp and Partee 1995)

       b. Kyle's car is an expensive BMW, though it's not expensive for a BMW. In fact, it's the least expensive model they make.
                                                 (Kennedy 2007)

In (25a), the standard for bigness changes depending on who does the building. In (25b), the standard for expensiveness is explicitly divorced from the head noun. The conclusion to draw, then, is not that such adjectives don't involve intersective interpretations. Rather, it is that in order to talk about adjective meanings in terms of sets, we should first adjust the membership of the set in a contextually appropriate way.

For this to be convincing, it would need to be spelled out more fully. Kennedy (2007) does this in especially explicit terms. One way of thinking about the issue along these lines (though the general idea dates to at least Wheeler 1972) is that adjectives take a contextually supplied comparison class as an argument, and that this argument is usually taken to be identical to the noun. This would mean that *big elephant* typically amounts to something like 'big-for-an-elephant elephant'. Compositionally, things might be as in (26), where $\mathbf{big}(x)(C)$ indicates that x is big when compared to the members of the comparison class C:

(26) $[\![big_C \ elephant]\!] = \lambda x . [\![big_C]\!](x) \wedge [\![elephant]\!](x)$
        $= \lambda x . \mathbf{big}(x)(C) \wedge \mathbf{elephant}(x)$

This is an intersective interpretation. The impression that something else might be going on comes from the fact that the value for C in most discourse contexts is **elephant**, obscuring the adjective's independence from the noun.[2] That said, this general analytical strategy – smuggling information about the noun into the interpretation of the adjective – need not be restricted to comparison-class arguments and is therefore potentially of use in analyzing at least some genuinely subsective adjectives as well (see section 2.3.4).

The crucial point, though, is that in the core cases of subsective modification, simply manipulating comparison classes in this way is insufficient. In *a beautiful dancer*, we can of course set the standard of beauty so that it is appropriate to dancers, but this won't explain why *a beautiful dancer* can be someone who merely dances beautifully.

In English, prepositions provide a nice way of distinguishing the two phenomena (Siegel 1976a,b):

(27) a. Olga is beautiful $\begin{Bmatrix} \text{for} \\ \text{as} \end{Bmatrix}$ a dancer.

b. Olga is skillful $\begin{Bmatrix} \text{for} \\ \text{as} \end{Bmatrix}$ a surgeon.

c. Olga is excellent $\begin{Bmatrix} \text{for} \\ \text{as} \end{Bmatrix}$ a chess player.

For provides a way of spelling out comparison classes and consequently occurs with adjectives that are dependent on a comparison class but not necessarily subsective. *As*, on the other hand, diagnoses subsective interpretations.[3]

2.2.4 Ordinary non-subsective adjectives

For the non-intersective adjectives we have so far encountered, it was possible to say that they are at least subsective. For other adjectives, however, even this fallback position is unavailable. Among these:

(28) an $\begin{Bmatrix} \text{alleged} \\ \text{probable} \\ \text{likely} \\ \text{potential} \end{Bmatrix}$ murderer

---

[2] For convenience, I'm equivocating here between function-talk and set-talk. If the comparison class argument really is to be a set, C would have to be the characteristic set of **elephant**.

[3] Indeed, it's possible to combine *for* and *as* phrases together, further demonstrating the independence of these issues:

(i) For an arthritic 90-year-old, Olga is skillful as a surgeon.

2.2 How adjectives and nouns combine: a typology

An intersective interpretation is impossible here: an alleged murderer is not a member of a set of 'alleged individuals'. There is no entailment along the lines of (29a), and one can't even make sense of what this non-entailment would mean:

(29) Olga is an alleged murderer.
   a. *does not entail:* #Olga is alleged.
   b. *does not entail:* Olga is a murderer.

Worse, though, (29b) – which is perfectly sensible – is not entailed either. The set of alleged murderers probably contains some actual murderers, but it also contains some innocent people too. So these adjectives aren't even subsective:

(30) $[\![alleged\ murderer]\!] \not\subseteq [\![murderer]\!]$

There is a standard conclusion to draw from these cases: because these adjectives aren't even subsective, and because their meaning can't be conceptualized as a set, we have no choice but to analyze them as a function that applies to the meaning of the noun (Montague 1970 and many since). It's hard to see how things could be any other way.

I'll illustrate this briefly with *alleged*, in a way that broadly parallels Heim and Kratzer (1998). Because *alleged* is inherently modal, it's necessary to use an intensional semantics. The denotation of *murderer* in (31a) therefore has a possible-world argument:[4]

(31) $[\![murderer]\!] = \lambda x \lambda w\ .\ \mathbf{murderer}(x)(w)$

The denotation of *alleged* applies to this, and yields something of the same type – that is, $[\![alleged]\!]$ is of type $\langle\langle e, st\rangle, \langle e, st\rangle\rangle$. It quantifies over the set of worlds compatible with what has been alleged (in the evaluation world w), represented here as $\mathbf{allegations}(w)$.[5] It requires that all such worlds be ones in which the individual is a murderer:

---

[4] This is equivalent to having simply written this:

   (i) $[\![murderer]\!] = \mathbf{murderer}$

Throughout the book, I will persist in spelling out the arguments in this strictly speaking needless fashion essentially just to make the types easier to discern.

[5] This abstracts away from several complications, including that allegations themselves are better construed as propositions.

24 THE LEXICAL SEMANTICS OF ADJECTIVES: MORE THAN JUST SCALES

(32) a. $[\![\text{alleged}]\!] = \lambda P_{\langle e, st \rangle} \lambda x \lambda w . \forall w' \in \textbf{allegations}(w) [P(x)(w')]$
b. $[\![\text{alleged murderer}]\!] = [\![\text{alleged}]\!] \, ([\![\text{murderer}]\!])$
  $= \lambda x \lambda w . \forall w' \in \textbf{allegations}(w) [\textbf{murderer}(x)(w')]$

This approach, in which the adjective takes a noun as an argument, reflects why it is so hard to make sense of the idea of a set of 'alleged individuals'. It also correctly predicts that such adjectives don't occur in predicative positions, where there is no noun for them to apply to:[6]

(33) #This murderer is $\begin{Bmatrix} \text{alleged} \\ \text{probable} \\ \text{likely} \\ \text{potential} \end{Bmatrix}$.

2.2.5 Privative adjectives, which may not exist

For some adjectives, a more striking effect emerges:[7]

(34) a $\begin{Bmatrix} \text{fake} \\ \text{pretend} \\ \text{fictitious} \\ \text{artificial} \end{Bmatrix}$ gun

These are PRIVATIVE adjectives, and they are distinguished by entailments (or apparent entailments) like (35c):

(35) That is a fake gun.
  a. *entails:* That is fake.
  b. *does not entail:* That is a gun.
  c. *entails:* That is **not** a gun.

The curious fact about these adjectives is that they seem to negate the meaning of the noun. Not only is it the case that fake guns don't constitute a subset of guns (as (36a) reflects); it's also the case that no fake

---

[6] Some of these adjectives can occur predicatively on eventive readings:

(i) Rain is $\begin{Bmatrix} \text{probable} \\ \text{likely} \end{Bmatrix}$.

[7] Sometimes temporal adjectives like *former* are included in this class. These raise some independent issues, however, so I have set them aside here (see section 2.4.2 for discussion).

2.2 How adjectives and nouns combine: a typology

gun is in the set of guns (i.e. the two sets have an empty intersection), as (36b) reflects:

(36)   a. $[\![\,\textit{fake gun}\,]\!] \not\subseteq [\![\,\textit{gun}\,]\!]$
         b. $[\![\,\textit{fake gun}\,]\!] \cap [\![\,\textit{gun}\,]\!] = \varnothing$

On one level, this seems obvious. On another, perhaps it shouldn't.

There is another difference between privative adjectives and ordinary non-subsective ones. We have no trouble making sense of the inference in 35a – that a fake gun is fake – and, more striking still, this inference turns out to be an entailment. Privative adjectives (of this class, anyway) behave this way systematically. A corresponding fact is that they happily occur in predicative positions:

(37)   This gun is $\begin{Bmatrix} \text{fake} \\ \text{pretend} \\ \text{fictitious} \\ \text{artificial} \end{Bmatrix}$.

This is surprising. One might have thought privative adjectives would be like modal non-subsective adjectives. They have a similar modal flavor, in that they introduce counterfactual possibilities (e.g. 'this isn't a gun, but it might have been').

Partee (2007) proposes a way of dealing with these facts that initially seems radical, but upon reflection is perfectly natural. She argues that privative adjectives as such don't actually exist. Rather, they are simply a species of subsective adjective with a notable additional property: they coerce the noun they modify into a looser interpretation than it otherwise would have received. The idea is that a fake gun is a gun after all, in an appropriately loose sense of *gun*. We occasionally resort to such loose interpretations in any case. One wouldn't be inclined to say something like (38) to a child:[8]

(38)   'Stop pointing your fake gun at your sister's face, and take your fake dinosaur out of her nose. Put away your fake truck, too.'

Instead, one would just refer to the fake gun as simply a gun, and so on. On this view, the apparent entailment in 35c that a fake gun is

---

[8] Martin Schäfer (p.c.) points out a cool subtlety: for something to be fake, there has to be a touch of deception about it. A toy gun in the relevant context would lack that property. Replacing *fake* with *toy* yields the same effect, though. One is still disinclined to say *toy* for each NP.

not a gun is a consequence of our unwillingness to coerce unmodified occurrences of *gun* to include fake guns without appropriate contextual support. It's a little trickier to explain the entailment in 35a, that is, that *fake gun* entails *fake*. But if privative adjectives are actually subsective, this entailment would parallel an inference (not really an entailment) that some other subsective adjectives systematically give rise to in appropriate discourse contexts. If the discourse is specifically concerned with surgery, we will generally conclude from *Floyd is a skillful surgeon* that *Floyd is skillful*. This can't be called an 'entailment', for the reasons that make this class of subsective adjectives difficult in general – namely, that one is not normally simply skillful in general. But at least in this discourse context, the inference goes through in a way that parallels the relevant entailment.

This also sheds light on a potentially deeper problem. Non-subsective adjectives such as *alleged* are impossible in predicative positions, and it is not clear how to even make sense of the notion of an individual being 'alleged'. The idea of an individual being fake is less mystifying. If privative adjectives were like *alleged*, this would be surprising; if they are actually subsective, it's expected. Of course, it's hard to evaluate these ideas without an explicit theory of how subsective adjectives are interpreted. That is the issue to which we will now turn.

2.3 THE TYPE OF ADJECTIVES AND THE NATURE OF SUBSECTIVITY

2.3.1 How powerful are adjectives?

If you're a linguistic expression that would like to impose its will on its phrase-structural neighbors, you will want to have a high type. Put another way: if you want to do something to your neighbor, first take that neighbor as an argument. Your argument is your hostage.

In the previous section, we've seen that many adjectives enter into fairly coequal partnerships with their nouns, and are interpreted intersectively (and hence symmetrically). These well-behaved adjectives can have a low type. Indeed, they **must**: to combine intersectively in the standard way, they must denote properties. Other adjectives, such as *alleged*, are not even subsective and insist on doing things to a noun that preclude this kind of coequal relationship. *Alleged* needs to push the semantic content of its noun across possible worlds, and therefore it needs to access this content directly. Such adjectives need to denote functions from noun meanings to noun meanings – that is, they need to denote PREDICATE MODIFIERS, type $\langle\langle e, st\rangle, \langle e, st\rangle\rangle$ (or, in extensional form,

2.3 The type of adjectives and the nature of subsectivity

$\langle\langle e,t\rangle, \langle e,t\rangle\rangle$). This is also sometimes referred to slightly more vaguely as a HIGHER-ORDER adjective meaning because it can't be expressed in first-order predicate logic. The term 'predicate modifier' is simply the name of a type, and, confusingly, is only indirectly related to Heim and Kratzer's (1998) rule of Predicate Modification, which applies only in the **absence** of a predicate modifier denotation.

So, in considering the semantic type of adjectives, we confront a question of power, or rather two closely related ones. First, are we wrong to think intersective adjectives are really property-denoting? If some adjectives require a higher type, perhaps all adjectives should be given it? This would mean that intersective adjectives in principle have as much power at their disposal as *alleged*, but for some reason (discretion?) choose not to use it. Or is it better to leave intersective adjectives as they are, and have a mixed theory in which different adjectives have denotations of different types? When Hans Kamp referred to 'two theories of adjectives' in the title of a widely cited paper (Kamp 1975), this is part of what he had in mind. It might seem an essentially aesthetic question that hinges on personal preferences in theory design, but interestingly – as we'll see in the next section – it turns out that it isn't.

The other question of power is where subsective adjectives fit in. Intuitively, they seem to occupy a middle ground between intersective and non-subsective, more complicated than the former but not as complicated as the latter. But as far as the types themselves are concerned, there is no middle ground to occupy. You denote either a property or a predicate modifier.

To make the first question more concrete, it will be necessary to spell out the two possible answers. In doing so, I'll adopt an intensional system to make *alleged* feel more at home. I've taken the liberty of assigning names to the two options, and provided sample denotations:

(39) ADJECTIVE TYPE HETEROGENEITY HYPOTHESIS

Intersective adjectives denote properties ($\langle e, st\rangle$) and are interpreted by a rule of (intensional) intersective interpretation such as Predicate Modification.

$[\![Canadian]\!] = \lambda x \lambda w . \textbf{Canadian}(x)(w)$

(40) ADJECTIVE TYPE HOMOGENEITY HYPOTHESIS

All adjectives, including intersective ones, denote predicate modifiers ($\langle\langle e, st\rangle, \langle e, st\rangle\rangle$).

$[\![Canadian]\!] = \lambda P_{\langle e, st\rangle} \lambda x \lambda w . \textbf{Canadian}(x)(w) \wedge P(x)(w)$

The reference to 'intensional intersective modification' in (39) is due solely to adopting an intensional system in general, but the operation is only slightly different from plain extensional Predicate Modification.[9] In (40), of course, there is a sense in which the intersective rule of semantic composition is built into the denotation of the adjective itself. One might regard this as suspicious, a generalization missed – or as an indication that intersectivity is a characteristic of adjective meanings that must, in the end, inevitably be stipulated.

Importantly, both of these hypotheses make precisely the same predictions about the truth conditions of simple attributive adjectives:

(41)   Assuming Adjective Type Heterogeneity:

   $[\![\,Canadian\ surgeon\,]\!]$

   $= \lambda x \lambda w\,.\,[\![\,Canadian\,]\!](x)(w) \wedge [\![\,surgeon\,]\!](x)(w)$
   (by intensional Predicate Modification)
   $= \lambda x \lambda w\,.\,\mathbf{Canadian}(x)(w) \wedge \mathbf{surgeon}(x)(w)$

(42)   Assuming Adjective Type Homogeneity:

   $[\![\,Canadian\ surgeon\,]\!] = [\![\,Canadian\,]\!]([\![\,surgeon\,]\!])$
   $= \lambda x \lambda w\,.\,\mathbf{Canadian}(x)(w) \wedge [\![\,surgeon\,]\!](x)(w)$
   $= \lambda x \lambda w\,.\,\mathbf{Canadian}(x)(w) \wedge \mathbf{surgeon}(x)(w)$

In light of this equivalence, distinguishing the two hypotheses empirically will require us to find other proving grounds.

Before doing so, though, there is an aesthetic point to be made. Famously, in the early years of formal linguistic semantics, Richard Montague introduced a tradition that became known as 'generalizing to the worst case'. The slightly jokey term reflects work like Montague (1973), in which the proper name *John* ultimately corresponds not as one might expect to an individual, type e, but a species of intensionalized generalized quantifier, type $\langle s, \langle \langle s, \langle \langle s, e \rangle, t \rangle \rangle, t \rangle \rangle$ (see Abbott 2010 for an especially clear discussion). The idea was that because at least **some** DP denotations must be of this type, **all** of them should

---

[9] This could be spelled out as:

(i)   INTENSIONAL PREDICATE MODIFICATION
      If a branching node α has as its daughters β and γ, and $[\![\,\beta\,]\!]$ and $[\![\,\gamma\,]\!]$ are both of type $\langle e, st \rangle$, then $[\![\,\alpha\,]\!] = \lambda x \lambda w\,.\,[\![\,\beta\,]\!](x)(w) \wedge [\![\,\gamma\,]\!](x)(w)$.

For discussion of questions that arise from the interaction of intensionality and intersective interpretation, see Musan (1997) and Keshet (2010).

2.3 The type of adjectives and the nature of subsectivity

be. Merely looking at the types, it seems perverse to suggest that $\langle s, \langle\langle s, \langle\langle s, e \rangle, t\rangle\rangle, t\rangle\rangle$ is more elegant than e. Nevertheless, there is a sense in which this is so. For all its commas and angle-brackets, the higher type made it possible to maintain a fixed correspondence between syntactic category and semantic type. It also meant that a single rule of semantic composition could be used for all members of this syntactic category. The more complicated type was thus the price of a simpler semantics overall. From a present-day perspective, these advantages are less important because we now generally assume a type-driven system with few specific rules of semantic composition and no necessary correspondence between syntactic category and semantic type. But, given the framework, the reasoning behind the type is almost unimpeachable.

Precisely the same reasoning applies to the choice between the two hypotheses at issue here. Consequently, Montague (1970) (and work contemporary with it including Wheeler 1972 and Lewis 1972) assumed Adjective Type Homogeneity. His adjectives were universally predicate modifiers. This means that the problem of subsective interpretations was easily set aside. If even ordinary intersective adjectives denote predicate modifiers, subsective adjectives would do so too. And if subsective adjectives have access to their nouns in this way, there is relatively little to explain. For *skillful*, for example, one might imagine that the core of the denotation is a predicate **skillful-as**, which is relativized to some role with respect to which one can be skillful:

(43) a. $[\![\textit{skillful}]\!] = \lambda P_{\langle e, st\rangle} \lambda x \lambda w \,.\, \textbf{skillful-as}(P)(x)(w)$
      b. $[\![\textit{skillful surgeon}]\!] = \lambda x \lambda w \,.\, \textbf{skillful-as}(\textbf{surgeon})(x)(w)$

This formulation doesn't overtly reflect the subsectivity of *skillful*, but one might further imagine that **skillful-as** is defined in a way that would require that its first argument (here, **surgeon**) hold of its second (x). Alternatively, one could add this entailment as an additional conjunct, as one would for an intersective adjective. The principal compositional challenge on this view, as Montague recognized, is not what to do with subsective adjectives, but rather what to do with adjectives (subsective or intersective) in predicative positions, as in (44):

(44) Floyd is $\left\{ \begin{array}{l} \text{skillful} \\ \text{lousy} \\ \text{Canadian} \\ \text{buoyant} \end{array} \right\}$.

Montague's solution – and the natural one in any theory that derives predicative adjectives from attributive ones – was to suppose that these cases involve an unpronounced noun, often a semantically bleached one such as *entity*. An independent account would have to be provided of why modal adjectives such as *alleged* can't be licensed in predicative positions in this way.[10]

This may seem a bit of a hack, but it has its advantages. For one, depending on the context, different unpronounced nouns might be involved – even contentful ones, such as *surgeon* – which would provide a way to model sensitivity to discourse context. For another, as Kennedy (2012a) points out, some languages genuinely seem to lack predicative adjectives and have, as their analogues to (44), sentences with overt semantically bleached nouns.

2.3.2 Siegel: the Doublet Theory

So must the choice between the two hypotheses above ultimately be made on aesthetic grounds? Siegel (1976a) convincingly demonstrated that the answer is no. Concrete linguistic facts can be brought to bear on the question, and viewed the right way, they seem custom-tailored to answer it.

The crucial observations concern a morphological alternation in Russian between two forms of adjective, a 'long form' and a 'short form':

(45)   RUSSIAN LONG- AND SHORT-FORM ADJECTIVES

	'good' (fem.)	'talented' (fem.)	'intelligent' (masc.)
long:	xorošaja	talantlivaja	umnyj
short:	xoroša	talantliva	umen

The clearest syntactic difference between the two is that the short forms don't occur in attributive positions (example from Matushansky 2008):

(46)   a. xorošaja   teorija
            good-LONG theory

       b. *xoroša   teorija
            good-SHORT theory

---

[10] The reason can't be just that modal adjectives are odd with semantically bleached nouns (?*alleged entity*), because at least in the case of *skillful*, it needs to be possible to delete contentful ones too. In a surgeon-oriented discourse, the deleted noun associated with predicative *skillful* would have to be *surgeon*.

2.3 The type of adjectives and the nature of subsectivity

In predicative positions, both forms are in principle possible (examples from Siegel 1976a):

(47) a. Naša molodež' talantlivaja i trudoljubivaja.
 our youth talented-LONG and industrious-LONG
 'Our youth is talented and industrious.'

 b. Naša molodež' talantliva i trudoljubiva.
 our youth talented-SHORT and industrious-SHORT

(48) Zimnie noči budut dolgimi / dolgi
 winter nights will.be long-LONG / long-SHORT
 'The winter nights will be long.'

There are a few further restrictions, but they aren't immediately relevant.

These morphological and syntactic facts on their own – without even touching on the semantics – have a bearing on the two hypotheses on the table. Clearly, there is a language with a systematic contrast in adjectives that is related to the predicative – attributive distinction, a distinction that is in turn related to the choice between property and predicate-modifier denotations. If we were to assume Adjective Type Heterogeneity, we would have an independently motivated tool relevant to accounting for the difference. If, on the other hand, we assumed Adjective Type Homogeneity, it would be necessary to find some other theoretical mechanism to account for these facts.

Beyond Adjective Type Heterogeneity, there are at least two further discoveries to be made here:

- Because short-form adjectives are exclusively predicative, they seem the natural choice for a simple property denotation. The long form would then be predicate modifiers. Given a standard modern semantics with a rule of intersective interpretation, this wouldn't yet explain why short-form adjectives are impossible in attributive positions. A property-denoting short form could simply combine intersectively with a property-denoting noun. Eliminating that rule, though, would render the two property-denoting expressions unable to combine, bringing about a type clash and thereby explaining the ungrammaticality. So this suggests – surprisingly, and interestingly – that a rule of intersective interpretation might not, in fact, be desirable after all.
- The situation in predicative positions is different. Here, the property-denoting short forms would be expected, consistent

with the facts. The predicate-modifier-denoting long forms, though, would not, because there is no adjacent noun to modify. Yet the long forms are possible in this position too. This would seem to be evidence for the idea independently broached earlier by Montague (1970) and others that there may be an unpronounced nominal in certain predicative positions. Such an unpronounced nominal would provide the long forms with a noun to modify, thereby licensing them.

All of these conclusions follow from distinctly linguistic, empirical arguments, not from a-priori aesthetic judgments. That's significant in itself. But notably, the conclusions so far arose before any reference to the semantics. Even if both forms of adjective meant precisely the same thing, this line of reasoning would present itself.

As it turns out, however, the two forms may not be semantically indistinguishable, in a way that bears on the question of how subsectivity works. Siegel reports a contrast in how long and short forms of 'intelligent' are interpreted:

(49) Studentka umna   / umnaja.
      student   intelligent-SHORT / intelligent-LONG
      '(The) student is intelligent.'

   a. *short form*: 'the student is generally intelligent'
   b. *long form*: 'the student is intelligent as a student'

The short-form interpretation in (49a) is a simple intersective one, in which the content of the adjective can be disentangled from the noun. If we take these facts at face value, the reading in (49b) would be a subsective one, in that it involves sensitivity to additional information provided by the head noun. It ascribes only academic intelligence to the student, and not, say, social intelligence.

Here, however, a caveat needs to be issued. The contrast in (49) may be absent for some speakers, perhaps even for many.[11] Luca Sbordone (p.c.) reports that one speaker he consulted characterized the contrast as something that might be found in a grammar more than in actual speakers. I don't know what to make of this observation, and it's not an issue this book can resolve. (This might be an interesting area for research, though.) For the sake of conveying Siegel's argument, however, let's assume the contrast is present.

---

[11] Thanks to Luca Sbordone and Vladislav Poritski for bringing this to my attention.

2.3 The type of adjectives and the nature of subsectivity

The connections between the short-form/long-form distinction and the intersective/subsective distinction run even deeper. In English, an out-of-the-blue predicative use of a subsective adjective of the *skillful* class would tend to elicit raised eyebrows:

(50)   Olga is skillful.

Without appropriate discourse support, this leaves the addressee adrift, uncertain about the nature of the skillfulness. Skillful at what? There is, marginally, a fallback option: skillful in general. English lacks a short-form/long-form distinction, so both the subsective skillful-at-what reading and the intersective skillful-in-general reading are possible, at least in principle. In light of that, the behavior of the Russian adjectives in (51) seems familiar:

(51)   Oleg umen   / umnyj.
        Oleg intelligent-SHORT / intelligent-LONG
        'Oleg is intelligent.'

   a. *short form:* 'Oleg is intelligent in general'
   b. *long form:* 'Oleg is intelligent as a ... what?'

Out of the blue, the short form is perfectly natural. It's intersective, and doesn't send us searching for a skillful-at-what argument. The long form, however, is subsective, and does exactly that. There is no common noun to suggest the nature of Oleg's intelligence, and we are left uncertain just as in (50).

The conclusion, then, seems to be not only that we should assume Adjective Type Heterogeneity, but also that the two types of adjectives correlate with the intersective/subsective distinction, with intersective adjectives denoting properties and subsective ones denoting predicate modifiers. Again, in this case the connection was not made on purely conceptual grounds – asking what type we need in order to write a plausible denotation for a subsective adjective – but rather on empirical ones. Siegel discovered an independent morphological way of identifying the semantic type of adjectives and found that this distinction correlated with the intersective/subsective distinction. In that respect, this is independent evidence for the view that subsective adjectives have higher-order denotations.

What, then, to conclude about adjectives outside of Russian? As one might expect, Siegel's suggestion is that the semantic facts are essentially the same, but that in English and most other languages the morphology doesn't overtly reflect them. Many English adjectives would then exist in two forms – 'doublets', she calls them – that happen to be homophonous. This explains why some adjectives, such as *beautiful* in *beautiful dancer*, give rise to an intersective/subsective ambiguity. It becomes simply a lexical ambiguity between two senses of the word *beautiful*, of precisely the same character as the lexical ambiguity in, e.g., *bank* (side of river versus financial institution).

It might seem a rather grand accident that vast numbers of adjectives in English should happen to be ambiguous in precisely the same way. But that's probably the wrong way to think about it. First, for some purely intersective adjectives, Siegel proposes an independent transformational mechanism that would license them in attributive positions without needing to stipulate a distinct predicate-modifier form. Second, non-subsective adjectives are never ambiguous in this way. Third, some adjectives that one might have expected to be ambiguous happen not to be. *Remiss*, for example, turns out to lack an attributive use (*a remiss surgeon*), even though it's quite easy to imagine what a subsective interpretation would mean (that is, what it would mean to be remiss as a surgeon). That suggests that there really is some irregularity here that must inevitably be stipulated in the lexicon.

Irrespective of the substantive claims about adjectives in the dissertation, though, the most memorable insight might be the methodological one: the elegant way in which linguistic facts are brought to bear on an issue that one might have thought couldn't be settled empirically.

2.3.3 Larson: events inside the nominal extended projection

There are, it seems to me, at least two difficulties facing the Doublet Theory, which tend to support an overall view of subsectivity advanced in Larson (1999).[12] First, because the Doublet Theory groups all subsective readings with predicate-modifier denotations, it unites subsective and modal adjectives into a single class. But empirically, they do seem to be distinct. The clearest respect in which this is so has to do with gradability. The biggest classes of subsective adjectives are gradable, while modal adjectives generally aren't:[13]

---

[12] Larson provides a simple independent counterargument to the Doublet Theory based on its prediction that attributive adjectives should never be ambiguous between subsective and intersective readings, as they are in English. For the Russian speakers available to me, though, this prediction goes through. Thanks to Pasha Koval and Vladislav Poritski for bringing this to my attention.

[13] One notable exception to this is *probable*: *the most/very probable killer*. The interaction of modality and degree modification has only relatively recently become an area of active research (Portner 2009; Lassiter 2010, 2011a,b; Klecha 2012). See section 3.7.5 for more discussion.

2.3 The type of adjectives and the nature of subsectivity

(52) a. the $\begin{Bmatrix} \text{more} \\ \text{most} \\ \text{very} \end{Bmatrix}$ beautiful dancer

   b. our $\begin{Bmatrix} \text{older} \\ \text{oldest} \\ \text{very old} \end{Bmatrix}$ friend

(53) *the $\begin{Bmatrix} \text{more} \\ \text{most} \\ \text{very} \end{Bmatrix}$ alleged murderer

This complicates any account of gradability. If the extended projections of gradable adjectives were all of the same type, the theory of gradability would have to simply ensure that this is the type that emerges once degree morphemes combine with adjectives. But it's not clear how such a theory could ensure that a single degree morpheme would yield a property when combining with some adjectives and a predicate modifier when combining with another. (One possible solution would be massive systematic two-way homophony extending across the full class of degree morphemes. Another would be a type shift for which there is no independent evidence. Neither of these is appealing.)

Second, the Doublet Theory predicts that the relative order of attributive adjectives should have no bearing on the availability of subsective interpretations. However there does seem to be a contrast between (54) and (55):

(54) an ugly beautiful dancer
   a. a person who is ugly and dances beautifully
   b. *a person who is beautiful and dances in an ugly way

(55) a beautiful ugly dancer
   a. *a person who is ugly and dances beautifully
   b. a person who is beautiful and dances in an ugly way

In both these examples, it is the higher adjective that receives the intersective reading and the lower one that receives the subsective one. In another context, Larson and Cho (2003) note a similar difference between *John's new old car* and *John's old new car*.

Larson (1998, 1999) argues that such facts as these show that the intersective/subsective distinction must be disentangled from the distinction between properties and predicate modifiers. He proposes instead that both intersective and subsective adjectives are property-denoting, and that the origin of subsective readings is fundamentally different. To appreciate the analytical intuition behind his idea, it helps to indulge in a momentary digression about manner adverbs. As a class, they have an odd characteristic: they all seem to be subsective (Bennett 1974), because of the failure of inferences such as (56) (see sections 5.3 and 5.4):

(56)   Olga danced beautifully.
        Olga sang.
        _____
        therefore: Olga sang beautifully.   (invalid!)

This, of course, mirrors the invalid reasoning behind concluding that Floyd is a skillful arsonist because he is an arsonist and skillful surgeon (in 10 above), rather than the valid reasoning behind concluding that he is a Canadian arsonist because he is an arsonist and Canadian surgeon (in 8). One might take this to show that manner adverbs, just like subsective adjectives, have to have predicate-modifier denotations.

But, as McConnell-Ginet (1982) notes, this is not the only way to prevent this inference from going through. The standard view is now that the source of the problem is entirely different: it is that manner adverbs are not predicates of individuals, but rather of Davidsonian events (Davidson 1967; see section 5.3.4). Thus, instead of a subsective predicate-modifier denotation as in (57a), the adverb receives an intersective property interpretation as in (57b) (I'll adopt an extensional framework for this section):

(57)   Olga danced beautifully.
        a. **beautifully**(**danced**)(**Olga**)
        b. $\exists e[\textbf{dance}(e) \land \textbf{agent}(e) = \textbf{Olga} \land \textbf{beautiful}(e)]$

The interpretation in (57a) involves a predicate modifier **beautifully** operating on **dance**, whereas the one in (57b) simply says that there was an event of dancing, that Olga was its agent, and it was beautiful.[14] Apart from being more explanatory, this explains the failure of the inference in 56. If there was a dancing event by Olga that was beautiful and a singing event by Olga, it doesn't follow that the singing event must have been beautiful.

---

[14] I have 'severed' the external argument from the predicate **dance** in the style of Kratzer (1996) – that is, rather that introducing Olga directly as an argument (i.e. **dance**(*e*)(**Olga**)), I've introduced her using the thematic-role predicate **agent**, which maps events to their agents. (See sections 5.4.2 and 5.4.3 for discussion.) This is not crucial for the most immediate point, but I will rely on it in my adaptation of Larson (1998, 1999) below.

2.3 The type of adjectives and the nature of subsectivity

Larson's core insight is that adjectival subsectivity might arise from precisely the same source: an event argument. In what follows, I will sketch a way of implementing this idea in a simplified framework that is likely to be more familiar for most readers. This requires significantly reformulating Larson's analysis, though the essential analytical insight is, I hope, preserved. I'll note the important differences once all the cards are on the table.

The first step is to observe that *dancer* can be understood very naturally in terms of events. A dancer is someone who habitually dances. This notion of 'habitually dancing' can be expressed with a generic quantifier **GEN** (Krifka et al. 1995; Chierchia 1995; among others):

(58)   Olga dances.
   a. **GEN** e [dance(e)(Olga)]
   b. **GEN** e : relevant$_c(e)$ [dance(e)(Olga)]

What (58a) says is that the generic or typical event is a dancing by Olga. This is too strong. Rather, what we really want is something closer to (58b), which says that the generic event among the ones relevant in the discourse context c is a dancing by Olga. Of course, what counts as relevant might vary dramatically from one discourse to another, but the crucial thing is that, under the relevant circumstances, Olga typically dances.

The next step is to incorporate this into the denotation of the noun *dancer* itself. This can be done by treating *dancer* as simply a property of dancing events:

(59)   ⟦ *dancer* ⟧ = λe . dance(e)

This looks more like a denotation for the verb *dance*, and it's not of the right type to occur in a nominal position, because it's a property of events (type $\langle v, t \rangle$) rather than of individuals ($\langle e, t \rangle$). If a determiner such as *the* were to combine with this directly, a type clash would occur:

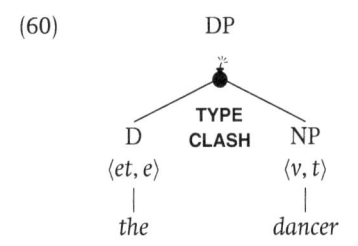

(60)
```
            DP
           /  \
          /    \
         /    TYPE
        D    CLASH   NP
      ⟨et, e⟩        ⟨v, t⟩
        |              |
       the           dancer
```

So there are two tasks in need of doing: a generic quantifier must be introduced, and this type clash must be avoided. One way of accomplishing this is to suppose that this quantifier is introduced by a node in the tree (corresponding to a functional head or perhaps reflecting the effect of a Partee 1987-style type shift):

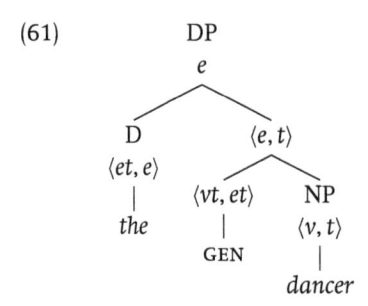

(61)
```
                DP
                 e
          ┌──────┴──────┐
          D           ⟨e,t⟩
        ⟨et,e⟩    ┌─────┴─────┐
          |     ⟨vt,et⟩       NP
         the      |          ⟨v,t⟩
                 GEN           |
                             dancer
```

The denotation of this morpheme will be as in (62):

(62) $[\![\text{GEN}]\!]^c = \lambda f_{\langle v,t \rangle} \lambda x \,.\, \textbf{GEN}\ e : \textbf{relevant}_c(e)\ [f(e) \wedge \textbf{agent}(e) = x]$

This applies to a property of events and yields a property of individuals, one that holds of an individual iff, for the generic event of the relevant type, the individual is the agent of that event and the event meets the description provided by the NP. The next step (henceforth I will omit the superscript c) is as follows:

(63) $[\![\text{GEN } dancer]\!] = [\![\text{GEN}]\!]\,([\![dancer]\!])$
$\ = \lambda x \,.\, \textbf{GEN}\ e : \textbf{relevant}_c(e)\ [[\![dancer]\!](e) \wedge \textbf{agent}(e) = x]$
$\ = \lambda x \,.\, \textbf{GEN}\ e : \textbf{relevant}_c(e)\ [\textbf{dance}(e) \wedge \textbf{agent}(e) = x]$

A dancer, then, is someone who is the agent of the typical dancing event (of the relevant sort).

The crucial issue here is how adjectives fit into this picture. The answer is straightforward. The only necessary wrinkle is that adjectives with both subsective and intersective readings like *beautiful* must be able to apply to either individuals or events. If the adjective occurs below GEN, as in (64), it will receive an event-based – and therefore subsective – reading:

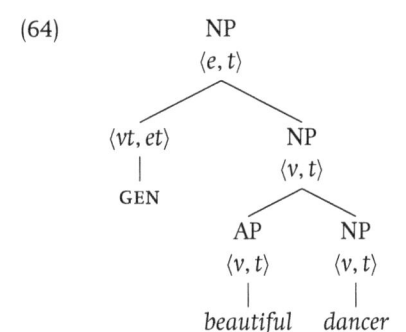

2.3 The type of adjectives and the nature of subsectivity

(64)
```
                NP
               ⟨e, t⟩
         ╱            ╲
    ⟨vt, et⟩            NP
       │              ⟨v, t⟩
      GEN         ╱          ╲
                AP            NP
              ⟨v, t⟩         ⟨v, t⟩
                │              │
             beautiful       dancer
```

The adjective can now be interpreted intersectively with the noun:

(65) a. $[\![\text{beautiful dancer}]\!] = \lambda e \,.\, [\![\text{beautiful}]\!](e) \wedge [\![\text{dancer}]\!](e)$
    $= \lambda e \,.\, \textbf{beautiful}(e) \wedge \textbf{dance}(e)$

  b. $[\![\text{GEN beautiful dancer}]\!] = [\![\text{GEN}]\!]([\![\text{beautiful dancer}]\!])$

   $= \lambda x \,.\, \textbf{GEN}\, e : \textbf{relevant}_c(e) \begin{bmatrix} [\![\text{beautiful dancer}]\!](e) \wedge \\ \textbf{agent}(e) = x \end{bmatrix}$

   $= \lambda x \,.\, \textbf{GEN}\, e : \textbf{relevant}_c(e) \begin{bmatrix} \textbf{beautiful}(e) \wedge \textbf{dance}(e) \wedge \\ \textbf{agent}(e) = x \end{bmatrix}$

On this reading, a beautiful dancer is someone who is the agent of the typical event that is beautiful and a dancing.

To achieve the intersective reading, the adjective simply has to occur higher in the tree, above GEN:

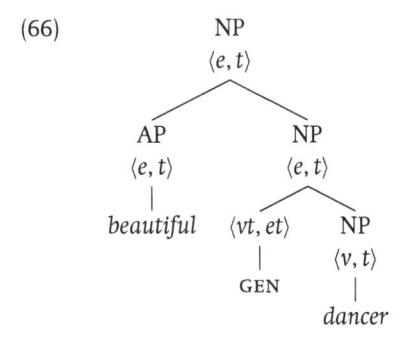

(66)
```
                 NP
                ⟨e, t⟩
          ╱            ╲
         AP             NP
       ⟨e, t⟩         ⟨e, t⟩
         │         ╱         ╲
      beautiful  ⟨vt, et⟩     NP
                   │        ⟨v, t⟩
                  GEN         │
                            dancer
```

The resulting interpretation would interpret *beautiful* intersectively with GEN *dancer*:

(67) a. $[\![\text{GEN dancer}]\!]$
    $= \lambda x \,.\, \textbf{GEN}\, e : \textbf{relevant}_c(e) \,[\textbf{dance}(e) \wedge \textbf{agent}(e) = x]$

b. ⟦ *beautiful* GEN *dancer* ⟧
   = λx . ⟦ *beautiful* ⟧ (x) ∧ ⟦ GEN *dancer* ⟧ (x)
   = λx . **beautiful**(x) ∧
         GEN e : **relevant**$_c(e)$ [**dance**(e) ∧ **agent**$(e) = x$]

This is the ordinary intersective reading. It requires simply that an individual be beautiful and a dancer.

This analysis naturally accounts for the adjective ordering facts. Just as the facts dictate, intersective readings are possible higher than subsective readings. It also assimilates subsective readings to intersective ones rather than to non-subsective ones, which better accords with the intuition that the two senses of *beautiful* have more in common with each other than either has with, e.g., *alleged*. Indeed, because *beautiful* need not be lexically ambiguous at all, there is no danger that the account of subsective readings will interfere with the account of its gradability.

This approach also has the advantage of scaling up: many forms of subsectivity can be understood in this way. But a crucial step, and one many people find somewhat less plausible, is introducing event arguments to nominals that don't wear their deverbal origins on their sleeve, as *dancer* does. For example, to accommodate the subsective reading of *old friend*, it's necessary to construe *friend* as having internal structure involving friendship states. Likewise, for the subsective reading of *just king*, *king* would have to be decomposed into an eventuality predicate of some kind (kingship states or reigning events). The analysis may also scale up so well as to overgenerate. Friendships can be rocky or brief or unfortunate, but there seem to be no subsective readings for #*rocky*/#*brief*/*unfortunate friend*. Nor is it clear how to extend this approach to, e.g., *big idiot* or *religious official*. Then again, these may both represent a fundamentally different kind of subsectivity in any case. Nevertheless, the larger picture that emerges is lovely and deeply explanatory: subsective readings are not an accident of the lexicon but rather a reflection of previously hidden aspects of the architecture of the extended nominal projection.

As noted earlier, I have taken the liberty of recasting Larson's analysis into a framework more consistent with the assumptions generally made elsewhere in this book. This has entailed some significant changes, though I hope the spirit of the proposal remains. It's worth flagging the biggest differences, though. First, Larson's proposal is cast in a framework in which the interpretation function itself is replaced by an interpretation relation so that a single linguistic

2.3 The type of adjectives and the nature of subsectivity

expression can correspond to multiple denotations (Larson and Segal 1995). In this case, any adjective–noun combination is related to both an intersective/individual and an subsective/event meaning. This arguably allows for a simpler syntax–semantics mapping. To the extent that this is so, it is an argument for this alternative framework. The second major difference has to do with the denotations themselves. Broadly in the spirit of Heim (1982), Larson adopts assumptions under which certain regions of trees can be mapped onto bits of a semantic representation by specialized rules of composition. This allows him to make a neat connection to how quantification in the verbal domain works. On the Mapping Hypothesis of Diesing (1990), the higher regions of the verbal extended projection are mapped onto the restrictor of a quantifier, and lower ones to its nuclear scope. Larson proposes that something similar happens in nominal extended projection and that adjectives can wind up either in the restrictor or in the nuclear scope of the generic quantifier. His actual denotation for the subsective reading of *beautiful dancer* is therefore closer to (68a):

(68)   a. $\lambda x \, . \, \textbf{GEN} \, e : \text{relevant}_c(e) \wedge \text{dance}(e) \wedge \text{agent}(e) = x$
$[\text{beautiful}(e)]$
        b. $\lambda x \, . \, \textbf{GEN} \, e : \text{relevant}_c(e) \wedge \text{dance}(e) \wedge \text{agent}(e) = x$
$[\text{beautiful}(e) \wedge \text{dance}(e) \wedge \text{agent}(e) = x]$

Because (68a) is equivalent to (68b), the difference between (68a) and the denotation provided here isn't as great as it initially appears. Indeed, because the contextually provided notion of relevance is quite flexible (notoriously so), it would be difficult to tease apart empirically whether the additional conjuncts in the restrictor are actually necessary or could be provided contextually via the predicate **relevant**. Either way, the broader connection to the Mapping Hypothesis isn't reflected in this adapted version.

2.3.4 The implicit-argument approach

Von Fintel and Heim (1999), Landman (2001), and Schäfer (2004, 2005) point out yet another analytical alternative that would, like Larson's, reduce subsective readings to intersective ones, even without accepting Larson's deeper explanation.

One could simply suppose that subsective adjectives do in fact have an additional argument position, but that this position is saturated within the extended projection of the adjective itself. The existence of *as*-phrases makes this especially appealing. The denotation of *skillful*, for example, could be as in (69) as suggested in section 2.3.1, but the first argument could be provided not by the noun, but by an *as*-phrase:

(69) a. $[\![\text{skillful}]\!] = \lambda P_{\langle e, st \rangle} \lambda x \lambda w \,.\, \textbf{skillful-as}(P)(x)(w)$
b. $[\![\text{skillful as a surgeon}]\!] = [\![\text{skillful}]\!]\,([\![\text{as a surgeon}]\!])$
  $= \lambda x \lambda w \,.\, \textbf{skillful-as}([\![\text{as a surgeon}]\!])(x)(w)$
  $= \lambda x \lambda w \,.\, \textbf{skillful-as}(\textbf{surgeon})(x)(w)$

In the attributive use, one might speculate that this *as*-phrase is implicit, so that *skillful surgeon* actually looks like (70) and is interpreted intersectively:

(70) $[\![\text{skillful }\overline{\text{as a surgeon}}\text{ surgeon}]\!]$
  $= \lambda x \lambda w \,.\, [\![\text{skillful }\overline{\text{as a surgeon}}]\!](x)(w) \wedge$
    $[\![\text{surgeon}]\!](x)(w)$
  $= \lambda x \lambda w \,.\, \textbf{skillful-as}(\textbf{surgeon})(x)(w) \wedge \textbf{surgeon}(x)(w)$

So long as the value of the implicit argument matches the noun, the resulting reading will be subsective. If its value is provided by context in some other way, an intersective reading should result. This all parallels the analytical move made for comparison classes in section 2.2.3, and in that respect hearkens back to Wheeler (1972) and others who leveled the distinction between sensitivity to comparison classes and to 'tasks' or 'roles'. Indeed, the talk of an 'implicit *as*-phrase' could more plausibly be replaced by a simple free variable in the tree, matching that discussion even more closely.

On its own, this sketch doesn't account for the full range of facts – one might like an explanation for why subsective readings occur lower, for example – but it demonstrates that a commitment to assimilating subsective adjectives to intersective ones can be maintained even without committing to the Larson analysis.

2.3.5 How much power is too much? Impossible adjectives

The available analytical options seem to converge on accepting the Adjective Type Heterogeneity Hypothesis. It seems that predicate-modifier denotations should, in fact, be reserved only for adjectives that really need them. If subsective adjectives can be assimilated to intersective ones, this would be very few indeed.

2.3 The type of adjectives and the nature of subsectivity

This has led von Fintel and Heim (1999) and Landman (2001) to feel some unease about predicate-modifier denotations in general. The worry is that such denotations are too powerful in principle. Suppose, for example, I were to attempt to coin an adjective *residentialous*, with the predicate-modifier denotation in (71):

(71) $\llbracket residentialous \rrbracket = \lambda P_{\langle e, st \rangle} \lambda x \lambda w . \exists y \begin{bmatrix} P(y)(w) \land \\ \text{reside-in}(y)(x)(w) \end{bmatrix}$

Thus a *residentialous city* is a resident of a city, and a *residentialous condo* is a resident of a condo:

(72) a. $\llbracket residentialous\ city \rrbracket = \lambda x \lambda w . \exists y \begin{bmatrix} \text{city}(y)(w) \land \\ \text{reside-in}(y)(x)(w) \end{bmatrix}$

b. $\llbracket residentialous\ condo \rrbracket = \lambda x \lambda w . \exists y \begin{bmatrix} \text{condo}(y)(w) \land \\ \text{reside-in}(y)(x)(w) \end{bmatrix}$

In purely formal terms, the denotation in (71) is beyond reproach. Yet we recoil in horror at this adjective. Clearly, this is not a possible adjective meaning. I've found that eliciting this judgment from speakers, irrespective of the language, often leaves them somehow indignant, outraged at the very suggestion that there should be such an adjective. Speakers rarely feel their judgments so viscerally.

But what could account for the outrage? One possibility would be to simply stipulate a constraint – perhaps crosslinguistic – that would prohibit such meanings. This may be the best we can do. It's roughly the course Landman charts. The theoretical status of this constraint would be a little unclear, but perhaps it's analogous to the (apparent) crosslinguistic ban on nonconservative determiners (Barwise and Cooper 1981; Keenan and Faltz 1985; Keenan and Stavi 1986; Keenan 2002). There is, however, an appealing alternative, which remains just out of reach: eliminating predicate-modifier adjective denotations from the grammar entirely. Such a categorical ban might do justice to the intuition. Although one would still confront the issue of how to implement such a ban theoretically – that is, precisely what kind of a rule can say this sort of thing – it would at least be the case that the ban would be a straightforward one involving possible semantic types for a syntactic category. But to my knowledge, no one has been able to reconcile such a ban with the existence of apparently unavoidably higher-order adjectives such as *alleged*.

2.4 THE MENAGERIE OF ADJECTIVES

2.4.1 A word about adjective classification

McNally (forthcoming) distinguishes between ENTAILMENT-BASED typologies of modifiers of the sort discussed so far and NOTIONALLY BASED typologies based on a modifier's descriptive content. Our next aim is to explore a handful of such notional adjective classes, ones distinguished by a coherent set of analytically tractable semantic characteristics. This task will be divided between this section and the next (section 2.5), which will focus on classes that give rise to a particular compositional problem in which an adjective appears to be interpreted outside the nominal.

What I will not do is provide a survey of adjective classes in general. There is considerable diversity among adjective classification schemes and in the terminology associated with them, and it's not always clear whether these classifications match those that formal semantic investigation would lead to. That said, work on the syntax of adjectives, especially on their relative order and typological properties, often frames adjective categories in semantic terms. For example, it is useful even for purely syntactic purposes to distinguish between evaluative adjectives such as *nice*, size adjectives such as *big*, shape adjectives such as *round*, and color adjectives.[15] Across languages, these tend to appear in that order when prenominal (that is, evaluative < size < shape < color); postnominally, they tend to occur either in the same order or in its mirror-image. For more on classifications of adjectives driven by syntactic goals, see Cinque (2010), a general, book-length investigation of the topic, or shorter work including Sproat and Shih (1988), Cinque (1994), Laenzlinger (2000), Scott (2002), Valois (2007), Demonte (2008), Truswell (2009), and Svenonius (2008b). For classifications driven by typological considerations, particularly what concepts various languages lexicalize with adjectives, see Hetzron (1978); Dixon (1982) and Dixon and Aikhenvald (2004). This syntactic and typological/descriptive work could serve as a good starting point for anyone interested in charting new empirical directions in the formal semantics of adjectives. The connection between such work and formal semantics has traditionally been undesirably remote, and it is distinctly uncomfortable that stating essentially syntactic ordering restrictions should require reference to natural classes that sound fundamentally semantic.

---

[15] Color adjectives have interesting semantic properties as well (see Kennedy and McNally 2010 and references cited therein).

2.4 The menagerie of adjectives

2.4.2 Temporal-ordering adjectives

For a few years after the 2008 United States presidential election, there was an acrimonious political dispute about whether (73) is true:

(73) The president was born in the United States.

One empirically well-founded argument against the truth of (73) was, to my knowledge, never made: the president is far too large to fit in a human birth canal.[16]

This would have convinced no one, but it's worth reflecting on why. The infant born in Hawaii to Barack Obama's parents was not president at the time of his birth. The past tense in (73) shifts the time associated with *born* into the past, but *president* remains resolutely anchored in the present. It's a neat design feature of language that we can refer to this infant with a definite description whose descriptive content could not in principle hold of it at the time. It might have been otherwise. One might imagine a language like English in which one has to say (74):

(74) The **future** president was born in the United States.

This leads to two observations.

First, nouns are often interpreted with respect to a time at which they hold, and this time need not correspond to event time of the sentence (Bach 1968; Kamp 1971; Enç 1981; Engdahl 1986; Musan 1995; Kusumoto 1999, 2005; Tonhauser 2002, 2005a,b, 2006). Other examples of this sort include (75):

(75) a. Due to the crash, all the passengers are dead.
      b. Many fugitives are now in jail.   (Musan 1995)

The corpses in (75a) are no longer passengers, and the prisoners in (75b) are no longer fugitives.

The second observation is that there are adjectives like *future* that manipulate the time associated with a noun. Others include (76):

(76) your $\begin{Bmatrix} \text{former} \\ \text{present} \\ \text{erstwhile} \\ \text{previous} \\ \text{old} \end{Bmatrix}$ spouse

---

[16] This example has the faint echo of Kamp's (1971) *A child was born that {will be/would become} king.*

These are what might be called TEMPORAL-ORDERING ADJECTIVES. There is another class of adjectives which could also be characterized as 'temporal' from which they should be distinguished. Those have come to be known as FREQUENCY ADJECTIVES:

(77) a(n) $\begin{Bmatrix} \text{quick} \\ \text{occasional} \\ \text{regular} \\ \text{daily} \end{Bmatrix}$ cup of coffee

Frequency adjectives pose some intricate compositional problems that temporal-ordering adjectives don't, so I'll address that class separately in section 2.5.2.

The analysis of temporal-ordering adjectives hinges partly on how the temporal sensitivity of nouns comes about. This is an issue beyond the scope of this book (though see Musan 1995; Kusumoto 1999; Tonhauser 2002, 2006). Most of the analytical options, though, would leave these adjectives as denoting predicate modifiers of one type or another. Dowty et al. (1981) proposed a denotation that, in its general outlines, has stood the test of time. For them, *former* asserts that the noun does not hold of its individual argument at the evaluation time but does at some time prior to it. They implemented this in a framework in which worlds and times are treated as indices on the interpretation function and manipulated together as pairs. Another way of achieving this with a more recent flavor would be to replace references to possible worlds with Kratzerian situations (Kratzer 1989), which are parts of worlds. Situations can have a temporal location, so one situation can precede another. I'll represent this ordering with $<_{time}$, the 'temporally precedes' relation:

(78) a. $[\![former]\!] = \lambda P_{\langle e, st\rangle} \lambda x \lambda s . \exists s'[s' <_{time} s \land P(x)(s') \land \neg P(x)(s)]$
      b. $[\![former\ president]\!] = [\![former]\!]([\![president]\!])$
      $= \lambda x \lambda s . \exists s' \begin{bmatrix} s' <_{time} s \land \textbf{president}(x)(s') \land \\ \neg \textbf{president}(x)(s) \end{bmatrix}$

Thus a former president in a situation is an individual that is not president in it, but was in an earlier one. The use of situations actually necessitates some further refinements, but for our purposes (78) will suffice.[17]

---

[17] The necessary additional refinements are reflections of general complexities situations bring with them. For example, this denotation would actually be true

2.4 The menagerie of adjectives

There is a twist here, however. In the presence of a possessive, an additional reading emerges (Larson and Cho 2003 and Partee and Borschev 2003):

(79) Mary's former mansion (Partee and Borschev 2003)
  a. something of Mary's that was formerly a mansion (but could now be a ruin)
  b. something that was formerly Mary's mansion (and now is someone else's)

The denotation in (78) would predict the reading in 79a:

(80) a. $[\![\text{former mansion}]\!] = [\![\text{former}]\!]([\![\text{mansion}]\!])$

$= \lambda x \lambda s \,.\, \exists s' \begin{bmatrix} s' <_{time} s \wedge \textbf{mansion}(x)(s') \wedge \\ \neg\textbf{mansion}(x)(s) \end{bmatrix}$

b. $[\![\text{Mary's former mansion}]\!]$

$= \lambda x \lambda s \,.\, [\![\text{Mary's}]\!](x)(s) \wedge [\![\text{former mansion}]\!](x)(s)$

$= \lambda x \lambda s \,.\, \textbf{Mary's}(x)(s) \wedge \exists s' \begin{bmatrix} s' <_{time} s \wedge \\ \textbf{mansion}(x)(s') \wedge \\ \neg\textbf{mansion}(x)(s) \end{bmatrix}$

But the reading 79b remains a mystery. Larson and Cho (2003) and Partee and Borschev (2003) both pursue accounts in which, intuitively, the possessive relation is placed under the scope of *former*. On the Larson and Cho analysis, this is taken as evidence that underlyingly, the structure is closer to (81a):

(81) a. $[\![\text{mansion of Mary's}]\!] = \lambda x \lambda s \,.\, \textbf{mansion}(x)(s) \wedge \textbf{Mary's}(x)(s)$
  b. $[\![\text{former}]\!]([\![\text{mansion of Mary's}]\!])$

$= \lambda x \lambda s \,.\, \exists s' \begin{bmatrix} s' <_{time} s \wedge \\ \textbf{mansion}(x)(s') \wedge \textbf{Mary's}(x)(s') \wedge \\ \neg[\textbf{mansion}(x)(s) \wedge \textbf{Mary's}(x)(s)] \end{bmatrix}$

As (81b) reflects, this yields the desired interpretation.

---

if *s* were in a world in which *x* is president at the time of *s* after all, but *x* happened not to be part of *s*. See Kratzer (1989, 2008) for discussion of such issues. Alternatively, one could simply treat the situation variable *s* as standing for a world-time pair in the spirit of Dowty et al.; or replace it with a time variable (and thereby ignore the world argument, since it's not relevant here); or treat nouns as having independent world and time arguments. This is of course in addition to going down **precisely** the path Dowty et al. go down, which is to treat world-time pairs as parameters provided to the interpretation function itself (i.e. $[\![\cdot]\!]^{w,t}$).

From this perspective, one might worry about the contrast in (82):

(82) a. Mary's former Japanese car
      b. Mary's Japanese former car

Only (82a) has the reading on which Mary's ownership is in the past; (82b) has only the reading on which the object's carhood is in the past. If the possessor-based readings arise because the possessor is actually interpreted quite low, this is unexpected. If, on the other hand, the possessor is interpreted high, above *Japanese*, but just below *former*, the correct result would follow. What syntactic or semantic principle could ensure that the structure that is interpreted has this shape is an interesting question. It's part of a larger set of questions about the relative order of adjectives, which we will return to in section 2.6.

An advantage of the predicate-modifier denotation for *former* is that it immediately accounts for its impossibility in predicative positions:

(83)   #That president is $\left\{ \begin{array}{l} \text{former} \\ \text{erstwhile} \\ \text{previous} \end{array} \right\}$.

Given the predicate-modifier type, adjectives of this class will always require a noun as an argument. Of course, if one adopts the Montague (1970) view that predicative adjectives apply to unpronounced nouns first, (83) would remain a problem, just like the impossibility of modal adjectives such as *alleged* in this position.

The particular situation-based implementation I've pursued here might feel vaguely familiar in light of the discussion of Larson (1998, 1999) in section 2.3.3. Situations and events are closely related, and one might imagine paraphrases of some of these meanings in terms of events. A former president, for example, is someone whose 'presidenting' events are in the past, and a former mansion is one whose mansion states are in the past. It would be a worthy enterprise to attempt to use these facts to provide an analysis of temporal-ordering adjectives in the Larson style. Among the major problems one would confront is the fact that *former* seems to be privative; that it's not clear what role a generic quantifier would play here; and that *former* is impossible in predicative positions.

2.4.3 Classificatory/relational adjectives

As section 2.3 noted, it may be both possible and desirable to assimilate many subsective adjectives to intersective ones. This project confronts a challenge in adjectives such as those in (84):

2.4 The menagerie of adjectives

(84) a. religious official
 b. legal conflict
 c. moral infraction
 d. technical architect

These are subsective (a legal conflict is a conflict), but they aren't straightforwardly intersective (a legal conflict is not simply something that's legal and a conflict). Nor is it clear how any of the ideas already raised could cope with this. In the spirit of Larson (1998), one might attempt to think of *religious official* as someone whose office-holder state is religious or who does their 'officialing' religiously, but that seems to be skating over dangerously thin ice. Or one could consider implicit-argument analysis, pursuing an analogy to 'an official who is religious as an official'. A possibility, perhaps, but again: thin ice. But what other options are there? Should we surrender to the higher-type denotation?

McNally and Boleda Torrent (2003) make the case for resisting this impulse. Following Bally (1944), they refer to this class as RELATIONAL ADJECTIVES (see also Bosque and Picallo 1996; Giorgi and Longobardi 1991; Demonte 2008).[18] Another term – possibly a more transparent one – for this general class is CLASSIFICATORY ADJECTIVES (Cinque 2010; Lin 2008; Morzycki 2004a, 2005a; Rutkowski and Progovac 2005), though some authors reserve this term for a subclass of relational adjectives (Bosque and Picallo 1996; Arsenijević et al. 2014). Other terms floating around in this general lexical field include 'associative adjectives' (Giegerich 2005) and 'pseudo-adjectives' (Alexiadou and Stavrou 2011).

McNally and Boleda Torrent observe that this class of adjectives has a number of characteristics that suggest they get a property interpretation. First, in Catalan they occur postnominally as in (85), a position from which predicate-modifier-denoting adjectives like *presumpte* 'alleged' are banned:

(85) a. arquitecte tècnic
  architect technical
  'technical architect'

 b. una malaltia pulmonar
  a disease pulmonary
  'a pulmonary disease'

---

[18] The term 'relational' isn't optimal, in that it suggests these adjectives should denote relations. It's also uncomfortably close to 'relative adjective', which has a number of other uses. See its glossary entry for details.

(86) a. un presumpte assassí
       'an alleged murderer'
    b. #un assassí presumpte

Relational adjectives also occur predicatively, again contrasting with *presumpte*:

(87) a. El domini del Tortosa va ser només territorial.
       'The dominance of the Tortosa [soccer team] was only territorial.'
    b. Aquest congrés és internacional.
       'This conference is international.'
    c. El conflicte és polític.
       'The conflict is political.'

(88) #L'assassí   era presumpte.
     the murder is alleged

Finally, they point out that relational adjectives can occur on their own, with no overt noun:

(89) a. Els joves van venir.
       'The young ones came.'
    b. *Els presumptes van venir.
       'The alleged ones came.'

They don't say this, but in this last characteristic they may have discovered a novel diagnostic for distinguishing adjective classes even in English, as the contrasts between *The young are foolish* and #*The alleged were indicted* reflects. One shouldn't put much weight on English in this context, though, because English is fairly restrictive in where it allows this phenomenon (essentially, in descriptions of humans, as Pullum 1975's term 'people deletion' suggests).

The challenge, then, is to provide these adjectives with a property denotation while capturing the fact that they lack the basic intersective entailment (from, e.g., *Floyd is a technical architect* to *Floyd is technical*). McNally and Boleda Torrent's idea is that the key to the puzzle is that these adjectives really aren't about ordinary individuals. Rather, they are about kinds (Carlson 1977). In a nutshell, a kind is an abstract sort of individual that, in English, is named by bare plurals like *dogs* or *screwdrivers*. Ordinary individuals ('objects') can be realizations of a kind. It's certainly true that an object of which the description *technical*

2.4 The menagerie of adjectives

architect holds is not itself technical, but the **kind** of architect that it instantiates is.

McNally and Boleda Torrent capture this by supposing that all nouns actually denote relations between kinds and individuals that realize them, as in (90a), and relational adjectives denote properties of kinds, as in (90b) (kind and object variables are distinguished with subscripts; similar ideas about a kind level within NP occur in Zamparelli 1995):

(90)   a. $[\![\textit{architect}]\!] = \lambda x_k \lambda y_o \,.\, \textbf{realizes}(x_k)(y_o) \land \textbf{architect}(x_k)$
        b. $[\![\textit{technical}]\!] = \lambda x_k \,.\, \textbf{technical}(x_k)$

These combine through the invocation of a new rule of semantic composition specialized for this purpose, and the kind argument is saturated with a contextually supplied value (k_k), yielding (91):

(91) $[\![\textit{technical architect}]\!] = \lambda y_o \,.\, \textbf{realizes}(k_k)(y_o) \land \textbf{architect}(k_k) \land \textbf{technical}(k_k)$

One might resist the idea that all nouns have both an object and a kind argument, and that they all therefore lexically encode the realization relation, but the basic analysis could be maintained even without this. One could also adopt a theory without a construction-specific semantic composition rule and still maintain the basic analysis. I'll sketch what that might look like. First, nouns could denote properties of kinds, as in (92a); they could then combine intersectively with a relational adjective, as in (92b):

(92)   a. $[\![\textit{architect}]\!] = \lambda x_k \,.\, \textbf{architect}(x_k)$
        b. $[\![\textit{technical architect}]\!] = \lambda x_k \,.\, \textbf{architect}(x_k) \land \textbf{technical}(x_k)$

At this point, some means of shifting this type to a property of objects is necessary. This could be done by positing a type shift (Partee 1987). Alternatively, a null morpheme could do this work. It would apply to a property of kinds and yield something that is true of an object iff it realizes a kind of which the property holds:

(93)   a. $[\![\text{REALIZE}]\!] = \lambda P_{\langle k, t \rangle} \lambda x_o \,.\, \exists y_k [P(y_k) \land \textbf{realize}(y_k)(x_o)]$
        b. $[\![\text{REALIZE } \textit{technical architect}]\!]$
           $= \lambda x_o \,.\, \exists y_k \begin{bmatrix} \textbf{architect}(y_k) \land \textbf{technical}(y_k) \land \\ \textbf{realize}(y_k)(x_o) \end{bmatrix}$

Thus (93b) denotes a property of objects that realize a technical-architect kind. A more sophisticated implementation of this variant of the approach might make use of the specialized type shifts of Chierchia (1984, 1998), which are designed specifically for manipulating kinds. One way or another, McNally and Boleda Torrent's core idea remains: that kinds play a role low in the nominal projection and that relational adjectives are predicates of kinds.

There seems to be some unclarity around whether adjectives of this class can occur predicatively:

(94)   a.   a medical doctor
       b.   ??That doctor is medical.

(95)   a.   an electric razor
       b.   That razor is electric.

The crucial issues in ruling out predicative uses would be whether an adjective can apply either to kinds or to objects, and whether the subject DP is kind-denoting. See McNally and Boleda Torrent for discussion.

One useful feature of this analysis is that it might explain certain otherwise mysterious effects of adjective order. Svenonius (1994) observes a truth-conditional difference in (96):

(96)   a.   dead dangerous animal
       b.   dangerous dead animal

A dead squirrel may well be a *dangerous dead animal* by virtue of being riddled with disease, but it is clearly not a *dead dangerous animal* because it isn't a *dangerous animal* at all (unlike, say, a lion). Neither of these adjectives is scope-bearing, so the contrast isn't expected. On the kind-based analysis, these might have the structures and denotations in (97):

(97)   a.   dead [REALIZE [dangerous animal]]
       b. $[\![\text{dangerous animal}]\!] = \lambda y_k . \textbf{dangerous}(y_k) \wedge \textbf{animal}(y_k)$
                                                (interpreted intersectively)
       c. $[\![\text{REALIZE}]\!]\,([\![\text{dangerous animal}]\!])$
$$= \lambda x_o . \exists y_k \begin{bmatrix} \textbf{dangerous}(y_k) \wedge \textbf{animal}(y_k) \wedge \\ \textbf{realize}(y_k)(x_o) \end{bmatrix}$$
       d. $[\![\text{dead [REALIZE [dangerous animal]] }]\!]$
$$= \lambda x_o . \exists y_k \begin{bmatrix} \textbf{dangerous}(y_k) \wedge \textbf{animal}(y_k) \wedge \\ \textbf{realize}(y_k)(x_o) \end{bmatrix} \wedge$$
$$\textbf{dead}(x_o) \quad \text{(interpreted intersectively)}$$

2.4 The menagerie of adjectives

(98)   dangerous [dead [REALIZE animal]]
  a. $[\![\text{REALIZE } animal]\!] = \lambda x_o . \exists y_k [\text{animal}(y_k) \wedge \text{realize}(y_k)(x_o)]$
  b. $[\![dead\ [\ \text{REALIZE } animal\ ]]\!] = \lambda x_o . \exists y_k [\text{animal}(y_k) \wedge \text{realize}(y_k)(x_o)] \wedge \text{dead}(x_o)$
  c. $[\![dangerous\ [\ dead\ [\ \text{REALIZE } animal\ ]]]\!] = \lambda x_o . \exists y_k [\text{animal}(y_k) \wedge \text{realize}(y_k)(x_o)] \wedge \text{dead}(x_o) \wedge \text{dangerous}(x_o)$

The lower occurrence of *dangerous* in (97) would thus be predicated of a kind, and the higher one in (98) of an object. Throughout, *dangerous* and *dead* are simply intersective. I don't know whether McNally and Boleda Torrent would endorse this analysis of *dangerous*, but the effect in (98) is just the sort of thing one might expect in light of their analysis.

2.4.4 The trouble with stone lions

There is a better-known puzzle that may be related, if indirectly, because it too may be amenable to a kind-based analysis. It is reflected in NPs like those in (99), with (99a) being a famous example from Kamp and Partee (1995):

(99)   a. stone lion
       b. paper plane
       c. porcelain ferret

The puzzle is that strictly speaking, these modifiers are privative: a stone lion is not a lion. Yet the clarity of that judgment melts away upon reflection: 'it isn't a lion, not **really**, but then again it sort of is, in a way, because it's, you know, pretty liony'. The puzzle is, primarily, how to compose the two elements semantically to get an appropriate result, and second, how to do it in a way that does justice to this intuition.

Before we move on, let's take a moment to be pedantic. It's conventional in discussions of *stone lion* and its kin to refer to *stone* as an adjective. This is eminently understandable. There are adjectives that behave in the relevant way (*wooden* is one), and in any case the syntactic category of *stone* isn't crucial to the discussion. All that's crucial is that it is some sort of adnominal modifier. It nevertheless warrants pointing out that *stone* is not actually an adjective, at least not yet, not in most people's grammars. Standard diagnostics for adjectives all fail:

(100) a. *That lion seems stone.
       b. *$\begin{Bmatrix} \text{more stone} \\ \text{stoner} \end{Bmatrix}$ than Clyde

c. *a very stone lion
d. *the stoneness of the lion

If this isn't an adjective, what is it? The obvious answer is that it's precisely what it looks like: a noun. What we need to explain is why it can occur in that position and how it's interpreted there. One possibility is to analyze these expressions as noun–noun compounds. I'm skeptical of this route too, though, for reasons that include the very un-compound-like predictability of their meanings (Morzycki 2004a, 2005a). So there is actually an interesting analytical problem here, and in referring to these expressions simply as 'adjectives', we obscure it. A better term – more syntactically accurate but otherwise analytically neutral – is 'attributive noun'. All that said, for many speakers some of these modifiers seem to be on their way to becoming adjectives, and *plastic* may already have gotten there.

The standard reference on *stone lion* and its kin is Kamp and Partee (1995). They suggest that the driving force behind the interpretation of such expressions is a principle that they establish on other grounds. Their paper advocates an inherent-vagueness/supervaluation approach to vagueness (see section 3.4 for extensive discussion). This provides a convenient and flexible way of thinking about how context affects the meaning of linguistic expressions. Normally, we would think of *lion* as having a single extension – the set of all lions – and any given individual is either in the set or it isn't. On a supervaluation approach, *lion* has two extensions: a positive extension, the set of things that are clearly lions, and a negative extension, the set of things that clearly aren't. Borderline cases are in neither. To see how this can help with *stone lion*, it helps to first consider a more prosaic example like *small elephant* (also discussed in section 2.2.3). On a naïve view, one might imagine *small elephant* would have nothing in its positive extension because no elephants are small. But of course, that's not how things work. Rather, Kamp and Partee suggest, we construe *small* in a way that's adapted to *elephant* by 'calibrating' it so that it has elephants in both its positive and its negative extension. The principle driving this is (101):

(101) NON-VACUITY PRINCIPLE
In any given context, try to interpret any predicate so that both its positive and its negative extension are non-empty.

This independent principle might guide us in how we construe *stone lion*. As with *small elephant*, one might imagine *stone lion* would have nothing in its positive extension because no actual lions are made of

2.4 The menagerie of adjectives

stone. But this is precisely what the Non-Vacuity Principle prohibits. In this case, for reasons that are slightly mysterious, it is the noun rather than its modifier that gets recalibrated (the more common term is 'coerced'). The process is otherwise the same. *Lion* is construed so as to include some stone things in its positive (and presumably negative) extension.

As Partee (2007) points out, it's worth reflecting on the relationship between this form of coercion and the one she posits for *fake gun* (see section 2.2.5). Both cases involve privative modifiers, and, by hypothesis, both involve coercion.[19]

While the framework they propose is spelled out very explicitly overall, the process by which we recalibrate *lion* is not spelled out in detail. In one respect, that seems natural. The conceptual machinery that allows us to work out how to extend the concept 'lion' to include stone things may not even be linguistic. In another, it's an unsatisfying place to wind up. There might, however, be a way of coping with this problem with the right tool, one that could equally well model linguistic and non-linguistic cognitive processes. As Oliver (2012) points out, Optimality Theory (Prince and Smolensky 1993) is just such a tool. At heart, Optimality Theory is an explicit way of modeling how language – or anything – resolves competing goals. In phonology, for example, language strives both to avoid complex consonant clusters and to avoid deleting sounds. These goals may conflict, and the grammar of a particular language can be construed as a ranking of such goals according to which should prevail when a choice between them must be made. Oliver proposes an account of how the coercion in *stone lion* works in Optimality-Theoretic terms, in which the competing goals to be resolved are preserving different elements of the meaning of *stone* and *lion*, such as animacy, being lion-shaped, or being made of stone. Hogeweg (2012) approaches the problem in a similar spirit, building on psycholinguistic facts about the processing of metaphor.

2.4.5 The attributive-with-infinitive construction

One of the strategies for dealing with subsectivity – explored in section 2.3.4 – was to provide adjectives with an implicit argument whose value is typically identical to the modified noun. If this idea is on the right track, we might expect to find cases in which the presence of an **overt**

---

[19] Thanks to Alan Bale for reminding me of the connection.

argument creates an interpretive effect precisely analogous to subsective readings.

Fleisher (2008a,b, 2011) examines a phenomenon that might have just this property, which he calls the ATTRIBUTIVE-WITH-INFINITIVE CONSTRUCTION (AIC). He doesn't actually make this claim, and the phenomenon is interesting for independent reasons; nevertheless, it would seem to be just such a case:

(102)   a. He's a [good __] person [to talk to].
            b. That is a [smart __] sofa [to buy].

In both these examples, the bracketed infinitive is an argument of the adjective, displaced from the complement position indicated with '__'. Both examples also give rise to a subsective but not intersective interpretation:

(103)   He's a [good __] person [to talk to].
            entails: He's a person.
            does not entail: He's good.

(104)   That is a [smart __] sofa [to buy].
            entails: That is a sofa.
            does not entail: That [sofa] is smart.

Just as the implicit-argument analysis would lead us to expect, the subsective reading depends on the argument. In its absence, only an intersective reading is available:

(105)   He's a good person.
            entails: He's a person.
            entails: He's good.

(106)   That's a smart sofa.
            entails: That is a sofa.
            entails: That [sofa] is smart.

This may not be all good news for an implicit-argument analysis of subsective adjectives. Such an analysis might also lead us to expect that the infinitive itself could be unpronounced and that the subsective reading would be available in (106) as well. One might avoid this by simply stipulating that the infinitive can't be left implicit in this way. For this to be convincing, of course, it would help to provide a general theory

2.4 The menagerie of adjectives

of the circumstances under which arguments of subsective adjectives can be implicit. Formulating such a theory strikes me as a worthwhile enterprise.

Fleisher distinguishes two flavors of this construction. One, the clausal AIC, is exemplified above. It differs from nominal AICs in that nominal AICs give rise to a sense of 'inappropriateness' and are possible with adjectives that don't independently license infinitive complements:

(107) a. *Middlemarch* is a long book to assign.
b. That is a well-made car to sell for scrap.

Uttering (107a) conveys the sense that it is inappropriate to assign a book as long as *Middlemarch*. Neither *long* nor *well-made* take infinitival complements:

(108) a. *It is long to assign *Middlemarch*.
b. *It is well-made to sell that car for scrap.

In (107a), there is the sense that it is inappropriate to assign as long a book as *Middlemarch*; in (107b), that the car is too well-made to sell for scrap. The two constructions pose slightly different analytical problems. I won't present Fleisher's analysis, but it's worth noting one of its most striking features: the inappropriateness flavor is derived from independently motivated assumptions about the modality associated with infinitival relative clauses.

2.4.6 Adnominal degree modifiers

Among the classes of subsective adjectives introduced in section 2.2.2 were examples like those in (109):

(109) a. Floyd is a $\begin{Bmatrix} \text{big} \\ \text{huge} \\ \text{colossal} \end{Bmatrix}$ idiot.

b. Floyd is a(n) $\begin{Bmatrix} \text{utter} \\ \text{complete} \\ \text{absolute} \end{Bmatrix}$ idiot.

These are subsective in slightly different ways. Size adjectives such as those in (109a) are ambiguous between intersective readings involving physical size and subsective readings involving the degree to which the predicate expressed by the noun holds. By contrast, expressions such as those in (109b) sometimes lack an intersective reading entirely, and it's not even clear conceptually what an intersective reading would look like – that is, what it would mean for an individual to 'be utter' or 'be absolute'.

The size adjective uses have begun to attract analytical attention (Morzycki 2005b, 2009b; Sassoon 2007, 2013b; de Vries 2010; Xie 2010; Constantinescu 2011). The other uses have been noted as examples of subsective interpretations since at least Siegel (1976a) and as examples of obligatorily attributive adjectives since at least Bolinger (1972) (and one suspects earlier), but they have attracted less attention (apart from Morzycki 2012b and Constantinescu 2011). The broader issue they both raise is actually as much about nouns as about adjectives, and about gradability. A great deal is known about gradability in adjectives, but in nouns it is more mysterious.

Because the analysis of these expressions unavoidably involves reference of scales and degrees – either explicitly in the semantics or else at some broader conceptual level – I won't discuss them in earnest in this chapter, which attempts to sidestep scalar issues. The main discussion of these puzzles is to be found in section 6.3.2. That said, even without too much further inspection, these modifiers suggest at least two broad conclusions relevant to the issues at hand.

First, they are a further indication of the diversity of the class of subsective modifiers. Whatever is going on in these cases, it seems quite different from the other cases we've seen. Of course, one could always treat these as denoting predicate modifiers without worrying about what precisely their lexical content is. The moment one starts worrying about the details, though, it becomes clear that the degree readings involved here are quite unlike any of the other readings we've seen.

Second, they raise a question that the *stone lion* examples also raise: are all such adnominal modifiers actually adjectives? Just as *stone* doesn't seem to pass standard diagnostics for adjectives (and is in fact a noun), so too *utter* seems to fail them:

(110) a. *That idiot seems utter.
 b. *a $\begin{Bmatrix} \text{more utter} \\ \text{utterer} \end{Bmatrix}$ idiot than Clyde
 c. *a very utter idiot
 d. *the utterness of the idiot

Absolute patterns similarly, and *complete* loses its degree reading in these cases.

2.5 ADJECTIVES WHERE THEY HAVE NO RIGHT TO BE: ADVERBIAL READINGS

2.5.1 A scope puzzle

One of the few things the underlined expressions in (111) have in common is that they are each interpreted with either clausal or VP scope:

(111) a. <u>Occasionally</u>, a sailor strolled by.
      b. Floyd had a cup of coffee <u>quickly</u>.
      c. <u>On average</u>, an American has 2.3 children.
      d. <u>It's not known</u> which hotel Solange stayed in.
      e. The ferret was <u>wholly</u> submerged.

In (111a), for example, *occasionally* combines with *a sailor strolled by*; in (111b), *quickly* with *had a cup of coffee*; and so on. The precise way these expressions combine with their phrase-structural neighbors is not immediately relevant here. The crucial thing is what they combine with. In light of that fact, it should come as a surprise that the meanings of these expressions can also be expressed with attributive adjectives:

(112) a. An <u>occasional</u> sailor strolled by.
      b. Floyd had a <u>quick</u> cup of coffee.
      c. The <u>average</u> American has 2.3 children.
      d. Solange stayed in an <u>unknown</u> hotel.
      e. The <u>whole</u> ferret was submerged.

The adjectives in (112) are embedded inside NPs. Yet they somehow give rise to meanings in which they seem to be interpreted elsewhere, as the paraphrases in (111) reflect. Put another way, to achieve their actual meanings, these adjectives would apparently have to combine with a much larger syntactic expression than their surface syntax would suggest, and – more troubling still – one in which they are deeply embedded. This is thoroughly bizarre behavior. It's as though these adjectives haven't been notified of how compositionality works. In fact, their behavior could even be viewed as counterevidence against the foundational assumption that natural languages are compositional.

These are called ADVERBIAL READINGS of adjectives because, in the prototypical cases, they give rise to paraphrases that involve an adverb (Stump 1981). The term originally referred only to a reading of frequency adjectives such as *occasional*, but, as the examples in (112) demonstrate, the overall phenomenon is more general. Indeed, it might be more general than this, extending to *same* and *different*, so perhaps the term NON-LOCAL READING (found in Schwarz 2005, 2006) is preferable. Each of the classes of adjectives that have this property is usually analyzed separately, and they typically aren't discussed under the single rubric of adverbial readings.

This section will explore some of the adjective classes that give rise to this puzzle. They may be bound together only by one thin empirical strand, their unexpected apparent scope. A more interesting hypothesis, though, is that their unexpected scope has a common cause. One reason to suspect that this might be so is that their unexpected scope correlates with two other facts that are logically independent. First, these readings often affect how the determiner is interpreted. Second, adverbial readings seem to be available only to adjectives in higher positions in the tree. The former property is widely noted, though not usually as a property of all these adjective classes together. The latter is often noted for, e.g., *occasional*, but otherwise usually seems to escape attention.

2.5.2 Frequency adjectives: the facts

The first corner of the grammar in which these problems were recognized was frequency adjectives, noted initially (rather offhandedly) in Bolinger (1967b).[20] Stump (1981) divided the readings of these adjectives into three classes. Perhaps the least startling one is the INTERNAL READING:

(113)   a. Floyd is an occasional sailor.
          'Floyd is someone who sails occasionally.'

   b. Floyd is a frequent contributor.
          'Floyd is someone who contributes frequently.'

   c. Floyd spoke to his daily visitor.
          'Floyd spoke to someone who visits him daily.'

Schäfer (2007) observed that this reading arises only with nouns that name a participant. It's less mysterious than the other readings in that

---

[20] Sometimes 'infrequency adjectives' (e.g. *infrequent*) are treated as a separate class. A similar phenomenon also received attention fairly early on. Hall (1973) observed that the work of P. G. Wodehouse is full of examples such as *He uncovered the fragrant eggs and I pronged a moody forkful* and *Somebody had opened a tentative window or two*, in which an adjective appears to get some sort of adverbial reading.

2.5 Adjectives where they have no right to be: adverbial readings

this one involves no scope acrobatics. But, to give it its due, there is still something to explain here. It's unlikely to be an accident that all these paraphrases involve an adverb, and simply saying that on this reading the adjective denotes a property of individuals wouldn't seem to do that justice.

The second reading is the ADVERBIAL READING. 'External reading' might be a better term, since (113) also involves adverbial paraphrases.[21] This is the scopally acrobatic reading:

(114) a. The occasional sailor strolled by. (Bolinger 1967b)
'Occasionally, a sailor strolled by.'

b. A periodic investigation would turn up a few new leads. (Stump 1981)
'Periodically, an investigation would turn up a few new leads.'

c. The monotony of North Dakota was interrupted by a sporadic billboard.
'Sporadically, the monotony of North Dakota was interrupted by a billboard.'

An adjective can get this reading even in the absence of an appropriate adverbial counterpart (*The odd sailor strolled by*; Larson 1999 attributes this observation to Ed Keenan). This reading can also give rise to scope ambiguities (Stump 1981):

(115) Every tourist saw an occasional sailor.

This can mean either that occasionally an event took place in which all the tourists saw a sailor, or that for each tourist, there were potentially separate occasional events of sailor-viewing.

There is a third reading whose status is more unclear: the GENERIC READING (the examples are from Stump):

(116) An occasional cup of coffee helps keep John awake.
  a. 'Having a cup of coffee occasionally helps keep John awake.'
  b. *'Occasionally, a cup of coffee helps keep John awake.'

---

[21] Bolinger (1967b) proposed the colorful term 'stroboscopic', after a device similar to a strobe light used to observe certain types of repetitive motion.

62 THE LEXICAL SEMANTICS OF ADJECTIVES: MORE THAN JUST SCALES

(117) Larry could tolerate an infrequent visit to the dentist.
  a. 'Visiting the dentist infrequently is something Larry could tolerate.'
  b. *'Infrequently, Larry could tolerate a visit to the dentist.'

(118) A periodic checkup never hurts.
  a. 'A checkup that takes place periodically never hurts.'
  b. *'Periodically, a checkup never hurts.'

As the (b) examples reflect, these readings can't be paraphrased the way adverbial readings can. Instead, Stump observed, they involve reference to kinds (in the sense of Carlson 1977), just as bare plurals like *bears* do. *An occasional cup of coffee*, for example, is a kind of thing that keeps John awake. This reading is oddly intermediate between the other two. On the one hand, it resembles the adverbial reading in that it doesn't involve reference to a particular object. On the other, it resembles the internal reading in that it gives rise to paraphrases that involve an adverb within the NP. For this reason, there is a certain impulse to assimilate the generic reading to one of the others. Gehrke and McNally (2010) treat it as a special case of the adverbial reading. I won't linger on it further, but for more discussion see also Stump (1981); Schäfer (2007) and DeVries (2010).

Two important additional observations need to be made about adverbial readings. First, they impose a curious requirement on the determiner that it be either *the*, *a*, or semantically bleached *your* (i.e. the colloquial-register *your* that means roughly 'the'; the % below indicates the absence of the adverbial reading):

(119) $\begin{Bmatrix} \text{The} \\ \text{An} \\ \text{Your} \\ \text{\%This} \\ \text{\%Every} \\ \text{\%Any} \end{Bmatrix}$ occasional sailor strolled by.

Moreover, the meaning of the sentence doesn't seem to change depending on which of the three licit determiners is chosen – somehow, the differences among them are leveled. Second, adverbial readings don't occur if the adjective is not adjacent to the determiner:

(120) %A well-dressed occasional sailor strolled by.

2.5 Adjectives where they have no right to be: adverbial readings

To be sure, strings like *a very infrequent visit* or *a relatively unknown hotel* are possible, but not on the adverbial reading.

2.5.3 The adverbial reading of frequency adjectives

There is one obvious answer to why some adjectives seem to be interpreted in adverbial positions: movement. One might imagine that the adjective simply moves out of the DP to adjoin to the VP or clause, and that it has an adverbial denotation. This would address some parts of the problem, but it has significant disadvantages (see Larson 1999 and Zimmermann 2003 for details). First, there is no independent evidence for such movement. Second, this movement wouldn't address why an adverbial expression would mysteriously find itself in the middle of a nominal in the first place.

Third, it's not clear how the semantics would cope with the resulting structure. The moved adjective might leave behind an individual-denoting trace, as is standard in movement of this type (Heim and Kratzer 1998). But this would lead to a type clash. An individual can of course combine with a property, but the result – a truth value (or proposition) – isn't an appropriate denotation for an NP and would clash with a determiner. Alternatively, the moved adjective might leave behind a trace of an appropriate type, or an uninterpreted trace, or perhaps no trace at all. These options aren't inherently objectionable, and there is some evidence for their utility elsewhere.[22] Nevertheless, the need for these semantic stipulations – on top of the stipulation of a movement operation for which there is no independent evidence – certainly doesn't add to the appeal of a movement analysis.[23]

Spurred on by the correlation between adverbial readings and odd interactions with the determiner, a number of people have taken the adjective–determiner relationship to be the heart of the problem instead. Analyses of this sort include Stump (1981), Larson (1998), Zimmermann (2000), and Zimmermann (2003). They all have in common that a 'complex determiner' is formed. This can be brought about

---

[22] The usual assumption about intermediate traces (ones that aren't in the base position of the moved element) is that they are ignored by the semantics, and this may be possible elsewhere too (Fox 1999). Thanks to Alan Bale for pointing this out.

[23] There may be particular implementations of this idea that make it more appealing. In a very loose sense, Barker (2007) – as we'll see – posits something in this spirit for *same*. He argues that in Type Logical Grammar, the desired effect can be achieved naturally without any unappealing assumptions.

by having the adjective syntactically incorporate into the determiner, in the same way that objects can incorporate into verbs (Baker 1988):[24]

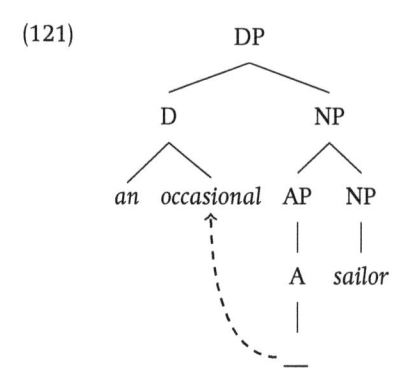

(121)
```
            DP
           /  \
          D    NP
         / \   / \
        an  occasional AP  NP
              ↑     |   |
              ┆     A  sailor
              ┆     |
              └─────┘
```

It's worth pointing out that there's something odd about this incorporation. Head movement normally occurs into a head from its complement (Travis 1984). Here, movement is from from an adjunct. This could be remedied by assuming an Abney (1987) syntax of attributive adjectives, in which adjectives take NPs as complements:

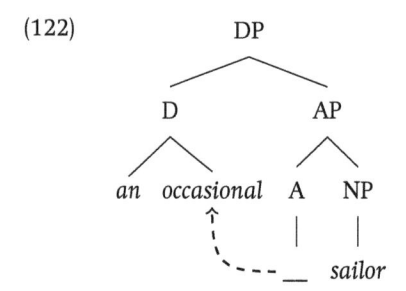

(122)
```
            DP
           /  \
          D    AP
         / \   / \
        an  occasional A   NP
              ↑        |   |
              ┆        └─ sailor
              └────────┘
```

This syntax, however, poses a number of major semantic problems, including how a common semantics could be provided for such adjectives and predicative adjectives and how degree morphemes should fit into this picture. On the other hand, there is independent overt evidence for movement of this kind. Svenonius (1994) argues that a certain class of adjectives in Norwegian can 'optionally behave as determiners'. Something similar might be said for English adjectives

---

[24] For convenience, I assume here that head movement doesn't leave a trace.

2.5 Adjectives where they have no right to be: adverbial readings

such as *many* or *two*, which are routinely analyzed as determiners. Perhaps *another* might be a kind of historical echo of the kinship between these two categories, with a historical source in the sequence *an other*.[25]

Once formed, the complex determiner can have access to clause-level material in the same way quantificational determiners generally can. Here is one way to implement this idea, roughly along the lines proposed by Zimmermann (2003) but radically simplified. First, it will be convenient to assume that a VP like *strolled by* denotes a relation between an individual stroller and the strolling event, as in (123a). The denotation of the complex determiner, then, can be as in (123b), which makes use of a special quantifier **OCCASIONAL**. This leads to a sentence denotation as in (123c):[26]

(123) a. $[\![\text{strolled by}]\!] = \lambda x \lambda e \,.\, \textbf{strolled-by}(x)(e)$

b. $[\![\text{an-occasional}]\!]$
   $= \lambda P_{\langle e, t \rangle} \lambda f_{\langle e, vt \rangle} \,.\, \textbf{OCCASIONAL } e[\exists x[P(x) \wedge f(x)(e)]]$

c. $[\![\text{an-occasional}]\!]([\![\text{sailor}]\!])([\![\text{strolled by}]\!])$
   $= \textbf{OCCASIONAL } e[\exists x[\textbf{sailor}(x) \wedge \textbf{strolled-by}(x)(e)]]$

---

[25] One might dismiss this as a historical quirk irrelevant to any speaker's individual grammar, but consider *a whole nother*. Although it's not customary to use *nother* in writing, this is probably the most common pronunciation. This structure would seem to have arisen by breaking apart *another* – perhaps a reflection of the historical memory that there was an adjective here (and of some confusion about where its morpheme boundaries lie).

[26] This implementation is also simplified in how the denotation of *strolled by* arises. This can be seen in cases in which *occasional sailor* is interpreted in an object position. In that case, the structure would involve binding the trace of the nominal's vacated position and creating via movement a lambda abstract with which it can combine (Heim and Kratzer 1998):

(i) Floyd saw an occasional sailor.

   a. $[_{\langle\langle e, vt\rangle, t\rangle}$ an-occasional sailor $]\,[_{\langle e, vt\rangle} \lambda x_1 \,[_{\langle v, t\rangle}$ Floyd saw $x_1 \,]]$
   b. $[\![\lambda x_1 \,[_{\langle v, t\rangle} \text{Floyd saw } x_1 \,]\!]] = \lambda x_1 \lambda e \,.\, \textbf{saw}(x_1)(\textbf{Floyd})(e)$
   c. $[\![\text{an-occasional sailor}]\!]([\![\lambda x_1 \,[_{\langle v, t\rangle} \text{Floyd saw } x_1 \,]\!]])$
      $= [\lambda f_{\langle e, vt \rangle} \,.\, \textbf{OCCASIONAL } e[\exists x[\textbf{sailor}(x) \wedge f(x)(e)]]]$
      $\qquad\qquad\qquad\qquad\qquad\qquad (\lambda x_1 \lambda e \,.\, \textbf{saw}(x_1)(\textbf{Floyd})(e))$
      $= \textbf{OCCASIONAL } e[\exists x[\textbf{sailor}(x) \wedge \textbf{saw}(x)(\textbf{Floyd})(e)]]$

Even in this more articulated structure, there are problems. Binding off the event variable, for example, can lead to problems further up the tree. See the more worked-out version in Zimmermann for details.

Of course, much hinges on the nature of the novel **OCCASIONAL** quantifier. Roughly, though, one can think of it as holding if there are sufficiently many events suitably distributed in time that satisfy its nuclear scope. Thus (123c) says that occasional events were ones of a sailor strolling by. One drawback of such an analysis is that it can't straightforwardly be extended to the generic readings. Indeed, Stump (1981) proposed a separate account of those cases.

It does, however, have the advantage of naturally accounting for both of the determiner-related properties of adverbial readings: that the adjective is obligatorily adjacent to the determiner and that the determiner doesn't get its usual interpretation. The adjacency follows from the incorporation. The abnormal determiner interpretation follows from the fact that on this view the determiners created by incorporation are simply different from the ordinary ones, with a distinct (by stipulation) denotation.

Gehrke and McNally (2010), building in part on Schäfer (2007), pursue a fundamentally different approach that doesn't rely on special determiners. They propose instead that adverbial readings of frequency adjectives are fundamentally about kinds – not just ordinary kinds of individuals, but also kinds of events (see also Gehrke 2011; Landman and Morzycki 2003; Landman 2006; Anderson and Morzycki forthcoming; Rett 2011b). This ultimately leads to denotations like (124):

(124) An occasional sailor strolled by.
$\exists x_k \exists e_k [\textbf{occasional}(\textbf{sailor})(x_k) \wedge \textbf{strolled-by}(e_k)(x_k)]$

The subscripts indicate whether a variable ranges over individuals (*e*) or kinds (*k*). What (124) says is that there is an individual-kind whose realizations are sailors distributed in time in an appropriately intermittent way, and that this kind participated in the event-kind of strolling by. Of course, much hinges on what it means for a kind to stroll by. Kinds, after all, can't **actually** stroll by in the ordinary sense – only their realizations can. To accommodate this fact, Gehrke and McNally define the **strolled-by** predicate so that, when it applies to kinds, the correct entailments follow about what this means for individual realizations of the kind. This means the compositional machinery is elegantly straightforward and requires no special tricks:[27]

---

[27] Strictly speaking, ⟦ *occasional* ⟧ should apply to an intensional property, type $\langle e, st \rangle$, not $\langle e, t \rangle$.

2.5 Adjectives where they have no right to be: adverbial readings

(125)   a. $[\![\textit{occasional}]\!] = \lambda P_{\langle e,t \rangle} \lambda x_k \,.\, \mathbf{occasional}(P)(x_k)$

       b. $[\![\textit{an occasional sailor}]\!]$

$$= \lambda f_{\langle e, vt \rangle} \,.\, \exists e_k \exists x_k \begin{bmatrix} \mathbf{occasional}(\mathbf{sailor})(x_k) \,\wedge\, \\ f(x_k)(e_k) \end{bmatrix}$$

       c. $[\![\textit{strolled by}]\!] = \lambda x \lambda e \,.\, \mathbf{strolled\text{-}by}(x)(e)$

       d. $[\![\textit{an occasional sailor}]\!] \,(\, [\![\textit{strolled by}]\!] \,)$

$$= \exists e_k \exists x_k \begin{bmatrix} \mathbf{occasional}(\mathbf{sailor})(x_k) \,\wedge\, \\ \mathbf{strolled\text{-}by}(x_k)(e_k) \end{bmatrix}$$

It's less clear on this approach what explains the adjective's obligatory proximity to the determiner on adverbial readings. DeVries (2010) points out another problem that a denotation along these lines must grapple with: the sailor-kind must be not only occasionally realized, but occasionally realized in strolling events (and not, say, runnings).

2.5.4 The internal reading of frequency adjectives

The less challenging of the readings, the internal one, generally doesn't get as much attention, but a major step in the direction of an account is provided in Larson (1999). As we saw in section 2.3.3, he proposes that there are events at play in the internal semantics of the NP and that certain adjectives can be predicated of these events as if they were adverbials. That alone helps explain the connection between the internal reading and NP-internal adverbial paraphrases. But it's possible to push the connection deeper. On Larson's analysis, the nominal event argument is quantified over by a generic quantifier. Frequency adverbials rather resemble quantificational adverbs such as *occasionally* and *frequently* (see section 5.8.2), so it wouldn't be unreasonable to think that on the internal reading, frequency adjectives also contribute a quantifier, one that binds the noun's event argument. Thus one might imagine a structure as in (126), with the denotation in (127):

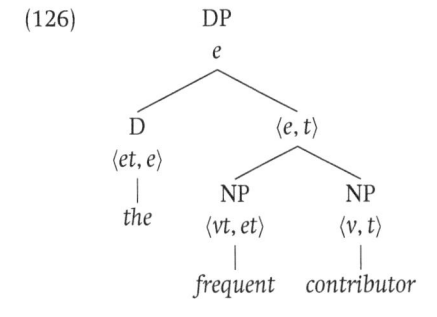

(126)
```
                DP
                e
               / \
              /   \
             D    ⟨e, t⟩
          ⟨et, e⟩  / \
             |    /   \
            the  NP    NP
               ⟨vt, et⟩ ⟨v, t⟩
                 |       |
              frequent contributor
```

(127) a. ⟦ frequent ⟧ = $\lambda f_{\langle v, t\rangle} \lambda x$. **MANY** $e[f(e) \wedge$ **agent**$(e) = x]$
b. ⟦ contributor ⟧ = λe . **contribute**(e)
c. ⟦ frequent ⟧ (⟦ contributor ⟧)
  = λx . **MANY** $e[$**contribute**$(e) \wedge$ **agent**$(e) = x]$

So a frequent contributor is someone who is the agent of many relevant contribution events.[28] This approach would also explain the contrast in (128):

(128) a. Olga is an occasional beautiful dancer.
b. Olga is a beautiful occasional dancer.

Normally, (128a) gets a reading in which Olga occasionally dances beautifully; in (128b), it is Olga that is beautiful. This would follow from this sort of Larsonian analysis. If subsective readings of *beautiful* arise from being interpreted below an event quantifier, and *occasional* contributes an event quantifier, *beautiful* should only be able to receive the subsective reading when below *occasional*. This is only a sketch of an analysis, but it does hint at further evidence that event arguments are involved in nominal semantics. That said, this approach doesn't fully resolve the issue of how such adjective denotations could be unified with the meaning of these adjectives on their other readings. Perhaps they don't need to be, but it seems a desirable goal.

2.5.5 Average Americans and parasitic scope

There is a certain stripe of linguist – Noam Chomsky being a notable example – that is skeptical of the entire enterprise of formal semantics. The reasons for this skepticism typically involve philosophical convictions about the nature of language, the proper aims of linguistic theory, and the relation between linguistic meaning and the world. This discussion sometimes takes place at such a level of abstraction that the connection to concrete linguistic observations seems remote. There is, however, at least one place where these rarified debates touch

---

[28] One could avoid using the **MANY** quantifier by making more sophisticated assumptions about plurality in events:

(i) $\lambda x . \exists e[$**contribute**$(e) \wedge$ **agent**$(e) = x \wedge |e| \geq$ **standard**$_c$(**many**)$]$

This says that there is a (plural) event of x contributing that is made up of a number of subevents that exceeds the contextually supplied standard for counting as 'many'. See section 6.2.1 for a more fully developed implementation.

2.5 Adjectives where they have no right to be: adverbial readings

very directly on a grammatical issue, one relevant here: the semantics of *average*.

On the classical view in formal semantics (though by no means the only one), the model that underlies the semantics is not a representation of the world; it *is* the world. This implies that whenever we claim that a linguistic expression denotes an object – an individual, an event, a property, whatever – we commit ourselves to the existence of that object in the mind-external world.[29] But Chomsky observes that there are certain linguistic expressions which don't seem to refer to anything in the real world:

(129)   The average American has 2.3 children.

(Carlson and Pelletier 2002)

There are two problems here. First, what does *the average American* denote? Which individual is the average American? Even if we could find some particular American – say, Steve – that is the most typical, it still seems strange to say *the average American* denotes Steve, and that every property Steve has is a property of the average American. Second, what does *2.3 children* denote? We're quite happy to judge (129) true without committing ourselves to the idea that there are fractional children.

There are various ways of responding to this concern (see Carlson and Pelletier 2002). Perhaps the most appealing on purely linguistic grounds is just to examine the grammar of the sentence more carefully. This impulse is what animates Kennedy and Stanley (2008, 2009). They observe that *average* has an adverbial paraphrase:

(130)   On average, an American has 2.3 children.

It's therefore natural to assimilate this problem to those we have already encountered in this section. With Larson (1999) and others, they assume that *average* incorporates into the determiner. This is consistent with the fact that other adjectives can't intervene between *average* and *the* (without getting a nonrestrictive reading; Carlson and Pelletier 2002), and the curious sense that *an average American* and *the average American* mean the same thing. (Indeed, *your average American* also means this, paralleling the frequency adjective facts.)

---

[29] See Bach (1989) for a particularly elegant exposition of another way of thinking about the issue.

At this point, things get slightly complicated. This is in part because the syntax–semantics of number terms is more complicated than it seems, and in part because averaging isn't as simple as it seems. Let's begin with the latter. If you were a survey-taker tasked with computing an average, you would need two pieces of information. First, would need to know who to direct your questions to. In this case, the answer is 'Americans'. Second, you would need to know what to ask them. In this case, it's 'how many children do you have?' You would then write down answers, a list of pairs of people and the number of their children: ⟨**Floyd**, 2⟩, ⟨**Greta**, 3⟩, ⟨**Clyde**, 19⟩, and so on. This structure – a set of pairs – is something one can think of as a relation between individuals and numbers, which we might call **have-children**. Thus: **have-children**(**Floyd**)(2), **have-children**(**Greta**)(3), **have-children**(**Clyde**)(19).[30]

The function for computing averages is like this census-taker. It needs two arguments: a property that indicates who or what the average is about, and a relation that reflects the information that's being averaged. To match the content of the sentence, this function, **average**, would need to behave as in (131):

(131)   **average**(**American**)(**have-children**) = 2.3

This isn't the only way an **average** function could work, of course, and this isn't an actual definition of this function, but it will suffice.[31]

Here, then, is a simplified version of Kennedy and Stanley's account. The denotation of *the-average*, the complex determiner created by incorporating *average* into *the*, will be (132), where n is a variable over

---

[30] A more elegant way to think about it might treat this predicate as a function from individuals to the number of their children (a function of this type is called a 'measure function'; see section 3.5.1). My reasons for not going down this road will become clear below.

[31] It could be defined this way:

(i) $\textbf{average} \stackrel{\text{def}}{=} \lambda P_{\langle e, t \rangle} \lambda f_{\langle e, nt \rangle} \cdot \dfrac{\sum\limits_{P(x)} \max\{n : f(x)(n)\}}{|P|}$

Where the type of real numbers is n; $|P|$ is to be read as 'the number (cardinality) of individuals that satisfy the function P'; and the **max** operator applies to a set and yields its maximal element (in this case the largest number; this is necessary because anyone that has three children also has two, but these shouldn't be counted separately in the average). Thus if $P = $ **American** and $f = $ **have-children**, this sums the number of children each American has and divides that by the number of Americans (in other words, it just calculates a mean). See Kennedy and Stanley (2009) for a full implementation.

2.5 Adjectives where they have no right to be: adverbial readings

(real) numbers as well as their type (ultimately, they should probably be treated as degrees; see section 3.5):

(132) $[\![\text{the-average}]\!] = \lambda P_{\langle e, t\rangle} \lambda f_{\langle e, nt\rangle} \lambda n \,.\, \mathbf{average}(P)(f) = n$

To yield the sentence denotation we're aiming at in 131, this will need to combine first with a property. That's easy enough: the complement to *the-average* is *American*, so the full DP will be as in (133):

(133) $[\![\text{the-average American}]\!] = [\![\text{the-average}]\!]([\![\text{American}]\!])$
       $= \lambda g_{\langle e, nt\rangle} \lambda n \,.\, \mathbf{average}(\mathbf{American})(g) = n$

The next point is more difficult: how to provide this with the **have-children** predicate it desires?

This is a syntactic question, and this is where the next layer of complexity arises. For Kennedy and Stanley, two steps are involved. First, the number term *2.3* moves out of its base position by Quantifier Raising, just as a quantified nominal like *every student* would have. That creates the structure in (134):

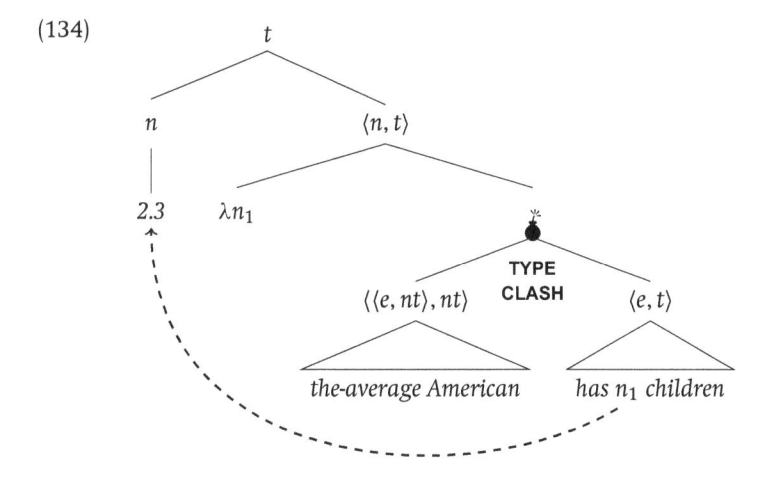

(134)

```
              t
           /     \
          n      ⟨n, t⟩
          |      /    \
         2.3   λn₁    💣
                     / TYPE \
                    /  CLASH \
              ⟨⟨e, nt⟩, nt⟩    ⟨e, t⟩
                  |              |
           the-average American  has n₁ children
```

The-average American will now have to move, due to a type clash. But in order to find itself next to a node of the right type, it will have to move to an unusual place: between *2.3* and the lambda its movement introduced:

(135)

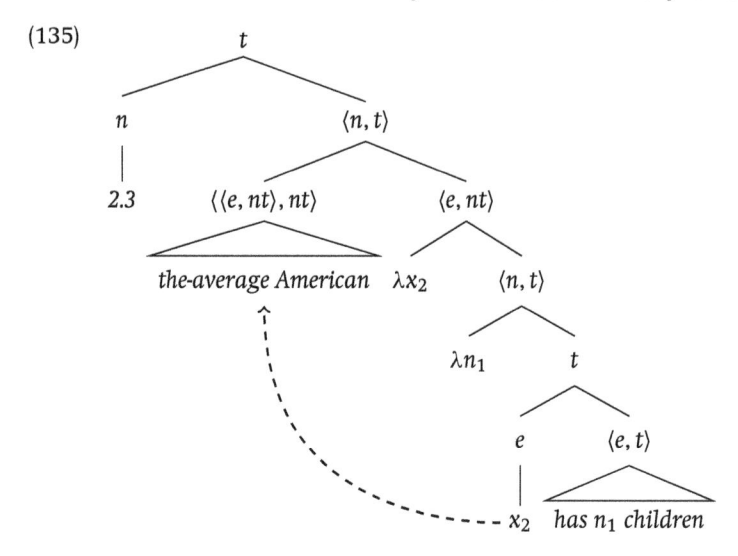

```
                        t
             ┌──────────┴──────────┐
             n                   ⟨n, t⟩
             │         ┌───────────┴───────────┐
            2.3    ⟨⟨e, nt⟩, nt⟩            ⟨e, nt⟩
                ┌──────┴──────┐         ┌──────┴──────┐
         the-average American  λx₂           ⟨n, t⟩
                                      ┌───────┴───────┐
                                     λn₁              t
                                              ┌───────┴───────┐
                                              e            ⟨e, t⟩
                                              │     ┌────────┴────────┐
                                             x₂    has n₁ children
```

In moving to between 2.3 and its lambda, *the-average American* itself creates a lambda, the λx_2 in (135). This variety of movement, in which an expression with a high type moves to a position that was itself created by movement of another expression, has been dubbed 'PARASITIC SCOPE' by Barker 2007. It turns out that there is independent evidence that such movement is necessary in a number of other contexts (Sauerland 1998, Bhatt and Takahashi 2007, 2011, and Matsui and Kubota 2012). Indeed, as we'll see in section 2.5.6, Barker proposed it in another context still (though his preferred implementation is in a distinct framework, Type Logical Grammar, in which there is no need to achieve its compositional effects through movement as such).

It's now possible to interpret (135). It will be easier to use English as a metalanguage for the first step:

(136)   a. $[\![\,has\ n_1\ children\,]\!] = \lambda x\,.\,x\ has\ n_1\ children$
       b. $[\![\,x_2\ has\ n_1\ children\,]\!] = [\![\,has\ n_1\ children\,]\!]\,([\![\,x_2\,]\!])$
           $= x_2\ has\ n_1\ children$
       c. $[\![\,\lambda x_2\ \lambda n_1\ x_2\ has\ n_1\ children\,]\!] = \lambda x_2 \lambda n_1\,.\,x_2\ has\ n_1\ children$

This denotes a relation between an individual and the number of children that individual has. This is precisely our **have-children** relation above, so:

(137) $[\![\,\lambda x_2\ \lambda n_1\ x_2\ has\ n_1\ children\,]\!] = $ **have-children**

2.5 Adjectives where they have no right to be: adverbial readings

This is also of the type that *the-average American* is looking for, so semantic composition can proceed:

(138)   a. $[\![\,\textit{the-average American}\ \lambda x_2\ \lambda n_1\ x_2\ \textit{has}\ n_1\ \textit{children}\,]\!]$
           = $[\![\,\textit{the-average American}\,]\!]\,(\,[\![\,\lambda x_2\ \lambda n_1\ x_2\ \textit{has}\ n_1\ \textit{children}\,]\!]\,)$
           = $[\![\,\textit{the-average American}\,]\!]\,(\textbf{have-children})$
    b. $[\![\,\textit{the-average American}\ \lambda x_2\ \lambda n_1\ x_2\ \textit{has}\ n_1\ \textit{children}\,]\!]\,(\,[\![\,2.3\,]\!]\,)$
           = $[\![\,\textit{the-average American}\,]\!]\,(\textbf{have-children})(2.3)$
           = $\textbf{average}(\textbf{American})(\textbf{have-children}) = 2.3$

The result is the one we sought.

The compositional machinery here is complicated, and it's possible to miss the analytical forest for the syntactic trees. With respect to the big-picture discussion about the foundations of semantics, the important point is that Kennedy and Stanley have provided an analysis of this sentence without making any exotic metaphysical commitments. The issue of whether there is a particular individual that is the average American doesn't arise, because *the average American* simply doesn't refer to an individual and nothing in its semantics entails the existence of such an individual. This is analogous to the question of what individual *no student* denotes. The answer, of course, is that this is the wrong question to ask because *no student* denotes a generalized quantifier, not an individual. To make the insight emerge, it was necessary to work out the semantics of *average* in some detail. This revealed that it is, indeed, complicated – but the complications are grammatical, not ontological. These complications are not specific to *average* alone. They are ones that play an independent role in the grammar. We've already seen that adjectives can be complicated in just this way.

This is not to say that similar theoretical challenges won't arise with other linguistic expressions. For example, Kennedy and Stanley don't provide an analysis of why *the average American* can introduce discourse referents (i.e. antecede subsequent pronouns: *The average American has 2.3 children. He votes infrequently.*) or extend their analysis to expressions like *Joe Sixpack*. Both of those are fertile ground for future research and, as Kennedy and Stanley demonstrate, may be tractable with sufficiently careful linguistic examination.

With respect to the more immediate question of how adjectives work and how they acquire wider-than-expected scope, several things have been achieved. First, we have examined an especially vexing additional example of the phenomenon. Second, we have encountered more evidence that incorporation into a determiner may be necessary to a general account of adverbial readings. Third, a new analytical tool has been put on the table: parasitic scope. A natural question to ask, then, is where else this tool might prove helpful.

2.5.6 Sameness and difference

A cottage industry has arisen around the semantics of *same* and *different*. It includes Nunberg (1984), Heim (1985), Carlson (1987), Keenan (1992), Moltmann (1992), Beck (2000), Lasersohn (2000), Majewski (2002), Alrenga (2006, 2007a,b), Barker (2007), and Brasoveanu (2011). Rather than trying to do it all justice, I will merely highlight the basic readings these adjectives receive and sketch a highly simplified analysis of one of them that, following Barker (2007), relies on parasitic scope. This entails sidestepping what these expressions reveal about plurals, reciprocals, discourse structure, imprecision, quantification, and other interesting issues.

Beck (2000) distinguishes three readings of *different*, two of which are also available for *same*. The first is the DISCOURSE ANAPHORIC READING (alternatively, 'deictic' or 'sentence-external' reading):

(139)   a. Floyd read a different book.
         b. Floyd read the same book.

The only way to interpret (139a) is as asserting that the book Floyd read is not the same as some book that was already present in the discourse, and (139b) is analogous. For slightly more complicated sentences, there is an NP-DEPENDENT READING (alternatively, 'internal reading'; Carlson 1987), so called because of a dependence on a preceding NP:

(140)   a. Floyd and Clyde read a different book.
         b. Floyd and Clyde read the same book.

The most natural way to construe (140a) is as (roughly) denying that the book Floyd read was the same as the one Clyde read. Finally, *different* also has a RECIPROCAL READING, which can be discerned in (141):

(141)   Floyd read different books.

Unless there is a plurality of books already salient in the discourse, the natural way to interpret (141) is as claiming that Floyd read a number of books that are different from each other (note the 'each other'; hence 'reciprocal reading'). This reading doesn't seem to be available for *same*. On such a reading, *Floyd bought the same cars* should be able to mean 'Floyd bought cars that are the same (as each other; e.g. both Hondas)'.

2.5 Adjectives where they have no right to be: adverbial readings

The most relevant reading for current purposes is the NP-dependent internal one. Here, again following Barker, I'll focus on *same*. The compositional challenge is a little harder to perceive here, since there is no obvious adverbial paraphrase, though *in common* is in the right ballpark:

(142) Floyd and Clyde read a book in common.

One can also get a sense of the scope problem by considering the range of expressions that make this reading possible, including plurals as in (143a), quantified nominals as in (143b), adverbs as in (143c), and even coordinated verbs as in (143d):

(143) a. The students read the same book.
       b. Every student read the same book.
       c. Floyd read the same book twice.
       d. Floyd praised and criticized the same book.

Accounting for all of these would take us far afield, but they reflect that *same* is sensitive to properties of the sentence that extend beyond the nominal in which it's located. The core case we'll concentrate on is (143a). Here, the problem in a nutshell is that *same* needs to know about not just books, but also and independently about the students, the ones who are similar in their book-reading. (See Barker 2007 for a complete exposition, or Keenan 1992 for an explicit proof.)

A very rough representation of the truth conditions of (143a) is in (144):

(144) $\exists z\,[\mathbf{book}(z) \wedge \forall y \in \mathbf{the\text{-}students}[\mathbf{read}(z)(y)]]$

This says that there is a book and every member of the plurality 'the students' read it. The notion of sameness is reflected here, crudely, in the wide-scope existential. This on its own doesn't remotely do it justice.[32] In keeping with the previous sections, I'll assume that *same* incorporates into the determiner (an assumption Barker doesn't make). The result is (145):

(145) ⟦ *the-same* ⟧ $= \lambda P_{\langle e,t\rangle} \lambda R_{\langle e,et\rangle} \lambda x\,.\,\exists z[P(z) \wedge \forall y \in x[R(z)(y)]]$

---

[32] Barker uses a choice function instead. A choice function is a way of picking an individual from a set and can be used to model the effect of indefinites: *A student died* could be thought of as saying roughly 'there is a choice function that picks from the set of students one that died' (or, alternatively, 'I have in mind a choice function that ...'). See Reinhart (1997), Winter (1997), Kratzer (1998), Matthewson (1998).

The question, then, is how to provide this denotation with the arguments it needs. The first argument is straightforward:

(146) 〚 the-same book 〛 = 〚 the-same 〛(〚 book 〛)
    = $\lambda R_{\langle e, et\rangle} \lambda x . \exists z[\textbf{book}(z) \wedge \forall y \in x[R(z)(y)]]$

In the simple case of 143a, the composition can in principle proceed with equal simplicity past this point, because *read* could denote a relation ($\langle e, et\rangle$), which is precisely what 〚 the-same book 〛 is looking for. But what if *read* has an event argument, for example, and therefore a type like $\langle e, \langle e, vt\rangle\rangle$? Or what if *the-same book* were not in object position?

It is for such cases that a more complicated tool – Barker's parasitic scope – is necessary. First, *the students* will move out of its base position by Quantifier Raising:

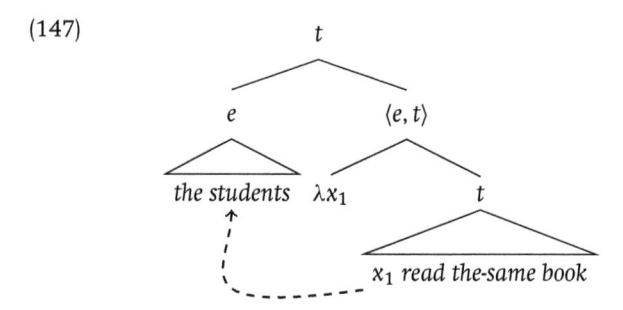

(147)
```
                    t
                   / \
                  /   \
                 e    ⟨e, t⟩
                / \   / \
         the students λx₁   t
                              / \
                             x₁ read the-same book
```

Next, *the same book* will move, thereby avoiding a possibility of a type clash. It will land in the only place where it can be interpreted: between *the students* and its lambda:

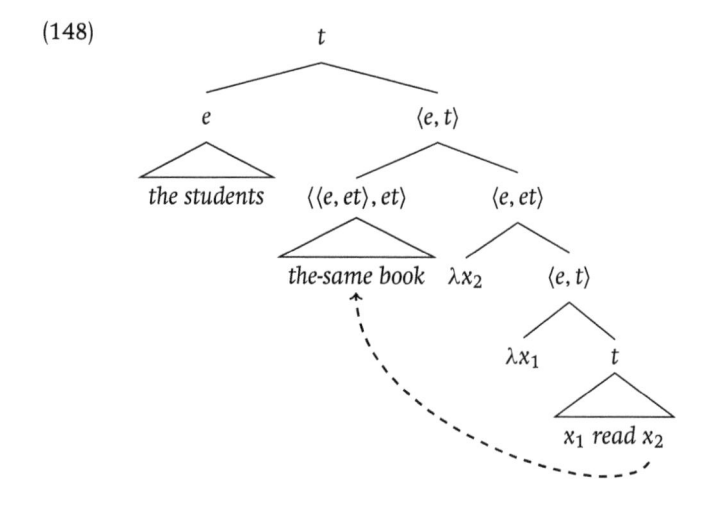

(148)
```
                         t
                        / \
                       /   \
                      e    ⟨e, t⟩
                     / \    / \
            the students ⟨⟨e,et⟩,et⟩  ⟨e,et⟩
                         / \        / \
                the-same book λx₂   ⟨e, t⟩
                                    / \
                                   λx₁  t
                                        / \
                                       x₁ read x₂
```

2.5 Adjectives where they have no right to be: adverbial readings

In moving, *the-same book* creates its own lambda, as (148) reflects. The interpretation will proceed as in (149) (with the the event argument omitted):

(149) a. $[\![\lambda x_2 \, \lambda x_1 \, x_1 \, \text{read} \, x_2]\!] = \lambda x_2 \lambda x_1 \, . \, \text{read}(x_2)(x_1)$

b. $[\![\text{the-same book}]\!] \, ([\![\lambda x_2 \, \lambda x_1 \, x_1 \, \text{read} \, x_2]\!])$

$= \lambda x \, . \, \exists z \left[\begin{array}{l} \text{book}(z) \wedge \\ \forall y \in x[\, [\![\lambda x_2 \, \lambda x_1 \, x_1 \, \text{read} \, x_2]\!] \, (z)(y) \,] \end{array} \right]$

$= \lambda x \, . \, \exists z[\text{book}(z) \wedge \forall y \in x[\text{read}(z)(y)]]$

c. $[\![\text{the students the-same book} \, \lambda x_2 \, \lambda x_1 \, x_1 \, \text{read} \, x_2]\!]$

$= [\![\text{the-same book} \, \lambda x_2 \, \lambda x_1 \, x_1 \, \text{read} \, x_2]\!] \, ([\![\text{the students}]\!])$

$= [\lambda x \, . \, \exists z[\text{book}(z) \wedge$
$\forall y \in x[\text{read}(z)(y)]]](\text{the-students})$

$= \exists z[\text{book}(z) \wedge \forall y \in \text{the-students}[\text{read}(z)(y)]]$

This is the desired result. Again, then, two ingredients added up to a theory of this adverbial reading of an adjective: incorporation into a determiner and parasitic scope. In light of that, some of the vexing behavior of *same* can be viewed as a special case of a wider problem.

2.5.7 Other adverbial readings and the bigger picture

Before moving on, it's worth briefly noting three other classes of adverbial readings of adjectives. First, *whole* and *entire* have an adverbial reading (Moltmann 1997, 2005; Morzycki 2002):

(150) a. The $\left\{ \begin{array}{l} \text{whole} \\ \text{entire} \end{array} \right\}$ ferret was submerged.

b. The ferret was $\left\{ \begin{array}{l} \text{wholly} \\ \text{entirely} \end{array} \right\}$ submerged.

The principal accounts of this rely either on tools used to account for distributive readings of plurals (Morzycki) or on situations (Moltmann). I won't elaborate, other than to observe that, once again, apparent incorporation into the determiner correlates with unexpected adverbial scope. The adverbial reading is lost when the adjective is not adjacent to the determiner as in (151a), or when the determiner is *every* as in (151b):

(151) a. The furry whole ferret was submerged.
b. Every whole ferret was submerged.

In both cases, the only reading possible is a non-adverbial one that means roughly 'structurally intact'.

Another class seems to consist of just one word, *wrong* (Larson 2000; Schwarz 2006):

(152) They arrested the wrong person.

The first thing to notice is the definite determiner. There are countless people that they shouldn't arrest, so we might expect that *a* would be obligatory. Yet *the* is the more natural choice – again, unexpected determiner behavior. The other crucial point is that no one can be said to be, once and for all, the wrong person. Rather, *the wrong person* is 'a person that it was wrong for them to arrest'. To build this meaning, though, the adjective must combine with a clausal denotation – indeed, that of the very clause in which it is embedded. There is no adverbial paraphrase, but the effect of combining with a clause is similar.

The third class of adjectives that have adverbial readings is the EPISTEMIC ADJECTIVES of Abusch and Rooth (1997):

(153) a. Dick Cheney is hiding at an undisclosed location.
b. You'll be staying at an unspecified hotel.

For a few years, (153a) was a kind of standing half-joke because the location became known primarily for being undisclosed. But of course, 'being undisclosed' is not really a characteristic of a place, and if at a moment of unusual candor Cheney were to reminisce fondly about his secret special place, he would be unlikely to say he misses how very undisclosed it was. Rather, the *undisclosed* says something about what information has been, well, disclosed: in (153a), something like 'Dick Cheney is hiding at a location, and it has not been disclosed what location he is hiding at'. Like *wrong*, these adjectives don't have adverbial paraphrases, but as this paraphrase reflects, they do require that the adjective combine with a clausal denotation. Abusch and Rooth propose an account of these facts couched in Discourse Representation Theory (Kamp 1981b). Again, I won't elaborate.

A few words about where all this leaves us. First, incorporation of adjectives into determiners seems to be the clearest mechanism by which adverbial readings can be achieved. But why should it be possible at all, given that it can't be performed by ordinary head-to-head movement?[33] Second, what characterizes the class of determiners

---

[33] Normally, movement of a head out of an adjunct isn't possible. This wouldn't be an issue if adjectives weren't adjuncts, as in Abney (1987).

that allow this incorporation, and how does it vary from one adjective to another? Finally, a broader question: I've grouped a number of adjective classes together under the rubric of 'adverbial readings', but they aren't normally treated as a single problem. This might be simply a historical accident. On the other hand, it's also possible – if, in my estimation, less likely – that these are genuinely unrelated puzzles, with no need for a unified theory. At the moment, all of these questions remain unresolved.

2.6 ADJECTIVE POSITION AND SYNTACTIC ISSUES

2.6.1 Attributive vs. predicative, prenominal vs. postnominal

We have already encountered a number of ways in which the relative order of adjectives has semantic consequences and a few differences between attributive and predicative adjectives. The aim of this section is to briefly address some additional issues in this domain.

The principal point that needs to be further explored is an essentially syntactic one: the fundamental difference between attributive and predicative adjectives. First, many adjectives in English and in numerous other languages are exclusively attributive. This effect goes beyond cases where this would be expected on semantic grounds such as *alleged*. Here are some examples from Bolinger (1967b), a pathbreaking paper on this topic:

(154) a. the main reason
b. *The reason is main.

(155) a. a crack salesman
b. *The salesman seems crack.

(156) a. a total stranger
b. *The stranger is total.

In some of these cases, one might wonder whether these are truly adjectives at all. For example, 154 might be better analyzed as some sort of attributive noun, though of course it's not obvious what the theoretical content of such a claim could be. (A simple compounding analysis is less plausible, since there is a genuine noun–noun compound *crack salesman*, but it means 'dealer of crack cocaine'. Unlike 155, the compound also has initial stress, a distinguishing characteristic of English compounding.) In 156, the alternative non-adjectival analysis might follow the lines of Morzycki (2009b, 2012b) (see section 2.4.6 and 6.3.2).

Other adjectives are exclusively predicative. In English, this includes a class of adjectives that all begin with *a-*:

(157) a. *an $\begin{Bmatrix} \text{asleep} \\ \text{alive} \end{Bmatrix}$ student

b. That student is $\begin{Bmatrix} \text{asleep} \\ \text{alive} \end{Bmatrix}$.

(158) a. *an aloft plane.
b. That plane is aloft.

(159) a. *some akimbo arms
b. Her arms were akimbo.

Others still have essentially unrelated meanings on their attributive and predicative uses:

(160) a. that poor man
b. That man is poor.

This amounts to saying that these are two different homophonous adjectives.

It is a terminologically inconvenient fact of English that it often allows adjectives that are obligatorily predicative to be used in attributive positions so long as they are to the right of the noun:

(161) a. every student $\begin{Bmatrix} \text{alive} \\ \text{awake} \end{Bmatrix}$
b. every plane aloft

This postnominal position is otherwise unavailable to English adjectives unless they have a complement (e.g. *a man proud* vs. *a man proud of his daughter*). The explanation for the apparent oddity of (161) may be that some such cases are derived by reduction of a relative clause (e.g. *every student that is alive*), a process Ross (1967) memorably dubbed 'whiz-deletion' ('*wh*-word + *is*'; see also Smith 1961, 1964; Sproat and Shih 1988; Kayne 1994; Larson 1999, 2000; Alexiadou 2001; Larson and Marušič 2004; Shimoyama 2011b).

That said, there are a few exceptional adjectives in English that are unexpectedly content postnominally even without a complement (e.g. *every firefighter available*, *every star visible*). Across languages – and especially in Romance – whether an adjective is pre- or postnominal correlates with its semantic properties in interesting ways.

There is substantial syntactic work in this area. In addition to work cited in section 2.4.1, this includes Crisma (1993), Alexiadou (2001),

2.6 Adjective position and syntactic issues

Bouchard (2002), Larson and Marušič (2004), Teodorescu (2006), Valois (2007), Vander Klok (2009), Aljović (2010), Centeno-Pulido (2010), and Kim (forthcoming), and historically oriented work including Fischer (2006) and Haumann (2010). Semantic or semantically oriented work that takes adjective-position observations as a starting point includes Truswell (2004, 2005), Champollion (2006), Katz (2007), and Morzycki (2008b) (see section 6.5 for discussion of some of this).

2.6.2 Indirect modification

The predicative–attributive distinction is so fundamental that some languages seem to lack either attributive or predicative adjectives entirely. Baker (2003) provides some examples. A language with only attributive adjectives is Vata (Niger-Congo; Baker cites Koopman 1984):

(162) a. kO! Kad-Ò
    man old
    'a big man, old man'
  b. *Wa (lÈ) kad-Uà
    they PRED old

A predicative-only language is Slave (an Athabaskan language, English pronunciation [sleɪvi]; Baker cites personal communication from Keren Rice and Rice 1989):

(163) a. Yenene (be-ghǫ) sho   hįlį
    woman 3-of   proud/happy 3-is
    'The woman is happy/proud (of him/her).'
  b. *yenene sho
    woman proud/happy
    'a proud/happy woman'

Japanese may also be such a language, though there is controversy on this point. (See Shimoyama 2011b for discussion and an argument against this claim.)

In light of facts like these, it's reasonable to ask how to translate a predicative adjective into Vata, or an attributive one into Slave. The answer, it turns out, is with additional grammatical equipment. Focusing on the Slave attributive case, Baker says the solution is a relative clause – that is, something like 'a woman that is proud'.[34]

This demonstrates a larger point, one first articulated by Sproat and Shih (1988): there are two ways of achieving adnominal modification.

---

[34] Baker doesn't include the relevant Slave example itself.

One of them, which they call DIRECT MODIFICATION, involves simple structures such as attributive adjectives. The other, INDIRECT MODIFICATION, involves additional structure layered on top of a predicative modifier so it can be used attributively. This typically takes the form of a relative clause, or a structure that could plausibly be analyzed as a reduced relative clause (of the sort mentioned in section 2.6.1 immediately above). Sproat and Shih provide examples in Mandarin:

(164)   a. fang-de   xiao-de   zhuo-zi
            square-DE small-DE table
            'small square table'

        b. *fang   xiao   zhuo-zi
            square   small   table

The presence of the additional morpheme *de* is required to approximate the effect of the direct modification attempted in (164b). This characterization abstracts away from a number of complications, one of which bears calling attention to. In fact, some direct modification is possible in Mandarin. Reversing the order of the adjectives in (164b) fixes the problem:

(165)   xiao   fang   zhuo-zi
        small   square table

What seems to be happening is that indirect modification provides a way of sidestepping restrictions on the relative order of attributive adjectives. Normally, size adjectives must precede shape adjectives, as in (165). But this holds only of truly attributive adjectives. Ones suffixed with *de* are not subject to the restriction. The ability to sidestep such restrictions may be a feature of indirect modification in general. For further discussion of these issues across a number of languages, see Larson and Takahashi (2007), Vander Klok (2009), Cinque (2010), Shimoyama (2011b), and Kim (forthcoming).

2.6.3 Stage-level/individual-level contrasts

One of the more striking effects of adjective position in English was initially observed by Bolinger (1972). It's most apparent in the few adjectives that can freely occur postnominally:

(166)   a. the stars visible
        b. the visible stars

(167)   a. the rivers navigable
        b. the navigable rivers

2.6 Adjective position and syntactic issues

(168) a. the responsible individuals
       b. the individuals responsible

These mean subtly different things. *The stars visible*, for example, are those we can see at a particular moment. *The visible stars* can mean this too, but it can also refer to those that are visible in principle, even if at the moment they are obscured by a cloudy night. The effect is similar in (167) and (168). It's especially clear in (168) because *irresponsible* is an antonym on only one of the relevant readings: one can be responsible or irresponsible as a character trait; with respect to any particular act, though, one can be responsible but not irresponsible.

Larson (1999) observed that this seems to be a contrast between STAGE-LEVEL and INDIVIDUAL-LEVEL predicates. (In a nutshell, a stage-level predicate is one that holds at a particular time, such as *drunk*, *hungry*, or *clothed*. An individual-level predicate such as *tall*, *Bolivian*, or *smart* characterizes an individual in general with no particular reference to time. Many constructions are sensitive to the distinction. See Carlson 1977; Kratzer 1995; and Jäger 1999 for an overview.) He also observed a similar effect of adjective order. If the same adjective is used twice, they are read in the two distinct senses. More strikingly, one has the intuition that the higher adjective is the stage-level one:

(169) a. the visible visible stars
       b. the responsible responsible individuals

Thus (169a) characterizes the stars that are visible in principle and actually visible at the moment. For the same reason, there is a clear contrast in (170) (Larson attributes this observation to Barbara Citko):

(170) a. the invisible visible stars
       b. the visible invisible stars

If some clouds are obscuring stars that would normally be visible, they can be described with (170a), but certainly not with (170b).

The outline of an analysis is provided by Larson's theory of event arguments inside the nominal projection (see section 2.3.3). The core idea is that there is a generic quantifier inside the extended NP. Individual-level properties can be construed as ones that hold generically (Chierchia 1995). If this quantifier binds off event arguments below it, we might expect that individual-level readings would be available only in its scope and therefore lower in the NP, near the noun. The stage-level readings would be available above it, and therefore higher in the NP. In a broadly similar spirit, one might also consider deriving stage-level adjectives from an underlying reduced relative clause source (i.e. from *visible stars that are visible*).

2.6.4 A focus position?

When adjectives occur in a non-canonical order, one doesn't normally have a clear-cut sensation of unacceptability. Rather, the result is just awkward. That's the case in (171b) and (171c):

(171) a. ugly big red ball
 b. ??big ugly red ball
 c. ??red ugly big ball

In some measure, the feeling is that there should be some kind of truth-conditional difference here (even though all these adjectives are intersective and consequently don't scope with respect to each other). One might account for this by supposing that some of the lower adjectives are kind-modifying and the higher ones aren't (Zamparelli 1995; McNally and Boleda Torrent 2003; Truswell 2004; Demonte 2008; Svenonius 2008a).

But that, while plausible, doesn't seem to suffice. Examples such as (171) most resemble sentences that, in a language with relatively free word order, have been scrambled (i.e. rearranged) without sufficient pragmatic justification. It's possible to get a taste of this in English in, e.g., *To the store, Floyd walked quickly*. The sentence is certainly not ungrammatical, but it requires a special context to be felicitous and would be odd out-of-the-blue.

So how to make sense of the similarity between pragmatically unmotivated scrambling and the effects in (171)? A number of researchers (those cited above, in fact) have suggested that what's going on is about focus.[35] On this view, adjectives that occur higher than the canonical order would dictate are simply focused – perhaps by occupying a specialized focus projection high in the extended NP – and as a consequence, are only felicitous in discourses in which it makes sense for the adjective to be focused. This would also account for why the odd sentences in (171) improve considerably if the first adjective is pronounced with focus intonation.

---

[35] Focus is the phenomenon that gives rise to truth-conditional differences primarily (in English) via prosodic prominence, in, e.g., *Greta only* TOUCHED *Floyd.* vs. *Greta only touched* FLOYD. (See Rooth 1996 for an overview.)

2.7 WHAT IS IT TO BE AN ADJECTIVE?

A few words are in order about what it is to be an adjective. This is oddly ambiguous between being a syntactic and a semantic question. 'Adjective' is, after all, a syntactic category, whatever its semantic properties might be. Yet it would not have been possible for this chapter to concern itself with the semantics of adjectives if there were no correlation between the syntax and the semantics.

Ideally, any answer to the question of what it is to be an adjective would need to extend across languages, so we might look across languages in search of such an answer. As it turns out, there is some controversy over whether adjectives are even present in all languages at all – and the controversy is complicated by uncertainty about the very issue we're trying to address (Dixon 1982; Déchaine 1993; Jelinek 1995; Demirdache and Matthewson 1996). It's hard to form a consensus on the distribution of adjectives across languages without a crosslinguistic definition of one.

It is here that it's natural to look to the semantics. This calls for great caution. The problem of whether the definitions of syntactic categories can legitimately make reference to semantic questions is an old one, and one that has been a bone of contention since before the twentieth century (Newmeyer 1980). Even so, one might be tempted to throw caution to the wind and conjecture that adjectives can be defined crosslinguistically as the syntactic category that expresses gradable notions. It's certainly the prototypical category for that. But even within English, gradability is neither a necessary condition for being an adjective (some adjectives aren't gradable, like *prime* and *wooden*) nor a sufficient one (many non-adjectives are gradable, like *hate* and *idiot*). Some languages even seem to be lacking in grammatical machinery specialized for manipulating gradable meanings (Stassen 1985, 2006; Bochnak 2013a,b). That suggests that this may not be the firm crosslinguistic foundation we are looking for – or in any case, that many caveats and refinements will be necessary in spelling out an explicit theory built on this idea.

In his magisterial work on the nature of syntactic categories, Baker (2003) takes a different tack. He treats adjectives as the elsewhere-case among categories. Nouns and verbs have distinctive definitional properties, which he articulates in detail. As for adjectives:

> What distinctive property do adjectives have that underlies their various morphological and syntactic characteristics? The strongest and

most interesting answer to this question would be to say that there is nothing special about adjectives.

This memorably elegant formulation is dangerously close to claiming that adjectives would be most interesting by being boring. Of course, Baker means this only in a syntactic sense, so perhaps this chapter has not been entirely a waste of time.

All things considered, though, there seems to be no easy resolution to the issue of what an adjective is and whether the semantics can help us figure it out. But whatever other accusations one might level at adjectives, it should at least be clear that one can't accuse them of failing to provide a wide array of puzzles and problems that are not primarily about gradability.

2.8 QUESTIONS FOR FURTHER REFLECTION AND DISCUSSION

- Do the proposals discussed here constitute an adequate theory of subsectivity? Indeed, is subsectivity a sufficiently unified phenomenon to call for a general theory, or has the term outlived its analytical usefulness?
- Is a fake gun in fact a gun (Partee 2007)? Is a stone lion a lion (Kamp and Partee 1995)? What is the nature of the coercion operations that may be necessary to answer 'yes' to this question? Is there something dangerously elusive about them? Could we pin them down more precisely? If not, is that an argument against their existence, or just evidence that such coercion is not at heart a purely grammatical phenomenon?
- The adjective classes discussed are not the only ones. It's worth reflecting on what other adjective classes there might be that behave in a semantically interesting and analytically tractable way.
- Could there be an analogue to adverbial readings in other categories? Could, for example, an adverb be interpreted in a way that is most naturally paraphrased with an adjective? (As we'll see in Chapter 5, the answer may well be yes.) What would this reveal?
- Most of the work discussed here focused on a single language at a time. How might languages vary with respect to these phenomena?

2.9 SUGGESTIONS FOR FURTHER READING

Good entry points into the literature cited in this chapter include the following:

- Bolinger (1967b), a classic descriptive article on the attributive/predicative distinction, rich in observations and insights that can serve as the foundation for further research.
- Siegel (1976a), also a classic and valuable not only for the substantive points it makes but also for the style of argumentation it demonstrates. Larson (1998) is a natural next step, and anyone interested in delving further into this area would be well advised to consider his analysis in its original form rather than (solely) in the adapted version here.
- For more on adverbial readings, Stump (1981) lays down a foundation. Gehrke and McNally (2010) is a good bridge to more recent work.
- Kamp and Partee (1995) is a foundational paper not only for its contributions to the study of particular kinds of adnominal modification but also for the insights it offers into the semantics of nouns and into how it relates to work in psychology and psycholinguistics.
- Exploration of the literature on *same* and *different* can begin with Beck (2000), though some of the older work cited is also quite accessible.
- Both Sproat and Shih (1988) and Baker (2003) address the nature of adjectives from a perspective that extends beyond Indo-European. The former is short and focused; the latter is a book-length presentation of a general theory of syntactic categories whose goals aren't primarily semantic but which nevertheless treads relatively deep into semantic waters.

3 Vagueness, degrees, and gradable predicates

3.1 INTRODUCTION

On a long car trip, one eventually encounters signs that say things like 'now entering Massachusetts'. That seems reasonable enough. Sometimes, though, one encounters signs that say things like 'scenic area'. This always struck me as faintly absurd. A government is perfectly entitled to draw lines on a map that define the precise boundaries between Massachusetts and adjacent states. But 'scenic'? Has a transportation department employee been dispatched to discern the precise boundaries within which things have become – officially and legally – scenic? Why not also erect signs that say 'ugly area' or 'disappointing region' or 'suburban sprawl'?

There are two linguistic issues that give rise to the sense of absurdity. One is important, but won't be our concern in this chapter: the subjective quality of adjectives like *scenic* that's incompatible with governments taking a position on them (see section 6.6). The other, however, is an aspect of a much larger question to which we will now turn. Even if we as a society decided to delegate our aesthetic judgments to regional transportation authorities, we would still find it odd for them to draw fixed borders between what's scenic and what isn't. Being scenic – like being ugly, disappointing, or suburban – is an inherently incremental notion.[1]

Such vagueness is an essential design feature of language. From a certain perspective, it is a problematic one. Formal semantics is founded on truth and falsity, binary notions that might seem to leave no wiggle room for the incremental. Yet in using language, we handle vagueness

---

[1] A parallel example: the US National Weather Service sometimes refers emotively in forecasts to 'bitter cold'. According to vaguely official-looking online charts, to be scientifically bitter, the temperature must be −19F/−28C to 0F/−18C (http://oceanservice.noaa.gov/education/yos/resource/JetStream/global/chill.htm). Bitterness apparently dissipates at lower temperatures, which are 'extremely cold'.

88

3.2 Vagueness 89

effortlessly. Sometimes, we cope with it by simply eliminating it: Clyde, we might say, is not merely *tall*, but *six feet tall* or *taller than Floyd*. At other times, we instead modulate the vagueness and assert that he is, for example, *a little too tall*. We do this with concrete grammatical tools, morphemes we can identify and subject to analytical scrutiny.

Broadly construed, this will be the task of this chapter and the next. The initial challenge is how to reconcile the incrementality of vagueness with the discreteness of truth conditions. That's only the first step. Examining the grammar of vague predicates turns out to shed light not just on vagueness itself and its conceptual cousin, gradability, but also on the underlying structure of adjective meaning, the role of notions like 'scale' and 'dimension' in the grammar, and the nature of the constructions and expressions that specialize in manipulating this sort of meaning.

The chapter begins with a discussion of vagueness in section 3.2. Section 3.3 gives a thumbnail sketch of theories of vagueness and gradability and explores one approach that hasn't much captured the imagination of formal semanticists. Sections 3.4 and 3.5 present two approaches that have. Section 3.6 compares them, considering what role the notion of 'degree' should have in the grammar. Finally, section 3.7 turns to scalar issues in the lexical semantics of adjectives.

3.2 VAGUENESS

3.2.1 Identifying vagueness

The first question to ask about vagueness is just what it is, precisely. When does a predicate count as vague? Perhaps the best answer is itself a kind of question. A predicate is vague if it gives rise to some version of the SORITES PARADOX ([sə'raɪɾiz]), the paradox of the heap ('sorites' is from Greek *soros* 'heap'). In its canonical form, this begins with a heap of sand. If we remove a single grain of sand from the heap, we still have a heap. If we remove another, again, the heap remains a heap. In fact, we are typically willing to commit to a general principle: removing a single grain of sand is never enough to turn the heap into something other than a heap. Yet if we repeat this process, we will ultimately wind up with a single grain of sand, which surely isn't a heap. But when did we lose the heap? Even in hindsight, we wouldn't be comfortable identifying the crucial grain that moved us over the threshold between heap and non-heap. So there is a paradox: removing a single grain can never eliminate the heap, and yet the heap is gone. It works in reverse, too: begin with a grain of sand. You have no heap. Adding a single additional grain is never enough to create a heap. Yet do this repeatedly, and sooner or later, voilà: heap.

Of course, not all vagueness is about sand. But analogues are easy to dream up for arbitrary vague predicates. Another standard example is *bald*. Floyd, who is balding, isn't actually bald. But what if we plucked a single hair from his head? And then another, and another? He will be, well, above all increasingly irritated, but also at some point bald. The crucial sequence of steps – removing grains of sand or hairs on his head – is called a SORITES SEQUENCE. Vague predicates systematically permit constructing one.[2]

Another way to look at the issue is in terms of BORDERLINE CASES. These are the points in a sorites sequence when our judgments begin to waver. There are people we consider bald and others we consider not bald, but there are some, the balding, that occupy the rather uncomfortable middle ground between bald and not bald. In some contexts and for some purposes and under some lighting conditions, we might consider them bald, and in others not. Such borderline cases are another hallmark of vague predicates.

Vagueness is virtually everywhere. It's in obvious places, such as in the semantics of GRADABLE ADJECTIVES – that is, adjectives that admit degree modification or can occur in comparatives and related constructions. Accordingly, that's the spot linguists have most concentrated on. But as the classic form of the sorites reflects, it's also found in nouns as well. One can construct sorites sequences for PPs like *across the quad*.[3] Verbs can be vague: *love* gives rise to borderline cases (for some people, apparently with alarming regularity), as can *run* (how fast must you go to count?). Indeed, it's not just vagueness that is ubiquitous. Its cousin, linguistic gradability is too (as Sapir 1944 and many subsequently have observed). As important as this is, some caution may be warranted. Gradability we can presumably take at face value, but certain instances of apparent vagueness might be better classified as imprecision (see section 3.2.3).

---

[2] The indifference we feel to the small changes that characterize each step in the sequence is termed TOLERANCE.

[3] The vagueness is even clearer with *near*, *close*, and *far*, which are sometimes mentioned as vague prepositions. But these may actually be adjectives, as their ability to occur as complements to *seem* and to form comparatives suggests:

(i)   He seemed $\begin{Bmatrix} \text{nearer} \\ \text{closer to} \\ \text{farther from} \end{Bmatrix}$ the quad.

3.2 Vagueness

3.2.2 Vagueness vs. ambiguity

When I was about about five years old growing up in Poland, I found myself confused about the metaphysical status of Montreal. I had been told with categorical certainty that it's in America, and with equal certainty that it isn't. I was baffled. What sort of magical fairy-tale city was this 'Montreal', that it could be and – at the same time – not be in a particular place? My mistake, of course, was failing to recognize that *America* can refer either to the New World as a whole or to the United States in particular. It is only AMBIGUITY, and not vagueness, that can lead an innocent child astray in this way. *The western part of North America*, for example, is vague. Is Manitoba in the western part of North America? It's unclear. Manitoba is a borderline case. But this would never lead a child to mistake Manitoba for an Alice-in-Wonderland enigma, because no one would confidently assert that Manitoba both is and is not in the western part of North America. A lack of confidence of this sort is the defining feature of borderline cases, and it contrasts sharply with the bewildering certainty I encountered about Montreal.

This encapsulates the essential difference between vagueness and ambiguity. An ambiguous linguistic expression has more than one distinct interpretation, and the interpretations are discrete and one can enumerate them. They don't give rise to borderline cases, at least not without an independent source of vagueness. Some instances of ambiguity involve two distinct words that happen to be homophonous (lexical ambiguity): *bank* can mean either 'side of a river' or 'financial institution'. Other instances arise due to multiple syntactic structures that lead to multiple semantic representations (structural ambiguity). Thus the shopworn introductory-linguistics example *We saw the deer with binoculars* has readings in which either we or the deer have binoculars, depending on whether *deer with binoculars* is a constituent. The distinction between vagueness and ambiguity is not always straightforward, and we should be cautious about relying too much on such purely descriptive terminology without first committing to an explicit theory with respect to which it can be defined. But there are some useful tests that can jog one's intuitions about the difference (see Zwicky and Sadock 1975, 1984; Martin 1982; Gillon 1990, 2004).

The most straightforward of these is simply denying one reading while asserting the other (an example of this general strategy can be found in section 2.2.2 and, inadvertently, in the use of *America* described above). One can do this with the deer example straightforwardly. In a normal deer-viewing scenario, the sentence is true on the reading in which we have binoculars and false on the reading in which the deer has them. We could therefore truthfully both assert and deny that that string of words characterizes the situation. Another angle on the same idea is finding a scenario that would render the sentence true on one reading and false on the other, and a distinct scenario that renders the previously true reading false and the previously false reading true. Thus in the deer example, the situation is reversed in a scenario in which we saw the deer unaided while the deer had binoculars.

A more subtle and interesting tool is ZEUGMA (['zugmə]),[4] the use of a word in two different senses simultaneously. It gives rise to a characteristic sense of anomaly that is absent in superficially similar non-zeugmatic structures. Suppose that we were interested in determining whether *expired* is lexically ambiguous between the meaning 'became out of date' and 'became dead', or whether it's a general cover term for both. The zeugmatic example in (1), due to Cruse (1986), might settle the question:

(1)   ?John and his driving license expired yesterday.

This predicates *expired* of *John* and *his driving license* in different senses. It feels odd – like a kind of half-joke – because *expired* is, indeed, ambiguous. In the absence of ambiguity, the odd feeling is absent too. Car doors are very different from house doors, and one might suspect that the word *door* is ambiguous between these two senses. But it isn't, as the lack of a zeugmatic flavor in (2) attests:[5]

(2)   Floyd's house and car both had a broken door.

As it turns out, *door* has a single meaning that encompasses both. One might say that *door* is therefore vague with respect to this distinction, though this kind of indeterminacy or underspecification probably isn't vagueness in the strictest sense. (What would a borderline case be? See Gillon 2004 for more.) In a way, it doesn't matter. What the zeugma

---

[4] A related term is 'syllepsis', apparently used mostly by literary scholars rather than linguists (Pinkal 1995 mentions it in scare quotes). It doesn't seem to have a consistently observed definition sufficiently rigorous to distinguish it from zeugma in way that is a grammatically principled and analytically useful.

[5] This contrasts with, for example:

(i)   ?Floyd and his car both had $\begin{Bmatrix} \text{an uncomfortable seat} \\ \text{a short fuse} \end{Bmatrix}$.

Sexist examples involving *rack* could also be constructed.

3.2 Vagueness

test shows is just that this isn't an ambiguity. Useful though the test is, it does depend precariously on the sensation of 'oddness'. Many things make us feel odd, only some of which are relevant here. Caveat emptor.

Before moving on, it's worth highlighting another form of indeterminacy: POLYSEMY. This describes the state of affairs in which a word has multiple senses that are clearly related. *A big country*, for example, can be one with a large population or a large landmass. A *bed* is normally what one sleeps on, but this meaning is related to uses like *a riverbed* or *a bed of lettuce*. It's not always clear when an ambiguity should be called a polysemy. From the usual perspective of formal semantics, nothing hinges on the difference: the typical analytical strategy is to simply treat polysemy as a special case of lexical ambiguity. Whether we should be embarrassed by this or proud of it is itself a little unclear. But there is certainly formally explicit work that wrestles with the issue without writing it off. It includes Nunberg (1995), Pustejovsky (1995), Pustejovsky and Bouillon (1995), Lascarides et al. (1996), Blutner (1998), Blutner (2008), Alrenga (2007b), Brasoveanu (2008b), Katz (2008).

It's also not clear whether the term 'polysemy' groups together a natural class of phenomena. The distinct interpretations of *skillful* in *a skillful surgeon* and *a skillful thief* or of *beautiful* on the two readings of *beautiful dancer* (see section 2.2.2 and indeed much of Chapter 2 generally) might be termed polysemy, yet they are rather different from the distinct meanings of *bed*. Moreover, in *beautiful dancer*, the two readings might arise – depending on the analysis – as the result of a structural ambiguity, or else as the result of an implicit argument that can receive distinct values from the discourse context. On the latter analysis, the context-dependence renders this more similar to vagueness than ambiguity after all.

This reinforces the conclusion that one shouldn't put too much stock in terminology. What matters is the analysis, and until we provide a sufficiently explicit one, we can't render a verdict about what semantic phenomenon is at issue.

3.2.3 Vagueness vs. imprecision

Vagueness, as we've seen, is distinguished by borderline cases, cases for which we are hesitant – however much we might be pressed – to assign a truth value. There is a superficially similar phenomenon that doesn't behave this way. It's reflected in the contrast between (3a) and (3b):

(3)   a. Floyd is tall.   (vague)
        b. Floyd is six feet tall.   (potentially imprecise)

To make things explicit, suppose (3b) is true, and Floyd is in fact six feet tall. Without further information, we don't know whether to judge (3a) true or false. This run-of-the-mill vagueness is completely resolved in (3b). We require no further information to judge (3) true or false. We know precisely what it would take for Floyd to be six feet tall. If we could shrink Floyd in tiny steps, we could construct a sorites sequence for (3a), but not for (3b). We would always in principle be able to identify the exact step that made him less than six feet tall.

The difference is apparent in everyday use. No reasonable person would agree to a bet that is to be determined on the basis of whether some as-yet-unseen individual turns out to be tall. There would be no objective way to resolve such a bet. This uncertainty contrasts with how we react to sentences such as (3b). A perfectly reasonable person might place a bet on whether someone turns out to be six feet tall. The MEASURE PHRASE *six feet* eliminates vagueness.

This seems relatively straightforward. But in some circumstances, the situation becomes murkier. If, for example, I have agreed to the bet that the unseen person is six feet tall, I might still find myself in an argument once this person – Floyd – has presented himself and agreed to be measured. It might turn out that Floyd is just barely shorter than six feet, by a few hundredths of an inch. Here, again, there seems to be a kind of uncertainty. Yet this uncertainty is of a quite different kind. If we have established conclusively that Floyd's height falls short of six feet, even by a fleetingly small amount, it would be very difficult for me to insist that he is nevertheless six feet tall. With this information, I could convince no one that (3b) is true. Any argument that breaks out is not about the truth value of (3b) as such. It is rather about how precisely we want to interpret the terms of the wager. To weasel out of it, I might accuse you of being unreasonable or pedantic in insisting that (3b) is false, but I could not accuse you of being wrong about it. So, despite the dispute, (3b) does not seem to be vague. It is, however, potentially IMPRECISE, and we can disagree about the intended level of precision.

Taken to its logical conclusion, this all has the odd consequence that, speaking absolutely strictly, it is improbable that anyone is (exactly) six feet tall. With sufficiently precise instrumentation, we would discover that virtually everyone falls at least an atom or two short, or is at least an atom or two too tall. This is sheer pedantry, of course – but again, it is not wrong. This is the insight that Lasersohn (1999) articulates in especially clear terms. In ordinary use, we are happy to judge true sentences that, if really pressed, we would be forced to admit are technically false. We allow ourselves what he called PRAGMATIC SLACK. Imprecision is at

3.2 Vagueness

heart not an issue of truth or falsity as such, but of how close an approximation of truth is pragmatically sufficient in a particular context.

Seem is sensitive to this distinction. It is compatible with vague predicates (Matushansky 2002), but not with ones that are merely imprecise:

(4)   Clyde seems (*six feet) tall.

The amount of pragmatic slack speakers give each other is of course not typically made explicit, but a variety of linguistic devices can help make it clear. *Precisely*, for example, restricts the amount of pragmatic slack available:

(5)   Floyd is precisely six feet tall.

For (5) to be judged close enough to be true, Floyd has to be closer to being six feet tall than if *precisely* were absent.

This distinction between these two flavors of linguistic uncertainty – vagueness and imprecision – is to be found in various forms and with various labels in Pinkal (1995), Lasersohn (1999), Kennedy and McNally (2005), Kennedy (2007), Sauerland and Stateva (2007, 2011), Morzycki (2011), van Rooij (2011b), Bouchard (2012), Klecha (2013), and Anderson (2013, 2014). Sometimes one of these notions is taken to include the other, as in Lewis (1979), who explicitly invokes 'standards of precision' and views it as a kind of vagueness. Sauerland and Stateva make a case for preferring the terms 'scalar vagueness' and 'epistemic vagueness' for (ordinary) vagueness and imprecision, respectively, but provide further evidence for a distinction. The variation of views is an indication that the distinction between vagueness and imprecision isn't an obvious one, and the issue of how best to think about it remains unsettled. Further work will, I hope, help clarify the situation.

Lasersohn (1999) conceptualizes imprecision in terms of PRAGMATIC HALOS. The pragmatic halo of an expression is a set of potential meanings of the same type as its denotation which differ in only 'pragmatically ignorable' ways. Thus, in most contexts, $[\![\,six\,feet\,]\!]$ has a halo around it consisting of lengths that are near enough to six feet not to make any difference: $5'11\frac{1}{2}''$–$6'\frac{1}{2}''$, say. Halos expand compositionally. The halo of $[\![\,six\,feet\,long\,and\,three\,feet\,wide\,]\!]$ combines the halos of $[\![\,six\,feet\,tall\,]\!]$ and $[\![\,three\,feet\,wide\,]\!]$, so that it might include objects that are $5'11\frac{1}{2}''$ tall and $2'11\frac{1}{2}''$ wide. Interestingly, to provide a semantics in this spirit for slack regulators like *precisely* (see also section 6.4), it's necessary for the compositional semantics to gain access to – and in that sense, to be interleaved with – the machinery by which halos are generated. Pragmatic halos, evidently, are not purely pragmatic.

3.2.4 Some foundational questions

In the discussion that follows, I will sidestep a number of interesting philosophical issues about vagueness in order to focus on the ones most directly relevant to linguistic semantics. Nevertheless, it's worth at least raising some foundational questions about the origin of vagueness.

One of these is whether vagueness is a property of linguistic expressions or objects in the world. We might be uncertain about the precise point at which the Sahara desert starts. Does that mean the proper name *the Sahara* is vague? Or is it the desert itself that is vague? The latter possibility is called ONTOLOGICAL VAGUENESS. The notion is rejected in Russell (1923) and Evans (1978) but has its defenders (see Sorensen 2012).

Even if we grant that it is language that is the locus of vagueness, we don't need to assume that it arises from an inherent indeterminacy in linguistic expressions. There is another way of thinking about it, due to Williamson (1994): vagueness might arise instead from our ignorance as speakers. On this view, it's not that some things are inherently incremental, but that our knowledge of them is inherently incomplete. The solution to the sorites paradox, then, is to reject the premise that removing a single grain of sand can't on its own eliminate a heap. There is simply a fact of the matter that is hidden from us: that a heap must have (let's suppose) 100,042 grains of sand. Reducing that number by one makes it no longer a heap. That we don't **know** this fact doesn't make it any less a fact. No one knows the precise number of grains of sand on Earth either, yet we don't dispute that there is a fact of the matter there. We just confess that we don't know (or care) what it is. Why, then, should we not take the same attitude to heaps?

At first, this idea – dubbed the EPISTEMIC VIEW of vagueness – seems counterintuitive, perhaps partly because the ubiquity of vagueness would entail a corresponding ubiquity of ignorance. But to paraphrase H. L. Mencken, no one ever lost money by overestimating human ignorance.[6] I think I know what *dead* means and generally have no hesitation in distinguishing the living from the dead. Yet there are tragic apparent borderline cases, and in those, I defer to doctors. (See Putnam 1975 for the classic argument that an individual speaker might have only partial knowledge of meaning in this way.) More or less similarly, I think I know what *winner* means in the context of an

---

[6] The original quote is 'no one ... has ever lost money by underestimating the intelligence of the great masses of the plain people' (1926; 'Notes on Journalism'; *Chicago Tribune*).

3.3 Theories of vagueness and gradability: a false start

election. Yet if told the vote count of a candidate but not the number of candidates or total votes cast, I couldn't determine whether she is the winner, or even the proportion of votes necessary to win. Despite this ignorance, I wouldn't be tempted to conclude that there is therefore no determinate winner or no specific vote quota the winner must reach. As a first step, it's enough to confess that other predicates might be roughly similar to these.

Williamson takes an important further step. In general, there are no authorities to tell us where sharp boundaries lie. A word on this view is defined instead by an unspoken and unconscious consensus among native speakers, so at any given moment, its meaning – and therefore the location of sharp boundaries – depends on a general patterns of use no individual speaker can track precisely. For most vague predicates, then, it is not just that we don't know where the boundaries lie. It's that we **can't** know. At a stroke, this would resolve the tension between vagueness and the methodological assumption that there are only two truth values.

All that said, we will proceed on the assumption that an account of the semantics of natural language must include an account of (at least some) vagueness.

3.3 THEORIES OF VAGUENESS AND GRADABILITY: A FALSE START

3.3.1 Three approaches

The literature contains various claims of the form 'there are n principal (classes of) theories of vagueness', where n varies. They are then enumerated in a way that adheres to certain general conventions but otherwise also varies. I mention this so that the reader will approach the next paragraph in the right spirit.

There are three principal classes of theories of vagueness. They are:

- Fuzzy-logic theories, in which there is a scale consisting of infinitely many truth values. They have not played a major role in formal linguistic semantics, except perhaps as a foil.
- What I'll call inherent-vagueness theories, which are often referred to with terms including 'supervaluation', 'delineation', and 'extension gap'. In these theories, certain sentences with vague predicates may lack a truth value and there is no direct representation of measurement.
- Degree-based theories, which introduce objects into the model called 'degrees' to directly represent measurement and assume these objects can serve as arguments to gradable predicates (or,

alternatively, can be what gradable predicates yield in place of a truth value).

Importantly, this lists semantic frameworks for analyzing vagueness and gradability rather than general views of what vagueness is (like, for example, the epistemic theory of vagueness, or the idea that vagueness stems from context-sensitivity).

3.3.2 Fuzzy logic

There is certainly a prima facie tension between the incremental quality of gradable predicates and the idea that there are only two truth values. Moreover, the idea that sentences must be simply true or false seems to fly in the face of common sense. It's hard to imagine a more banal truism than that life is not in black and white but full of shades of gray. So why should the semantics be founded on something so deeply unintuitive?

The answer emerges in considering what the alternative would look like. The most dangerously seductive option is to allow an infinite number of truth values, including all real numbers between 0 and 1. One could be more cautious and simply introduce a single additional truth value, but that doesn't scratch the relevant analytical itch – life is full of **shades** of gray, not full of black, white, and gray. Embracing infinitely many truth values is what distinguishes FUZZY LOGIC from classical logic (Zadeh 1965, 1983; Pelletier 2000 points out that infinite-valued logics without the catchy name date to Łukasiewicz 1920).

Fuzzy logic has for the most part not played a prominent role in formal linguistics (a notable exception is Lakoff 1973), so I will only sketch some of the difficulties it presents. (See Kamp 1975; Fine 1975; and Kamp and Partee 1995 for further discussion.) First, it makes odd predictions about the truth values of coordinated sentences such as (6):

(6)   a. Floyd is tall or he isn't tall.
        b. Floyd is tall and he isn't tall.

Intuitively, if Floyd is a borderline case for *tall*, we would probably want these to have different truth values: (6a) is true, and (6b) false.[7] On at

---

[7] The latter judgment might be clouded by linguistic conventions like saying 'Is he tall? Well, he is and he isn't, depending.' The cloudiness may be dispelled with various rewordings:

(i)   a. It's true that Floyd is tall and it's true that he isn't.
        b. It is and is not the case that Floyd is tall.
        c. It's true that Floyd is tall and it's false that Floyd is tall.

3.3 Theories of vagueness and gradability: a false start

least one natural implementation of fuzzy logic, however, that's not what would happen. Fuzzy connectives could be defined as in (7) (Zadeh 1965; Kamp and Partee 1995; I've translated the set-theoretic characterization into its logical counterpart):

(7) a. $[\![\,not\,\phi\,]\!] = 1 - [\![\,\phi\,]\!]$
b. $[\![\,\phi\,and\,\psi\,]\!]$ = the lower of these truth values: $[\![\,\phi\,]\!], [\![\,\psi\,]\!]$
c. $[\![\,\phi\,or\,\psi\,]\!]$ = the higher of these truth values: $[\![\,\phi\,]\!], [\![\,\psi\,]\!]$

The idea behind (7a) is that the negation of a proposition is exactly as true as the original proposition was false. If it's mostly true that I'm tall, it's mostly false that I'm not. What (7b) reflects is that conjoined proposition is as true as its least true conjunct: the claim that I'm tall and triangles have four sides is simply false, no matter my height. What (7c) reflects is the corresponding fact about disjunction: the claim that I'm tall or triangles have four sides is precisely as true as it is that I'm tall. With this in mind, suppose *Floyd is tall* has a truth value of 0.5. Following these rules, the same truth value, 0.5, would be assigned to its negation, *Floyd isn't tall*, and therefore also to both (6a) and (6b). Bad news.

Second, one of the things one might want from a theory of vagueness is some insight into gradability and comparison. On a fuzzy-logic approach, comparatives might be interpreted by comparing truth values directly:

(8) a. Floyd is taller than Clyde.
b. $[\![\,Floyd\,is\,tall.\,]\!] > [\![\,Clyde\,is\,tall.\,]\!]$

There is something uncomfortable about this. Judgments about relative height feel subjectively very different from judgments about relative truth. There is a world of difference between asserting (8) and asserting, for example, that it would be more of a lie to claim that Clyde is tall than it would to claim that Floyd is tall. Perhaps these subjective impressions are misleading, and there is a way of disentangling them from the fuzzy machinery. But they require some explanation – and it doesn't bode well for the approach when it must explain away grammatical intuitions right from the outset. Moreover, as Nouwen et al. (2011a) point out, putting all comparatives on the same scale – that of truth values – means it should be possible to interpret comparatives composed of arbitrary pairs of sentences, as in (9):

(9) a. #Floyd is taller than this is a ferret.
b. #Floyd is taller than Clyde is unpleasant.

Perhaps (9a) can be ruled on out purely syntactic grounds. That seems unsatisfying, since it feels like something has gone wrong semantically too in a way we might want the semantics to reflect. But even if we were to set it aside, this mode of explanation is unavailable for (9b), which is syntactically pristine. Yet of course, tallness and unpleasantness manifest a fundamental INCOMMENSURABILITY. Setting aside some complications (see sections 4.3.6 and 4.3.7), comparatives built around unrelated properties are systematically ill-formed in just this way. Having a single scale might be desirable for certain purposes (Bale 2006, 2008), but this isn't the right way to achieve it.

3.4 THE INHERENT VAGUENESS APPROACH

3.4.1 Extension gaps

If we must resist the siren song of fuzzy truth values, it would be nice to hold on at least to the intuition that for borderline cases, vague predicates are neither true nor false. It turns out that we can. On a standard semantics, a predicate like *tall* has as its extension the set of tall people. In a slight terminological modification, we could call this the POSITIVE EXTENSION of *tall*, and call everything that isn't tall its NEGATIVE EXTENSION. This would suffice in a world of absolutes, but we'd like to find a place for the borderline cases. These, it might be said, fall into an EXTENSION GAP: the set of things in neither the positive nor the negative extension of *tall*; that is, the set of things of which it is neither true nor false. Correspondingly, sentences in which a vague predicate is predicated of a borderline case fall into a TRUTH-VALUE GAP.

This idea lies at the heart of one class of approaches (Fine 1975; Kamp 1975, and Klein 1980, 1982 develop the core framework, building on formal tools in van Fraassen 1966; work broadly in this spirit includes Lewis 1970; McConnell-Ginet 1973; Ballweg 1983; Pinkal 1983; Larson 1988; Kamp and Partee 1995; Sassoon 2013a, 2007, 2013b, 2010c; van Rooij 2008; Krasikova 2009; Doetjes 2010; Doetjes et al. 2011). The names by which people refer to these theories – or various subsets of them – aren't consistent, and generally involve picking the name of a certain component of the theory as a name for the whole. These include 'supervaluation(ist)', 'delineation', 'comparison class', 'precisification', 'vague predicate' (with 'theory' or 'approach' appended, of course).[8]

---

[8] The term 'delineation theory' has a catchy ring, but it strikes me as less than ideal. 'Delineation' refers to the sharpening of a vague predicate by eliminating

3.4 The inherent vagueness approach

Depending on the author, these might not pick out precisely the same class of ideas, but they are part of the same broad intellectual current. At the risk of compounding the problem, I'll refer to them by yet another term, as 'inherent vagueness' theories, to reflect that they build on the intuition that vagueness is inherent in vague predicates themselves rather than – as on a degree-based theory – the result of how they enter into the compositional semantics.[9]

What I'll present here is a version of the idea mostly in the spirit of Klein (1980, 1982). First, we need to introduce extension gaps into the system. This can be done by assuming that vague predicates denote partial functions, ones that are simply undefined when applied to individuals in their extension gap. The most familiar use of partial functions in natural language semantics is as a means of analyzing presuppositions, so this represents a departure. (Though it's worth reflecting on what similarities to presupposition there might be.)

A second crucial component is discourse contexts. What counts as a borderline case varies from one context to another.[10] If we're discussing basketball players, many people we might ordinarily describe as tall would instead be borderline cases, and therefore in the extension gap of *tall*. If we're discussing children, many people who might

---

borderline cases, a cut-off used in doing so, or a function associated with either. The term hardly occurs in work that established the approach – none of van Fraassen (1966), Fine (1975), Kamp (1975), Klein (1980, 1982), Ballweg (1983), Pinkal (1983), Larson (1988), or Kamp and Partee (1995) use it. (The sole exception is McConnell-Ginet 1973.) More important, both the concept and the term are no less at home in degree-based theories. Barker (2002), for example, explicitly treats delineations as functions that map a gradable predicate to a degree, which is fully consistent with the (apparently) original use of the term in Lewis (1972). Setting aside independent differences, this is also what the standard-determining predicate does in the degree-based analysis of Kennedy (2007) – and, indeed, in this book. For similar reasons, 'the comparison class approach' doesn't seem like an ideal term either.

[9] This is presumably the intuition behind the term 'vague predicate analysis' as well, but I avoid it because 'vague predicate' is a useful pre-theoretical descriptive term to describe predicates that are vague, without regard to how their vagueness is analyzed.

[10] This essential analytical impulse is an aspect of what is referred to in the philosophical literature as CONTEXTUALISM. With respect to vagueness, this emphasis on contexts leads to a view of sorites sequences in which each step is a kind of incremental coercion of one context into another (Kamp 1981a). See Stanley (2003) for an ingenious and alarming counterargument to this from ellipsis, and van Rooij (2011b) for a counterargument to the counterargument. It's worth pointing out that – in the particular versions presented here – this view of sorites sequences is in principle compatible with both inherent-vagueness and degree-based approaches.

otherwise be borderline cases would instead fall in the positive extension of *tall*. In one context, *tall* would mean something like 'tall for a basketball player', and in the other, 'tall for a child'. These sets of individuals – basketball players or children – are distinct COMPARISON CLASSES. They must be at least part of what a context supplies. (Beyond that, I will remain noncommittal on how contexts should be represented. Less Klein-influenced implementations of this approach use another formal tool, partial models, instead.)

With that in place, one can venture a denotation. The following predicates will be useful:

(10) a. $\mathbf{gap}_c(P)(x) \stackrel{\text{def}}{=} 1$ iff x is in the extension gap of P in context c
     b. $\mathbf{pos}_c(P)(x) \stackrel{\text{def}}{=} 1$ iff x is in the positive extension of P in context c
     c. $\mathbf{neg}_c(P)(x) \stackrel{\text{def}}{=} 1$ iff x is in the negative extension of P in context c

I will use c as a variable for contexts, which will be introduced as an index on the interpretation function $[\![\cdot]\!]$. Thus, using the colon notation below to express a restriction on the value of x (and therefore that this is a partial function; Heim and Kratzer 1998):

(11) $[\![tall]\!]^c = \lambda x : \neg\mathbf{gap}_c(\mathbf{tall})(x) \,.\, \mathbf{pos}_c(\mathbf{tall})(x)$

To yield a result, this function requires that the individual it applies to, x, must not be in the extension gap of **tall** in context c. If this requirement is satisfied, the function will yield 1 if x is in the positive extension and 0 otherwise (i.e. if x is in the negative extension).

3.4.2 Precisification and supertruth

The next crucial component is the observation that contexts aren't static. As the discourse unfolds, old contexts are extended and elaborated into new ones. One way this can happen is by the accumulation of information that allows the interlocutors to close in on a consensus about, for example, who counts as tall (see Barker 2002 for an especially direct implementation of this insight). Indeed, in some cases, one can even imagine interlocutors explicitly assigning various borderline cases to the positive and negative extension of *tall*: 'Clyde? He's tall-ish, but I wouldn't really say he's tall. As for Floyd, he's **definitely** tall.' One can even imagine, hypothetically, that the discourse could continue to the point that no extension gap remains. A context such as this – one in which the extension gap is empty – is called a total

3.4 The inherent vagueness approach

PRECISIFICATION (or a 'completion', or one that provides a 'delineation' of the predicate).[11]

Precisifications play at least two key roles. One of them is that they keep us from running aground on the shores that doomed the fuzzy-logic approach. Its undoing was in part the failure to ensure that (12a) is always true and (12b) always false:

(12)   a. Floyd is tall or he isn't tall.
        b. Floyd is tall and he isn't tall.

To arrive at the right result, though, it will be necessary to nudge the notion of truth slightly from its customary place. If Floyd is a borderline case, these sentences both come out simply undefined. That's assuming that extension gaps are represented as in (11) and that the assignment of truth values to sentences – the VALUATION – works as it does in most textbooks. This isn't good enough, though, because the sentences in (12) are true or false irrespective of whether Floyd is a borderline case. But there is an interesting twist. On any total precisification, (12a) will come out true. If we assign Floyd to the positive extension of *tall* in a precisification, the sentence will be true because of the first conjunct; if we assign him to the negative extension, because of the second. An assignment of truth values on the basis of all total precisifications is a SUPERVALUATION, and it renders a sentence such as (12a) SUPERTRUE. Precisely the same reasoning renders (12b) SUPERFALSE.

As these examples demonstrate, it seems to be supertruth and superfalsehood that really count in reflecting our intuitions. Indeed, one can say that this is the case for all sentences, even simple ones like *Floyd is tall*. Previously, we'd have said this sentence would be true in a context if Floyd is in the positive extension of *tall* in that context. But it's true on all precisifications of that context, too. Precisifications, after all, remove members of extension gaps, not of positive or negative extensions. So one could define truth and falsity this way:

(13)   a. A sentence is true in a context c iff it is true on all total precisifications of c.
        b. A sentence is false in a context c iff it is false on all total precisifications of c.

---

[11] For a context to count as a precisification of another, it must meet conditions including, informally, not eliminating members of the positive or negative extension, and respecting orderings already present in the model. (A brief discussion follows in section 3.4.3; see Klein 1980, 1982 for details, or Kennedy 1997 for an especially accessible exposition.)

What if Floyd is in the extension gap of *tall* in a context? The result would be the same as it was: certain precisifications would put him in the positive extension, others in the negative extension. By this definition, then, *Floyd is tall* in this context would be neither true or false.

3.4.3 Comparatives

The other major role for precisifications is in the semantics of comparatives. Again, assuming that Floyd is in the extension gap of *tall*, we'd still like (14) to be able to come out true:

(14)   Floyd is taller than Clyde.

A similar move – quantifying over precisifications – will accomplish this. If Floyd is actually taller than Clyde, a total precisification could do one of three things (individuals are listed in descending order of height):

(15)   a. assign both Floyd and Clyde to the positive extension:

$$\left.\begin{array}{l}\text{Greta}\\ \text{Floyd}\\ \text{Clyde}\end{array}\right] \textit{positive extension}$$

$$\text{Herman} \;] \;\textit{negative extension}$$

   b. assign both Floyd and Clyde to the negative extension:

$$\text{Greta} \;] \;\textit{positive extension}$$

$$\left.\begin{array}{l}\text{Floyd}\\ \text{Clyde}\\ \text{Herman}\end{array}\right] \textit{negative extension}$$

   c. assign Floyd to the positive extension and Clyde to the negative extension:

$$\left.\begin{array}{l}\text{Greta}\\ \text{Floyd}\end{array}\right] \textit{positive extension}$$

$$\left.\begin{array}{l}\text{Clyde}\\ \text{Herman}\end{array}\right] \textit{negative extension}$$

What a precisification could **not** do is assign Clyde to the positive extension and Floyd to the negative one. There is no way of drawing the boundary between the tall and the not-tall that would count a taller person as not-tall and a shorter one as tall. But the crucial case is (15c).

3.4 The inherent vagueness approach

That precisification is only possible because Floyd is, in fact, taller than Clyde.

So we've arrived at the truth conditions of a comparative: *Floyd is taller than Clyde* is true iff there is a way of drawing the boundary between the tall and not-tall that leaves Floyd in the tall group and Clyde in the not-tall group. More precisely, it's true iff there is a precisification on which Floyd winds up in the positive extension and Clyde doesn't:

(16) $[\![\textit{Floyd is taller than Clyde}]\!]^c$

$= \exists c' \in \textbf{precisifications}(c) \begin{bmatrix} [\![\textit{tall}]\!]^{c'}(\textbf{Floyd}) \wedge \\ \neg [\![\textit{tall}]\!]^{c'}(\textbf{Clyde}) \end{bmatrix}$

Where **precisifications**(c) is the set of total precisifications of c. Because we're dealing with total precisifications, we can disregard the partiality of the functions (on a total precisification, they are defined for all individuals in the domain).[12] Thus (16) amounts to:

(17) $[\![\textit{Floyd is taller than Clyde}]\!]^c$

$= \exists c' \in \textbf{precisifications}(c) \begin{bmatrix} \textbf{pos}_{c'}(\textit{tall})(\textbf{Floyd}) \wedge \\ \neg \textbf{pos}_{c'}(\textit{tall})(\textbf{Clyde}) \end{bmatrix}$

$= \exists c' \in \textbf{precisifications}(c) \begin{bmatrix} \textbf{pos}_{c'}(\textit{tall})(\textbf{Floyd}) \wedge \\ \textbf{neg}_{c'}(\textit{tall})(\textbf{Clyde}) \end{bmatrix}$

The last step is licit because, when the extension gap is empty, if Clyde isn't in the positive extension he must be in the negative one, and vice versa. (That said, even on a partial precisification, the effect of the comparative would be achieved even without having taken this last step.)

Importantly, this correctly predicts that the comparative does not license inferences to the POSITIVE FORM of the adjective (the bare, morphologically unmarked form): we can't conclude from *Floyd is taller than Clyde* that he is tall. This follows because the precisifications stay resolutely inside the scope of the existential quantifier. With respect to the main, matrix context of evaluation, everything remains just as it was: the inhabitants of the positive and negative extensions and the extension gap are unchanged.

This approach – quantifying over something similar to potential continuations of the discourse context – anticipates a major mechanism

---

[12] The restriction to total precisifications here is only for conceptual clarity. The partiality of the function $[\![\textit{tall}]\!]$ would be harmless even on a partial precisification.

in theories of dynamic semantics that would be developed later, such as Heim (1982), Kamp (1981b), and their many intellectual descendants. On such views, quantificational expressions (determiners, modals, adverbs) also quantify over ways of extending a discourse context. This isn't always apparent in work in the inherent-vagueness framework in part because the 'extending the context' language either wasn't used or wasn't emphasized until Pinkal (1995) and Barker (2002). An explicit connection isn't necessarily drawn between this account of the comparative and the dynamic treatment of quantifiers (more precisely, between quantifying over precisifications and quantifying over assignment functions). The nature of such connections, and if indeed there are any, is a question worth pondering.

But how to arrive at the desired truth conditions compositionally? The denotation of the comparative morpheme (*-er/more*) should be as in (18), where α is a gradable adjective:

(18) $[\![\text{more } \alpha]\!]^c = \lambda x \lambda y . \exists c' \in \textbf{precisifications}(c) \left[\begin{array}{c} [\![\alpha]\!]^{c'}(x) \wedge \\ \neg [\![\alpha]\!]^{c'}(y) \end{array} \right]$

This isn't a fully compositional denotation, though, because it fails to assign a denotation to *more* on its own, independent of the adjective. The difficulty is that *more* needs access to the context parameter of the adjective it combines with. If it simply gathered up an adjective meaning (type $\langle e, t \rangle$), it wouldn't get this access. What it actually needs is a function that it can feed precisified contexts into, something of type $\langle c, et \rangle$, where c is the type of contexts. One way of achieving this is with a new rule of semantic composition, a close cousin to ordinary functional application that stands in roughly the same relation to it as intensional functional application does:

(19) CONTEXT-ACCESSING FUNCTIONAL APPLICATION

If a branching node α has as its daughters β and γ, and $[\![\beta]\!]^c$ applies to expressions of type $\langle c, \ldots \rangle$ and $[\![\gamma]\!]^c$ is of type $\langle \ldots \rangle$, then $[\![\alpha]\!]^c = [\![\beta]\!]^c (\lambda c' . [\![\gamma]\!]^{c'})$

Accessing a context index in this way may be useful in other analytical circumstances (Schlenker 2003). Indeed, Klein points out that functions from contexts to extensions are precisely what Kaplan (1989) proposed in his groundbreaking work on demonstratives. (In Kaplan's terminology, a function of type $\langle c, \ldots \rangle$ is the 'character' of a function of type $\langle \ldots \rangle$.)

3.4 The inherent vagueness approach

With this in place, a compositional denotation is possible (I assume *than* is not interpreted):

(20)   a. $[\![\,more\,]\!]^c = \lambda f_{\langle c, et\rangle} \lambda x \lambda y . \exists c' \in \textbf{precisifications}(c)$
$$[f(c')(x) \wedge \neg f(c')(y)]$$

    b. $[\![\,more\ tall\,]\!]^c = [\![\,more\,]\!]^c\,(\lambda c''.\,[\![\,tall\,]\!]^{c''})$
$$= \lambda x \lambda y . \exists c' \in \textbf{precisifications}(c)$$
$$[[\lambda c''.[\![\,tall\,]\!]^{c''}](c')(x) \wedge \neg [\lambda c''.[\![\,tall\,]\!]^{c''}](c')(y)]$$
$$= \lambda x \lambda y . \exists c' \in \textbf{precisifications}(c)$$
$$[[\![\,tall\,]\!]^{c'}(x) \wedge \neg [\![\,tall\,]\!]^{c'}(y)]$$
$$= \lambda x \lambda y . \exists c' \in \textbf{precisifications}(c)$$
$$[\textbf{pos}_{c'}(\textbf{tall})(x) \wedge \neg \textbf{pos}_{c'}(\textbf{tall})(x)]$$

    c. $[\![\,more\ tall\ than\ Clyde\,]\!]^c = [\![\,more\ tall\,]\!]^c\,([\![\,than\ Clyde\,]\!]^c)$
$$= [\![\,more\ tall\,]\!]^c\,(\textbf{Clyde})$$
$$= \lambda y . \exists c' \in \textbf{precisifications}(c)$$
$$[\textbf{pos}_{c'}(\textbf{tall})(x) \wedge \neg \textbf{pos}_{c'}(\textbf{tall})(\textbf{Clyde})]$$

The syntax-semantics interface assumptions behind this structure – that *more tall* denotes a relation between individuals – certainly aren't sufficient to account for the range of English comparatives, but they will suffice for now. Chapter 4 will present some more general, and therefore more sophisticated, options. This chapter will, for the sake of simplicity, stubbornly persist in this mistake.

3.4.4 Degree words

A theory of gradability should include not just a means of understanding comparatives, but also degree words such as *very*. This approach offers that possibility.

Klein suggests that degree words like *very* have, sensibly enough, precisely the same type as the degree morpheme *more*: functions from characters to extensions, type $\langle\langle c, et\rangle, et\rangle$. This is natural, since they have the same syntactic category. Comparatives accomplish their work by quantifying over contexts, so one might expect *very* to do this too. The question, then, is what effect *very* has on the context with respect to which a gradable adjective is evaluated.

Klein's answer is that it changes the comparison class. The gradable predicate is interpreted not with respect to the current context's comparison class, but rather a comparison class that consists only of the members of its current positive extension. Someone who is *very tall* is 'tall even compared to the people we've already established are tall', or, more pithily, 'tall (even) for a tall person'. The denotation and a first step in semantic composition are in (21) and (22):[13]

(21)   a. $[\![\text{very}]\!]^c = \lambda f_{\langle c, et \rangle} \lambda x . f(c')(x)$

where c' is identical to c except that the comparison class in c' is $\{y : f(c)(y)\}$

b. $[\![\text{very tall}]\!]^c = [\![\text{very}]\!]^c (\lambda c'' . [\![\text{tall}]\!]^{c''})$

$= \lambda x . [\lambda c'' . [\![\text{tall}]\!]^{c''}](c')(x)$

where c' is identical to c except that the comparison class in c' is $\{y : [\lambda c'' . [\![\text{tall}]\!]^{c''}](c)(y)\}$

$= \lambda x . [\![\text{tall}]\!]^{c'}(x)$

where c' is identical to c except that the comparison class in c' is $\{y : [\![\text{tall}]\!]^c (y)\}$

$= \lambda x : \neg \textbf{gap}_{c'}(\textbf{tall})(x) . \textbf{pos}_{c'}(\textbf{tall})(x)$

where c' is identical to c except that the comparison class in c' is $\{y : \textbf{pos}_c(\textbf{tall})(y)\}$

Other degree morphemes could receive a similar treatment. Measure phrases such as *six feet* could too – it would trigger evaluation with respect to a modified context in which the boundary of the positive extension is drawn at six feet.

3.4.5 Degree functions and comparatives revisited

Klein calls functions that manipulate the extensions of gradable predicates – such as the ones *very* and *six feet* denote – DEGREE FUNCTIONS. As it turns out, the idea is more generally useful. One application is to the comparative itself. Instead of quantifying over precisifications directly, a comparative could quantify over degree functions:

(22)   a. $[\![\text{more}]\!]^c$

$= \lambda f_{\langle c, et \rangle} \lambda x \lambda y . \exists d \in \textbf{degree-functions}(c) \begin{bmatrix} d(f)(x) \wedge \\ \neg d(f)(y) \end{bmatrix}$

---

[13] For clarity, I've written $\{y : f(c)(y)\}$ for the characteristic set of $f(c)$ rather than merely writing $f(c)$. More noticeably, the prose bits are unwieldy. Klein (1980) writes $c[X]$ to represent a context identical to c except that the comparison class in that context is X. Thus (21a) could be written as:

(i) $[\![\text{very}]\!]^c = \lambda f_{\langle c, et \rangle} \lambda x . f(c[\{y : f(c)(y)\}])(x)$

3.5 The degree-based approach

b. $[\![\text{more tall}]\!]^c$

$$= \lambda x \lambda y . \exists d \in \textbf{degree-functions}(c) \begin{bmatrix} d(\textbf{tall})(x) \wedge \\ \neg d(\textbf{tall})(y) \end{bmatrix}$$

This says that there is a degree function that precisifies gradable predicates in accord with c and would precisify **tall** so that x falls in its positive extension and y doesn't. To put it another way: there is a cut-off (such as six feet) that would leave x on the positive side and y on the negative one. This amounts to the same truth conditions as before. So why bother?

One reason is just that it reflects more directly the connection between comparatives, degree morphemes, and measure phrases. Another is that, as it will turn out, this denotation looks very much like a comparative denotation in standard implementations of the degree-based approach to the semantics of gradability and is therefore important in comparing the two approaches. A third reason is pointed out in Doetjes et al. (2011): many degree functions are ordered with respect to each other (e.g. $[\![5\,feet]\!] < [\![six\,feet]\!]$), and this is useful. It draws the two classes of theories even closer together. Degree functions can play many of the roles degrees simpliciter play in the other kind of theory. This other kind of theory is next on the agenda.

3.5 THE DEGREE-BASED APPROACH

3.5.1 Degrees

The key element in degree-based theories is, well, DEGREES. What these are precisely can vary from one theory to another, but what they have in common on all of them is that they provide a direct way of representing measurement along a scale. They are all measures of some property. One can be tall to the degree 'six feet', for example, or cold to the degree '−15C'. This way of putting it brings out the other distinguishing element of these theories: they generally treat gradable predicates as having DEGREE ARGUMENTS. Thus *tall*, for example, isn't simply the property tall people have. It's slightly more complex than that. Anyone that is tall is tall to some degree. There is no such thing as being tall without some associated point on a scale. *Tall*, therefore, shouldn't denote a property, but rather a **relation** between individuals and degrees.

An alternative way of construing the same insight links it more closely to resolving the tension between vague language and discrete semantics. One reason fuzzy logic has a certain appeal is that it accords with our feeling that borderline cases satisfy a vague predicate 'less' than clear cases. What we're groping for when we feel this intuition is, perhaps, not the idea that vague predicates fail to yield discrete truth values, but instead that they yield some abstract measure of the extent to which a gradable property holds. It's not that **tall(Floyd)** yields 1 if Floyd is seven feet tall and, say, 0.8 if he is six feet tall. The very fact that one is forced to pick '0.8' out of thin air – even when we know his precise height – should be alarming. Rather, what we really want to say is that **tall(Floyd)** yields a measure of his tallness: if he's seven feet tall, 'seven feet', and if he's six feet tall, 'six feet'. This is not equivalent to the view that gradable predicates denote relations, but it's in the same family. On this version of the theory, articulated in Kennedy (1997), gradable predicates denote MEASURE FUNCTIONS: functions from individuals to degrees.

What's important for current purposes is what these ideas have in common – the notion of degrees, and the idea that a gradable predicate associates an individual with a degree.[14] There is a great variety of degree-based theories on the market, as this two-pronged introduction begins to attest. Within linguistics, they have proven more popular than inherent-vagueness/supervaluation approaches. One reason may be their general merit, but another is just that they are easier to work with. Research in this tradition is so extensive as to defy easy citation, but includes Seuren (1973), Cresswell (1976), von Stechow (1984), Heim (1985), Bierwisch (1989), Rullmann (1995), Kennedy (1997, 2007), Schwarzschild and Wilkinson (2002), Kennedy and McNally (2005) and countless others, many of which will come up throughout the book.

What I'll present here will be a relatively standard exemplar of such a theory, except that it is considerably pared down to avoid presupposing a highly articulated syntax and to simplify the compositional process. (We will return to those issues in Chapter 4.) First, some assumptions about degrees themselves. Intuitively, to measure anything, one needs a SCALE, a kind of an abstract measuring stick. We'll represent a scale as simply a set with certain properties, chief among them that it comes with an ORDERING RELATION, similar to the $\leq$ relation that orders numbers.[15] Degrees are members of such a set. They will not be constructed

---

[14] These two characteristics go together, but they need not. One could have degrees in the model without using either degree arguments or measure functions, introducing them through some more indirect means. This possibility is explored in Morzycki (2012b).

[15] For a bit more on all the order-related terminology here, including more general definitions, consult the glossary.

3.5 The degree-based approach

out of anything else, so they're primitives, atomic types in the model. Not just any set of degrees is a scale, of course. A scale has to be LINEAR, that is, TOTALLY ORDERED: every degree is ordered with respect to every other degree. It is also common to suppose that scales are perfectly gradient rather than granular; that is, the scale has a DENSE ordering relation: for every pair of degrees, however close, there is a degree between them. More formally, degrees are elements of the domain of degrees, D_d; the variables used for them will be $d, d', d'', \ldots$; and scales meet the requirements in (23):

(23)   a set of degrees S with the ordering relation $\leq$ is a scale iff
$\forall d, d' \in S$:
   a. $\leq$ is total: $d \leq d' \vee d' \leq d$
   b. $\leq$ is dense: $d \leq d' \rightarrow \exists d'' \in S[d \leq d'' \wedge d'' \leq d']$

Because $\leq$ is a non-strict order, it is also TRANSITIVE, ANTISYMMETRIC, and REFLEXIVE.[16] It has a counterpart $<$ defined in the natural way ($d < d' \stackrel{\text{def}}{=} d \leq d' \wedge d \neq d'$). Neither of the assumptions in (23) is inevitable, and the consequences of eliminating or weakening them are potentially interesting. (For more on (23a) and linearity, see Bale 2011; for more on (23b) and granularity, see Fox and Hackl 2006; Sauerland and Stateva 2007; Nouwen 2008; Abrusán and Spector 2011; van Rooij 2011b, and Cummins et al. 2012.)

An important feature of this arrangement is that while all degrees on the same scale can be compared (because they are ordered with respect to each other), degrees can't be compared across scales (because no degrees on different scales are ordered with respect to each other). This means that each scale can be matched to a DIMENSION of measurement: length, temperature, weight, etc. As a consequence, degrees like 'six feet' and '−15C' will remain appropriately distinct and incommensurable.

---

[16] That is, $\forall d, d', d'' \in S$:

(i)   a. $\leq$ is transitive: $[d \leq d' \wedge d' \leq d''] \rightarrow d \leq d''$
'If one degree is at least as small as a second, and the second at least as small as a third, then the first is at least as small as the third.'
   b. $\leq$ is antisymmetric: $[d \leq d' \wedge d' \leq d] \rightarrow d = d'$
'Two degrees can be at least as small as each other only if they are actually identical.'
   c. $\leq$ is reflexive: $d \leq d$
'Every degree is at least as small as itself.'

The paraphrases are, of course, approximate.

3.5.2 Gradable predicates

With these assumptions in place, the denotation of a gradable predicate will be a relation between an individual and a degree (type $\langle d, et \rangle$):[17]

(24) $\;\;\;\;$ $[\![\,tall\,]\!] = \lambda d \lambda x \,.\, \mathbf{tall}(d)(x)$

There is an analytical decision to be made here about the relative order of the two arguments: whether the type should be $\langle d, et \rangle$ or $\langle e, dt \rangle$. The choice hinges entirely on what syntactic assumptions one adopts (particularly with respect to whether one assumes a version of the internal subject hypothesis). The type above better accords with a more surface-oriented syntax, for reasons that will become evident.

The first hurdle to get over is how to get from (24) to a denotation for a simple sentence like *Floyd is tall*. In order to get there, it helps to first make a detour that might superficially seem unnecessary into an apparently more complicated structure, the one in (25):

(25) $\;\;\;\;$ Floyd is [six feet tall].

One nice feature of degrees is that we already have a natural denotation for *six feet*, without any need for the more complicated degree functions of the inherent vagueness approach. On the current view, *six feet* can directly denote a degree, type d:

(26) $\;\;\;\;$ $[\![\,six\,feet\,]\!] = \mathbf{6\text{-}feet}$

From here on, the pieces click into place:

(27) $\;\;\;\;$ a. $\;\;$ $[\![\,six\,feet\,tall\,]\!] = [\![\,tall\,]\!] ([\![\,six\,feet\,]\!]) = \lambda x \,.\, \mathbf{tall}(\mathbf{6\text{-}feet})(x)$
$\;\;\;\;\;\;\;\;\;\;\;\;$ b. $\;\;$ $[\![\,Floyd\,is\,six\,feet\,tall\,]\!] = [\![\,is\,six\,feet\,tall\,]\!] ([\![\,Floyd\,]\!])$
$\;\;\;\;\;\;\;\;\;\;\;\;\;\;\;\;\;\;$ = $\mathbf{tall}(\mathbf{6\text{-}feet})(\mathbf{Floyd})$

It's in this construction and, as we'll see, in the comparative that the degree approach works most straightforwardly.

For the unmodified positive form, more must be said. This might at first seem unintuitive. *Floyd is tall* is, after all, a simpler sentence

---

[17] A common alternative is to express this relational meaning with the use of a measure function **tallness** (usually written as just **tall**) that maps individuals to their highest degree of height:

$\;\;\;\;$ (i) $\;\;\;\;\;\;\;\;$ $[\![\,tall\,]\!] = \lambda d \lambda x \,.\, \mathbf{tallness}(x) \geq d$

As will emerge from the discussion that follows, this is equivalent to what's intended by the denotation provided in the main text.

3.5 The degree-based approach

than *Floyd is six feet tall*, so we might expect a simpler semantics. But this is misleading. Whether the syntax is indeed simpler is not a question that can be resolved at a glance, without investigating it in more detail. Moreover, there is no particular reason in any case to expect that a simpler syntax should necessarily correlate with a simpler semantics. Indeed, the bare positive form is in an important respect manifestly **more** semantically complicated than the measure-phrase form, since only the former is vague.

A better way to think about it is that there are two bits of syntax-semantics that are in complementary distribution (that is, never occur in the same structure): measure phrases and vagueness. When two bits of syntax are in complementary distribution – say, English modal auxiliaries and tense morphemes – the conclusion to draw is that they compete for the same syntactic position. That's the conclusion we should draw here, too: vagueness competes for the same syntactic position as the measure phrase. But what does it mean for an abstraction like 'vagueness' to compete for a syntactic position? There is only one way to make sense of this: the source of vagueness (of this sort) must be a morpheme in the syntax that is capable of occupying, and therefore competing for, a syntactic position. It has no phonological content, but its semantic content is clearly discernible.

This morpheme is standardly called POS. I'd like to remain relatively neutral about the syntax at this stage in the discussion – despite the syntactic mode of argumentation I just indulged in – but in broad terms, placing it 'in the same position as' the measure phrase would yield a structure like (28):

(28)   Floyd is [POS tall].

The task this morpheme has to perform is to introduce vagueness. In the inherent vagueness approach, vagueness emerged as a form of context-sensitivity. That will be the case here, too. Again, we will need to index the interpretation function with a context parameter. Instead of retrieving from the context the positive extension of a predicate, on this approach one normally takes a more direct route: the context provides a STANDARD, the smallest degree on a scale consistent with satisfying the predicate – that is, the cut-off point that divides, say, the tall from the non-tall. Thus (28) asserts that Floyd has a degree of height that exceeds the contextually supplied standard for tallness:[18]

---

[18] The assumption is often made that it's sufficient to meet the standard without necessarily exceeding it, in which case the denotation in (29) could be written

(29) $[\![\textit{Floyd is } \text{POS } \textit{tall}]\!]^c = \exists d[d > \textbf{standard}_c(\textbf{tall}) \wedge \textbf{tall}(d)(\textbf{Floyd})]$

The standard for the **tall** predicate in context c is written here as **standard**$_c$(**tall**) (sometimes it is also indicated with a single contextually supplied variable; 'norm' is also occasionally used, following Bierwisch 1989, though that tends to be tied to the idea that the standard retrieved is a 'normal' value). Although it's important to investigate how exactly contexts supply standards, it's not necessary to have a complete answer to this question in order to make progress. A wide variety of answers are compatible with the framework. All that's necessary to get off the ground is a placeholder for such answers. In this respect, this isn't so different from the inherent vagueness theory, which in principle is compatible with various accounts of how a context determines the cut-off for membership in the positive extension.[19]

There is another aspect of (29) that merits attention. The denotation involves existential quantification over degrees. This seems inconsistent with how we normally talk about heights. We usually use definite descriptions such as 'the height of Floyd' to talk about heights, not indefinites. So why the existential? There are two ways of addressing this. One pushes back against the objection, and the other embraces it. The first, which is more standard and is the course we will take for now, is that this intuition is at odds with how heights (and therefore degrees) actually behave. Consider a sign next to a roller coaster with the content in (30), along with a horizontal line indicating the required height:

(30)   You must be this tall to ride the roller coaster.

The horizontal line is a naturally occurring counterpart of a degree. Of course, no one would interpret this as admitting only people whose height is precisely the same as the line. Rather, we take anyone who is at least as tall as the line – or taller – to be tall to this degree. We talk in a way that reflects this, too. If the horizontal line is known to be precisely six feet off the ground (an odd roller coaster, this), we might even say (31):

---

with $\geq$ in place of $>$ (or even as simply **tall**(**standard**$_c$(**tall**))(**Floyd**)). These are hard to distinguish empirically.

[19] Indeed, there is nothing to stop us from introducing extension gaps into a degree-based system. One would simply need to introduce two distinct standards, **pos-standard** and **neg-standard**, the cut-offs for membership in the positive and negative extension.

3.5 The degree-based approach

(31) It's obvious Floyd can ride this roller coaster. He's clearly six feet tall. In fact, he's at least 6′4″.

So it seems that anyone who is tall to the degree **6-feet** is also tall to every smaller degree. This is sometimes referred to as the MONOTONICITY of adjectives.

The principal alternative response to the sense that an individual only has a single height is to encode it into the semantics by having a gradable predicate denote a measure function that returns the **maximal** height of an individual (Kennedy 1997). This makes it possible to avoid existential quantification in the denotation of POS and other degree morphemes, but it requires other additional assumptions to accommodate the fact that gradable predicates are of a type that doesn't yield truth values (see section 4.2.4). Adopting a built-in maximality semantics doesn't actually require measure function denotations, though (von Stechow 1984; Rullmann 1995; Sharvit and Stateva 2002 have a nice discussion of the issue).

To derive the denotation in (31) compositionally, the contribution of the POS morpheme has to introduce the quantifier and the standard:

(32) $[\![\text{POS}]\!]^c = \lambda G_{\langle d, et \rangle} \lambda x . \exists d [d > \textbf{standard}_c(G) \wedge G(d)(x)]$

The composition process then proceeds as in (33) (I assume *is* is not interpreted):

(33) a. $[\![\text{POS } tall]\!]^c = [\![\text{POS}]\!]^c ([\![tall]\!]^c)$
   = $\lambda x . \exists d [d > \textbf{standard}_c(\textbf{tall}) \wedge \textbf{tall}(d)(x)]$
   b. $[\![\textit{Floyd is } \text{POS } tall]\!]^c = [\![\text{POS } tall]\!]^c ([\![\textit{Floyd}]\!]^c)$
   = $\exists d [d > \textbf{standard}_c(\textbf{tall}) \wedge \textbf{tall}(d)(\textbf{Floyd})]$

What distinguishes this from the measure-phrase sentence denotation, then – and what introduces vagueness into the picture – is the notion of dependence on contextually supplied standards.

3.5.3 Borderline cases and context-dependence

There is no single answer in this system to how to handle borderline cases. It isn't tailor-made for that in the way a theory based on extension gaps is. It would be possible to introduce an extension gap into this picture – but equally, it would be possible to accommodate other treatments of borderline cases as well. That's one of the strengths of the approach. The theoretical tools it makes available are versatile, easily adaptable to a wide variety of analytical goals and theoretical and methodological inclinations. The moving parts move smoothly. This certainly helps in syntax–semantics interface questions, as we'll see, but it also helps in adapting the system to broader goals linguists share with philosophers, including acquiring a deeper understanding of the status of borderline cases.

An illustration of this can be found in Graff (2000). She argues that a crucial ingredient in vagueness is the interests of interlocutors in a particular context. Part of what makes us willing to take the steps in a sorites sequence, on this view, is that the steps are not large enough to be salient in the light of those interests. A vague predicate in its positive form therefore requires exceeding a standard to an extent sufficiently large to be salient in the context. This doesn't mean the standard won't still depend on the comparison class as well. Indeed, comparison classes often are provided not by context but by a *for* phrase as in *tall for a basketball player*, so some account of them is necessary on any theory (see also Kennedy 2007, Bale 2011, and Solt 2011c). To reflect these considerations, Graff adopts a POS morpheme that looks roughly like the one in (34).[20] The 'saliently greater than' relation is !>, and **norm** combines with an adjective (G) and a comparison class property (P) and returns the normal degree associated the comparison class:

(34) a. $[\![\text{POS}]\!]^c = \lambda G_{\langle d, et \rangle} \lambda P_{\langle e, t \rangle} \lambda x . \exists d [G(x)(d) \wedge d \mathrel{!>} \text{norm}(G)(P)]$

b. $[\![\text{POS tall}]\!]^c = [\![\text{POS}]\!]^c ([\![\text{tall}]\!]^c)$

$= \lambda P_{\langle e, t \rangle} \lambda x . \exists d [\, \text{tall}(d)(x) \wedge d \mathrel{!>} \text{norm}(\text{tall})(P) \,]$

c. $[\![\text{POS tall for a basketball player}]\!]^c$

$= [\![\text{POS tall}]\!]^c ([\![\text{for a basketball player}]\!]^c)$

$= [\![\text{POS tall}]\!]^c (\textbf{basketball-player})$

$= \lambda x . \exists d \begin{bmatrix} \text{tall}(d)(x) \wedge \\ d \mathrel{!>} \text{norm}(\text{tall})(\textbf{basketball-player}) \end{bmatrix}$

The result, then, is something that is true of an individual *x* iff *x* is tall to a degree that exceeds the normal height for a basketball player in a

---

[20] I've reframed this to accord with the compositional assumptions in this section. Graff calls her POS morpheme ABS, following Kennedy (1997). This abbreviates 'absolute', another term for the positive form. One advantage of that term is that it avoids having to describe certain occurrences of the negative member of an antonym pair such as *short* as being a 'positive negative adjective'. (A disadvantage is that 'absolute' is also used in other senses. See the glossary for more terminological griping.) Graff further assumes, with Kennedy, that gradable adjectives denote measure functions, which changes the denotation:

(i) $[\![\text{ABS}]\!] = \lambda G_{\langle e, d \rangle} \lambda P_{\langle e, t \rangle} \lambda x . G(x) \mathrel{!>} \text{norm}(G)(P)$

3.5 The degree-based approach

contextually salient way. In the absence of the *for* PP spelling out the comparison class, its value is supplied by context.

To be sure, no small part of the theory lies obscured behind the !> symbol, and I have provided only the faintest glimpse of it. But the larger point is that it is easily stated in terms of degrees, and in a way that instantly relates Graff's subtle philosophical concerns to the grammatical architecture of the expression. Philosophy and syntax have intermingled effortlessly. This is exciting and is a point in favor of the theoretical framework that brought it about. (See Stanley 2003 and Kennedy 2007 for further discussion relevant to Graff's approach.)

Inherent vagueness theories, on the other hand, tend to be wedded to a view of vagueness that relies on an extension gap. Graff's approach has no need – and no use – for one.

The careful reader might observe I have subtly moved the goalposts in this section. The discussion of 'vague predicates' in the inherent vagueness theory has turned into a discussion of 'gradable predicates' here. This is a reflection of another fact about degree-based accounts. They work beautifully for gradable adjectives, but a theory of other vague predicates – nouns, verbs, even prepositions – doesn't fall out automatically. Providing such a theory isn't trivial, but of course that's precisely what makes it interesting (discussion can be found in section 6.3 and in Nakanishi 2004a,b, 2007; Morzycki 2005b, 2009b, 2012b; Kennedy and Levin 2008; Rett 2008b; Wellwood et al. 2012; Anderson forthcoming).

3.5.4 The tautology and contradiction issue

For the sake of consistency, we should look again at the tautology and contradiction that doomed the fuzzy-logic approach, to verify that the degree approach isn't similarly doomed:

(35)   a. Floyd is tall or he isn't tall.
       b. Floyd is tall and he isn't tall.

Returning to our simpler original POS morpheme, the denotations would be as in (36):

(36)   a. $[\![\text{Floyd is tall or he isn't tall.}]\!]^c$
       = $\exists d\,[\text{tall}(d)(\text{Floyd}) \land d > \text{standard}_c(\text{tall})] \lor$
       $\neg \exists d\,[\text{tall}(d)(\text{Floyd}) \land d > \text{standard}_c(\text{tall})]$

       b. $[\![\text{Floyd is tall and he isn't tall.}]\!]^c$
       = $\exists d\,[\text{tall}(d)(\text{Floyd}) \land d > \text{standard}_c(\text{tall})] \land$
       $\neg \exists d\,[\text{tall}(d)(\text{Floyd}) \land d > \text{standard}_c(\text{tall})]$

A quick glance verifies that these have the form ⌜$\phi \vee \neg\phi$⌝ and ⌜$\phi \wedge \neg\phi$⌝ respectively – the former necessarily true, the latter necessarily false – so the right result emerges unproblematically.

3.5.5 Comparatives

Comparatives – and other DEGREE CONSTRUCTIONS such as equatives and superlatives – are an area where a degree-based theory excels. One natural way to think about a comparative such as *Floyd is taller than Clyde* on this approach is that it requires that there be a degree of tallness that Floyd has and Clyde lacks:

(37) 〚*Floyd is taller than Clyde*〛^{c}
= $\exists d[\textbf{tall}(d)(\textbf{Floyd}) \wedge \neg\textbf{tall}(d)(\textbf{Clyde})]$

Compositionally, this can be assembled straightforwardly from the comparative morpheme in (38a) (which I'll again represent as *more*, and again I'll assume *than* is not interpreted):

(38) a. 〚*more*〛$^c = \lambda G_{\langle d, et \rangle} \lambda x \lambda y . \exists d[G(d)(y) \wedge \neg G(d)(x)]$
b. 〚*more tall*〛^{c} = 〚*more*〛^{c} (〚*tall*〛^{c})
= $\lambda x \lambda y . \exists d[\textbf{tall}(d)(y) \wedge \neg\textbf{tall}(d)(x)]$
c. 〚*more tall than Clyde*〛^{c} = 〚*more tall*〛^{c} (〚*than Clyde*〛^{c})
= $\lambda y . \exists d[\textbf{tall}(d)(y) \wedge \neg\textbf{tall}(d)(\textbf{Clyde})]$

Because there is no reference to a contextually provided standard, no entailment is predicted to the positive form. Nothing in (38) tells us anything about whether an individual exceeds that standard for tallness.

As we'll see in Chapter 4, it's customary to adopt a more sophisticated syntactic representation than the surface-oriented one adopted in (38), but for the moment this will suffice. It's worth pointing out, though, that one reason degree theories often invoke a more sophisticated syntax is that they're especially good at handling it. In particular, they offer an option that isn't available in principle on the inherent vagueness approach: they can have linguistic expressions denote not just functions that play a degree-like role, but actually degrees themselves. The best an inherent vagueness approach could do would be to have an expression denote a degree function. That's not a bad approximation, but it doesn't have quite the same graceful simplicity.

There are of course other possible treatments of the comparative (as there are for POS). We'll consider alternatives in Chapter 4. For now, it's worth just pointing out that many of these use the > relation, which seems especially natural in the context of a degree-based theory.

3.5 The degree-based approach

The version here, which Schwarzschild (2008) dubs the 'A-not-A' analysis, nevertheless has much to recommend it and is for that reason widespread. For one thing, given the structure of scales, an equivalent denotation could actually be written that **does** use >, just not as simply. Another advantage of this way of expressing it is that the overt negation explains in an especially clear way why comparative clauses (*than*-clauses) license negative polarity items (NPIs) such as *anyone* or *ever*: *than anyone is, than he ever has*. It does so without assuming anything beyond that negation licenses NPIs. As we'll see in section 4.5.2, many languages even express comparatives explicitly as coordinate structures with a negated conjunct.

3.5.6 Degree words

The degree-based theory lends itself very naturally to expressing degree modifiers, a topic to which we will return repeatedly (including in sections 3.7.2 and 3.7.4). For the sake of comparison with the inherent vagueness approach, a degree-based denotation for *very* might look like this:

(39) $[\![very]\!]^c = \lambda G_{\langle d, et \rangle} \lambda x . \exists d [G(d)(x) \wedge d \gg_c \textbf{standard}_c(G)]$

This is identical to the simple POS denotation, except that it requires exceeding the contextually provided standard by a large degree, where the context determines what counts as large (this relation is what $\gg_c$ expresses). On this view, a *very* predication is doubly context-sensitive: it relies both on the usual contextually provided standard and on a contextual definition of what counts as exceeding it by a large amount. There are, however, many other options. In a degree-based theory, one could also express (39) by predicating largeness directly of the difference between a degree and the standard:

(40) $[\![very]\!]^c = \lambda G_{\langle d, et \rangle} \lambda x . \exists d [G(d)(x) \wedge \textbf{large}_c(d - \textbf{standard}_c(G))]$

Yet another alternative is to simply adopt Klein's *very* into this framework, which can also be done straightforwardly (Kennedy and McNally 2005).

3.5.7 Varieties of degrees

As presented here, degrees are atomic types, simply points on a scale abstractly representing measurement. This is not the only option. We'll encounter various alternatives over the course of the book, but it makes sense to mention a few of them now to convey a sense of the available options.

First, one could represent degrees not as points but rather as intervals, sets of points portions of a scale (Kennedy 1997; Schwarzschild and Wilkinson 2002). This arguably makes some of the system simpler and may have welcome consequences for scope ambiguities, measure-phrase licensing, and capturing the distinction between antonymous adjectives (e.g. *short* vs. *tall*; for scope issues, see section 4.2.8, and for the others, section 3.7.1).

One could also adopt an earlier idea, due to Cresswell (1976), that constructs degrees out of equivalence classes of individuals. An equivalence class is a set of individuals that have the same measure along some dimension: height, weight, size, pleasantness, etc. (More formally, an equivalence class is any subset whose members stand in an equivalence relation to each other, where an equivalence relation – like 'has the same height as' – is like a partial order except that instead of being antisymmetric, it is symmetric.) This has the advantage of metaphysical parsimony. It would mean there is one fewer atomic type in the model. This approach yields a less flexible notion of degrees, though. It has trouble with the meaning of measure phrases in differential comparatives such as *Floyd is two feet taller than Clyde*, where *two feet* couldn't plausibly denote everything that measures two feet and it's not clear how to achieve the effect of adding or subtracting degrees. In light of this, it wouldn't be unreasonable to doubt whether such a theory really counts as a degree-based theory.

Some other possibilities:

- model at least some degrees numerically (using real or rational numbers depending on the author; Hellan 1981; Bale 2006, 2008)
- model degrees as concrete property manifestations ('tropes') of the sort that e.g. *the height of Floyd* might refer to (Moltmann 2007, 2009)
- model degrees as kinds of states (Anderson and Morzycki forthcoming)
- construct degrees out of several more basic elements, such as a property, a measure, and a measured object (Grosu and Landman 1998)
- recognize more than one type of degree (Bale 2006, 2008; see section 4.3.8)

For most purposes, the standard approach sketched in the preceding sections is easiest to work with.

3.6 DEGREE OR NOT DEGREE? THAT IS THE QUESTION

Now that both the inherent vagueness and degree-based approaches are on the table, we can consider them in relation to each other.

The differences between the approaches at first glance seem profound. This is at least partly misleading. The most important difference is probably that one theory treats degrees as objects in the model and makes use of degree arguments. But of course, to say that degrees are 'objects in the model' is not to say much, given that they don't need to be primitives (i.e., atomic types). If a theory in which degrees are constructed out of something else counts as a degree theory, well, then it has that in common with an inherent vagueness theory that has degree functions, which are also 'in the model' but not atomic types. Of course, the types involved in degree functions are more complicated, but perhaps that's not particularly important.

A point of clear similarity is their treatment of comparatives, at least as I have presented them here (van Rooij 2008; Doetjes et al. 2011; and Nouwen et al. 2011a make a similar point):

(41)   Floyd is taller than Clyde.

   a. *inherent vagueness theory:*
      $\exists d \in \textbf{degree-functions}(c)[d(\textbf{tall})(\textbf{Floyd}) \wedge \neg d(\textbf{tall})(\textbf{Clyde})]$

   b. *degree-based theory:*
      $\exists d[\textbf{tall}(d)(\textbf{Floyd}) \wedge \neg \textbf{tall}(d)(\textbf{Clyde})]$

This similarity is precarious, and it could melt away with only minor changes. Nevertheless, many changes in one theory might find analogues in the other, since both are manipulating something like degrees.

One deep difference between the two classes of approaches is that an extension gap theory is tightly bound to a particular view of vagueness. One could certainly enrich it in various ways, but it would lose a major component of its character if the extension gap element were gone. What's especially troubling about this is that extension gaps have significant shortcomings as a theory of vagueness. They certainly reflect the existence of borderline cases, but what about the boundary between borderline and clear cases? The theory suggests that it should be completely sharp, but that's not consistent with our intuitions. There are certainly some borderline cases that are clearly borderline cases, but there are also ones that are borderline cases of borderline cases. This phenomenon, called HIGHER ORDER VAGUENESS, strikes at the heart of the theory. If vagueness is simply due to extension gaps, what accounts for vagueness about the extension gaps themselves?

Additional difficulties are pointed out in Kennedy (1997). One of them involves incommensurability, the ill-formedness of comparatives (and related constructions) formed from adjectives that measure along different dimensions:

(42) #My copy of *The Brothers Karamazov* is heavier than my copy of *The Idiot* is old. (Kennedy 1997)

It's not that inherent-vagueness theories leave no room for explanations of such effects. The problem with these examples, one might say, is conceptual rather than semantic. Perhaps one just can't make sense of a comparison between weight and age? If that were so, however, we would expect (43) to be just as bad:

(43) My copy of *The Brothers Karamazov* is higher on a scale of heaviness than my copy of *The Idiot* is on a scale of age. (Kennedy 1997)

Yet this sentence is fine – or rather, it's odd in precisely the way a conceptual oddness might feel. It seems strange that anyone would want to make such a comparison, but there is no sense of semantic anomaly. He notes further problems having to do with several varieties of comparative. The most important property of inherent-vagueness theories that gives rise to these problems is that they don't offer a sufficiently articulated notion of scales. To be sure, they involve orderings among individuals, orderings that are present in the model itself. But on these theories the comparative (ultimately) involves quantification over precisifications rather than over degrees on a particular scale, so arbitrary cross-scale comparisons are expected to be licit. Moreover, operations that are easily defined in a degree theory – such as measuring the difference between degrees in, for example, differential comparatives like *two feet taller* – are problematic.

On the other hand, inherent-vagueness theories have at least two apparent advantages over degree theories. First, they take the positive form of the adjective to be basic and define the comparative in terms of it. A degree theory, arguably, does precisely the opposite, because it assigns a semantics to a positive adjective that involves an ordering relation: a positive adjective has a meaning of the form 'more G than the standard for G'. Yet across languages, the positive form is the less syntactically complicated one (or in any case, that's what the syntax superficially suggests). This is potentially a deep problem, and an

3.6 Degree or not degree? That is the question

oft-mentioned one. In principle, one can imagine a vaguely functionalist response that goes like this: In any language, the more often-used form is likely to be the one that involves the most phonological and syntactic reduction, and the less often used one will be the one with overt bells and whistles. It may simply be that positive adjectives are more common than comparatives, across languages, and apparently structurally simpler for that reason alone. But that doesn't necessarily tell us anything about the relative complexity of the semantics – for insight into that, we must ask about truth conditions, not count overt morphemes.

Second, inherent-vagueness theories provide a better understanding of the ubiquity of vagueness. It's not just adjectives that are vague, after all. A degree-based theory weds vagueness to degree arguments, and therefore in turn to gradability. It's certainly true that vagueness and gradability are closely related, but they're not indistinguishable. *Heap*, for example, isn't directly gradable.[21] So, on a degree-based theory, what is to be said about it? Do we give it a degree argument, and thereby – in the face of the grammatical evidence – a gradable semantics? That seems unappealing, particularly when it has to be extended to other syntactic categories as well. If the answer is no, then an independent theory of the vagueness of these expressions is required. Whatever that independent theory is, it would likely result in an account of adjectival vagueness too, which would mean adjectival vagueness would be explained twice over. The generative linguist's instinctive drive for simplicity recoils at this possibility. On an inherent-vagueness theory, vagueness is treated as a single unified phenomenon, and these issues don't arise.

This too is a deep problem. Again, though, one could argue the other way: we know adjectives are the primary gradable category. A theory should reflect that, as introducing degree arguments does. Any theory that levels the distinction between gradable adjectives and non-gradable vague predicates in other categories fails to explain why adjectives are so good for grading. And here again a reply is available: what's special about adjectives that makes them especially gradable is a subtle fact about their lexical semantics, not a crude fact about their type: they have meanings that just lend themselves, conceptually, to gradability.

This dialogue could continue, and no doubt should (elsewhere). But before leaving it, it's worth pointing out an intermediate position. Perhaps **both** approaches are right. Although this sounds superficially like

---

[21] It can enter into constructions such as *more of a heap*, of course.

a mealy-mouthed compromise, one shouldn't reject it out of hand. Running the theories in parallel would decouple general vagueness and gradability. That might be what's empirically necessary. Caution is warranted, of course. Combining competing theories can yield the union of their flaws and the intersection of their virtues. Even so, there might be a way to, as Doetjes et al. (2011) suggest, integrate them insightfully. One might, for example, eliminate the extension gaps themselves, but maintain the idea that vague predicates lack degree arguments and have their extensions fixed by context – and perhaps even that gradability can be understood in terms of degree functions and quantification over precisifications.

3.7 SCALES AND THE LEXICAL SEMANTICS OF ADJECTIVES

3.7.1 Antonyms

Chapter 2 focused on non-scalar issues in the lexical semantics of adjectives. We now have the tools in place to handle the scalar ones too. Among the more obvious of these is the relation between adjectives and their antonyms:

(44) tall ⟷ short
      wide ⟷ narrow
      old   ⟷ young
      fast ⟷ slow
      hot   ⟷ cold

Many adjectives are like this. Unsurprisingly, the marked member of each pair is called a NEGATIVE ADJECTIVE. This is a terrible term. It makes the other member of the pair, inevitably, a POSITIVE ADJECTIVE. This term is already used to designate the morphologically unmarked form of the adjective too, so some negative adjectives occur in the positive form. This might suggest that we should reserve 'positive' for this sense and refer to the morphologically unmarked form as just 'unmarked', except that the term 'unmarked' is taken, too – and for precisely this purpose. *Tall* and *short* are the 'unmarked' and 'marked' members of an antonym pair. There's nothing to be done but to press on.

The first question to ask about this distinction is how one knows which member of the pair is the negative one. Intuitions about being 'positive' are not an adequate guide. There are some clear diagnostics, though (Seuren 1978; Bierwisch 1989; Kennedy 2001; Rett 2008a,b; Sassoon 2010a). Negative adjectives never accept measure phrases (setting aside comparatives):

3.7 Scales and the lexical semantics of adjectives

(45)   a. six feet $\begin{Bmatrix} \text{tall} \\ \text{\#short} \end{Bmatrix}$

       b. six feet $\begin{Bmatrix} \text{wide} \\ \text{\#narrow} \end{Bmatrix}$

       c. six years $\begin{Bmatrix} \text{old} \\ \text{\#young} \end{Bmatrix}$

Of course, many positive adjectives don't accept measure phrases either: #80 mph fast, #−15C cold. Negative adjectives are also dispreferred with factor phrases like *twice* in the equative:

(46)   twice as $\begin{Bmatrix} \text{tall} \\ \text{?short} \\ \text{wide} \\ \text{?narrow} \\ \text{old} \\ \text{?young} \end{Bmatrix}$

Negative adjectives don't occur in nominalizations that name the dimension along which they measure:

(47)   The $\begin{Bmatrix} \text{length} \\ \text{\#shortness} \\ \text{width} \\ \text{\#narrowness} \end{Bmatrix}$ of the coffee table is 4 feet.

In *wh*-questions, negative adjectives give rise to a presupposition:

(48)   a. How $\begin{Bmatrix} \text{tall} \\ \text{short} \end{Bmatrix}$ are you?

       b. How $\begin{Bmatrix} \text{wide} \\ \text{narrow} \end{Bmatrix}$ is this coffee table?

Short in (48a) gives rise to the presupposition that you're short, and *narrow* in (48b) to the presupposition that the coffee table is narrow. No analogous presupposition arises for the positive form. A similar effect happens in the equative:

(49)   a. Floyd is as $\begin{Bmatrix} \text{tall} \\ \text{short} \end{Bmatrix}$ as Clyde.

       b. The coffee table is as $\begin{Bmatrix} \text{wide} \\ \text{narrow} \end{Bmatrix}$ as the couch.

Short in (49a) gives rise to the entailment that Floyd and Clyde are short, and *narrow* in (49b) to the entailment that the coffee table and couch are narrow.

A more subtle but notable difference is that negative adjectives in the comparative can give rise to ambiguities involving modals, sometimes called the (Seuren-)Rullmann ambiguity (Seuren 1978; Rullmann 1995; Heim 2006a; Rett 2008b; Beck 2013):

(50) The helicopter was flying lower than a plane can fly.
  (Rullmann 1995)
  a. The helicopter was flying lower than the the **lowest** level a plane can fly.
  b. The helicopter was flying lower than the the **highest** level a plane can fly.

The corresponding positive form (i.e. with *higher*) is unambiguous.

These all serve both as diagnostics for the negative member of a pair, and as data to be explained. One additional fact needs to be added to this mix. Antonym pairs can give rise to CROSS-POLAR ANOMALY (so dubbed by Kennedy 1997, 2001) in comparatives:

(51) a. ??Floyd is shorter than Clyde is tall.
  b. ??This table is wider than that one is narrow.
  c. ??Your nephew is younger than your grandmother is old.

These reflect that the adjective in the matrix and comparative clause must either both be positive or both be negative. Büring (2007b) observes that sentences with essentially the same meaning are improved when one of the adjectives isn't the polar antonym:

(52) a. The ladder is shorter than the house is high.
  (Büring 2007b)
  b. My yacht is shorter than yours is wide.

This also demonstrates that the problem in (51) can't be due to a constraint on forming comparatives with non-identical adjectives.

Kennedy (2001) proposed an account of these facts based on a particular ontology of degrees. The idea is that there are two sorts of degrees: positive and negative, both of which are intervals. Positive adjectives measure in positive degrees, and negative adjectives measure in negative degrees – and never the twain shall meet. The two sorts are related, obviously. They use the same sets of points, but they are on different scales because they have different orderings, one the

3.7 Scales and the lexical semantics of adjectives

mirror-image of the other. Given this way of thinking, then, 'Floyd's tallness' and 'Floyd's shortness' are distinct degrees. 'Floyd's tallness' is what one might expect: if he's six feet tall, it's a positive degree that extends upwards from (just above) 0 to 6 feet. 'Floyd's shortness', however, is a little surprising. It extends to six feet, but, because it's negative, it gets there from the opposite direction – from above – by extending **downwards**. This of course means it can't start at 0. The scale has no opposite end, however: there is no maximum height in principle. So the degree of his shortness extends from infinity down to six feet:

(53) a. Floyd's tallness: $(0, 6\text{ft}]$
      b. Floyd's shortness: $(\infty, 6\text{ft}]$

Two results follow naturally from this very intuitive set-up.

First, cross-polar anomaly is explained, though things look a little different in the A-not-A theory of comparatives we've so far assumed than in Kennedy's formulation:

(54) a. #Floyd is taller than Clyde is short.
      b. $\exists d\,[\textbf{tall}(d)(\textbf{Floyd}) \land \neg\textbf{short}(d)(\textbf{Clyde})]$

What goes wrong in (54b) is that it's necessarily true (if Floyd has any tallness at all): only degrees of tallness can satisfy the first conjunct, and no tallness degree is a degree to which someone is short, satisfying the second conjunct. Sentences that are necessarily true by virtue of their structure are generally unusable. Kennedy adopts another way of representing the meaning of a comparative that actually leaves (54a) undefined. He assumes that comparatives require one degree to exceed another on a single scale (see Chapter 4). The comparison in (54a) would then require comparing a tallness degree on the same scale as a shortness degree – which, by hypothesis, is precisely what isn't defined. A rough intuitive approximation of the idea is simply that there's no way to compare how tall people are to how tall others aren't.

Second, the measure-phrase facts also fall into place. This is because measure phrases denote positive rather than negative degrees. It would be odd if it were otherwise: measure phrases have to start measuring relative to a fixed point, so they must denote intervals that extend from an origin point on a scale. A negative interval wouldn't have one.

Heim (2006a) (see also Büring 2007c; Heim 2008) takes a different approach, building on Rullmann (1995). She takes as her point of departure the Rullmann ambiguity in (50) and winds up with a syntactic rather than ontological solution. It is based on two intuitions. First, we do want something that resembles negation associated with negative adjectives. In many cases, negative adjectives have overtly negative morphology (e.g. *impure, unmanageable, implausible*). Second, as Rullmann noticed, precisely the same ambiguity emerges when *lower* is replaced by *less high*:

(55)   The helicopter was flying less high than a plane can fly.
                                                        (Rullmann 1995)
   a. The helicopter was flying lower than the the **lowest** level a plane can fly.
   b. The helicopter was flying lower than the the **highest** level a plane can fly.

This suggests that *lower* spells out the same structure as *less high* does. But these forms are both in the comparative. Obviously, not all negative adjectives are comparative. So if we are to generalize this decomposition, we need to find a way to factor out the comparative morphology. A way to do that is revealed by paradigms like those in (56):

(56)   a. He $\left\{\begin{array}{l}\text{knows}\\ \text{expects}\end{array}\right\}$ $\left\{\begin{array}{l}\text{little}\\ \text{less}\\ \text{the least}\end{array}\right\}$.

   b. We have $\left\{\begin{array}{l}\text{little}\\ \text{less}\\ \text{the least}\end{array}\right\}$ water.

In this way, *little* is a counterpart of *much*:

(57)   a. He $\left\{\begin{array}{l}\text{knows}\\ \text{expects}\end{array}\right\}$ $\left\{\begin{array}{l}\text{much}\\ \text{more}\\ \text{the most}\end{array}\right\}$.

   b. We have $\left\{\begin{array}{l}\text{much}\\ \text{more}\\ \text{the most}\end{array}\right\}$ water.

This shows that *less* is simply the comparative form of *little*: *-er little* (Bresnan 1973). This in turn means *less high* is really *-er little high*, as in (58a). And if *lower* spells out the same structure as *less high*, it too must be *-er little high* underlyingly, as in (58b):[22]

---

[22] I have switched from representing the comparative morpheme as *more* to *-er* since, on this view, *more* could be *-er much*.

3.7 Scales and the lexical semantics of adjectives

(58)   a. *[-er little] high* ⇒ *less high*
           b. *-er [little high]* ⇒ *-er low* ⇒ *lower*

So we've arrived at a way to factor out the comparative from *lower*: *low* alone is *little high*. It can't actually be pronounced that way in natural-sounding English, but this may be a morphological quirk of the language. German, Heim says, permits it. This how Rullmann (1995) explains why *less high* and *lower* both give rise to the Rullmann ambiguity. Heim considers this approach but ultimately rejects it, but it is embraced and further developed in Büring (2007b,c) (see also Heim 2008).

This decomposition is of course just a start. The actual scope-taking machinery necessary to account for the ambiguity is complex and presupposes syntactic and semantic assumptions we won't have in place until the following chapter (see Heim 2006a, 2008 and Büring 2007b,c). Nevertheless, it's possible to sketch an analysis that connects to the basic insight behind Heim (2006a), which is this: *little* expresses a mode of negation specialized for degrees and gradable predicates. In our terms, it might look like (59a), meaning that *low* (underlyingly *little high*) will have the denotation in (59b) (we will now depart significantly from Heim):

(59)   a. $[\![\textit{little}]\!] = \lambda G_{\langle d, et \rangle} \lambda d \lambda x . \neg G(d)(x)$
           b. $[\![\textit{little high}]\!] = [\![\textit{little}]\!] ([\![\textit{high}]\!])$
               $= \lambda d \lambda x . \neg [\![\textit{high}]\!] (d)(x)$
               $= \lambda d \lambda x . \neg \mathbf{high}(d)(x)$

To get to a sentence denotation, of course, we must go via POS. Our current POS denotation won't suffice, however, since it would predict that an individual x is POS *little high* iff there's a degree above the standard to which x isn't high, as in (60) (I'll omit context super/subscripts from now on):

(60)   a. $[\![\textsc{pos}]\!] = \lambda G_{\langle d, et \rangle} \lambda x . \exists d [G(d)(x) \wedge d > \mathbf{standard}(G)]$
           b. $[\![\textsc{pos}\ \textit{little high}]\!] = [\![\textsc{pos}]\!] ([\![\textit{little high}]\!])$

$$= \lambda x . \exists d \left[\begin{array}{l} [\![\textit{little high}]\!] (d)(x) \wedge \\ d > \mathbf{standard}([\![\textit{little high}]\!]) \end{array} \right]$$

$$= \lambda x . \exists d \left[\begin{array}{l} \neg \mathbf{high}(d)(x) \wedge \\ d > \mathbf{standard}(\lambda d \lambda x . \neg \mathbf{high}(d)(x)) \end{array} \right]$$

This is far too weak. Unless x is high to every degree, there will always be a degree above a standard to which x isn't high.

Heim instead adopts an alternative denotation advanced by von Stechow (2005) (see also Beck 2011). Von Stechow suggests that positive and negative adjectives both use the same scale, with two cut-offs. For example, being low might require being below 12 feet, and being high might require being at at least 100 feet. Von Stechow calls this middle ground between the antonyms the 'delineation interval', which I'll represent with a predicate **middle-ground**.[23] His POS, modified significantly to match our current assumptions, requires that an individual satisfy a gradable predicate to all the degrees in the middle ground:

(61) a. $[\![\text{POS}]\!] = \lambda G_{\langle d, et \rangle} \lambda x . \forall d \in \textbf{middle-ground}[G(d)(x)]$
 b. $[\![\textit{The helicopter is POS high.}]\!]$
  = $\forall d \in \textbf{middle-ground}[\textbf{high}(d)(\text{the-helicopter})]$

Thus the helicopter is high iff it is high to every degree from the *low* cut-off to the *high* cut-off – so it must be at least as high as the *high* cut-off. Combining this with *little* yields a semantics for *low*:

(62) a. $[\![\textit{little high}]\!] = \lambda d \lambda x . \neg\textbf{high}(d)(x)$
 b. $[\![\textit{The helicopter is POS little high.}]\!]$
  = $\forall d \in \textbf{middle-ground}[\neg\textbf{high}(d)(\text{the-helicopter})]$

Thus the helicopter is low iff it fails to be high to any degree from the *low* cut-off to the *high* cut-off – so it must be less high than the *low* cut-off.[24]

In the comparative, the pieces fit together elegantly:

(63) a. $[\![\textit{-er}]\!] = \lambda x \lambda y . \exists d[\textbf{high}(d)(y) \wedge \neg\textbf{high}(d)(x)]$
 b. $[\![\textit{-er little high}]\!] = \lambda x \lambda y . \exists d \begin{bmatrix} [\![\textit{little high}]\!](d)(y) \wedge \\ \neg [\![\textit{little high}]\!](d)(x) \end{bmatrix}$
  = $\lambda x \lambda y . \exists d[\neg\textbf{high}(d)(y) \wedge \neg\neg\textbf{high}(d)(x)]$
  = $\lambda x \lambda y . \exists d[\neg\textbf{high}(d)(y) \wedge \textbf{high}(d)(x)]$
 c. $[\![\textit{The helicopter is -er little high than the plane}]\!]$
  = $\exists d[\neg\textbf{high}(d)(\text{the-helicopter}) \wedge \textbf{high}(d)(\text{the-plane})]$

---

[23] I'll leave off any indication of which scale is at issue, though this could be done by simply providing the gradable predicate as an argument.
The delineation interval is a little like an extension gap, but not quite. First, it's an interval on a degree scale, not a set of individuals. Second, it demarcates the area between, e.g., *low* and *high*, not between *not high* and *high*.

[24] This all predicts an asymmetry between the two cut-offs: being precisely at the *low* cut-off doesn't render you low, but being precisely at the *high* cut-off does render you high.

3.7 Scales and the lexical semantics of adjectives

Thus the helicopter is lower than the plane iff there's a degree to which the plane is high to which the helicopter isn't. This is the right result. It's not a complete theory of the Rullmann ambiguity, but by enriching this with more sophisticated compositional assumptions (such as ones we'll adopt in Chapter 4), one can reassemble these basic ingredients in multiple ways that do provide such a theory (see Rullmann 1995; Heim 2006a, 2008; Büring 2007b,c). For discussion of cross-polar anomaly in light of Heim (2006a), see Heim (2008).

While Kennedy (2001) and Heim (2006a) focus on different puzzles, one shouldn't lose sight of the bigger picture, the more general puzzle they both address: polar antonymy and the semantics of negative adjectives. I think that there's something revealing about considering them together. First, they both begin with puzzles that might seem small, peripheral, or arcane, and yet in both cases these are the keys to deep insights of very general importance. Second, surely it's staggeringly cool that the same empirical phenomena may lead to insights into either the ontology of natural language or the syntax–semantics interface – and that further discussion about these fundamentally different modes of analysis will also be guided by concrete linguistic observations.

3.7.2 Open and closed scales

Over roughly the past decade, it has emerged that another semantic distinction among adjectives – indeed, a range of predicates – is no less important than antonymy. It can be glimpsed in the contrasts reflected in (64) and (65):

(64)   a. The glass is $\begin{Bmatrix} \text{half} \\ \text{mostly} \end{Bmatrix}$ full.

   b. Her eyes were $\begin{Bmatrix} \text{half} \\ \text{mostly} \end{Bmatrix}$ closed.

   c. These images are $\begin{Bmatrix} \text{half} \\ \text{mostly} \end{Bmatrix}$ invisible.

(65)   a. ??A 15-year-old horse is $\begin{Bmatrix} \text{half} \\ \text{mostly} \end{Bmatrix}$ old.

   b. ??That car was $\begin{Bmatrix} \text{half} \\ \text{mostly} \end{Bmatrix}$ expensive.

   c. ??Clyde seemed $\begin{Bmatrix} \text{half} \\ \text{mostly} \end{Bmatrix}$ tall.

The PROPORTIONAL MODIFIERS *half* and *mostly* turn out to be just the tip of the iceberg, a reflection of a distinction with broader consequences. But what is this distinction, precisely? How should it be represented formally?

Kennedy and McNally (2005) and Rotstein and Winter (2004) provide an answer: these adjectives differ in the structure of their scales. (I'll frame the discussion along the lines of the former.) There are many aspects of how scales are organized that one might describe as 'scale structure', but the one that's relevant here has to do with what happens at the ends of a scale. There are four options, which can be best appreciated by thinking degrees on a scale in terms of real numbers between 0 and 1. One option is for a scale to include 0 and 1 in addition to the numbers between them. This would be a CLOSED SCALE, so called because it is a closed interval: one that includes minimal and maximal values. The natural alternative is for a scale to exclude 0 and 1, including only the real numbers between them. This is an OPEN SCALE. It doesn't include a minimal or maximal value. It **approaches** 0 and 1 at its extremes, but never reaches them – there is no smallest non-zero between 0 and 1, and no largest non-one number either. There are, of course, two other possibilities – a scale could include 1 and leave out 0, or vice versa. This can be stated set-theoretically:

(66)   SCALE TYPES

   a. *closed*: $\{d : 0 \leq d \leq 1\}$
   b. *open*: $\{d : 0 < d < 1\}$
   c. *upper closed*: $\{d : 0 < d \leq 1\}$
   d. *lower closed*: $\{d : 0 \leq d < 1\}$

Here is a visual representation:

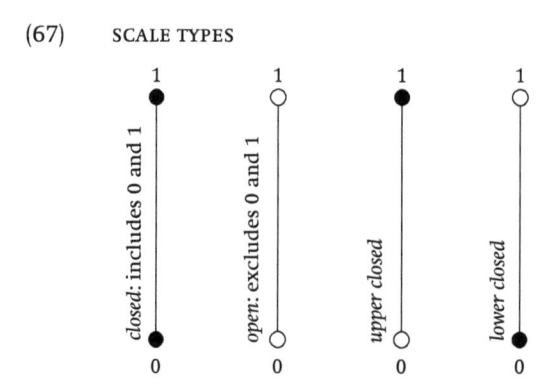

(67)   SCALE TYPES

3.7 Scales and the lexical semantics of adjectives

Because these are intervals, a standard notation for intervals can be used. The closed interval is [0, 1], the open one (0, 1), the upper closed (0, 1], and the lower closed [0, 1).

This is purely a formal distinction, which might well have turned out to be linguistically irrelevant. But it isn't. It provides a way of representing scale boundedness, the intuition that scales can vary with respect to whether they have a highest or lowest degree. That's the idea behind Kennedy and McNally's account of proportional modifiers. Proportions are about bounded quantities. If I ask you how much coffee you'd like, you can't reasonably reply 'half'. Analogously, the degree modifier *half* also needs a bounded quantity, in this case, a bounded – that is, closed – scale.

This can be represented in the semantics straightforwardly. The intuition behind *half* is that it locates a degree whose distance from the bottom of a scale is the same as the distance from the top. To say this more formally, we need some tools. First, we'll need a **scale** function that applies to a gradable predicate and returns its scale. Second, we'll need two functions, **max** and **min**, which return the maximum (i.e., top) and the minimum (i.e., bottom) of a scale.[25] Third, we'll need a function for measuring the difference (i.e., distance) between degrees on a scale. Let's call that **diff**. On Kennedy and McNally's approach, then, *half* will be as in (68a), and precisely the same tools give us *mostly* as well:

(68) a. $[\![half]\!] = \lambda G_{\langle d, et \rangle} \lambda x . \exists d \begin{bmatrix} G(d)(x) \wedge \\ \textbf{diff}(\textbf{max}(\textbf{scale}(G)))(d) = \\ \textbf{diff}(d)(\textbf{min}(\textbf{scale}(G))) \end{bmatrix}$

b. $[\![mostly]\!] = \lambda G_{\langle d, et \rangle} \lambda x . \exists d \begin{bmatrix} G(d)(x) \wedge \\ \textbf{diff}(\textbf{max}(\textbf{scale}(G)))(d) > \\ \textbf{diff}(d)(\textbf{min}(\textbf{scale}(G))) \end{bmatrix}$

These are like POS in that they are degree words and they saturate the degree argument. Taking one additional step:

---

[25] The **min** and **max** functions will recur elsewhere in the book. Here are their definitions (S is a set of degrees or a scale construed as such):

(i) a. $\textbf{max}(S) \stackrel{\text{def}}{=} \iota d[d \in S \wedge \forall d' \in S[d' \leq d]]$
'the unique degree in S such that every degree in S is smaller than (or identical to) it'

b. $\textbf{min}(S) \stackrel{\text{def}}{=} \iota d[d \in S \wedge \forall d' \in S[d \leq d']]$
'the unique degree in S that is smaller than (or identical to) any degree in S'

(69) $[\![\textit{half}]\!]([\![\textit{full}]\!]) = \lambda x . \exists d \begin{bmatrix} \textbf{full}(d)(x) \wedge \\ \textbf{diff}(\max(\textbf{scale}(\textbf{full})))(d) = \\ \textbf{diff}(d)(\min(\textbf{scale}(\textbf{full}))) \end{bmatrix}$

So something is half full if it is full to a degree that is the same distance from the minimum and maximum of the scale.[26]

These denotations also explain what goes wrong for adjectives incompatible with proportional modifiers – that is, for adjectives with open or partly open scales. In a case like *half old*, the maximality and minimality operators will apply to the scale of age. But (at least) the maximality operator simply isn't defined for the scale of age because it doesn't have a maximum. The sentence, therefore, comes out undefined.

Similar reasoning can accommodate modifiers that are sensitive to only one end of the scale. The MAXIMALITY MODIFIERS *fully* and *completely* are of this class:

(70) CLOSED SCALE

a. The flower was fully $\begin{Bmatrix} \text{open} \\ \text{closed} \end{Bmatrix}$.

b. The monkey was fully $\begin{Bmatrix} \text{visible} \\ \text{invisible} \end{Bmatrix}$.

(71) OPEN SCALE

a. ??Floyd is fully $\begin{Bmatrix} \text{tall} \\ \text{short} \end{Bmatrix}$.

b. ??This table is fully $\begin{Bmatrix} \text{wide} \\ \text{narrow} \end{Bmatrix}$.

(72) UPPER CLOSED SCALE VS. LOWER CLOSED SCALE

a. We are fully $\begin{Bmatrix} \text{certain} \\ ??\text{uncertain} \end{Bmatrix}$.

b. The treatment is fully $\begin{Bmatrix} \text{safe} \\ ??\text{unsafe} \end{Bmatrix}$.

The examples in (72) require special attention. The first adjective in each pair is upper closed (lower open), and its antonym is lower closed (upper

---

[26] Well, that's not quite true. Alan Bale points out a neat subtlety: because anything that's full to one degree is also full to every degree below it, (69) would be true of something that is completely full because it is full to a degree at the midpoint of the scale too. Yet we can't say without contradiction that a glass is both half full and completely full. The problem here is inherited from Kennedy and McNally. Bochnak (2010) provides a denotation along these lines that remedies this.

3.7 Scales and the lexical semantics of adjectives

open). This all reveals that *fully* has a semantics that requires reference to the maximum on a scale, but not to a minimum:

(73) $[\![fully]\!] = \lambda G_{\langle d, et \rangle} \lambda x . G(\mathbf{max}(\mathbf{scale}(G)))(x)$

Consequently, *fully* will be incompatible with any scale for which a maximum degree isn't defined, but it will be indifferent to the presence of a minimum degree. Sometimes *slightly* is suggested as an example of a modifier that requires lower-closed scales, but the judgments it evokes are less clear and Kennedy and McNally don't mention it.

There is a more important insight to be gleaned from (73), however. The distribution of degree modifiers shows that the scales of polar antonyms are identical except in direction of the ordering – metaphorically, in which end is up. The maximum of one scale is the minimum of the other, and vice versa. If an adjective has a maximum, its antonym will always have a minimum. This is an important insight relevant to a general theory of antonymy, and thus has consequences far beyond the distribution of the degree modifiers.

The semantics of positive forms is one area where these differences turn out to be crucial:

(74) UPPER CLOSED SCALE VS. LOWER CLOSED SCALE

a. The rod is $\left\{ \begin{array}{l} \text{straight} \\ \text{bent} \end{array} \right\}$.

b. The soap is $\left\{ \begin{array}{l} \text{pure} \\ \text{impure} \end{array} \right\}$.

c. The child is $\left\{ \begin{array}{l} \text{healthy} \\ \text{sick} \end{array} \right\}$.

All of these adjectives have partially closed scales (as combining them with, e.g., *fully* would reveal). In each of these cases – and more generally – the standard associated with the scale always corresponds to the closed end. For example, *straight* is upper closed and lower opened, and *bent* is therefore the opposite. Across contexts, the standard for *straight* is set at the maximum on the scale: something is straight iff it's fully straight. *Bent* is a mirror-image. Across contexts, the standard for *bent* will be set at the minimum on the scale: something is bent iff it has any amount of bend at all.[27] For fully closed scales, there

---

[27] It's possible to imagine contexts in which one might say something is straight even if it has a tiny, pragmatically irrelevant amount of bend. Kennedy and McNally argue convincingly that this involves imprecision, not vagueness (see section 3.2.3).

is a complication: there are two natural endpoints. In these cases, the adjective must simply resolve the matter lexically. Open-scale adjectives pose the opposite problem: not a surfeit of endpoints but too few. *Tall* and (therefore) *short* are open scale, so their scales include no natural boundary one might use as a standard. Without reliance on context, there is no way to determine conclusively where the standard lies. And so, in these cases, that's precisely what we do – rely on context, giving rise to vagueness.

Because of this fundamental difference, Kennedy and McNally dub adjectives with at least partly closed scales ABSOLUTE ADJECTIVES because their standard is fixed at the closed end of the scale. Open-scale adjectives like *tall* have no closed end, so their standard is context-dependent. They dub these RELATIVE ADJECTIVES.[28] Of course, absolute adjectives can be subdivided further, into those with minimum standards and those with maximum ones. Older terms for these, which are still very much in use, are PARTIAL and TOTAL adjectives (Yoon 1996; Rotstein and Winter 2004). Fully closed-scale adjectives are a bit less tidy: they are absolute adjectives, and their standard is always at one end, but which end needs to be stipulated in the lexicon.

To account for this effect, the POS morpheme must be changed. As it stands, it requires exceeding a contextually provided standard. This is doubly problematic. First, it suggests all adjectives should be context-dependent, not just relative adjectives. Second, for maximum standard adjectives, it would impose an impossible to meet requirement: if the standard is at the top of a scale, it's impossible to exceed it. That could be addressed by changing the ordering relation from $>$ to $\geq$, so that it's only necessary to meet the standard rather than exceed it. But this leaps out of the frying pan and into the fire: for minimum-standard adjectives, any degree on the scale meets or exceeds the standard, so any positive-form predication involving a minimum-standard adjective would be true. Kennedy and McNally propose working around this by encoding the degree ordering relation into the semantics of the **standard** predicate itself. A version of their POS is in (75):

(75) $\quad [\![\text{POS}]\!] = \lambda G_{\langle d, et \rangle} \lambda x \,.\, \exists d[\textbf{standard}(G)(d) \wedge G(d)(x)]$

---

[28] Neither term is ideal because both have other uses. 'Absolute' is sometimes used to refer to the positive form of an adjective (Kennedy 1997), and 'relative' is sometimes used as a synonym for 'gradable' or for 'subsective' (Bartsch and Vennemann 1973; Siegel 1976a).

3.7 Scales and the lexical semantics of adjectives

This requires that there be a degree that stand in the right relation to the standard. What that relation is, precisely, depends on the adjective provided, as does whether the standard is dependent on context. Subsequently, attempts have been made to shed some light on this. Kennedy (2007) seeks to derive this effect from an economy principle. The idea is that context-dependence is inherently costly, and that there is a general linguistic preference for relying on non-contextual, lexically provided meaning as much as possible. This would, of course, include information about scale structure. Potts (2008) suggests that this principle can actually be derived from independent principles in game theory that govern the strategies participants settle into when they interact.

These scale–structure distinctions are relevant to how adjectives behave in comparatives and other degree constructions as well. In her extensive examination of these effects, Rett (2008b,a) observes that in the equative, closed scale adjectives systematically license inferences to the positive form (as in (76)), unlike open-scale adjectives (as in (77)):

(76)   a. This is as opaque as that.
            entails: This is opaque.

        b. This is as transparent as that.
            entails: This is transparent.

(77)   Floyd is as tall as Clyde.
        does not entail: Floyd is tall.

Rett's general framework is discussed a bit more in section 4.4. For more on scale-structure sensitivity across syntactic categories, see Bochnak (2010), Kennedy and Levin (2008), and section 6.3.

For reference, (78) lists some antonyms pairs according to this aspect of scale structure. Many adjectives don't have clear antonyms, of course. A few of the examples are less clear-cut than the others, and such cases may reflect opportunities for further refinements to the theory.

(78)   ANTONYMOUS ADJECTIVES AND THEIR SCALE TYPES

open	closed	upper closed	lower closed
tall/short	empty/full	clean	dirty
heavy/light	transparent/opaque	dry	wet
high/low	open/closed	straight	bent
wide/narrow	visible/invisible	pure	impure
big/small	cooked/raw	safe	unsafe

3.7.3 Dimensional and non-dimensional adjectives

Bierwisch (1988b, 1989) identified a scalar lexical-semantic distinction among adjectives that is manifestly related to questions of open and closed scales, but nevertheless is probably distinct. He provided a sustained argument for distinguishing between two natural classes, DIMENSIONAL and NON-DIMENSIONAL adjectives. He actually called the latter class EVALUATIVE adjectives, but I will avoid the term because it is used in a number of other ways and there is quite enough ambiguity in adjective terminology as it stands (see section 4.4).[29]

Dimensional adjectives include *tall*, *heavy*, and *hot*. Non-dimensional adjectives include *stupid*, *ugly*, and *lazy*. The crucial intuition behind the distinction is that non-dimensional adjectives are 'less clearly delimited and less systematically structured' (Bierwisch 1988b).

This intuition alone doesn't get us very far, of course, but it correlates with a number of contrasts that are relatively clear. One of them is that dimensional adjectives come in positive–negative antonym pairs:

(79)   tall ⟷ short
        heavy ⟷ light
        hot ⟷ cold

Non-dimensional adjectives, on the other hand, lack a single clear antonym. Rather, they involve groups of adjectives clustered at each pole of a scale:

---

[29] It's also used to mean adjectives that simply imply some evaluative judgment such as *good* or even *unknown* (Cinque 2010), particularly in discussions of the relative order of adjectives or of implicational universals about what concepts are lexicalized as adjectives (e.g. Hetzron 1978; Laenzlinger 2000; Scott 2002; Cinque 2010). This sense of the expression is not confined to syntactic and typological literature, though (Kiefer 1978; Geuder 2000; van Rooij 2008). A closely related use characterizes subsective adjectives of the *skillful* class (Beesley 1982; see 2.2.2). Neeleman et al. (2004) and Rett (2008a,b) use it to characterize degree constructions that license inferences to the positive form. All these uses are related to Bierwisch's sense, but none is identical to any of the others, and all things being equal a four-way (or more than four, if we include adverbs) polysemy is probably best avoided. See also sections 2.4.1, 4.4, 5.5.2, and 5.7.

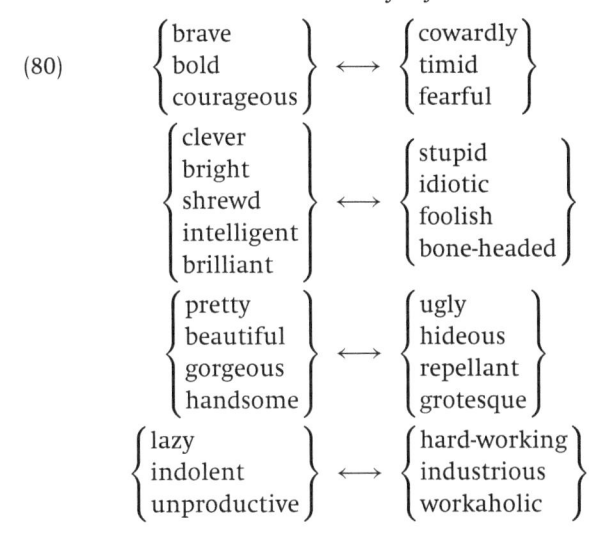

3.7 Scales and the lexical semantics of adjectives

(80) $\begin{Bmatrix} \text{brave} \\ \text{bold} \\ \text{courageous} \end{Bmatrix} \longleftrightarrow \begin{Bmatrix} \text{cowardly} \\ \text{timid} \\ \text{fearful} \end{Bmatrix}$

$\begin{Bmatrix} \text{clever} \\ \text{bright} \\ \text{shrewd} \\ \text{intelligent} \\ \text{brilliant} \end{Bmatrix} \longleftrightarrow \begin{Bmatrix} \text{stupid} \\ \text{idiotic} \\ \text{foolish} \\ \text{bone-headed} \end{Bmatrix}$

$\begin{Bmatrix} \text{pretty} \\ \text{beautiful} \\ \text{gorgeous} \\ \text{handsome} \end{Bmatrix} \longleftrightarrow \begin{Bmatrix} \text{ugly} \\ \text{hideous} \\ \text{repellant} \\ \text{grotesque} \end{Bmatrix}$

$\begin{Bmatrix} \text{lazy} \\ \text{indolent} \\ \text{unproductive} \end{Bmatrix} \longleftrightarrow \begin{Bmatrix} \text{hard-working} \\ \text{industrious} \\ \text{workaholic} \end{Bmatrix}$

One might reasonably doubt that these do in fact involve the same scale. *Shrewd* and *clever* seem to mean slightly different things, after all. But making such distinctions makes it no easier to identify a unique antonym for each of these.

Non-dimensional adjectives also have in common that they have minimal standards in the Kennedy and McNally (2005) sense. This wasn't how Bierwisch put it, due to his temporal precedence and lack of clairvoyance, but it seems a fair reformulation in more contemporary terms. (It may not be perfectly equivalent.) This means that in the comparative, they license inferences to the unmarked form:

(81)   NON-DIMENSIONAL

    a. Clyde is stupider than Floyd.
       entails: Floyd is stupid.

    b. Clyde is lazier than Floyd.
       entails: Floyd is lazy.

    c. Clyde is uglier than Floyd.
       entails: Floyd is ugly.

As we've seen, this is not how dimensional adjectives behave:

(82)   DIMENSIONAL

    a. Clyde is taller than Floyd.
       does not entail: Floyd is tall.

b. This is heavier than that.
does not entail: That is heavy.

Having minimal standards also ensures that unlike dimensional adjectives, non-dimensional adjectives are systematically compatible with *slightly*:

(83) DIMENSIONAL

a. #Clyde is slightly tall.
b. #This board is slightly long.

(84) NON-DIMENSIONAL

a. Clyde is slightly stupid.
b. Clyde is slightly lazy.

The conclusion Bierwisch draws from all this is initially startling: that non-dimensional adjectives are essentially not gradable, and therefore have no degree argument. This is immediately worrying because non-dimensional adjectives straightforwardly form comparatives, as (81) already showed, and occur with degree modifiers, as in (85):

(85) Clyde is $\left\{\begin{array}{l}\text{really}\\ \text{a little}\\ \text{shockingly}\end{array}\right\} \left\{\begin{array}{l}\text{stupid}\\ \text{lazy}\\ \text{ugly}\end{array}\right\}$.

To bridge the gap, Bierwisch proposes a type shift that exploits orderings already present in the domain. Another, related possibility is that this is evidence for combining an inherent-vagueness and degree-based approach. That would make it possible to deprive non-dimensional adjectives of their degree argument without sacrificing the idea that they could indirectly become gradable. For this to be convincing, of course, it would need to be fully spelled out, and it would need to be demonstrated that this is in fact necessary to account for the differences Bierwisch observed. The minimal-standard facts alone would not be sufficient to make this case, because an alternative and independently motivated account of those is already available, as section 3.7.2 showed.

3.7.4 Extreme adjectives

Certain adjectives present a puzzle to which all three of the preceding sections might be relevant. Just as many adjectives have polar antonyms, others have counterparts that, intuitively, correspond to not the opposite end of a scale but merely an extreme end of it. Among

3.7 Scales and the lexical semantics of adjectives

them are *gigantic, gorgeous,* and *fantastic* (Cruse 1986; Paradis 1997, 2001; Rett 2008b; Morzycki 2009a, 2012a).[30] One piece of evidence that these EXTREME ADJECTIVES (henceforth EAs) are a natural class is that they occur with EXTREME DEGREE MODIFIERS (henceforth EDMs):

(86) Your shoes are $\begin{Bmatrix} \text{downright} \\ \text{flat-out} \\ \text{positively} \\ \text{full-on} \end{Bmatrix} \begin{Bmatrix} \text{gigantic} \\ \text{gorgeous} \\ \text{fantastic} \\ \text{??big} \\ \text{??pretty} \\ \text{??OK} \end{Bmatrix}$!!!

Big, for example, is not extreme, so it resists extreme degree modification. This raises several questions: what makes an extreme adjective extreme? How is this reflected in their denotations? What makes EDMs sensitive to it? The remainder of this section will touch on some answers, distilling Morzycki (2009a, 2012a).

In addition to their ability to occur with EDMs, Cruse (1986) points out that many EAs are set apart by their ability to be 'intensified' via prosodic prominence:[31]

(87) a. That van is $\begin{Bmatrix} \text{huuuuuuuuge} \\ \text{?biiiiiiiiiiiiiiiig} \end{Bmatrix}$!

b. Kevin Spacey is $\begin{Bmatrix} \text{fantaaaastic} \\ \text{?goooooooood} \end{Bmatrix}$!

In (87a), it is possible to convey greater degrees of size by pronouncing the EA *huge* with an unnaturally long vowel, and likewise for *fantastic* in (87b). This is not possible with ordinary adjectives.[32]

Another property that distinguishes EAs, first noted by Bolinger (1967a), is a resistance to comparatives and other degree constructions.

(88) ??A is more excellent than B. (Paradis 1997)

---

[30] Cruse, following Sapir (1944), called these 'implicit superlatives'. I avoid the term because it's not clear whether there is actually a deep connection to superlatives.
[31] The particular intonational contour involved in this lengthening might be crucial.
[32] The observation that such prosodic intensification is possible, and that it is sensitive to some notion of extremeness, goes back at least to Bolinger (1972), who observed a similar contrast in nouns. This phenomenon does not seem to be simply focus, at least not in a straightforward sense – both the meaning achieved and the prosodic contour are different.

(89) a. ?Godzilla is more gigantic than Mothra.
b. ?Monkeys are less marvelous than ferrets.
c. ?Everything is more scrumptious than natto.

The strength of this resistance varies among speakers and among adjectives. Nevertheless, there is a class of EA comparatives whose ill-formedness is especially robust, in which a extreme and ordinary adjectives are compared:

(90) a. #Godzilla is more gigantic than Mothra is big.
b. #Godzilla is bigger than Mothra is gigantic.

Echoing Kennedy (1997, 2001)'s term 'cross-polar anomaly', I dubbed this (less euphonically) CONFLICTING-INTENSITY ANOMALY.

There is a further distinction within the class of EAs: some are LEXICAL EXTREME ADJECTIVES, others merely CONTEXTUAL EXTREME ADJECTIVES. *Calm*, for example, can be an EA, as its compatibility with the EDM *flat-out* in (91a) attests, but this effect melts away in the context in (91b):

(91) a. Clyde didn't panic during the earthquake – he was flat-out calm.
b. ??In his transcendental meditation class, Clyde was flat-out calm.

The crucial difference seems to be that calmness is unexpected during earthquakes, but expected during meditation. Even out-of-the-blue, expectations that the rest of the sentence gives rise to can bring about this contrast:

(92) Those $\begin{Bmatrix} \text{professors} \\ \text{??toddlers} \end{Bmatrix}$ are downright illiterate.

Lexical EAs don't manifest this sensitivity. Athletes participating in the Olympics are all outstanding at their sport. But even in this context, *outstanding* seems to be an EA:

(93) Clyde impressed everyone in the triathlon. He was downright outstanding.

The expectation that everyone is outstanding does nothing to diminish the acceptability of the EDM. Rather, what one seems to do in such examples is adjust the comparison class (or the standard of comparison)

3.7 Scales and the lexical semantics of adjectives

as needed. In this sense, of course, these adjectives are context-sensitive as well – but their extremeness seems to persist.

This distinction helps make sense of the comparative and degree modification data. Contextual EAs don't resist either:

(94)   a. Clyde is $\begin{Bmatrix} \text{richer} \\ \text{more offensive} \\ \text{more dangerous} \end{Bmatrix}$ than Floyd.

     b. Clyde is very $\begin{Bmatrix} \text{rich} \\ \text{offensive} \\ \text{dangerous} \end{Bmatrix}$.

This also correlates with another difference: lexical EAs often have 'neutral' counterparts to which they license entailments (*gigantic* entails *big*), but contextual EAs do not.

The account in Morzycki (2012a) is built on an analogy to quantification generally. When we assert that *Everyone left*, we don't actually commit to the entire population of the globe having (improbably) left. Rather, we confine the domain of the quantifier to a smaller set of individuals (Westerståhl 1985; von Fintel 1994 among many others). This seems to be how natural language quantification works in general. That being the case, we should expect the existential quantifier in POS to be similarly restricted. This, in turn, means that in any given context of use, we don't attend to an entire degree scale. Rather, we attend only to salient degrees, which constitute only a part of the scale, which I called the PERSPECTIVE SCALE. With other forms of quantification, there are morphemes that signal we should extend the domain to include individuals we might not otherwise have, such as *any* or *ever* (Kadmon and Landman 1993). EAs can be viewed as analogous. They lexically encode that we should consider a degree outside of the perspective scale. Concretely, one can represent the set of salient degrees (the perspective scale) with a contextually supplied variable, C, leading to denotations like those in (95) and (96):

(95)   ORDINARY ADJECTIVE

    a. $[\![\,big_C\,]\!] = \lambda x \lambda d \,.\, d \in C \wedge \textbf{big}(d)(x)$
    b. $[\![\,\text{POS } big_C\,]\!] = \lambda x \,.\, \exists d[d \in C \wedge \textbf{big}(d)(x) \wedge d > \textbf{standard}(\textbf{big})]$

(96)   EXTREME ADJECTIVE

    a. $[\![\,gigantic_C\,]\!] = \lambda x \lambda d \,.\, d > \textbf{max}(C) \wedge \textbf{big}(d)(x)$
    b. $[\![\,\text{POS } gigantic_C\,]\!] = \lambda x \,.\, \exists d \begin{bmatrix} d > \textbf{max}(C) \wedge \textbf{big}(d)(x) \wedge \\ d > \textbf{standard}(\textbf{big}) \end{bmatrix}$

The ordinary adjective *big* is interpreted exactly as we'd expect, with the additional twist that the degree quantifier now has a contextual domain restriction. The EA *gigantic*, on the other hand, lexically encodes that a degree must exceed (the maximum degree of) the set of salient degrees *C*, thereby capturing the sense that to be *gigantic* is not merely to be very big, but to be big to degrees that exceed contextual expectations. This mechanism makes possible an account of how lexical EAs behave in comparatives and equatives as well, and might provide a way of thinking about imprecision via perspective scale granularity (along lines suggested by Sauerland and Stateva 2007).

What EDMs do is manipulate perspective scales. The general idea is this: because EAs differ from ordinary adjectives in the degrees that satisfy them, EDMs can impose the requirement that makes them compatible only with EAs by simply having certain presuppositions about the scale structure of the adjective they combine with.

3.7.5 Gradable modal adjectives

There is another type of gradation that has long attracted the attention of semanticists: the kind associated with modals, including most prominently modal auxiliaries. In evaluating claims involving modals, it's frequently necessary to consider various non-optimal circumstances. It's true, for example, that the law is that if you murder Floyd, you must go to jail. But the law also says that you must not murder Floyd in the first place. A world in which Floyd murdered someone and went to jail accords better with the law than one in which he did so and got away, but neither accords with it fully. So when evaluating what the law says must happen, the worlds that we have to take into account can't be only the ones in which all laws are fully met. Some of them need to be worlds that fail to fully accord with the law. The classical analysis of Kratzer (1981) therefore has as a crucial ingredient an ordering among worlds (Lewis 1973) according to how fully they accord with a set of requirements (an ORDERING SOURCE) such as the law. This ordering relation on its own is already suggestive of a potential connection to degree orderings, but there is in fact more to it. Kratzer goes on to rigorously define notions like 'slight possibility' and 'human possibility' (expressed in ordinary language as *a good possibility*), and even 'comparative possibility' (the analogue of *it's more likely than*). So, as Portner (2009) points out, these questions of modality land us directly on the turf of degree semantics.

The question, then, is what to conclude from this. If these modal tools are sufficient to account for gradability in general, we should try to use those, since they also account for an independent set of facts. If not,

3.7 Scales and the lexical semantics of adjectives

the situation becomes more complicated. Of course, it is, in fact, more complicated. One difficulty a theory based on ordering worlds has is with sentences like (97):

(97)   a. It's twice as likely that Godzilla will eat Mothra.
          b. There is a 50% probability that Godzilla will eat Mothra.

The problem is making sense of apparently numerical notions like '50%' and 'twice' in a theory that has no way to represent them. Swanson (2006), Villalta (2007), Yalcin (2007), Portner (2009), Lassiter (2010, 2011a,b), Klecha (2012, 2013) have in various ways taken up the challenge of reconciling or combining the standard way of thinking about gradation and modality with the kind of data for which degree semantics is designed.

The most natural place to make this connection is, naturally enough, gradable modal adjectives like *likely*, *possible*, and *certain*. One satisfyingly direct move, explored from a linguistic perspective most extensively by Lassiter, is to treat these adjectives as involving direct measures of probability.[33] This would, of course, represent a major departure from the classical treatment of modals – and if that departure is warranted for these adjectives, it might suggest that the account of other modals should undergo a similar shift. So a great deal is at stake. Klecha (2012) seeks to chart a middle course that preserves aspects of the classical analysis of modals on a degree semantics for these adjectives. Part of the interest of this area is that it lies at the intersection of two well-studied areas of the grammar, with consequences for both and opportunities to ask questions that relate the two. One can, for example, examine the scale structure of gradable modals and their interaction with degree modifiers – and indeed, Lassiter (2011a) and Klecha (2012) both do.

3.7.6 On scales and categories

Chapter 2 ended on a slightly pessimistic note about whether one could find straightforward crosslinguistic semantic correlates of being an adjective. This section returns to that question in a more optimistic spirit.

It's certainly true that not all adjectives are gradable and not all gradable categories are adjectives. As we've seen, vagueness is

---

[33] The idea of introducing probability measures into the grammar is older, dating to at least Kamp (1975), and in some form as far as Black (1937). Thanks to Daniel Lassiter (p.c.) for pointing this out.

ubiquitous, and one of the principal ways of thinking about it – the inherent vagueness approach – makes no deep compositional distinction between adjectives and other predicative categories. Yet this draws attention to an important contrasting property of the degree-based approach. Foundational to it is the idea that gradable adjectives have a different type from other predicates. That type might be $\langle d, et \rangle$ or $\langle e, dt \rangle$ or $\langle e, d \rangle$, but one way or another, a degree is directly involved. Might this type difference provide a way of matching a syntactic category with a type? Types are, after all, the building blocks of a kind of parallel syntax running inside the semantics, with its own conditions on well-formedness and legal modes of combination.

I suspect the answer is no, but I wouldn't bet on it. Kennedy and Levin (2008) and Piñón (2008), for example, invoke degrees in the semantics of verbs, and Morzycki (2005b, 2009b) does so for nouns. On the other hand, Rett (2011b) makes the case against verbal degree arguments, and Morzycki (2012b) backpedals about just how big a role degrees play in nouns too. Perhaps one way of splitting the difference is to suppose that outside of adjectives, degrees are involved but never as arguments. Alternatively, it may be that they are involved, but only in certain lexically exceptional cases – that is, that only the most adjective-like nouns and verbs have degree arguments.[34]

This isn't a question of degree arguments alone, however. There do seem to be generalizations about the scalar properties of syntactic categories that draw distinctions independently of any particular theory of gradability. It is an old observation that adjectives frequently involve a single dimension or 'quality', whereas nouns involve many (see Hamann 1991 and references therein). To be *blue*, for example, one must have a single, irreducible quality: blueness. To be a chair, one must have many qualities, and we could enumerate at least some of them. Because we couldn't make a full list of necessary and sufficient conditions, though, it's probably better to view noun meanings in terms of prototypes: a chair must be sufficiently like a prototypical chair (Rosch 1973; Osherson and Smith 1981, 1997; Kamp and Partee 1995). That would make nouns even more unlike adjectives.

A skeptic might object that comparing chairs and blue things is a way of rigging the game by picking extreme examples – of course chairs are more complicated than blue things, but that's an insight into home furnishings, not language. But then consider the canonical example of vagueness we began with, which involved a noun: *heap*. There are at

---

[34] We will return to the issue of non-adjectival gradability in section 6.3.

3.8 Questions for further reflection and discussion 147

least two ways of failing to be a heap, or of becoming only a borderline case of a heap: by having too few grains, as in the sorites paradox, or by being too flat. An agglomeration of many grains of sand that is perfectly spread out, one grain deep, is definitely not a heap. So there are two qualities or dimensions here, independently discernible. In contrast, there is only one way of failing to be tall: by being too short. Again, one might object that in both cases, our choice of simple adjectives rigged the game. There are more complicated adjectives. Bierwisch's non-dimensional adjectives may be an example. Indeed, Sassoon (2013a,b) explicitly argues that many adjectives involve multiple dimensions (but nevertheless handle those dimensions differently from nouns).

So where does this leave us? Perhaps we can't find a single, simple, rigorous, and crosslinguistic semantic definition of adjectives. But there is certainly room for identifying semantic correlates of syntactic category, particularly with respect to the connection between adjectives and scales. At a minimum, we can say with some confidence that there are certain semantic characteristics that, if not perfectly correlated with adjectivehood, are at least unmistakably adjectivey.

3.8 QUESTIONS FOR FURTHER REFLECTION AND DISCUSSION

- How much should linguistics care about vagueness as such rather than gradability? Is there a difference between vagueness and imprecision?
- In light of section 3.6: Degree or not degree? That is the question.
- Even more than the previous chapter, work in this chapter tended to focus on data from a single language. Indeed, it was generally English. Is that a problem? The obvious answer is 'yes', but for this answer to be convincing one would have to provide a careful empirical characterization of some relevant differences as well as a compelling argument that they offer new theoretical insights. Attempting to do this is of course an important and valuable project. On the other hand, if the answer to the question is 'no' – even for some remote corner of the area covered in this chapter – that too requires explanation. Why would certain aspects of the grammar be less prone to crosslinguistic variation?
- What other kinds of degree modifiers are there? How is their distribution constrained? What do they reveal about the lexical semantics adjectives they combine with (including their scale structure, how they represent antonymy, and so on)?

3.9 SUGGESTIONS FOR FURTHER READING

Good entry points into the literature cited in this chapter include the following:

- For more on vagueness generally from a perspective that is especially relevant to linguistic concerns, see Graff (2000) and the rejoinder in Stanley (2003). For a more extensive book-length philosophical discussion, see Williamson (1994).
- The classic descriptive work on degree modification and related issues is Bolinger (1972), which provides a wealth of puzzles, analytical intuitions, and observations.
- To further explore imprecision, Lasersohn (1999) is the most natural next step.
- For a full-fledged articulation of an inherent-vagueness theory, see Klein (1980) and Klein (1982) (the latter might be more accessible). Its degree-based counterpart is probably von Stechow (1984). Kennedy (1997) is a beautifully clear articulation of the choices involved between the two theories, and of the merits of degree-based approaches. Kamp (1975) and Fine (1975) are both important, of course, but moving directly to them may prove difficult.
- Kennedy and McNally (2005) is the natural next step for anyone interested in the scalar lexical semantics of adjectives and in scale structure generally.

4 Comparatives and their kin

4.1 INTRODUCTION

Florence Nightingale suffered from two afflictions:

- She had one leg shorter than the other.
- She also had one leg longer than the other.

This is according to the comedian Graeme Garden, who was lying.[1] (Her legs were fine, both of them.) In doing so, he was playing on some relatively subtle intuitions about the semantics of the comparative. The joke would still have worked, more or less, if he had said this:

(1)   She also had one leg not as long as the other.

But this would be worse, or in any case less funny than just weird:

(2)   She also had one leg not as short as the other.

What the joke depends on – to kill it by explanation – is that the two afflictions entail each other, on either the original formulation or (1). The problem with (2) is that it introduces an unwelcome additional entailment: that her legs were short. Why the difference in entailments?

This chapter will examine the semantics of comparatives and their grammatical relatives, such as the equative, which positively bristle with such subtle and often vexing puzzles. These puzzles provide insight into a surprisingly wide array of issues: the nature of comparison, of course, but also the ontology of degrees, scope-taking mechanisms, ellipsis, negative polarity items, modality, focus, type-shifting, contextual domain restrictions, imprecision, and semantic

---

[1] This paraphrases remarks made on the BBC Radio 4 show *The Unbelievable Truth* (series 8, episode 4, first broadcast in 2012). Lying was appropriate in the discourse context.

crosslinguistic variation. This will also give us an opportunity to address the syntax of the extended AP in earnest for the first time.

Section 4.2 confronts the mapping between syntax and semantics in the adjectival extended projection, with special attention to the comparative. Section 4.3 provides a tour of other degree constructions, including differential comparatives, equatives, superlatives, and others. Section 4.4 is the one most directly relevant to the puzzle we began the chapter with: the question of why the entailments of apparently very similar degree constructions differ subtly. Finally, section 4.5 concludes with a discussion of the crosslinguistic picture. Throughout this chapter, I will assume a degree-based framework. This is chiefly because most of the work in this area does so – but that too is for a reason.

4.2 THE SYNTAX AND SEMANTICS OF THE EXTENDED AP

4.2.1 Getting terminology out of the way

Before proceeding, it will help to introduce or reintroduce some terminology:[2]

- I'll call the family of constructions to which the comparative belongs – including *as* constructions, superlatives (*-est*), *too* constructions – DEGREE CONSTRUCTIONS. *As*-phrases are EQUATIVES. Sometimes one encounters SUFFICIENCY CONSTRUCTION for *enough* and EXCESSIVE CONSTRUCTION for *too*.
- A less Anglo-centric term for a *than*-clause is COMPARATIVE CLAUSE. What it contributes is a STANDARD OF COMPARISON. A language-neutral term for expressions such as *than* that mark standards of comparison is STANDARD MARKER.
- The morphologically unmarked base form of an adjective is the POSITIVE FORM.
- *More*, *less*, *-er*, *very*, *slightly*, and the like are DEGREE MORPHEMES or DEGREE WORDS, members of the syntactic category Deg.

4.2.2 The unpronounced in comparative clauses

One additional prefatory point: in English, as in many languages, comparative clauses tend not to be fully pronounced. This won't affect the subsequent discussion, but when large chunks of the sentences under discussion are missing, something should be said.

---

[2] More information on terminological issues can, of course, be found in the glossary.

4.2 The syntax and semantics of the extended AP

This state of affairs can come about in several ways. First, it can involve ordinary verb phrase ellipsis:

(3)   Floyd will seem taller than Clyde will ~~seem tall~~.

Second, it can involve COMPARATIVE DELETION (Bresnan 1973), in which an adjective phrase is elided:

(4)   Floyd will seem taller than Clyde will seem ~~tall~~.

These processes differ in that VP ellipsis can only target full VPs as in (5a), rather than merely APs as in (5b):

(5)   a. Floyd will seem tall, and Clyde will ~~seem tall~~ too.
       b. *Floyd will seem tall, and Clyde will seem ~~tall~~ too.

Consequently, (4), where *seem* is left behind, can't be attributed to VP ellipsis. Another difference between the two processes is that VP ellipsis is optional, so (5a) could be pronounced fully as well. By contrast, comparative deletion is generally obligatory, so (4) would be ungrammatical or at least strange if fully pronounced. A third process distinct from both is the more radical COMPARATIVE ELLIPSIS (Bresnan 1975; Lechner 1999):

(6)   Floyd will seem taller tomorrow than ~~he seemed tall~~ today.

Yet a fourth deletion operation is, from a contemporary perspective, less obviously deletion at all. Nevertheless, the term COMPARATIVE SUB-DELETION has stuck:

(7)   a. The table is wider than it is ~~that~~ long.
       b. Floyd knows fewer philosophers than Clyde knows ~~that many~~ linguists.

I have included overt expressions in (7) to suggest why one might regard this as deletion, but the choice of expression is semi-arbitrary. Sentences like (7) are sometimes called SUBCOMPARATIVES.

At first blush (or indeed afterward), it's not obvious where PHRASAL COMPARATIVES, in which the *than*-phrase is smaller than a clause, fit in, and whether they involve ellipsis (Hankamer 1973; Napoli 1983; Heim 1985; Lechner 1999, 2001; Xiang 2005; Merchant 2009, forthcoming; Bhatt and Takahashi 2007, 2011; and Matsui and Kubota 2012). One of their more notable characteristics, though, is an ambiguity they give rise to that is not present in clausal comparatives:

(8) Greta deloused her ferret more often than Clyde.
  a. Greta deloused her ferret more often than Clyde deloused her ferret.
  b. Greta deloused her ferret more often than she deloused Clyde.

Rooth (1992) notes that this ambiguity can actually be eliminated via focus (roughly, prosodic prominence):

(9) a. [FOCUS **Greta**] deloused her ferret more often than Clyde.
  b. Greta deloused [FOCUS **her ferret**] more often than Clyde.

In (9a), it must be the ferret that has been deloused; in (9b), it must be Clyde. Interestingly, Japanese has an overt morpheme, *hoo*, that can achieve this disambiguation (Matsui and Kubota 2012):

(10) a. Watashi-no-<u>hoo</u>-ga John-yori neko-o aishiteiru
    I-GEN-hoo-NOM John-than cats-ACC love.NONPAST
    'I love cats more than John loves cats.'
    not: '...than I love John'

  b. Watashi-wa John-yori neko-no-<u>hoo</u>-o aishiteiru
    I-TOPIC John-than cats-GEN-hoo-ACC love.NONPAST
    'I love cats more than I love John.'
    not: '...than John does'

4.2.3 First steps

Given the (degree-based) semantics for the positive form and for measure phrases in Chapter 3, a relatively straightforward and historically traditional view of the AP would suffice. On such a view, both measure phrases and degree words occupy the specifier position of AP. The crucial denotations are repeated in (11) and the corresponding trees are in (12) (see section 3.5.2 for the full computations):

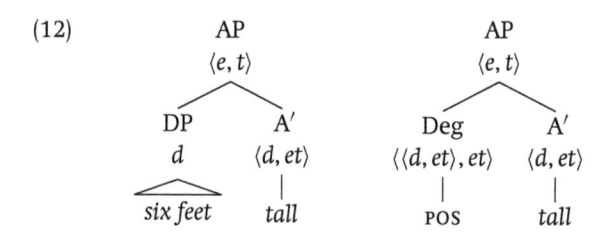

(11) a. $[\![tall]\!] = \lambda d \lambda x . \textbf{tall}(d)(x)$
  b. $[\![six\ feet]\!] = \textbf{6-feet}$
  c. $[\![\text{POS}]\!] = \lambda G_{\langle d, et \rangle} \lambda x . \exists d\ [d > \textbf{standard}(G) \wedge G(d)(x)]$

(12)
```
        AP                        AP
       ⟨e,t⟩                     ⟨e,t⟩
       /   \                     /   \
     DP    A'                  Deg    A'
      d   ⟨d,et⟩            ⟨⟨d,et⟩,et⟩  ⟨d,et⟩
      |     |                   |         |
  six feet tall                POS       tall
```

4.2 The syntax and semantics of the extended AP

In comparatives, the semantics clicks right into place as well:

(13) $[\![\text{more}]\!] = \lambda G_{\langle d, et \rangle} \lambda x \lambda y \,.\, \exists d \, [G(d)(y) \wedge \neg G(d)(x)]$

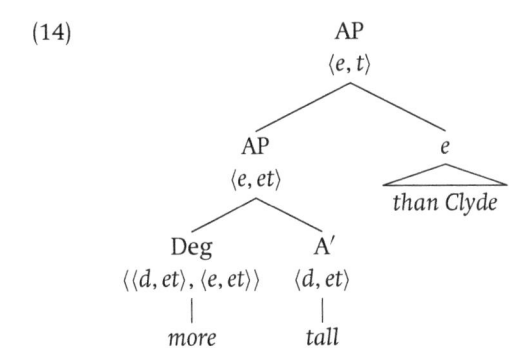

(14)
```
                        AP
                       ⟨e, t⟩
                      /      \
                    AP         e
                  ⟨e, et⟩     /  \
                 /      \    than Clyde
               Deg       A'
      ⟨⟨d, et⟩, ⟨e, et⟩⟩  ⟨d, et⟩
               |           |
             more         tall
```

Nevertheless, some significant refinements will need to be made here.

The principal flaw in this comparative denotation is the assumptions it makes about the *than*-phrase, which it treats as individual-denoting. As we'll see in section 4.5.3, this may be the right approach in some languages and perhaps for cases like (14) in English, but it doesn't generalize to cases like those in (15):

(15) a. Floyd is taller than six feet.
 b. Floyd is taller than Clyde is ~~tall~~.

In (15a), the *than*-phrase hosts a (presumably) degree-denoting expression. In (15b), it hosts a full clause, which can't plausibly denote an individual.

To correct the problem, it's best to begin with the simpler case, (15a). The denotation we should aim for is in (16) (I'll continue to represent *-er* as underlyingly *more*):

(16) $[\![\text{[more tall] than six feet}]\!] = \lambda x \,.\, \exists d \, [\textbf{tall}(d)(x) \wedge d > \textbf{6-feet}]$

An individual x will satisfy this iff x is tall to a degree greater than six feet. Working backwards, if we assume (17a), *more* should have the denotation in (17c):[3]

---
[3] One often finds the ordering relation > subscripted with something, such as the adjective denotation G, indicating whether degrees are being compared on, e.g., the scale of height or of weight. I won't do this, chiefly for convenience. Instead I'll assume that the > relation is defined only for degrees on the same scale, so requiring that d is a degree of tallness ensures that d' must be a tallness degree as well.

(17) a. ⟦ *than six feet* ⟧ = **6-feet**
      b. ⟦ *more tall* ⟧ = $\lambda d' \lambda x . \exists d\, [\textbf{tall}(d)(x) \wedge d > d']$
      c. ⟦ *more* ⟧ = $\lambda G_{\langle d, et \rangle} \lambda d' \lambda x . \exists d\, [G(d)(x) \wedge d > d']$

This puts us in a better position to cope with the clausal case. To combine with (17c), the comparative clause *than Clyde is ~~tall~~* would have to denote a degree – more precisely, the degree of tallness one would have to exceed in order to be *taller than Clyde is ~~tall~~*. That degree is Clyde's height, the maximal degree to which Clyde is tall. (Not just any degree will do: Clyde is no doubt also tall to the degree **1-foot**, but it wouldn't be sufficient to exceed that.) The maximality operator **max** introduced in Chapter 3 is what we need.

Previously, **max** was defined for sets of degrees, but it will be useful to use it for properties of degrees, too. Because properties and sets are two sides of the same coin, the definition is essentially the same (I will use D for properties of degrees):[4]

(18) $\textbf{max}(D) \stackrel{\text{def}}{=} \iota d [\forall d'\, [D(d') \rightarrow d' \leq d]]$

This yields the largest degree that satisfies D. This makes it possible to state the intended denotation for the clause as in (19):

(19)   ⟦ *than Clyde is ~~tall~~* ⟧ = $\textbf{max}(\lambda d\, . \textbf{tall}(d)(\textbf{Clyde}))$

That said, it's common to confine oneself to the set-based definition of **max** and to write such a denotation equivalently as (20):

(20)   ⟦ *than Clyde is ~~tall~~* ⟧ = $\textbf{max}\{d : \textbf{tall}(d)(\textbf{Clyde})\}$

Throughout this chapter, one may safely replace any instance of $\textbf{max}(\lambda d \ldots)$ with $\textbf{max}\{d : \ldots\}$. Either way, this is a definite description of a degree. Comparing (19) and (20) to the definition of **max** in 18 makes that clear: it is *the* maximal height of Clyde. As an empirical matter, definite descriptions also include a maximality element. This is reflected in the fact that *the height of Clyde* refers to his maximal height, but also in more ordinary uses. In a context with three equally salient ferrets, *the ferrets* picks out all three, and can't be interpreted to mean any pair of them. Likewise, *the water* picks out the largest (i.e. maximal)

---

[4] The definite description operator ι yields the only element that could replace d and make the formula in the scope of ι true.

4.2 The syntax and semantics of the extended AP

portion of water in the context, and you haven't mopped up the water unless you've mopped up all of it.[5]

This isn't the only path we could have taken, but it is a well-trodden one (Russell 1905; von Stechow 1984; Rullmann 1995). An alternative is to have the comparative clause denote a property of **all** the degrees to which Clyde is tall, with further manipulation to happen in the denotation of *more*. This further manipulation might itself involve a maximality operator. (See Heim 1985; Beck 2011 for such an analysis.)

Arriving at the denotation in (20) isn't trivial. The standard course is to assume, following Chomsky (1977), that the comparative clause is analogous to a relative clause in which *wh*-movement of a null operator, ∅, has taken place:

(21) a. the ferret [$_{CP}$ ∅ λx_1 Clyde deloused x_1]
     b. than [$_{CP}$ ∅ λd_1 Clyde is ~~d_1 tall~~]

In English relatives, the null operator has a pronounced counterpart, *which*. English comparatives seem to lack one, although some speakers accept (22) (or at least fail to reject these very strongly):[6]

(22) a. That table is longer than how long that other table used to be.
     b. That table is much larger than what it should be.

Many other languages are not so impoverished and systematically permit an overt *wh*-expression in this position. Further evidence for movement can be adduced from island effects (*taller than Greta doubts the claim that Clyde is ~~d tall~~).[7] The source of the movement is the measure phrase position – the null operator is essentially a *wh*-measure phrase – so the degree trace it leaves behind can be interpreted as a measure phrase:

(23) a. $[\![d_1\ tall]\!] = \lambda x . \text{tall}(d_1)(x)$
     b. $[\![Clyde\ d_1\ tall]\!] = \text{tall}(d_1)(\textbf{Clyde})$

---

[5] Sets of degrees are more like mass than count individuals (Schwarzschild and Wilkinson 2002; Schwarzschild 2005), so the analogy to the latter is closer.
[6] Thanks to Alan Bale for pointing this out.
[7] Islands are syntactic structures from which an expression can't be moved without creating ungrammaticality, such as the complex DP in *Who λx_1 do you believe [the claim that Clyde killed x_1]?

The ∅ operator is not interpreted (following the Heim and Kratzer 1998 approach to relative clauses), so the result for the CP is (24):

(24)   ⟦ ∅ λd₁ Clyde is d̶₁̶ ̶t̶a̶l̶l̶ ⟧ = λd₁ . **tall**(d₁)(**Clyde**)

To take us from this to the intended comparative clause denotation in 19, *than* would need to be as in (25a), leading to (25b), as (26) illustrates:

(25)   a. ⟦ *than* ⟧ = λD₍d, t₎ . **max**(D)
       b. ⟦ *than* ⟧ (⟦ ∅ λd₁ Clyde is d̶₁̶ ̶t̶a̶l̶l̶ ⟧)
          = **max**(λd₁ . **tall**(d₁)(**Clyde**))

(26)

```
                    d
                   / \
              ⟨dt,t⟩  ⟨d,t⟩
                |    / \
              than  ∅  ⟨d,t⟩
                    ↑  / \
                   λd₁   t
                    \   / \
                     Clyde is d̶₁̶ ̶t̶a̶l̶l̶
```

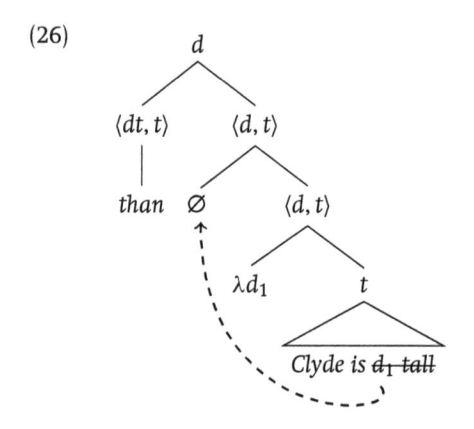

This is, of course, equivalent to the denotation we were looking for: the maximal degree to which Clyde is tall.

The next step is to combine this with the comparative itself:

(27)   a. ⟦ *more* ⟧ = λG₍d, et₎ λd'λx . ∃d [G(d)(x) ∧ d > d']
       b. ⟦ *more tall* ⟧ = λd'λx . ∃d [**tall**(d)(x) ∧ d > d']
       c. ⟦ *more tall* ⟧ (⟦ ∅ λd₁ Clyde is d̶₁̶ ̶t̶a̶l̶l̶ ⟧)
          = λx . ∃d [**tall**(d)(x) ∧ d > **max**(λd₁ . **tall**(d₁)(**Clyde**))]

So an individual *x* is taller than Clyde iff there's a degree to which *x* is tall that exceeds the maximal degree to which Clyde is tall.

This denotation works both for full comparative clauses and for e.g. *than six feet*, but it would fail for our original example, the humble phrasal comparative (e.g. *than Floyd*). Both *than* and *more* are now incompatible with this use. Assuming both forms have two homophonous variants might seem stipulative. One could avoid this by deriving the phrasal comparative syntactically from the clausal one. As it turns

4.2 The syntax and semantics of the extended AP

out, though, some languages distinguish their phrasal and clausal comparatives with different standard markers (Merchant 2009, forthcoming), precisely as one might expect if the English case involves an ambiguity. Moreover, some languages have only phrasal comparatives or only clausal ones (Bhatt and Takahashi 2007, 2011). Both of these facts suggest that one shouldn't work too hard at integrating them. (This is briefly discussed further in section 4.5.3.)

4.2.4 The big DegP view

There are two competing ideas about the syntax of the extended adjectival projection. They both involve recognizing a phrasal projection called DegP, but disagree about where it is and what it is. I'll call one the 'big DegP view' and the other the 'small DegP view'. Each view correlates with a certain view of the semantics, although it's possible to disentangle the two at least to some extent.

The small DegP view is the older one and is sometimes described as the 'classic' view. It's probably more popular among semanticists at the moment. The syntax associated with the big DegP view is more recent, but not by much. It was originally proposed more than a quarter of a century ago by Abney (1987), with refinements and variations in Larson (1988), Corver (1990, 1993), Grimshaw (1991), and Kennedy (1997) (and, in a significantly different form, Corver 1997 and Lechner 1999). The basic insight behind the structure is that degree morphemes are functional heads, just as determiners are in DP. At one point, it had been standard to construe determiners as specifiers of NP. Abney (among others) convinced most syntacticians of a certain stripe that determiners are better treated as heads in themselves instead, ones which take an NP as a complement:

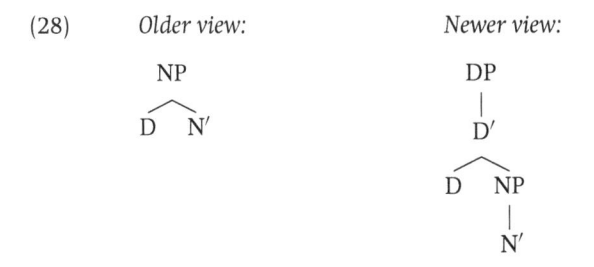

(28)   Older view: Newer view:

          NP   DP
          /\ |
        D N'   D'
                             /\
                          D NP
                              |
                              N'

Much of the appeal of X' Theory is in the crosscategorial parallels it reveals, so the change to DP should prompt reexamination of other categories. Structural parallelism would seem to dictate that degree words should also be heads:

(29)　　Older view:　　　　　　Newer view:

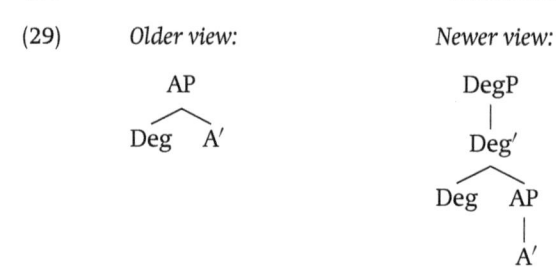

```
        AP                    DegP
       /  \                    |
     Deg   A'                 Deg'
                              /  \
                            Deg   AP
                                   |
                                   A'
```

This accords with the Grimshaw (1991) vision that every lexical category (NP, AP, VP) projects layers of functional structure on top of it. It would be rather odd if AP were alone in failing to do so.

This structure opens up two positions where previously there was one. There is a head position, which can be occupied as before by degree morphemes. But there is also a specifier of DegP position, where we would expect a phrasal category. This is the natural home of measure phrases.

This additional phrase-structural flexibility makes possible certain analytical options that on the previous structure were unavailable or less appealing. Chief among them is what is proposed in Kennedy (1997): taking adjectives to denote measure functions, type $\langle e, d \rangle$. To make this work, it's necessary to suppose there is some maximality built in. If each individual is mapped to only one degree, it has to be the maximal one. For Kennedy, the preferred implementation of this is to suppose degrees are INTERVALS, uninterrupted stretches of a scale. The height any individual is mapped to is an interval extending from the bottom of the scale to their maximal height. The elegance of such an approach is striking:

(30)　　a.　$[\![\, tall \,]\!] = \lambda x \,.\, \textbf{tallness}(x)$
　　　　b.　$[\![\, \text{POS} \,]\!] = \lambda G_{\langle e, d \rangle} \lambda x \,.\, G(x) > \textbf{standard}(G)$
　　　　c.　$[\![\, \text{POS } tall \,]\!] = \lambda x \,.\, \textbf{tallness}(x) > \textbf{standard}(\textbf{tallness})$

The POS morpheme now simply determines the degree to which x is mapped on the scale associated with G and requires that this degree exceed the standard. The structure is in (31) (I omit irrelevant layers):

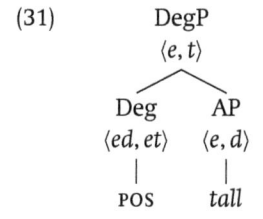

(31)
```
              DegP
             ⟨e, t⟩
             /    \
           Deg     AP
         ⟨ed, et⟩ ⟨e, d⟩
            |       |
           POS     tall
```

4.2 The syntax and semantics of the extended AP

Comparatives are similarly elegant:[8]

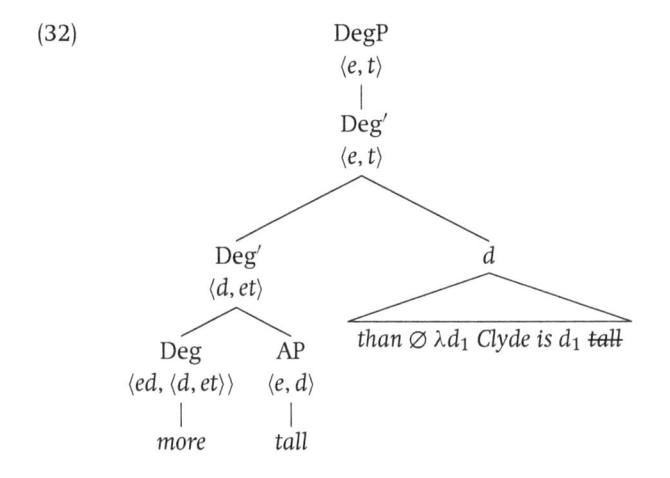

(32)
```
                        DegP
                        ⟨e,t⟩
                         |
                        Deg'
                        ⟨e,t⟩
                       /     \
                    Deg'       d
                   ⟨d,et⟩     / \
                  /    \    than ∅ λd₁ Clyde is d₁ t̶a̶l̶l̶
                Deg     AP
             ⟨ed,⟨d,et⟩⟩ ⟨e,d⟩
                 |        |
                more     tall
```

(33) a. $[\![more]\!] = \lambda G_{\langle e,d \rangle} \lambda d \lambda x . G(x) > d$

b. $[\![more]\!]([\![tall]\!])([\![than\ \emptyset\ \lambda d_1\ Clyde\ is\ d_1\ \text{t̶a̶l̶l̶}]\!])$
   $= \lambda x . \textbf{tallness}(x) > \textbf{max}(\lambda d_1 . \textbf{tallness}(\text{Clyde}) = d_1)$
   $= \lambda x . \textbf{tallness}(x) > \textbf{tallness}(\text{Clyde})$

This will be true iff the tallness of x exceeds the tallness of Clyde.[9] Introducing measure phrases into this picture requires slightly more work, so I will set them aside.

Perhaps the most important thing to notice about this view is that it commits itself to the idea that there are no scope-bearing elements (like quantifiers or a maximality operator) contributed by degree morphemes, and, somewhat less deeply, that the structure of the extended AP is relatively rigid, without any need for elements of it to move around at Logical Form. This is probably the most substantial difference between this approach and its principal competitor.

4.2.5 The small DegP view

The alternative view takes the extended AP to have a different shape entirely (Chomsky 1965; Bresnan 1973; Heim 2000; Bhatt and Pancheva

---

[8] Indeed, the maximality operator in the comparative clause could instead be an ordinary ι (definite description) operator.

[9] The final step is possible because the maximal degree that is identical to **tallness(Clyde)** is, of course, **tallness(Clyde)** itself.

2004 among others). It's based in part on the observation that degree words seem to idiosyncratically select the head of their standard of comparison. For example, *more* requires the standard marker *than* rather than, say, *as*; *as*, on the other hand, requires another *as*; *so* requires *that*; *too* and *enough* license infinitives. On the big DegP view, the comparative clause is an adjunct. Heads don't normally impose selectional restrictions on their adjuncts, so this is suspicious. Another potential worry is that, because comparative clauses are adjuncts, we might expect to be able to stack them. But this isn't normally possible.[10] To be sure, it follows from the semantics provided, which takes the comparative clause as an argument of which there is only one. Nevertheless, there does seem to be an imperfect fit between the adjoined modifier-like syntax and the argument-like semantics. Finally, and most seriously, a fundamental prediction that the big DegP analysis is designed to capture appears not to be borne out, as we will see in section 4.2.6: that there are never any scope interactions involving a scope-bearing element contributed by the degree morpheme.[11]

To begin we will need to rearrange the puzzle pieces slightly. If a head imposes selectional restrictions on something, it's reasonable to suppose that it's actually its complement. That suggests that the complement of a degree morpheme is a standard phrase, and that (34) is a constituent:

(34)   more than $\varnothing$ λd_1 Clyde is ~~d_1 tall~~

Of course, this doesn't surface overtly in *Floyd is taller than Clyde is*. Before we can get to that issue, we need to identify what this constituent is and where to put it. The what question has a simple answer: it's a projection of a Deg, so it's a DegP. The where question is simple too: the whole thing goes in the specifier of AP. The overall picture, with potential types, would be as in (35):

---

[10] It doesn't seem to be impossible in principle. Bhatt and Pancheva (2004) point to examples like these:

(i) a. John is much taller than Mary than Bill is.
     b. John has much more CDs than Mary than Bill does.

The semantics of these is mysterious.

[11] This doesn't preclude the possibility that the comparative clause rather than the degree morpheme might be scope-bearing, of course (von Stechow 1984; Alrenga et al. 2012).

4.2 The syntax and semantics of the extended AP

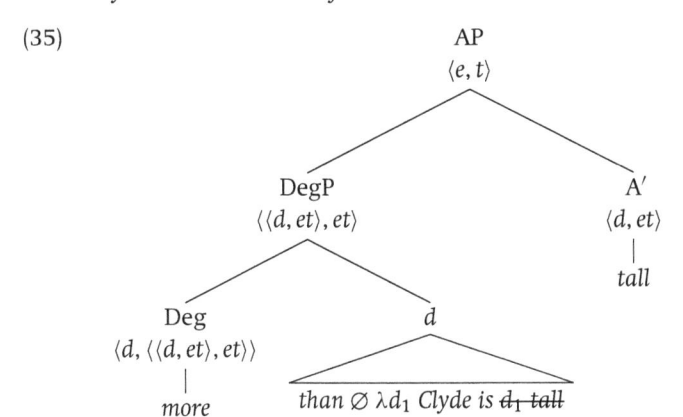

(35)

```
                    AP
                   ⟨e, t⟩
                  /      \
               DegP        A'
           ⟨⟨d, et⟩, et⟩   ⟨d, et⟩
             /    \          |
           Deg     d        tall
       ⟨d, ⟨⟨d, et⟩, et⟩⟩
           |       \
         more    than ∅ λd₁ Clyde is d₁ tall
```

This could all be achieved by simply manipulating the order of arguments in the denotations considered in section 4.2.3. To achieve the surface order, the comparative clause would have to extrapose to the right (see Bhatt and Pancheva 2004 for a contemporary implementation).

There's an analytical opportunity being lost here, though. The type assigned to the DegP – ⟨⟨d, et⟩, et⟩ – is complex. This is slightly awkward. After all, the location the DegP occupies is precisely the same one that measure phrases can occupy, and they, on this view, are simply of type d. So is there a way to simplify this? It turns out that there is, with a more abstract syntax. Since von Stechow (1984), it has been standard to take this additional step. The crucial analogy is to the behavior of generalized quantifiers. The standard assumption there is that a generalized quantifier has a denotation of type ⟨et, t⟩, and when it finds itself in a position where only type e would fit compositionally, it moves (by Quantifier Raising), leaving behind a type e trace that it can then bind:

(36) a. [every ferret] λx_1 Floyd deloused x_1
      b. [[*every ferret*]] = λ$P_{⟨e, t⟩}$. ∀x[**ferret**(x) → P(x)]
      c. [[*every ferret*]] ([[λx_1 Floyd deloused x_1]])
         = ∀x[**ferret**(x) → [[λx_1 Floyd deloused x_1]] (x)]
         = ∀x[**ferret**(x) → **deloused**(x)(**Floyd**)]

Precisely the same sort of analytical strategy is available in the degree domain:

(37)

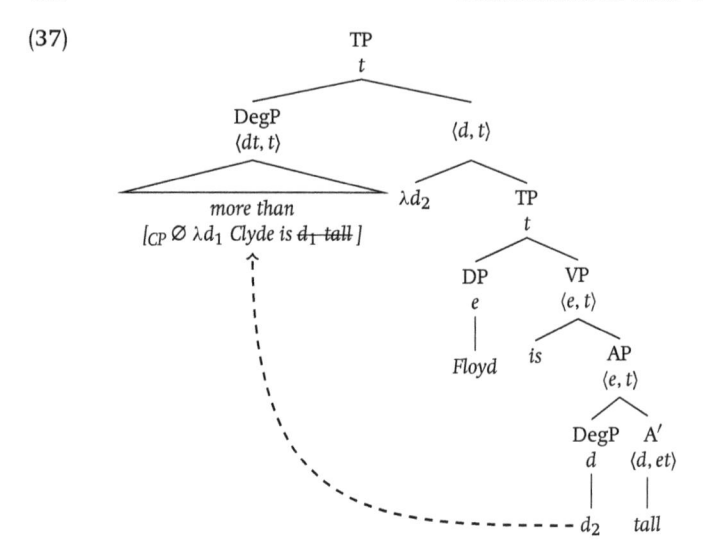

```
                    TP
                    t
         ┌──────────┴──────────┐
       DegP                   ⟨d,t⟩
       ⟨dt,t⟩                  λd₂    TP
   ┌─────┴─────┐                      t
 more than   λd₂              ┌───────┴───────┐
[CP ∅ λd₁ Clyde is d₁ tall]   DP              VP
                              e             ⟨e,t⟩
                              │         ┌─────┴─────┐
                            Floyd      is          AP
                                                  ⟨e,t⟩
                                              ┌────┴────┐
                                            DegP        A'
                                              d       ⟨d,et⟩
                                              │         │
                                              d₂       tall
```

More can now denote a relation between the degree expressed by the comparative clause and a property of degrees created by movement of the DegP it heads. Two ways of doing this are in (38):

(38)   a. $[\![more]\!] = \lambda d' \lambda D_{\langle d,t\rangle} . \exists d[D(d) \wedge d > d']$
       b. $[\![more]\!] = \lambda d' \lambda D_{\langle d,t\rangle} . \mathbf{max}(D) > d'$

The existentially quantified approach in (38a) is older, and the maximality one in (38b) is arguably more elegant and otherwise desirable (Heim 2000; Beck 2011). Assuming (38b), this would combine with the comparative clause – which itself has a maximality operator – to yield (39):

(39)   a. $[\![than]\!]$ ($[\![\varnothing\ \lambda d_1\ Clyde\ is\ d_1\ tall]\!]$)
           = $\mathbf{max}(\lambda d_1 . \mathbf{tall}(d_1)(\mathbf{Clyde}))$
       b. $[\![more\ than\ \varnothing\ \lambda d_1\ Clyde\ is\ d_1\ tall]\!]$
           = $\lambda D_{\langle d,t\rangle} . \mathbf{max}(D) > \mathbf{max}(\lambda d_1 . \mathbf{tall}(d_1)(\mathbf{Clyde}))$
       c. $[\![\lambda d_2\ Floyd\ is\ d_2\ tall]\!] = \lambda d_2 . \mathbf{tall}(d_2)(\mathbf{Floyd})$
       d. $[\![more\ than\ \varnothing\ \lambda d_1\ Clyde\ is\ d_1\ tall]\!]$ ($[\![\lambda d_2\ Floyd\ is\ d_2\ tall]\!]$)
           = $\mathbf{max}([\![\lambda d_2\ Floyd\ is\ d_2\ tall]\!]) > \mathbf{max}(\lambda d_1 . \mathbf{tall}(d_1)(\mathbf{Clyde}))$
           = $\mathbf{max}(\lambda d_2 . \mathbf{tall}(d_2)(\mathbf{Floyd})) > \mathbf{max}(\lambda d_1 . \mathbf{tall}(d_1)(\mathbf{Clyde}))$

Thus the maximal degree of Floyd's height must exceed the maximal degree of Clyde's. The analogy to individual quantification really is deep: the DegP denotes a generalized quantifier over degrees (that

4.2 The syntax and semantics of the extended AP

is, type $\langle\langle d,t\rangle,t\rangle$. This account is of a comparative, but POS and other degree morphemes can be treated similarly.

On the elegance front, this isn't a no-brainer. The types are simpler, the trace left behind is satisfyingly analogous to a measure phrase, and the denotation of the comparative is elegantly pared down to just the bare essentials of manipulating degrees. But there's no denying the phrase-structural complexity brought about by the movement. The kind of movement itself – Quantifier Raising – is independently motivated, and this would be simply a special case of it, so it requires no major additional stipulations to achieve. Indeed, arguably, it would establish a desirable parallel: if this is how quantification works for individuals, why shouldn't it work just the same for degrees?

Before indulging too much in such aesthetic reflection, though, it behooves us to ask the empirical question: do the movement and non-movement approaches make different predictions? It turns out that they do: movement predicts scope ambiguities and lack of movement doesn't. The next question, then: do degree morphemes actually give rise to scope ambiguities?

4.2.6 Scope and degree operators

The scopal behavior of degree quantifiers is a vexed and complicated matter. The crucial structures are intricate, the judgments often vertigo-inducing, the facts mysterious, and the theoretical consequences profound. At stake are theories of the syntax and semantics of the extended AP, of course, but also the nature of scope-taking mechanisms, the syntax of extraposition, ellipsis, and syntactic reconstruction, and – for surprising reasons – even the ontology of degrees. We'll only touch on the broad issues.

The story begins with a twist right at the start. One might expect to detect scope ambiguities in fairly simple cases, like (40):

(40)   Some linguist is taller than six feet.

The movement view leads us to expect two scope configurations here. As it turns out, though, they have identical truth conditions:[12]

---

[12] This is also a nice demonstration of the fact that a sentence with multiple syntactic structures need not have multiple readings, and that – contrary to what one might tell introductory linguistics students – assigning multiple structures therefore can't suffice to explain an ambiguity without some semantic assumptions.

(41) a. $\exists x[\textbf{linguist}(x) \wedge \textbf{max}(\lambda d_1 . \textbf{tall}(d_1)(x)) > \textbf{6-feet}]$
b. $\textbf{max}(\lambda d_1 . \exists x[\textbf{linguist}(x) \wedge \textbf{tall}(d_1)(x)]) > \textbf{6-feet}$

In (41a), there is a linguist whose height is greater than six feet. In (41b), the maximum height reached by a linguist is greater than six feet. In both cases, the result is the same: some linguist must be taller than six feet.

To make a scope ambiguity perceptible, more complicated examples are required (Heim 2000):

(42) Floyd is six feet tall. Every linguist is less tall than that.

I'll take the *that* to directly denote a degree, and *less* to have the denotation in (43b):

(43) a. $[\![\textit{that}_{\textbf{6-feet}}]\!] = \textbf{6-feet}$
b. $[\![\textit{less}]\!] = \lambda d' \lambda D_{\langle d, t \rangle} . \textbf{max}(D) < d'$

There are two structures for (42). The first merely involves moving only the DegP, as in (44a); the second involves then moving *every linguist*, as in (44b):

(44) a. [less tall than that] λd_1 [every linguist is d_1 tall]
b. [every linguist] λx_1 [less tall than that] λd_1 [x_1 is d_1 tall]

They give rise to different interpretations. First, (44a):

(45) [less tall than that] λd_1 every linguist is d_1 tall
a. $[\![\textit{less than that}_{\textbf{6-feet}}]\!] = \lambda D_{\langle d, t \rangle} . \textbf{max}(D) < \textbf{6-feet}$
b. $[\![\lambda d_1 \textit{ every linguist is } d_1 \textit{ tall}]\!]$
  $= \lambda d_1 . \forall x[\textbf{linguist}(x) \rightarrow \textbf{tall}(d_1)(x)]$
c. $[\![\textit{less than that}_{\textbf{6-feet}}]\!] ([\![\lambda d_1 \textit{ every linguist is } d_1 \textit{ tall}]\!])$
  $= \textbf{max}(\lambda d_1 . \forall x[\textbf{linguist}(x) \rightarrow \textbf{tall}(d_1)(x)]) < \textbf{6-feet}$

The maximal degree this picks out is the greatest height that all the linguists have reached. That is the height of the shortest linguist. So this says that the shortest linguist is shorter than six feet. But this is much weaker than what the sentence actually means. The sentence requires **every** linguist to be under six feet, not just the shortest one.

Quantifier-Raising *every linguist* addresses the problem:

(46) [every linguist] λx_1 [less tall than that] λd_1 x_1 is d_1 tall
a. $[\![\lambda d_1 \, x_1 \textit{ is } d_1 \textit{ tall}]\!] = \lambda d_1 . \textbf{tall}(d_1)(x_1)$

4.2 The syntax and semantics of the extended AP

b. $[\![\text{less than that}_{\text{6-feet}}]\!] ([\![\lambda d_1 \, x_1 \text{ is } d_1 \text{ tall}]\!])$
   = $\max(\lambda d_1 \, . \, \text{tall}(d_1)(x_1)) < \text{6-feet}$
c. $[\![\text{every linguist}]\!] ([\![\lambda x_1 \text{ less than that}_{\text{6-feet}} \, \lambda d_1 \, x_1 \text{ is } d_1 \text{ tall}]\!])$
   = $\forall x[\text{linguist}(x) \rightarrow \max(\lambda d_1 \, . \, \text{tall}(d_1)(x_1)) < \text{6-feet}]$

This, correctly, requires that for every linguist, the maximum degree of tallness the linguist reaches is less than six feet.

It seems, then, that the scopal approach has run into a problem. It predicts an ambiguity where there is none. The alternative Kennedy-style measure-function approach fares better:

(47) a. $[\![\text{less}]\!] = \lambda G_{\langle e, d \rangle} \lambda d \lambda x \, . \, G(x) < d$
      b. $[\![\text{less}]\!] ([\![\text{tall}]\!])([\![\text{than that}_{\text{6-feet}}]\!])$
         = $\lambda x \, . \, \text{tallness}(x) < \text{6-feet}$
      c. $[\![\text{every linguist is less tall than that}_{\text{6-feet}}]\!]$
         = $\forall x \, [\text{linguist}(x) \rightarrow \text{tallness}(x) < \text{6-feet}]$

This predicts only one reading – precisely the correct one.

If things were as simple as this, the issue would be easily settled. But they aren't. Suppose a student has been assigned to write a paper, and there is a length requirement. This could take two forms: a minimum required length or a maximum permitted length. Suppose further that the student has written a ten page paper. She might be told:

(48) The paper is required to be less long than that.

Has the student been told she has met the requirement, or failed to meet it? As it turns out, it could be either, as the continuations in (49) reflect:

(49) The paper is required to be less long than that,
      a. ... so you have to shorten it.
      b. ... so you don't need to lengthen it.

In (49a), there must have been a cap on paper length. In (49b), there must have been a minimum length requirement.[13] The observation – and the example – is due to Heim (2000). The ambiguity arises from

---

[13] The reader may find this example slightly mind-bending. Other examples of the class are generally no easier, but they include comparatives with *exactly* differential measure phrases:

(i)   The paper is $\left\{\begin{array}{l}\text{required}\\ \text{allowed}\end{array}\right\}$ to be exactly five pages longer than that.

the relative scope of the comparative and *required* (for convenience, I assume *the paper* remains in the subject position of the infinitive at logical form):

(50)   a. is required [less long than that] λd_1 the paper to be d_1 long
           it's required that the paper be shorter than that
      b. [less long than that] λd_1 is required the paper to be d_1 long
           the length the paper is required to have is shorter than that

To represent this formally, we'll need to switch to an intensional system, though I'll subscript the world variables (**permitted$_w$** is the set of worlds compatible with what is permitted in w; this is a deontic accessibility relation):

(51)   a. $[\![\,long\,]\!] = \lambda d \lambda x \lambda w \,.\, \mathbf{long}_w(d)(x)$
      b. $[\![\,less\,]\!] = \lambda d' \lambda D_{\langle d, st \rangle} \lambda w \,.\, \mathbf{max}(\lambda d \,.\, D(d)(w)) < d'$
      c. $[\![\,required\,]\!] = \lambda p_{\langle s, t \rangle} \lambda w \,.\, \forall w' \in \mathbf{permitted}_w\,[p(w')]$

Required asserts that the proposition it combines with holds in all permitted worlds. The interpretation of (50a), then, is:

(52)   is required [[less long than that] [λd_1 the paper to be d_1 long]]

      a. $[\![\,less\ long\ than\ that_{\text{10-pages}}\,]\!]$
         $= \lambda D_{\langle d, st \rangle} \lambda w \,.\, \mathbf{max}(\lambda d \,.\, D(d)(w)) < \mathbf{10\text{-pages}}$
      b. $[\![\,\text{the paper to be } d_1 \text{ long}\,]\!] = \lambda w \,.\, \mathbf{long}_w(d_1)(\mathbf{the\text{-}paper})$
      c. $[\![\,\lambda d_1 \text{ the paper to be } d_1 \text{ long}\,]\!]$
         $= \lambda d_1 \lambda w \,.\, \mathbf{long}_w(d_1)(\mathbf{the\text{-}paper})$
      d. $[\![\,less\ long\ than\ that_{\text{10-pages}}\,]\!]\,([\![\,\lambda d_1 \text{ the paper to be } d_1 \text{ long}\,]\!])$
         $= \lambda w \,.\, \mathbf{max}(\lambda d \,.\, \mathbf{long}_w(d)(\mathbf{the\text{-}paper})) < \mathbf{10\text{-pages}}$

See Heim (2000) for discussion. Alrenga et al. (2012) mention a simpler example that involves a different kind of comparative but illustrates a roughly similar ambiguity:

(ii)   California voters have been required to decide more ballot measures than Nevada voters.
      a. 'The requirement was that California voters decide more ballot measures than Nevada voters.'
      b. 'The number of ballot measures California voters have been required to decide is greater than the number of ballot measures Nevada voters have been.'

4.2 The syntax and semantics of the extended AP

e. $[\![\text{is required}]\!] \left(\begin{bmatrix} \textit{[less long than that}_{\text{10-pages}}\textit{]} \\ \lambda d_1 \textit{ the paper to be } d_1 \textit{ long} \end{bmatrix} \right)$

$= \lambda w . \forall w' \in \textbf{permitted}_w$
$[\max(\lambda d . \textbf{long}_{w'}(d)(\textbf{the-paper})) < \textbf{10-pages}]$

This is the length-cap reading. The requirement – what must be the case in all permitted worlds – is that the (maximal, i.e., full) length of the paper is less than ten pages. The other reading:

(53) [less long than that] [λd_1 is required [the paper to be d_1 long]]

a. $[\![\lambda d_1 \textit{ is required [the paper to be } d_1 \textit{ long]}]\!]$
$= \lambda d_1 \lambda w . \forall w' \in \textbf{permitted}_w [\textbf{long}_{w'}(d_1)(\textbf{the-paper})]$

b. $[\![\textit{less long than that}_{\text{10-pages}}]\!]$
$([\![\lambda d_1 \textit{ is required [the paper to be } d_1 \textit{ long]}]\!])$

$= \lambda w . \max \begin{pmatrix} \lambda d . \forall w' \in \textbf{permitted}_w \\ [\textbf{long}_{w'}(d)(\textbf{the-paper})] \end{pmatrix} < \textbf{10-pages}$

This is the minimum-length requirement reading. First, it identifies the lengths the paper is required to reach (that is, the lengths it reaches in all permitted worlds). We need the plural 'lengths' because if a paper is required to reach nine pages, it is also required to reach 8, 7, 6 and so on.[14] On this reading, then, the greatest length the paper is required to reach is less than ten pages.

So, a scope ambiguity has been discovered, and the evidence is therefore mixed. The theory on which comparatives are scope-bearing predicts some ambiguities where there are none, but successfully predicts others. The theory on which comparatives aren't scope-bearing predicts the absence of scope ambiguities where some are found. The challenge is making sense of this situation. Scope ambiguities are found only in limited circumstances, so on a movement theory, constraints must be imposed to explain why many expected scope ambiguities are blocked. The alternative theory must be supplemented with an explanation of what's going on in the Heim example.[15]

---

[14] In other words, if a paper reaches nine pages in all required worlds, it also reaches 8 pages in them. This follows from the monotonicity assumption that any paper that is 9 pages is also 8 pages. See section 3.5.2.

[15] Interestingly, the scope of the comparative quantifier correlates with the surface position of the comparative clause (Gawron 1995; Bhatt and Pancheva 2004), which may make it possible to attribute some of the vexing scope properties not to the comparative morpheme but rather to the standard marker *than* (Alrenga et al. 2012).

Perhaps because it's generally easier to block readings than to create them, most semanticists currently seem to favor the movement view. It was always the better-established one in any case. But it's in large measure on this treacherous empirical terrain that the question may have to be decided. This has been a lively area of research (Kennedy 1997; Heim 2000; Schwarzschild and Wilkinson 2002; Sharvit and Stateva 2002; Bhatt and Pancheva 2004; Grosu and Horvath 2006; Heim 2006b; Bhatt and Takahashi 2007, 2011; van Rooij 2008; Beck 2011, 2012; Alrenga et al. 2012).

4.2.7 The Russell ambiguity

Before we leave this topic, a historical note. Bertrand Russell noticed an ambiguity involving comparatives, which he illustrated with an example that has since become famous (1905):

(54) I thought your yacht was larger than it is.

This might be uttered by a disappointed yachting enthusiast with a bigger-is-better mindset. The crucial observation is that this has two readings, one of which attributes to the speaker belief in a contradiction:

(55) a. I thought your yacht was a certain size. That size exceeds its actual size.
      b. I thought, 'the size of your yacht exceeds the size of your yacht'.

What accounts for the ambiguity? One traditional answer was scope. A degree quantifier can scope either outside of *thought*, yielding the rational reading in (56a), or inside *thought*, yielding the irrational reading in (56b) (@ represents the actual world and **thoughts**$_@$ represents the worlds compatible with what the speaker thinks in the actual world; that is, the epistemically accessible worlds):

(56) a. $\max(\lambda d . \forall w \in \textbf{thoughts}_@[\textbf{large}_w(d)(\text{your-yacht})]) > \max(\lambda d . \textbf{large}_@(d)(\text{your-yacht}))$

b. $\forall w \in \textbf{thoughts}_@ \left[\begin{array}{l} \max(\lambda d . \textbf{large}_w(d)(\text{your-yacht})) > \\ \max(\lambda d . \textbf{large}_w(d)(\text{your-yacht})) \end{array} \right]$

This seems alarmingly familiar. There is a major difference, however. Because what's at issue here is a propositional attitude predicate, this can be assimilated to an ambiguity of a different kind, the DE RE/DE DICTO ambiguity (see section 5.3.2 or Heim and Kratzer 1998 for a brief

4.2 The syntax and semantics of the extended AP

introduction to the phenomenon). The current prevailing wisdom is that such ambiguities are not actually about scope. For one thing, the movement operation that would be necessary to achieve the required scope would take the degree quantifier out of a finite clause, which is not possible syntactically. An alternative, preferable explanation can be achieved by indexing predicates in the object language with world variables that can then be bound (or not) by higher intensional operators (Percus 2000; Heim 2000; see also von Stechow 1984, an early idea in a broadly similar spirit). Despite its fame and general neatness, the Russell sentence won't help us here.

4.2.8 Quantification and comparative clauses

Matters of quantification and scope also figure in connection with quantifiers in the comparative clause.

One fact any theory of comparatives should capture is that comparative clauses license negative polarity items (NPIs; Hoeksema 1983):

(57) a. Floyd is taller than <u>any</u> linguist <u>at all</u>.
      b. Floyd complained more than I <u>ever</u> have.

This follows most clearly from the sort of denotation for the comparative the chapter began with (what Schwarzschild 2008 called the 'A-not-A' theory), in which an overt logical negation is involved. Other theories of the comparative also capture this fact, though. On the classical view of Ladusaw (1980), NPIs are licensed in DOWNWARD-ENTAILING ENVIRONMENTS, environments that license inferences from supersets to subsets. Comparative clauses do, in fact, do this:

(58) Floyd is taller than any linguist.
      entails: Floyd is taller than any phonologist.

That's reflected in the maximality semantics. In (58), the maximality operator invites one to examine all linguists, note the height of each, and pick the highest value. Because phonologists are a subset of linguists, the examination of all linguists included all phonologists. This in turn means that the maximum value initially arrived at could not be exceeded by looking only at phonologists.

On the other hand, comparative clauses have a systematic prohibition on negation and quantifiers that are themselves downward-entailing (von Stechow 1984; Rullmann 1995):

(59) #Floyd is taller than $\left\{ \begin{array}{l} \text{Clyde isn't} \\ \text{none of the phonologists is} \\ \text{no linguist is} \end{array} \right\}$.

Again, this follows from a maximality semantics. To determine whether Floyd is taller than no linguist is, one would first have to determine the maximum height that no linguist reaches. Well, no linguist is twelve feet tall – or 13, or 14, or 15, ... Of course, there is no such maximum, so the maximality operator will be undefined for such a case.

Finally, there are thorny problems concerning other quantifiers in comparative clauses. As Larson (1988), Schwarzschild and Wilkinson (2002), and Heim (2006b) observe, quantifiers in the comparative clause take unexpectedly wide scope:

(60) a. Floyd is taller than every linguist is.
   b. [more than $\emptyset$ λd_1 every linguist is d_1-tall] λd_2 Floyd is d_2 tall
   c. $[\![$ than $\emptyset$ λd_1 every linguist is d_1-tall $]\!]$
      = $\mathbf{max}(\lambda d_1 . \forall x[\mathbf{linguist}(x) \rightarrow \mathbf{tall}(d_1)(x)])$
   d. $[\![$ [more than $\emptyset$ λd_1 every linguist is d_1-tall] λd_2 Floyd is d_2 tall $]\!]$
      = $\mathbf{max}(\lambda d_2 . \mathbf{tall}(d)(\mathbf{Floyd})) >$
         $\mathbf{max}(\lambda d_1 . \forall x\ [\mathbf{linguist}(x) \rightarrow \mathbf{tall}(d_1)(x)])$

This denotation asks us to survey the linguists to determine the greatest height they have all reached – that is, the height of the shortest linguist. It then asserts that Floyd's height exceeds this. This isn't a possible reading. (Any sense of déjà vu one might be experiencing in light of section 4.2.6 is not accidental.)

If the universal could scope outside the comparative, the right reading would result:

(61) a. [every linguist] λx_1 [more than $\emptyset$ λd_1 x_1 is d_1-tall] λd_2 Floyd is d_2 tall
   b. $[\![$ every linguist $]\!] = \lambda P_{\langle e, t \rangle} . \forall x[\mathbf{linguist}(x) \rightarrow P(x)]$
   c. $[\![$ [than $\emptyset$ λd_1 x_1 is d_1-tall] $]\!]$
      = $\mathbf{max}(\lambda d_1 . \mathbf{tall}(d_1)(x_1))$
   d. $[\![$ [more than $\emptyset$ λd_1 x_1 is d_1-tall] λd_2 Floyd is d_2 tall $]\!]$
      = $\mathbf{max}(\lambda d_2 . \mathbf{tall}(d)(\mathbf{Floyd})) > \mathbf{max}(\lambda d_1 . \mathbf{tall}(d_1)(x_1))$
   e. $[\![(61a)]\!] = \forall x \begin{bmatrix} \mathbf{linguist}(x) \rightarrow \\ \mathbf{max}(\lambda d_2 . \mathbf{tall}(d)(\mathbf{Floyd})) > \\ \mathbf{max}(\lambda d_1 . \mathbf{tall}(d_1)(x_1)) \end{bmatrix}$

The scope-taking operation that would be required to achieve this configuration is precisely the sort that isn't possible: Quantifier Raising (QR) doesn't operate across finite clause boundaries.[16] Worse, here the

---

[16] Of course, this might be evidence that there is no such restriction after all (it's the sort of movement that would also be required for a scopal account of

4.3 Other degree constructions

impossible would have to be not only possible but obligatory. We need not only to generate (61) but also to avoid generating (60). Worse still, as Schwarzschild and Wilkinson point out that the same problem can be discerned with FLOATED QUANTIFIERS like the one in (62) (Sportiche 1988), which don't undergo QR:

(62) Lucy paid more for her suit than they both paid in taxes last year (Schwarzschild and Wilkinson 2002).

These kinds of facts remain an area of active research (in addition to work already cited, see Krasikova 2008b; van Rooij 2008; Gajewski 2009; Beck 2010). Larson (1988) proposed coping with the problem by changing what is being lambda-abstracted over in the comparative clause (not degrees but properties). Schwarzschild and Wilkinson take a radically different tack: they suggest that what is necessary is a different way of thinking about degrees. On the usual approach, a degree represents only a single point on a scale – say, a single height. But, they suggest, when there are quantifiers in the comparative clause, degrees need to represent more than one height at a time. This can be accomplished by assuming that instead of ordinary degrees, comparatives manipulate intervals. In a different way and for different reasons, Kennedy (1997) proposed this, too. (There is a slight terminological difficulty here: one could reserve the term 'degree' for degrees-qua-points, or one could generalize it to include degrees-qua-intervals. The usual choice is the former. Kennedy suggests 'extents' for degrees-qua-intervals.) One intriguing aspect of this work is the way it relates assumptions about scope-taking mechanisms – ultimately a syntactic matter as much as a semantic one – to assumptions about the ontology of degrees, a matter that would have seemed distant from syntactic considerations like movement constraints.

4.3 OTHER DEGREE CONSTRUCTIONS

4.3.1 Differential comparatives and measure phrases

Ordinary comparatives do not, of course, exhaust the full range of degree constructions. We should consider some of the others.

Among the better-studied are DIFFERENTIAL COMPARATIVES. These are simply comparatives with a measure phrase:

> DE RE/DE DICTO ambiguities and of specific indefinites), but this would run counter to a well-established consensus.

(63)   Floyd is three inches $\begin{Bmatrix} \text{taller} \\ \text{less tall} \end{Bmatrix}$ than Clyde is.

To cope with these, one move is simply to add an additional argument to the comparative morpheme. For the remainder of this chapter, we'll stick with the relatively standard small DegP movement approach to comparatives. Thus we move from (64a) to (64b):

(64)   a. $[\![more]\!] = \lambda d \lambda D_{\langle d, t \rangle} . \mathbf{max}(D) > d$
        b. $[\![more]\!] = \lambda d \lambda d' \lambda D_{\langle d, t \rangle} . \mathbf{max}(D) - d \geq d'$

The differential degree d' now serves to measure the difference between the maximal degree associated with the clause and the degree provided by the comparative clause complement of *more*. The syntax of the DegP is as in (65), and the full denotation in (66):

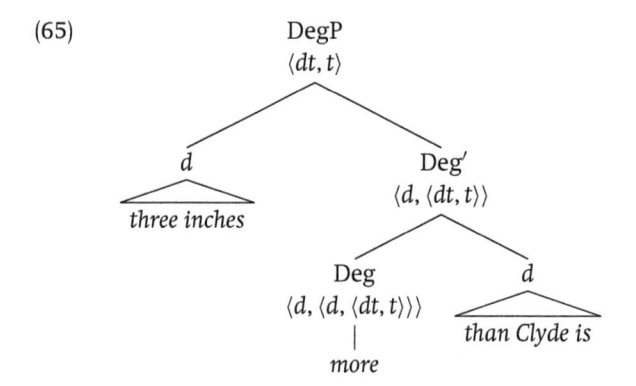

(65)
```
                    DegP
                   ⟨dt, t⟩
                  /       \
                 d         Deg'
                /\        ⟨d, ⟨dt, t⟩⟩
          three inches    /      \
                        Deg        d
                  ⟨d, ⟨d, ⟨dt, t⟩⟩⟩  /\
                        |      than Clyde is
                       more
```

(66)   a. [three inches more than Clyde] λd_1 Floyd is d_1 tall
        b. $[\![\text{three inches more than Clyde}]\!]$
            = $[\![more]\!] ([\![\text{than Clyde is}]\!]) ([\![\text{three inches}]\!])$
            = $[\![more]\!] (\mathbf{max}(\lambda d_2 . \mathbf{tall}(d_2)(\mathbf{Clyde})))(\mathbf{3\text{-}inches})$
            = $\lambda D_{\langle d, t \rangle} . \mathbf{max}(D) -$
            $\qquad \mathbf{max}(\lambda d_2 . \mathbf{tall}(d_2)(\mathbf{Clyde})) \geq \mathbf{3\text{-}inches}$
        c. $[\![\text{three inches more than Clyde}]\!] ([\![\lambda d_1 \text{ Floyd is } d_1 \text{ tall}]\!])$
            = $[\![\text{three inches more than Clyde}]\!] (\lambda d_1 . \mathbf{tall}(d_1)(\mathbf{Floyd}))$
            = $\mathbf{max}(\lambda d_1 . \mathbf{tall}(d_1)(\mathbf{Floyd})) -$
            $\qquad \mathbf{max}(\lambda d_2 . \mathbf{tall}(d_2)(\mathbf{Clyde})) \geq \mathbf{3\text{-}inches}$

Does this require stipulating that *more* and *less* each come in two homophonous forms, one with a differential argument and one without? Not necessarily. There are ways of elaborating the structure of the

4.3 Other degree constructions

comparative or changing its basic meaning that make it possible for a single denotation to accommodate a measure phrase. Discussion of differential comparatives can be found in Schwarzschild (2005), Xiang (2005), Brasoveanu (2008a), Rett (2008b), Schwarzschild (2008), Solt (2009), Sawada and Grano (2011), Grano and Kennedy (2012), and they often come up in older, more general work as well (such as von Stechow 1984).

A related phenomenon is FACTOR PHRASES, also known as RATIO PHRASES, which seem to involve degree multiplication:

(67) The coffee table is two times wider than the armchair.

In English, these are more natural with equatives:

(68) The coffee table is two times as wide as the armchair.

Gobeski (2009) points out that languages vary in which of these forms they permit with factor phrases, with Macedonian insisting on the comparative (as do Hebrew and Russian; Sassoon 2010a):

(69) a. Jon je dva puti po visok od Mari.
John is two times more tall from Mary
'John is two times as tall as/taller than Mary.'

b. *Jon je dva puti visok kolku Mari.
John is two times tall as Mary

Even in English, Gobeski observes, only the equative occurs with *twice* (*twice taller than Mary*). Writing a denotation for a factor phrase might seem relatively straightforward, but a number of deeper issues lurk beneath the surface. One of them is simply how to arrange the pieces compositionally in an insightful way. Apart from the Gobeski observation and related puzzles (does being *two times taller* entail being at least twice as tall, or more than twice as tall? How do these relate to adverbial uses?), there are also broader questions about what operations on degrees are possible in principle (Sassoon 2010b).

4.3.2 Equatives

The standard assumption about equatives is that they require meeting or exceeding the standard degree:

(70) $[\![as]\!] = \lambda d \lambda D_{\langle d, t \rangle} . \mathbf{max}(D) \geq d$

(71) a. Floyd is as tall as Clyde is.
b. $\mathbf{max}(\lambda d_1 . \mathbf{tall}(d_1)(\mathbf{Floyd})) \geq \mathbf{max}(\lambda d_2 . \mathbf{tall}(d_2)(\mathbf{Clyde}))$

Discussion of the equative can frequently be found in discussions of the comparative, but recent work includes Bale (2006), Alrenga (2007b), Bhatt and Pancheva (2007); Schwarz (2007); Brasoveanu (2008a); Rett (2008b, 2010, 2011b); Anderson and Morzycki (forthcoming); Beck (2012). For discussion specifically of the choice between = (an exactly identical reading) vs ≥ (an at-least reading), see Bhatt and Pancheva (2007), Rett (2008a,b) and, briefly, section 4.4.

4.3.3 Superlatives

Things get more complex with superlatives:

(72)   Floyd is the tallest.

For this to be true, Floyd must be taller than everyone else. There are a number of ways to cash this out, but here's one:

(73) $\quad \forall x \begin{bmatrix} x \neq \textbf{Floyd} \rightarrow \\ \quad \textbf{max}(\lambda d \,.\, \textbf{tall}(d)(\textbf{Floyd})) > \\ \quad \textbf{max}(\lambda d' \,.\, \textbf{tall}(d')(x)) \end{bmatrix}$

This universally quantifies over all non-Floyd individuals, requiring that he be taller than all of them.

How is this denotation built? The answer depends largely on what explains a well-known ambiguity (Ross 1964, Szabolcsi 1986, and many since) between ABSOLUTE and COMPARATIVE readings:

(74)   Floyd climbed the highest mountain.

   a. *comparative reading*:
      'Everyone else climbed a mountain shorter than the one Floyd climbed.'

   b. *absolute reading*:
      'All other mountains are shorter than the one Floyd climbed.'

There are two approaches to explaining the ambiguity. One, the older of the two, is based on the scope of the degree operator (I'll lapse partly into ordinary English to simplify things):

(75)   a. *comparative reading*:

$\quad \forall x \begin{bmatrix} x \neq \textbf{Floyd} \rightarrow \\ \quad \textbf{max}\begin{pmatrix} \lambda d \,.\, \textbf{Floyd} \text{ climbed} \\ \text{a } d\text{-high mountain} \end{pmatrix} > \\ \quad \textbf{max}(\lambda d' \,.\, x \text{ climbed a } d'\text{-high mountain}) \end{bmatrix}$

4.3 Other degree constructions

b. *absolute reading*:

Floyd climbed the mountain such that:
$$\forall x \begin{bmatrix} x \neq \textbf{Floyd's-mountain} \rightarrow \\ \max\begin{pmatrix} \lambda d \,.\, \textbf{Floyd's-mountain is} \\ \text{a } d\text{-high mountain} \end{pmatrix} > \\ \max(\lambda d' \,.\, x \text{ is a } d'\text{-high mountain}) \end{bmatrix}$$

The crucial difference is in whether the mention of climbing occurs inside the scope of **max**. If it does, the maximal degree will depend on the relative heights of mountains that were climbed. If it doesn't, it will depend only on the heights of mountains. To arrive at these readings compositionally, the superlative morpheme must be able to scope at different levels, so this approach favors theories in which degree morphemes move. The implementation tends to be complicated, so I won't go into further detail here (that can be found in Heim 1995 and Sharvit and Stateva 2002 among others).

The alternative approach is simpler. Its outlines can be perceived by considering slightly different paraphrases of precisely the same meanings:

(76) a. *comparative reading*:
'Of the mountains climbed, the one Floyd climbed is the highest.'

b. *absolute reading*:
'Of all the mountains, the one Floyd climbed is the highest.'

In each case, the paraphrase begins with an *of* PP that restricts the domain of quantification, in one case to mountains climbed and in the other to mountains generally. This is rather like what happens with any run-of-the mill quantifier. *Everyone left* doesn't require total depopulation of the planet, but only that the contextually relevant people have left. The usual way to represent this is with a RESOURCE DOMAIN VARIABLE C that contains all relevant individuals (Westerståhl 1985; von Fintel 1994):

(77) a. Everyone$_C$ left.
b. $\forall x \in C \,[\textbf{person}(x) \rightarrow \textbf{left}(x)]$

Natural language quantification generally seems to work this way, so it would be odd if the quantifier in the superlative, and therefore in the mountain sentence, weren't similarly restricted:

(78) Floyd climbed the mountain such that:
$$\forall x \in C \begin{bmatrix} x \neq \text{Floyd-mountain} \rightarrow \\ \max\begin{pmatrix} \lambda d\,.\,\text{Floyd-mountain is} \\ \text{a } d\text{-high mountain} \end{pmatrix} > \\ \max(\lambda d'\,.\,x \text{ is a } d'\text{-high mountain}) \end{bmatrix}$$

This representation looks virtually identical to the absolute reading. But because there is now a contextual domain restriction, everything hinges on its content. If the discourse is concerned with all mountains, C contains them all and the result is the absolute reading. If the discourse is concerned only with mountains climbed, C consists only of those, and the comparative reading results.

One interesting aspect of the two competing proposals is that they disagree on how to diagnose the problem. On the scope view, this is a structural ambiguity; on the contextual view, something else (arguably, something closer to vagueness, inasmuch as it relies on an indeterminate C). This illustrates again that these distinctions aren't always clear without first articulating an analysis – and then the choice between them may hang on the relative merits of alternative analyses.

For more on superlatives, consult Partee (1986), Szabolcsi (1986), Gawron (1995), Heim (1995), Farkas and Kiss (2000), Sharvit and Stateva (2000), Sharvit and Stateva (2002), Büring (2007a), Geurts and Nouwen (2007), Matushansky (2008), Aihara (2009), Beck (2009), Gutiérrez-Rexach (2010), Sleeman (2010), Cohen and Krifka (2011), and Krasikova (2011).

4.3.4 Sufficiency and excess

Certain degree constructions require an intricate intermingling of degrees and possible worlds (Meier 2003; Hacquard 2006). In English, they are headed by *too* and *enough*:

(79) a. Floyd is too old to ski.
     b. Floyd is old enough to ski.

What (79a) says, very roughly, is something about worlds consistent with norms about the appropriate age for safe (or good or enjoyable) skiing. The precise nature of the accessibility relation – that is, precisely what worlds are being quantified over – need not concern us here. The crucial thing is just the fact of the modality itself. To represent it, we will need to momentarily return to an intensional system (with @ representing the actual world):

(80) a. Floyd is too old to ski.
     b. $\forall w \in \textbf{safe-skiing-worlds} \begin{bmatrix} \max(\lambda d\,.\,\textbf{old}_@(d)(\textbf{Floyd})) > \\ \max(\lambda d\,.\,\textbf{old}_w(d)(\textbf{Floyd})) \end{bmatrix}$

4.3 Other degree constructions

This says that in all the worlds in which safe skiing practices are observed, Floyd's age is lower than in the actual world.[17] *Old enough* would simply be the existential counterpart (with, in this case, a different accessibility relation).

These structures have not received nearly as much attention as has been lavished on other degree constructions. A fully developed theory is, however, presented in Meier (2003), who assimilates them to conditionals, and in Hacquard (2006), who explores whether the content of the infinitive is an entailment.

4.3.5 Degree exclamatives and degree questions

Questions and exclamatives are not primarily about degrees. Both have their own intricate and independent grammar. Nevertheless, degree expressions can enter into both of these structures, and when they do, there is an opportunity to examine the interaction of degrees and a complicated and independent subsystem of the grammar.

In English – and indeed in many languages – degree questions and degree exclamatives are formed with the same *wh*-word:

(81)   a. How tall are you?   (question)
       b. How tall you are!   (exclamative)

We can't indulge here in an extensive digression on the grammar of questions and exclamatives, but it's possible to perceive at least one interesting puzzle. Part of the meaning of the exclamative in (81b) is roughly paraphrasable as 'you're very tall'. Although *how* and *very* are both degree modifiers, it seems unlikely that *how* is responsible for the 'very' meaning because *how* also occurs in (81a), which has no such meaning. The challenge, then, is to derive this meaning from an independent general property of exclamative structures. That crucial property may be the sense of surprise or unexpectedness that exclamatives convey. But how to assemble these pieces? What is the basic meaning of *how*? What is the basic meaning of exclamatives? Why does the 'very' paraphrase seem not to do justice to the full meaning of (81b)? If the exclamative structure itself can create a semantic effect similar to that created by the degree word *very*, might this reveal something about various ways to give rise to degree-modifier meanings? One might begin a search for answers with Zanuttini and Portner

---

[17] This toy denotation isn't strong enough, because (80a) further requires that Floyd's age be the reason his skiing is unsafe. Thanks to Alan Bale for pointing it out. Consult Meier (2003) for a proper implementation.

(2003), Portner and Zanuttini (2005), Castroviejo Miró (2007, 2008b,c, 2013), Potts and Schwarz (2008), Rett (2008b), Sæbø (2010), Bylinina (2011), Rett (2011a) and Miró (2012).

4.3.6 Metalinguistic comparatives

Among the more exotic forms of comparative are METALINGUISTIC COMPARATIVES, which, according to one common description, compare not the meanings of words but rather the appropriateness of their use:

(82) a. George is more dumb than crazy.
b. Clarence is more a syntactician than a semanticist.

The idea is that these are like METALINGUISTIC NEGATION, which is 'metalinguistic' in the sense that it doesn't negate the semantic content of an expression but rather 'reject[s] the language used by an earlier speaker' (Horn 1985):

(83) He didn't call the ['poʊlis]. He called the [pə'lis].

This is especially striking because it **can't** be the meaning that's negated. Semantically, one sentence is simply the negation of the other, so they can't both be true. It's that the language itself is at issue, not the content.

There are several ways in which metalinguistic comparatives differ from ordinary ones. First, they are never possible as SYNTHETIC comparatives, the kind with -er (the other kind, with more, are called ANALYTIC):

(84) a. *George is dumber than crazy.
b. *Dick is crazier than dumb.

In ordinary comparatives, both dumb and crazy generally require the synthetic form (i.e., dumber rather than more dumb). Metalinguistic comparatives also permit than-phrases that would otherwise be impossible:

(85) a. George is more dumb than crazy.
b. *George is dumber than crazy.

And they are robustly crosscategorial:

(86) a. George more [VP felt the answer] than [VP knew it].
b. George is more [AP afraid of Dick] than [PP in love with him].

Some languages even use distinct morphemes for metalinguistic comparison (Sawada 2007; Giannakidou and Yoon 2011):

4.3 Other degree constructions

(87) GREEK
Ta provlimata sou   ine perissotero ikonomika para nomika.
the problems yours are more   financial   than legal
'Your problems are financial more than legal.'

(88) JAPANESE
Taroo-wa sensei-to iu-yori   gakusya-da.
Taroo-TOP teacher-as say-than scholar-PRED
'Taroo is more a scholar than a teacher.'

Morzycki (2009c, 2011) argued that such comparatives are not actually 'metalinguistic' in the sense that metalinguistic negation is. If they compared the appropriateness of the use of linguistic expressions, it should be possible to compare pronunciations metalinguistically just as it's possible to negate them. As it turns out, it generally isn't:

(89)   #He more called the [pəˈlis] than the [ˈpoʊlis].

Another significant difference is that metalinguistic comparatives don't actually seem to compare along a vague generalized 'appropriateness' dimension. Suppose Herman has entered a kindergarten class and said to the children, 'George is an asshole.' Clarence might reasonably take him aside and say (90a), but not (90b):

(90) a. It's more appropriate to say 'He is a bad man' than to say 'He is an asshole'.
     b. ??He's more a bad man than an asshole.

One can't compare aesthetic appropriateness this way either. If Coleridge had just presented you with a poem that begins 'in Xanadu did Kubla Khan / a stately pleasure dome requisition', you can respond with (91a) but not (91b):

(91) a. It's more appropriate/better (metrically) to say he decreed it than to say he requisitioned it.
     b. ??He more decreed it than requisitioned it.

This suggests that we can do better than a vague appeal to 'appropriateness'.

Instead, I argued that these are actually about comparing IMPRECISION, the pragmatic slack we afford each other in communicating (see section 3.2.3; Lasersohn 1999). The idea is that we're comfortable describing someone as *six feet tall* even if they're a few molecules shorter than that because it's close enough for most contexts. In Lasersohn's terms, such a height falls in the PRAGMATIC HALO around *six feet*. What metalinguistic comparatives do, then, is compare halo size, or degrees of precision required to render something true. What *more dumb than crazy* means is that *George is dumb* is true at a higher level of precision than *George is crazy*. To implement this, it's natural to construe halos as having a size measured in degrees and to add such degrees of precision as an index to the interpretation function. Thus:

(92) $[\![$ *George is more dumb than crazy* $]\!]^{d'}$

= $\max(\lambda d. [\![$ *George is dumb* $]\!]^{d}) > \max(\lambda d. [\![$ *George is crazy* $]\!]^{d})$

This may have other applications. One could ask, for any given degree modifier, whether it manipulates lexically provided degrees or contextual imprecision degrees (see also Bouchard 2012; Klecha 2013; Anderson 2014, 2013).[18]

Giannakidou and Stavrou (2008); Giannakidou and Yoon (2009, 2011) instead emphasize modal notions, so that *George is more α than β* means something like 'I prefer to say that George is α than to say that he is β.' Importantly, though, both approaches agree that metalinguistic comparatives are part of the grammar rather than an extra-grammatical, purely pragmatic phenomenon.

4.3.7 Comparison of deviation

Outside of metalinguistic comparatives, comparisons across scales are generally impossible (see also sections 3.6 and 3.3.2):

(93) a. #My copy of *The Brothers Karamazov* is heavier than my copy of *The Idiot* is old. (Kennedy 1997)
  b. #My monkey is uglier than this book is long.

This is INCOMMENSURABILITY, and it's one of the selling points of a degree-based semantics that it naturally accounts for it. Kennedy (1997)

---

[18] Bouchard (2012) makes the useful point that using the terms 'precise' and 'imprecise' for independently vague predicates departs from their ordinary meaning. In the ordinary sense, we wouldn't say e.g. #*He's precisely bald/tall*. On the other hand, *Bald/tall is precisely what he is* or ... *is precisely the right term* are both fine, which suggests the former oddness is a grammatical rather than a conceptual one. (Clearly, there are some such grammatical idiosyncrasies: *We'll arrive at precisely/??imprecisely three o'clock*.) Nevertheless, there might be something to be said for adopting a term like 'truth-conditional aptness'.

4.3 Other degree constructions

observed that distinct adjectives of distinct polarities can nevertheless sometimes support comparatives (his examples):

(94) a. Robert is as short as William is tall.
      b. Alex is as slim now as he was obese before.
      c. It's more difficult to surf Maverick's than it is easy to surf Steamer Lane.

He dubbed this COMPARISON OF DEVIATION because what's apparently being compared is the amount by which the standard has been exceeded. In what would seem to be a telling parallel to metalinguistic comparatives, he points out that such readings seem to be impossible for synthetic comparatives:

(95) San Francisco Bay is $\begin{Bmatrix} \text{more shallow} \\ \text{\#shallower} \end{Bmatrix}$ than Monterey Bay is deep.

At a very broad level of description, these also resemble metalinguistic comparatives in their meaning. But it may be wise to resist the temptation to unify them. Comparison of deviation readings license inferences to the positive form:

(96) Alex is as slim now as he was obese before.
      entails: 'Alex is slim now.'

The inference is not cancelable, as we would expect of an entailment.

(97) ??Alex is as slim now as he was obese before, but he's not slim now.

Metalinguistic comparatives, on the other hand, give rise to an **implicature** that the positive form holds, but not an entailment:

(98) Clarence is more tall than ugly.
      implicates but does not entail: Clarence is tall.

Being only an implicature, it **is** cancelable:

(99) Clarence is more tall than ugly, but he's not (really) tall either.

4.3.8 Indirect comparison

Yet another kind of comparison that might be mistaken for either of the previous two is INDIRECT COMPARISON (Bale 2006, 2008; van Rooij

2011c; Doetjes et al. 2011).[19] Such cases still involve comparatives with distinct adjectives (examples are from Bale 2008):

(100) a. Let me tell you how pretty Esme is. She's prettier than Einstein was clever.
b. Although Seymour was both happy and angry, he was still happier than he was angry.
c. Seymour is taller for a man than he is wide for a man.

Unlike either of the other two varieties of cross-adjective comparatives, these are possible with *-er*. And unlike comparison of deviation, these don't license inferences to the positive form. Bale asks us to consider a scenario in which Mary is known to be stupid, and he would like to convey that he is unattractive. He might say (101):

(101) Unfortunately, Mary is more intelligent than I am beautiful.
does not entail: Mary is intelligent.
does not entail: I am beautiful.

Indeed, in this context, there isn't even an implicature to this effect. This is important because it's relatively easy to dismiss metalinguistic comparatives and comparison of deviation as peripheral kinds of comparative, not ones upon which the analysis of comparatives generally should rest.

These cases, however, can't be dismissed so easily. Nor are they a quirk of English: he shows that they occur across a number of languages, with precisely the same morpheme as ordinary comparatives. They may therefore provide a window onto all comparatives. What they reveal, Bale argues, is that comparison is inherently a two-part affair, and that we've been overlooking half of it. The first part involves degrees similar to the ones we've been dealing with, determined by the lexical semantics of particular gradable predicates. The other part involves what he calls 'the universal scale': an abstract all-purpose scale consisting of (or isomorphic to) the rational numbers (all numbers that can be expressed as fractions). What indirect comparatives reveal is that the comparative morpheme deals in universal-scale degrees, not

---

[19] Doetjes et al. (2011) refer to this as 'relative comparison'. The term is perhaps more transparent but also taken several times over. Van Rooij (2011c) opts for 'interadjective comparison', which is also helpfully transparent, but risks leaving us in the position of saying that comparison of deviation and metalinguistic comparison isn't interadjective comparison despite being, in the informal sense, precisely that.

their lexical counterparts. See Bale (2006, 2008) for the articulation of the idea (and van Rooij 2011c for an alternative view).

4.4 NEUTRALIZATION AND POSITIVE-ENTAILINGNESS

On any semantics we've considered, the comparative should not give rise to inferences to the positive form. Degree theories expect such inferences only when the comparative morpheme's denotation includes some crucial element of the denotation of POS: a contextually provided standard, or something like one.

In light of this, (102) should be alarming:

(102) a. This surface is more opaque than that one.
entails: This surface is opaque.

b. This surface is more transparent than that one.
entails: This surface is transparent.

c. This cough syrup is sweeter than that one.
entails: This cough syrup is sweet.

Equally alarming are similar facts about equatives (already encountered in section 3.7.1):

(103) a. Floyd is as short as Clyde.
entails: Floyd is short.

b. The coffee table is as narrow as the couch.
entails: The coffee table is narrow.

These are in fact related to the example the chapter began with:

(104) She also had one leg not as short as the other.
entails: She had one leg that was short.

Neither the comparative nor the equative denotations predict this. What's going on?

Before we address this question, a brief terminological interlude is in order. I've been using the cumbersome phrase 'licenses inferences to the positive form'. It would be useful to have a simple unambiguous term for this property. One candidate is EVALUATIVE, used in this sense by Neeleman et al. (2004), Rett (2008a,b), but this is certainly not unambiguous. It's more often used in several other senses with respect to adjectives (see the glossary). Another established term is 'NORM-RELATED' (Bierwisch 1989). This is unambiguous, but may be too specific. First, it suggests that inferences to the positive form necessarily involve a norm (rather than some other form of standard; Kennedy 2007, who cites Bogusławski 1975). Second, the term is misleading for absolute adjectives. *Dry*, for example, has a standard of complete dryness – an umbrella isn't dry if it's even slightly wet – yet it would be odd to claim that the norm is for things to be completely dry. Third, Bierwisch himself intended for the term to be restricted to dimensional adjectives. So, for lack of a better alternative, I will use the cumbersome term 'POSITIVE-ENTAILING' (though of course *positive* in itself has multiple uses). There is a better term for the **failure** to license inferences to the positive: NEUTRALIZATION (see, e.g., Winter 2001).

So, to ask the question again, this time more precisely: what accounts for the positive-entailing reading of various degree constructions?

This is the question Rett (2008a,b) addresses. She begins with the insight that positive-entailingness may be independent of the degree relation an adjective provides. She proposes that it actually comes from an optional independent morpheme, EVAL, whose sole contribution is that a degree exceeds the standard:

(105) $[\![\text{EVAL}]\!] = \lambda D_{\langle d, t \rangle} \lambda d \, . \, D(d) \wedge d > \textbf{standard}(D)$

Importantly, this is a predicate-modifier type – it maps from properties of degrees to properties of degrees. It can therefore plug into a tree with minimal disruption.

Because EVAL can optionally be inserted anywhere, a simple positive form will now have two possible structures, one with it and one without. In its absence, the positive will have a structure like the one in (106) (I will take certain liberties with her framework for convenience):

(106) $[\![\exists \text{ is } d \text{ [Floyd tall]}]\!] = \exists d \, [\textbf{tall}(d)(\textbf{Floyd})]$

This assumes the order of the arguments of the adjective is switched, that is, that it is type $\langle e, dt \rangle$ rather than $\langle d, et \rangle$, and that the subject therefore starts low in the structure (Bhatt and Pancheva 2004). It also assumes that the measure-phrase position is occupied by a degree variable, d, which is then bound by a general-purpose existential closure operation (Heim 1982). What's notable about (106) is that it has extremely weak truth conditions: it just requires that Floyd have **some** degree of height. This is unusably uninformative. If this is all a positive adjective ever meant, no one would be able to use one.

But of course, there is another reading, one that is informative and will therefore always be preferred. That's associated with the different but homophonous structure that contains EVAL:

4.4 Neutralization and positive-entailingness

(107) ⟦ ∃ is d [EVAL [Floyd tall]] ⟧
 = ∃d[**tall**(d)(**Floyd**) ∧ d > **standard**(D)]

Unlike (107), this structure has a reasonable meaning: precisely that of the actual meaning of the positive form.

Things become more interesting still in the equative. Rett assumes an 'exactly' semantics, as in (108):

(108) ⟦ as ⟧ = λdλD$_{⟨d, t⟩}$. **max**(D) = d

This will turn out to be crucial. As for the positive form, a simple equative will have two structures, one with EVAL and one without:

(109) Floyd is as tall as Clyde.
 a. ⟦ [as as Clyde] ∅ λd$_1$ is d$_1$ [Floyd tall] ⟧
  = $\begin{bmatrix} \mathbf{max}(\lambda d_1 \,.\, \mathbf{tall}(d_1)(\mathbf{Floyd})) = \\ \mathbf{max}(\lambda d \,.\, \mathbf{tall}(d)(\mathbf{Clyde})) \end{bmatrix}$
 b. ⟦ [as as Clyde] ∅ λd$_1$ is d$_1$ EVAL [Floyd tall] ⟧
  = $\begin{bmatrix} \mathbf{max}(\lambda d_1 \,.\, \mathbf{tall}(d_1)(\mathbf{Floyd}) \wedge d_1 > \mathbf{standard}(D)) = \\ \mathbf{max}(\lambda d \,.\, \mathbf{tall}(d)(\mathbf{Clyde})) \end{bmatrix}$

The positive-entailing form in (109b) means the same thing as (109a), except that it adds the requirement that the maximal degree of Floyd's tallness is above the standard. This is simply a stronger version of (109a), so the form might as well not exist. Any use of it could equally well be taken as an instance of the weaker one. This seems a good result. It correctly predicts that equatives such as (109) aren't positive-entailing.

In equatives that involve negative adjectives, though, the picture changes. Those aren't neutralizing, as we've seen. Here's what the account predicts for these cases:

(110) Floyd is as short as Clyde.
 a. ⟦ [as as Clyde] ∅ λd$_1$ is d$_1$ [Floyd short] ⟧
  = $\begin{bmatrix} \mathbf{max}(\lambda d_1 \,.\, \mathbf{short}(d_1)(\mathbf{Floyd})) = \\ \mathbf{max}(\lambda d \,.\, \mathbf{short}(d)(\mathbf{Clyde})) \end{bmatrix}$
 b. ⟦ [as as Clyde] ∅ λd$_1$ is d$_1$ EVAL [Floyd short] ⟧
  = $\begin{bmatrix} \mathbf{max}(\lambda d_1 \,.\, \mathbf{short}(d_1)(\mathbf{Floyd}) \wedge d_1 > \mathbf{standard}(D)) = \\ \mathbf{max}(\lambda d \,.\, \mathbf{short}(d)(\mathbf{Clyde})) \end{bmatrix}$

The result is largely the same. However, there's an important fact to notice about the relationship between (110a) and (109a): they mean precisely the same thing. If Floyd and Clyde have the same maximal tallness, they also have the same maximal shortness. So the two neutral versions of the equative have identical truth conditions. This, Rett argues, is inherently an unstable situation: two adjectives with opposite polarity and yet precisely the same meaning in the same construction. Just as nature abhors a vacuum, language abhors losing its polarity distinctions. There is, she suggests, a general principle that makes us favor only one form in this case, and favor the unmarked – that is, positive – adjective in particular. This means that the only way to express the positive-entailing meaning is with the positive adjective, (109a). The only way the negative form could achieve any meaning other than what the positive form means is on the reading in (110b). And that is, in fact, its actual meaning.

For more on how these considerations interact with scale structure, and in particular the open- and closed-scale distinction, see Rett (2008b).

4.5 THE CROSSLINGUISTIC PICTURE

4.5.1 Measure phrases

In its classical form, the degree analysis takes as its starting point examples like (111), in which a positive adjective has a measure phrase.

(111)　Floyd is six feet tall.

But there is something deeply misleading about this, Schwarzschild (2005) points out. This construction is present in German and English – which perhaps accounts for its familiarity to semanticists – but otherwise the combination of a measure phrase and positive adjective isn't particularly crosslinguistically common. A more common state of affairs is to permit differential measure phrases in comparatives, but not with positive adjectives. This is the case in Russian (Matushansky 2002), Japanese (Snyder et al. 1995), and Spanish (Bosque 1999), for example. Even in languages that do permit measure phrases with positive adjectives, the choice of adjectives that permit it varies. English doesn't permit #*two tons heavy*, #*two kilometers far*, or #*35C hot*, Schwarzschild observes, but other languages do:

(112)　a.　quasi　due tonnellate　　　　　　　　　　　(Italian)
　　　　　　almost two tons

　　　　b.　twee kilometer ver　　　　　　　　　　　　(Dutch)
　　　　　　two　kilometer far

4.5 The crosslinguistic picture

    c. 35C heiss   (German)
       35C hot

Schwarzschild deals with the issue by treating positive adjectives in general as unable to take measure phrases, but allowing for certain lexical exceptions to be created by a rule that shifts their semantic type to one more closely resembling that of a comparative. This licenses positive-form measure phrases essentially by assimilating them to the ones in differential comparatives.

4.5.2 Comparison strategies

In his typological examination of comparatives, Stassen (1984, 1985, 2006) offered a characterization of variation in this area that formal semanticists have recently turned to as a kind of challenge. Perhaps unsurprisingly, comparatives of the type most familiar to Indo-European speakers are not especially common. These are what he terms PARTICLE COMPARATIVES because they use a specialized particle (like *than*) as a standard marker.

One of the main alternative possibilities is the CONJOINED COMPARATIVE (examples throughout this section are from Stassen 2006, with his citations):

(113)   AMELE (PAPUAN)
        jo   i   ben, jo   eu   nag
        house this big   house that small
        'This house is bigger than that house.'   (Roberts 1987: 135)

(114)   MENOMINI (ALGONQUIAN)
        Tata'hkes-ew, nenah teh kan
        strong-3SG   I   and not
        'He is stronger than me.'   (Bloomfield 1962: 506)

In one sense, this seems quite different from English comparatives. In another, it's reassuringly familiar. The semantics for the comparative we began with, the A-not-A analysis (to use Schwarzschild 2008's useful term), was as in (115):

(115) $[\![more]\!] = \lambda G_{\langle d, et\rangle} \lambda x \lambda y . \exists d[G(d)(y) \wedge \neg G(d)(x)]$

This has the shape of a conjoined comparative: two conjuncts with one negated. This denotation was not arrived at by reference to Menomini, of course, so the connection is striking. The underlying semantic structure that English obscures – and which can be glimpsed only with hard-won analytical insights – Menomini wears on its sleeve. One shouldn't get over-excited (one might grudgingly tell oneself). There is no overt degree morphology in such comparatives, and that alone constitutes a major difference and hints at a broader crosslinguistic question about the status of degrees, as we'll see in the next section. (For an explicit analysis of this kind of comparative, see Bochnak 2013a,b.)

Another strategy is the EXCEED COMPARATIVE, in which a verb like English 'exceed' is used:

(116) THAI
kǎw sǔuŋ kwaà kon túk kon
he tall exceed man each man
'He is taller than anyone.'   (Warotamasikkhadit 1972: 71)

This isn't reminiscent of any particular denotation for the comparative, but it is faintly echoed in English constructions like *His height exceeds everyone's*.

A third class of strategies are what Stassen calls LOCATIONAL COMPARATIVES. These involve the use of adpositions or case morphology to mark the standard of comparison. The preposition or case can be 'from' or 'out of' (which he calls 'separative'); 'to', 'for', or 'over' ('allative'); or 'in', 'at', or 'on' ('locative'):

(117) MUNDARI (AUSTRO-ASIATIC, MUNDA)
sadom-ete hati mananga-i
horse-from elephant big-3SG.PRES
'The elephant is bigger than the horse.'   (Hoffmann 1903: 110)

(118) MAASAI (NILO-SAHARAN, NILOTIC)
sapuk olkondi to lkibulekeny
big hartebeest to waterbuck
'The hartebeest is bigger than the waterbuck.'
(Tucker and Mpaayi 1955: 93)

4.5.3 How much degree is there in your degree constructions?

The view of degrees that has developed has them doing a lot of work. They are arguments. They can be bound, like pronouns, and in that guise occupy syntactic positions. They can be associated with operator movement of the relative-clause sort. They can be the referents of measure phrases, which name them just as proper names name individuals. They can be referred to with definite descriptions, too, in the form of comparative clauses. They can be quantified over by generalized quantifiers. They can power your hybrid vehicle and taste great in your breakfast cereal.

4.5 The crosslinguistic picture

In light of all this, Beck et al. (2004) – and a stream of research in a similar spirit – broached an interesting and deep theoretical question: can languages vary with respect to how they use degrees, and how **much** they use them? The consensus that seems to be forming is that they can and that they do.

The hypothesis space in this domain is vast: one can imagine various ways in which a language might fail to avail itself of all the available machinery, and various possibilities have been explored and refined. Beck et al.'s key idea about this, though, was as in (119):

(119) DEGREE ABSTRACTION PARAMETER
A language {does/does not} have binding of degree variables in the syntax.

Choosing the 'does not' option would mean that a language would not be able to form comparative clauses via lambda abstraction over degrees. Such a language would lack comparatives that can only be formed in this way.

One such case might be comparatives that operate across adjectives but on the same scale (subcomparatives; see section 4.2.2):

(120) The shelf is taller than $\emptyset$ λd_1 the door is d_1 wide.

This structure as written would of course be ruled out by (119). Beck et al. are especially interested in cases like these because they don't lend themselves to alternative analyses that attempt to work around using degree-binding. So if a language lacks (120), one might suspect it of having chosen the 'does not' option in (119). And indeed, Japanese seems to be just such a language:

(121) *Tana-wa [doa-ga   hiroi yori (mo)] (motto) takai
       shelf-TOP door-NOM wide yori (mo) (more) tall
       'The shelf is taller than the door is wide.'

Japanese doesn't permit direct measure phrases or degree questions (e.g. *how tall?*) either, just as one would expect in the absence of degree abstraction.

How might one get around such a restriction? One possibility is in terms of what Kennedy (2007, 2011) later called 'implicit' and 'explicit' comparison. English can make use of both of these styles:

(122) a. *explicit:* Floyd is taller than Clyde.
      b. *implicit:* Compared to Clyde, Floyd is tall.

In the implicit case, the *compared to Clyde* clause doesn't seem to be overtly manipulating degrees. There is no hint of degree of morphology anywhere to be found. Rather, what this sentence seems to do is modify the context by changing the comparison class in a particular way. So this is another strategy of comparison: using contextual tools. Beck et al. proposed that Japanese favors this approach.

There is another way an expression that provides the standard of comparison might fail to make use of degrees, one we have already encountered. The chapter began with a comparative morpheme specialized for phrasal comparatives like *than Clyde* rather than clausal ones. On that view, the phrasal comparative simply denoted an individual, which the comparative morpheme took as an argument:

(123) a. $[\![more]\!] = \lambda G_{\langle d, et\rangle} \lambda x \lambda y . \exists d[G(d)(y) \wedge \neg G(d)(x)]$
       b. $[\![more]\!]([\![tall]\!])([\![than\ Clyde]\!])$
       $= \lambda y . \exists d[\textbf{tall}(d)(y) \wedge \neg \textbf{tall}(d)(\textbf{Clyde})]$

Perhaps this wasn't the right analysis for English – though this is hardly self-evident – but it could still very well be the right analysis for other languages. Bhatt and Takahashi (2007, 2011) pursue exactly this possibility. Following Heim (1985), they refer to comparative denotations like (123a) – which take as arguments a gradable predicate and two compared individuals – as the DIRECT ANALYSIS of comparatives. A language that runs its comparative this way would have less use for degrees than English does. Even so, such a language need not go so far as to commit itself to a negative setting for the Degree Abstraction Parameter.

There is in this discussion an unmistakeable echo of another one: the discussion over whether to adopt an inherent-vagueness or degree-based approach to gradability (see section 3.6). One way of viewing the current issue is in these terms. It might be that the choice between these options should not be made once and for all on behalf of language in general. Instead, perhaps some languages favor strategies that look more degree-based, and others favor ones that look more like inherent vagueness, and others still some combination of the two.

This discussion continues in a very lively vein, and even the correct characterization of Japanese is in dispute (Shimoyama 2011a, 2012 provides a bracing reassessment). Further work on the status of degrees and degree constructions across languages includes Xiang (2003, 2005), Pancheva (2006, 2010), Tanaka (2006), Kennedy (2007a), Lin (2007), McCready and Ogata (2007), Krasikova (2008a), Oda (2008), Aihara (2009), Merchant (2009, forthcoming), Sawada (2010), Pancheva and Tomaszewicz (2011), van Rooij (2011a), Sawada and Grano (2011), Yoon

4.7 Suggestions for further reading 191

(2011), Alrenga et al. (2012), Bochnak (2013a,b), Matsui and Kubota (2012), Sawada (2011), Beltrama and Bochnak (forthcoming).

4.6 QUESTIONS FOR FURTHER REFLECTION AND DISCUSSION

- Which is preferable, the small or big DegP? What kinds of considerations might bear on this question? Superficially, it's a syntactic one, but of course the choice affects the semantics. For that reason, one could make either syntactic or semantic arguments in either direction.
- What should we conclude about the scope properties of degree quantifiers? Whatever it is, might this also tell us something about the expressions they do and don't scope with respect to? How might an approach on which adjectives denote measure functions be modified or further developed to accommodate the facts? On the other hand, how could a theory that predicts many scope interactions be constrained to block nonexistent ones?
- What might the semantics of degree constructions – including their scope properties and their interaction with various kinds of measure phrases – reveal about the ontology of degrees? If degrees support some notion of subtraction (in differential comparatives) and perhaps even multiplication (in factor phrases), what is the range of operations available?
- What do the typological facts reveal about degree constructions? What analytical moves would be necessary to explain the different grammatical strategies languages use? And what should a theory of crosslinguistic variation in this domain look like? Should it have parameters, choices a language has to make once and for all? If so, what is the theoretical status of these parameters? That is, how are they represented in the grammar?

4.7 SUGGESTIONS FOR FURTHER READING

Good entry points into the literature cited in this chapter include the following:

- The usefulness of exploring Bolinger (1972); Klein (1980, 1982); von Stechow (1984), and Kennedy (1997) has not diminished since the previous chapter.

- For more on the scope of comparatives, consult Heim (2000). Some of that work responds to points made in Kennedy (1997), so looking at that work can be helpful in this respect, too. The more recent work cited in the text is a natural next step.
- For the syntax of comparatives, Bhatt and Pancheva (2004) provide a highly semantically informed analysis. Classical work in the area includes Bresnan (1973, 1975).
- For superlatives, a pivotal work was Szabolcsi (1986). For most of the degree constructions discussed here, though, the reader will now be equipped to move directly to the work cited in the course of the discussion without too much difficulty.
- The work mentioned in the discussion of the crosslinguistic picture will also be accessible, but Beck et al. (2004) makes for a natural beginning for that journey.

5 Adverbs

5.1 INTRODUCTION

If adverbs were sentient, we might pity them. Sometimes, they are treated as nothing more than adjectives crudely tarted up with some minor ornamental morphology. At other times, they are treated as the 'wastebasket category', because 'adverb' is what you call a word when you've run out of other names to call it. All sorts of stray mystery particles have been described as adverbs, for the most tenuous of reasons or for no particular reason at all. Worse still, the term is often taken to include not just a motley assortment of scarcely related lexical riffraff but also whole phrases without regard to their syntactic category. Loiter around the peripheries of a clause for too long, and you too might be accused of being an adverb.

To be mistreated unjustly is bad. It's worse when it's precisely what you deserve. The prototypical exemplars of adverbs are genuinely very adjective-like, and languages don't always bother to make the distinction. And these expressions really do seem alarmingly and confoundingly promiscuous in their distribution. Even so, whatever their internal properties, the question of how they fit into the semantics of larger expressions is interesting. Equally interesting is what about their semantics accounts for their versatility. Adverbs in this more restricted sense – adjective-like things in non-adjective-like positions – will be the focus of this chapter. For the most part, modifiers of other categories will enter the discussion only to the extent that their semantic contribution resembles that of adverbs proper. More generally, I will observe a distinction between 'adverb', the name of a syntactic category, and 'adverbial', the collective term for phrases headed by adverbs and for phrasal modifiers of verbal projections and clauses.

Part of the focus on adverbs in the more restricted sense is practical. Discussing adverbials as a class would entail discussing virtually all of formal semantics. There's hardly any area of the field that hasn't been concerned to a large extent with some class of adverbials in one way or another, and in certain areas – such as temporal semantics – the analysis of adverbials constitutes much of the enterprise. Unavoidably, though, I'll briefly touch on some adverbials whose serious examination is best undertaken by looking elsewhere (say, a book on temporal semantics). Many issues that fall under the broad rubric of 'adverbials' will also be taken up in Chapter 6 as instances of crosscategorial phenomena.

As for this chapter, section 5.2 considers how some taxonomical organization can be imposed on the chaos of adverbs. Section 5.3 then takes the first steps toward an analysis, wrestling with basic compositional questions. Section 5.4 examines two classes of adverbs (manner and subject-oriented) in more detail. Section 5.5 turns to adverbs that occur higher in the clause. Section 5.6 introduces some facts and tools relevant to locative adverbials. Section 5.7 turns to the ill-understood phenomenon of adverbs as modifiers of adjectival projections. Section 5.8 mostly just sets aside temporal and quantificational adverbials. Section 5.9 concludes by revisiting the question of the relative order of adverbs.

5.2 CLASSIFYING ADVERBIALS

One of the odder properties of adverbs is that their interpretation seems to change radically with their syntactic position. In (1), for example, each instance of *happily* contributes something different to the sentence (this is a version of a sentence in Jackendoff 1972):

(1) Happily, Floyd would happily play the tuba happily.

This could be paraphrased as 'it is fortunate that Floyd would be happy to play the tuba in a happy way'. This raises a number of puzzles. Just what are all these readings, precisely? How should they be represented? How do they come about compositionally? Is it the same lexical item in each instance? If so, what gives rise to the distinct readings?

Adverbs in general are a notoriously heterogeneous class – even when you set aside non-adverb adverbials – so a natural way to begin is to divide the problem by organizing adverbs into more tractable natural classes.

A number of general classification schemes for adverbs have been proposed. Many of the finer-grained ones are due in large measure to syntacticians (Bellert 1977; Cinque 1999; Ernst 2002; see Delfitto 2007 for a summary). Semanticists have usually focused on slightly different distinctions and, perhaps in part because of that, for the most part wound

5.2 Classifying adverbials

up with fewer categories (Bonami et al. 2004 is a general overview). In broad terms, we'll follow a version of the classification found in Ernst (2002)'s magisterial volume on syntax of adjuncts, which is in many respects quite semantically oriented, but the basic distinctions we'll need to get off the ground were present in some form even in Jackendoff (1972). Ernst's first distinction is between PREDICATIONAL ADVERBS and others. All the adverbs in (1) are predicational. Ernst summarizes their properties this way:

- They are (or are related to) gradable predicates.
- In English, they almost always end in *-ly*.
- They typically don't quantify over individuals or events (modal quantificational adverbs such as *probably* and *certainly* do belong in this class).

This excludes quantificational adverbs like *always* and *frequently*, domain adverbs like *mathematically*, focus particles like *only*, and adverbials that do things like introduce new participants to an event (*for Floyd, with a knife*). Expressions like *almost* are among the many grammatical particles sometimes referred to as adverbs, perhaps unhelpfully, but they certainly wouldn't be predicational either (see section 6.4).

The predicational adverbs can be further divided into at least three classes. We'll discuss each class, but a preview might be helpful:

- The class of EVENT ADVERBIALS includes MANNER ADVERBIALS, which characterize the manner in which an event took place (such as *softly* or *tightly*). It also includes certain temporal or locative adverbials. RESULTATIVE ADVERBS such as *fatally* (in *wounded fatally*) or *coarsely* (in *chop coarsely*; Parsons 1990) might or might not be a species of manner adverb (Geuder 2000; Bonami et al. 2004).
- SUBJECT-ORIENTED ADVERBS are sensitive to properties of the subject and give rise to entailments involving it. The class includes *accidentally*, *deliberately*, and *unwillingly*. Many manner adverbs, such as *foolishly*, *cleverly*, and *rudely*, have subject-oriented readings as well.[1] Within this class, Ernst (along with Geuder 2000) distinguishes between mental-attitude adverbs (*reluctantly*, *calmly*, *willingly*, *anxiously*) and agent-oriented ones (*cleverly*, *stupidly*, *wisely*, *rudely*).

---

[1] The two readings can be distinguished by position:
(i)   a.   SUBJECT-ORIENTED: Foolishly, the senator has been talking to reporters.
(Ernst 2002)
        b.   MANNER: The senator has been talking foolishly to reporters.

- SPEAKER-ORIENTED ADVERBIALS are more heterogeneous. They include EVALUATIVE ADVERBS, which express the attitude of the speaker toward a proposition (*amazingly, surprisingly, unfortunately*); SPEECH-ACT ADVERBS, which characterize the speech act itself (*frankly, honestly, briefly, confidentially*); and EPISTEMIC ADVERBS, which include various gradable modal adverbs (*probably, certainly, clearly*).

Naturally, this brief and informal characterization is a bit fuzzy at the margins, but it serves as a reasonable first approximation.

Speaker-oriented adverbials are also often characterized syntactically as SENTENCE ADVERBIALS, on the grounds that they attach to a sentence rather than a VP. This is a convenient term, but it may have become less enlightening over the years. The main difficulty is that it presupposes a syntactic analysis rather than providing a pretheoretical description. This means that subject-oriented adverbials may be construed as sentence adverbials or VP adverbials, depending on one's analysis. Worse, if one has a more refined view of verbal and clausal projections in which there are more than two attachment sites, 'sentence' and 'VP' are – at best – crude proxies for 'high attachment' and 'low attachment'. Indeed, the latter two are probably more useful terms, because they don't give the impression of being anything other than vague.

It's worth noting some features of other classification systems. Some authors distinguish a category of FRAMING or FRAME(-SETTTING) ADVERBIALS, a useful term for adverbials that occur very high in the clause (in English and German, on the left) and specify the general circumstances – especially spaciotemporal circumstances – with respect to which the clause should be evaluated (Maienborn 2001 provides an especially thorough semantic characterization, though the term itself is older):

(2) a. <u>In Japan</u>, the elderly don't seem to be disposable.
     b. <u>In the Middle Ages</u>, sadism and dentistry weren't easily distinguished.
     c. <u>In linguistics</u>, one must choose between disappointment and delusion.

Their precise status and how one might subdivide this class is, as for the others, a matter of discussion. In this case, one can understand the issue as one of properly characterizing the notion of 'frame-setting'.

The cartographic tradition in syntax – concerned with creating fine-grained structural maps of constructions – has arrived at a correspondingly fine-grained inventory of adverbs. Cinque (1999) is the most

5.3 The compositional puzzle

comprehensive undertaking of this sort, which carefully teases out many crosslinguistic distributional differences – especially correlations between adverbs and functional morphemes with which they co-occur – to arrive at the inventory in (3). Each adverb class is labeled with the label of a corresponding functional head, given here in descending order:

(3) speech-act: *frankly*; evaluative: *fortunately*; evidential: *allegedly*; epistemic: *probably*; past: *once*; future: *then*; irrealis: *perhaps*; necessity: *necessarily*; possibility: *possibly*; habitual: *usually*; repetitive I: *again*; frequentative I: *often*; volitional: *intentionally*; celerative I: *quickly*; anterior: *already*; terminative: *no longer*; continuative: *still*; perfect: *always*; retrospective: *just*; proximative: *soon*; durative: *briefly*; generic/progressive: *characteristically*; prospective: *almost*; singular completive I: *completely*; plural completive: *tutto* (Italian); voice: *well*; celerative II: *fast, early*; repetitive II: *again*; frequentative II: *often*; singular completive II: *completely*

It's easy – too easy – to point out that this inventory is huge and may therefore fail to distill broader generalizations about adverb order or classification. But this kind of detailed crosslinguistic description is a natural first step toward distilling such broader generalizations. It's important too that these names, arrived at on syntactic grounds, should sound so inherently semantic: it suggests that these are semantic as much as syntactic generalizations. The observation of a correlation between adverbs and functional heads with a similar meaning is obviously semantically important as well.

5.3 THE COMPOSITIONAL PUZZLE

5.3.1 Modifiers of propositions?

In Chapter 2, we traced developments in thinking about adjectives from the early idea that they were generally PREDICATE MODIFIERS (functions that apply to and yield the same type), to a later consensus that more and more of them were actually INTERSECTIVE (properties that combine with other properties via conjunction). Thinking about the semantics of adverbs in some respects paralleled that, though the connection is not generally made. Indeed, one might have imagined that adjectives and adverbs would have been a common joint object of study, but as it turns out, the two are usually treated independently, though there are exceptions (e.g., work like Geuder 2000 and Schäfer 2005, which explicitly examine adjectives and adverbs in light of each other).

Early on, the most common approach was a variant of the predicate-modifier one. It treated adverbs as functions from propositions to propositions.[2] This idea, advanced by Clark (1970), Montague (1970), Parsons (1972), Cresswell (1973, 1974), is simply a generalization of another, better established idea: that modal adverbs like *necessarily* and *possibly* are of this type.

Here's how that works. The first step is to construe modals, classically, as quantifiers over worlds. *Necessarily* requires that the proposition it applies to be true in all relevant worlds, and *possibly* that it be true in some relevant worlds. In order to represent the contribution of such expressions, we will of course need to adopt an intensional system. That makes it possible to define *necessarily* and *possibly* as in (4), where R is an appropriate contextually provided accessibility relation (which I've represented as a contextually supplied function that provides a set of worlds accessible from the evaluation world; this may include worlds compatible with what is known, for example, or worlds compatible with what is required):

(4) a. $[\![\,necessarily_R\,]\!] = \lambda p_{\langle s,t \rangle} \lambda w \, . \, \forall w' \in R(w)[p(w')]$
     b. $[\![\,possibly_R\,]\!] = \lambda p_{\langle s,t \rangle} \lambda w \, . \, \exists w' \in R(w)[p(w')]$

This gives rise to interpretations like (5) ($\mathbf{died}_w(x)$ means x died in w):

(5) a. Possibly$_R$, Floyd died.
     b. $[\![\,Floyd\ died\,]\!] = \lambda w \, . \, \mathbf{died}_w(\mathbf{Floyd})$
     c. $[\![\,Possibly_R,\ Floyd\ died\,]\!] = [\![\,possibly_R\,]\!] \, ([\![\,Floyd\ died\,]\!])$
         $= \lambda w \, . \, \exists w' \in R(w)[\mathbf{died}_w(\mathbf{Floyd})]$

So (5) is true iff there is a world accessible from the evaluation world – say, one compatible with the known facts in the evaluation world – in which Floyd died.

This is all relatively straightforward, but one would like to extend it to other adverbs. Should we treat a manner adverb like *quietly*, for example, in a similar way? If by 'in a similar way' one means 'using the

---

[2] That's not so different from treating them as modifiers of predicates. It's typical to think of propositions as predicates of possible worlds: the proposition $[\![\,Floyd\ fell\,]\!]$ holds of any world in which Floyd fell. More precisely, if we define 'predicate modifier' as simply anything of type $\langle \tau, \tau \rangle$ for any predicate type τ, propositional operators qualify because they are type $\langle st, st \rangle$ (where s is the type of worlds).

5.3 The compositional puzzle

same type', then the answer is probably not. The idea that adverbs in general – rather than just in some specific cases – apply to propositions has been largely set aside. One reason can be perceived intuitively. It makes sense to have *possibly* combine with a proposition because we know precisely what it means for a proposition to be possible. But *quietly*? What would it mean for a proposition to be quiet? Something seems awry in this. Although the question isn't unanswerable in principle, any answer would swim against the tide of our intuitions. It certainly doesn't bring us any closer to a treatment in which it's a property, which is what would be necessary to achieve a parallel with adjectives. Still, on their own, these are just general conceptual observations, not arguments. It's possible to make the case much more explicitly, as we'll see in the next section.

5.3.2 Subject-oriented adverbs and the predicate-modifier approach

Precisely such an explicit case against treating adverbs as functions from propositions to propositions was made by Thomason and Stalnaker (1973). The empirical foundation of the argument is the behavior of subject-oriented adverbs like *intentionally*:

(6)   Floyd intentionally killed Clyde.

Pursuing the analogy to *necessarily*, the natural thing would be to have *intentionally* combine with the whole sentence *Floyd killed Clyde*. But Thomason and Stalnaker notice a subtle asymmetry in how *intentionally* affects subjects and objects that militates against this view.

The key notion in this asymmetry is the DE RE/DE DICTO ambiguity, which we've already encountered in in Chapter 4. A simple case is in (7), which involves the investment banking firm Morgan Stanley:

(7)   Floyd thinks the chairman of Morgan Stanley is a jerk.

Floyd may think (7) by virtue of his opinions about investment bankers, even though he's never met the chairman of Morgan Stanley. He may subsequently unknowingly meet this person, who has been introduced to him only by his name, which we'll suppose is R. Clyde Weaselraptor. Floyd may find him not at all a jerk. Given that the name *R. Clyde Weaselraptor* and the definite description *the chairman of Morgan Stanley* refer to the same individual, it should be possible to substitute one for the other and wind up with a sentence true under precisely the same circumstances. But not so:

(8)   Floyd thinks R. Clyde Weaselraptor is a jerk.

This, of course, is false. This failure of substitutability is called REFER-ENTIAL OPACITY. The problem is that (7) is ambiguous between two readings, which could be represented as in (9) (notational assumptions: @ is the actual world; **belief**$_@$**(Floyd)** is the worlds compatible with Floyd's beliefs in @; **the** applies to a property and yields the only individual that satisfies it):

(9)   a. *de dicto*:
$$\forall w \in \mathbf{belief}_@(\mathbf{Floyd})[\,\mathbf{jerk}_w(\mathbf{the}(\mathbf{chairman\text{-}of\text{-}MS}_w))\,]$$
     b. *de re*:
$$\forall w \in \mathbf{belief}_@(\mathbf{Floyd})[\,\mathbf{jerk}_w(\mathbf{the}(\mathbf{chairman\text{-}of\text{-}MS}_@))\,]$$

The *de dicto* (Latin for 'from what is said') reading is about whoever the chairman is in the worlds compatible with what Floyd believes. That's why **chairman-of-MS** is subscripted with w, the bound variable associated with Floyd's belief worlds. The *de re* ('about the thing') reading is about the person who is the chairman in the **actual** world, R. Clyde Weaselraptor. It's this latter belief that is expressed in (8) – where **the-chairman-of-MS** is subscripted with the actual world, @ – and it's the one Floyd doesn't hold.

This turns out to be relevant to adverbs. It's a signature property of intensional operators that they create such referentially opaque contexts. Thomason and Stalnaker observe that *intentionally* does do this, but only with respect to the object. They provide an example that is to be interpreted against the background of *Oedipus Rex*, the plot of which revolves around failure to recognize one's parents:

(10)   Oedipus intentionally married Jocasta.
            Jocasta is Oedipus' mother.
            ―――――――――――――――――――
            therefore: Oedipus intentionally married his mother.   **(invalid)**

This is, of course, not a valid inference, despite the fact that the name *Jocasta* and the definite description *his mother* refer to the same person in the actual world. Oedipus was confused about Jocasta's identity, so it's perfectly reasonable for him to have intended to marry her but not to marry his mother. Yet in the subject position, things work differently:

(11)   Oedipus intentionally married Jocasta.
            Oedipus is the son of Laius.
            ―――――――――――――――――――
            therefore: The son of Laius intentionally married Jocasta.   **(valid)**

One might have expected a similar failure of substitutability.

5.3 The compositional puzzle

Thomason and Stalnaker conclude from this that *intentionally* must be inherently intensional, but that it must apply not to the whole sentence but only to the VP, as in (12):

(12) $[\![intentionally]\!] = \lambda P_{\langle e, st \rangle} \lambda x \,.\, \mathbf{intentionally}(P)(x)$

It therefore leaves the subject out of its scope and so out of the opaque context it creates. The two readings of (13a) can be represented as (13b) and (13c):

(13) Oedipus intentionally married his mother.
  a. *de dicto*:
  $\mathbf{intentionally}(\lambda x \lambda w \,.\, \mathbf{married}_w(\mathrm{his}(\mathrm{mother}_w))(x))(\mathrm{Oedipus})$
  b. *de re*:
  $\mathbf{intentionally}(\lambda x \lambda w \,.\, \mathbf{married}_w(\mathrm{his}(\mathrm{mother}_@))(x))$
  (Oedipus)

And, of course, it's on the *de dicto* reading that the inference fails.

This is a first step toward a theory of subject-oriented adverbials. But what does this tell us about ordinary manner adverbs like *quietly*? Well, at the very least, it suggests that it may apply to a VP meaning rather than a proposition. It might also lead us to expect that it's intensional, like *intentionally*. As it turns out, though, it doesn't create opaque contexts:

(14) Oedipus quietly married Jocasta.
  Jocasta is Oedipus' mother.
  _____
  therefore: Oedipus quietly married his mother. **(valid)**

In this respect, *quietly* doesn't seem to be intensional. Perhaps that's to be expected. It's natural enough to think of *intentionally* as quantifying, say, over worlds compatible with Oedipus' intentions. But what worlds would be quantified over by *quietly*?

So we've seen good evidence that at least some adverbs should be treated as applying to properties rather than propositions. The argument was based on a fact about intensionality. Yet that same argument can't be made in the case of manner adverbs like *quietly*. That suggests an important difference. To interpret such adverbs, we need to explore a different strategy.

5.3.3 Problems for the intersective approach

One reason intensionality matters here is the parallel to adjectives. Many adjectives are intersective and denote simple properties rather than predicate modifiers. This approach isn't available, though, for intensional adjectives. *Alleged*, for example, needs to apply to the noun it combines with, because we can't think of *alleged burglar* as simply the intersection of people who are alleged and burglars (see Chapter 2 for extensive discussion). It seems reasonable to suppose that the adjectival and adverbial domains are similar to each other, and so that some adverbs have intersective interpretations. Pairs such as *quiet* and *quietly* cry out for a parallel analysis. If manner adverbs are crucially intensional, though, we can't treat them as intersective – and if they aren't, perhaps we can.

The previous section revealed that indeed *quietly* doesn't behave as though it's intensional, so let's try to do things intersectively:

(15) a. $[\![$ *quietly married Jocasta* $]\!]$
      $= \lambda x . [\![$ *quietly* $]\!] (x) \wedge [\![$ *marry Jocasta* $]\!] (x)$
   b. $[\![$ *Oedipus quietly married Jocasta* $]\!]$
      $= [\![$ *quietly* $]\!] (\mathbf{Oedipus}) \wedge [\![$ *marry Jocasta* $]\!] (\mathbf{Oedipus})$

The combinatorics work, but the result is wrong. This would require Oedipus to be quiet, not the marriage. Even if the intensionality facts point in the right direction, it seems we still can't pull off an intersective interpretation.

There is another problem with an intersective approach. To appreciate it, it helps to consider adjectives first. Suppose we live in a world in which all linguists are professors, and all professors are linguists. This would mean that, in this world, *linguist* and *professor* have the same extension: they pick out precisely the same people. Staying in this world, then, (16a) and (16b) have the same truth conditions, as do (17a) and (17b):

(16) a. I met a linguist.
      b. I met a professor.

(17) a. I met a friendly linguist.
      b. I met a friendly professor.

Because *friendly* in (17) is interpreted intersectively, it can't do anything to block this effect. This seems to accord with intuitions about this (admittedly bizarre) scenario.

In light of that, let's return to adverbs. This time, we'll suppose that we live in a world in which everyone who ran also juggled and vice versa. In this world, *juggled* and *ran* have the same extension. Now (18a) and (18b) should mean the same thing, as should (19a) and (19b):

5.3 The compositional puzzle

(18)   a. Floyd juggled.
        b. Floyd ran.

(19)   a. Floyd juggled quickly.
        b. Floyd ran quickly.

The judgment about (18) is that the sentences do indeed have the same truth conditions. But something odd happens in (19). If *quickly* were interpreted intersectively, these sentences should mean precisely the same thing, but in fact, they don't. Even in this bizarre world, they don't entail each other.[3]

This argument, modeled on McConnell-Ginet (1982) and Larson (1999), seems to suggest that *quickly* isn't intersective. Perhaps it even suggests that *quickly* must be intensional after all, contrary to the result in the previous section. The sentences in (19) might fail to entail each other in the relevantly weird world because the adverb applies to intensions of the verbs, and those differ even when their extensions are the same.

There are now two reasons to conclude manner adverbs aren't intersective. Yet there is another argument that points in precisely the opposite direction. Again, the first step is to consider adjectives. A sequence of intersective adjectives gives rise to the DIAMOND ENTAILMENT PATTERN illustrated in (20), where the arrows indicate entailment:

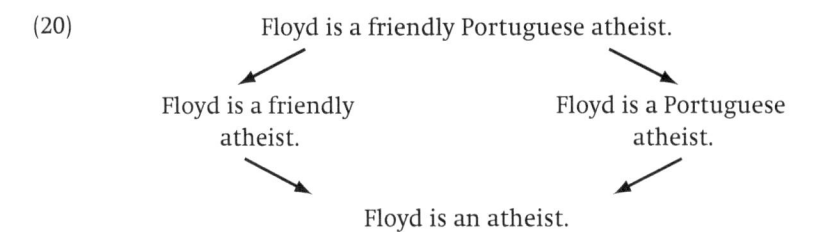

(20)   Floyd is a friendly Portuguese atheist.
        ↙   ↘
Floyd is a friendly   Floyd is a Portuguese
     atheist.   atheist.
        ↘   ↙
                  Floyd is an atheist.

If the original sentence is true, dropping – that is, omitting – any of the adjectives will also result in a true sentence. Intersective adjectives are DROPPABLE in this way.[4]

---

[3] I've cheated slightly in replacing our previous example, *quietly*, with *quickly* to make the judgment a little easier. With a bit of contemplation, though, *quietly* should work the same way.

[4] The term seems to be due to Wyner (1994). On this definition, intersective modifiers aren't actually droppable in downward-entailing contexts. *No one is a Portuguese atheist*, for example, doesn't entail *No one is an atheist*.

Many adverbs give rise to the same pattern of entailments:[5]

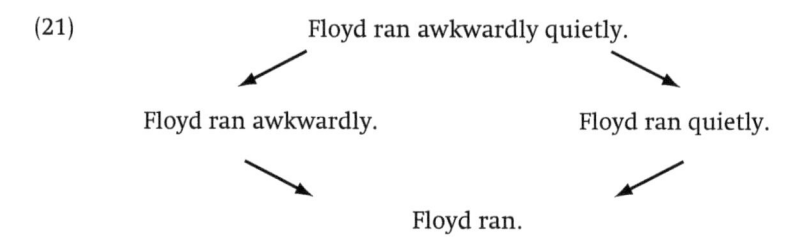

(21) Floyd ran awkwardly quietly.

Floyd ran awkwardly.   Floyd ran quietly.

Floyd ran.

This is the same pattern, of course. As it turns out, in the right semantic environments, all intersective modifiers behave this way. It's precisely what we'd expect to happen with an interpretation framed in terms of conjunction, because this is precisely how conjunction behaves. One can verify this by dropping conjuncts from *Floyd knows Norwegian and Quechua and Dutch*.

So we now have two reasons to think manner adverbs aren't intersective and one reason to think they are. There is reason to think that they aren't intensional, and reason to think that they are. It's therefore also not clear whether to treat them as predicate modifiers either. This is a real quandary.

5.3.4 Davidsonian events: the intersective approach redeemed

A lovely solution to all this emerges from Davidson (1967). He shows that in fact, manner adverbs – and many others – should in fact be analyzed intersectively. Perhaps surprisingly, the key is not to adjust our compositional assumptions, but rather our ontological ones.[6] To make his case, Davidson often uses adverbial PPs rather than adverbs, and I'll follow him in this. The crucial conclusions generally carry over to manner adverbs.

For mysterious reasons, Davidson begins by reporting that someone seems to have perpetrated an inexplicably illicit act of clandestine buttering:

(22) Jones buttered the toast in the bathroom with the knife at midnight.

---

[5] Adjacent adverbs that end in *-ly* tend to sound odd. That's not relevant here. This can be fixed by moving one adverb into a medial position (*awkwardly ran quietly*).

[6] This is reminiscent of the way compositional questions shed light on the ontology of degrees (see Chapter 4).

5.3 The compositional puzzle

In their indictment, prosecutors from the Ministry of Baked Good Enforcement might later allege of Jones' infraction that it had the following properties:

(23) a. It was done with the knife.
      b. It was done at midnight.
      c. It was done in the bathroom.

The pronouns especially are worth noticing. They refer to what Jones did, whatever it was. What such pronouns refer to, Davidson proposed, is EVENTS. Events are objects in the model just as individuals or times or degrees are. Reasons for thinking so include that we can refer to them (*John's buttering the toast*), that pronouns can refer back to them (as *it* does in (23)), and – most important in the current context – that we can ascribe properties to them. That's what the prosecutors do in making the allegations in (23): they ascribe properties to John's buttering event. (See Parsons 1990 for further argumentation and discussion.)

Davidson argues that this is the crux of what adverbials do, too. The way to interpret a sentence like (22) is by predicating each adverbial not of an individual or even of a property, but rather of an event. The meaning should be rendered as in (24):

(24) $\left[\!\!\left[\begin{array}{l} \textit{Jones buttered the toast in the bathroom with the knife} \\ \textit{at midnight.} \end{array} \right]\!\!\right]$

$= \exists e \left[\begin{array}{l} \textbf{buttered}(\textbf{the-toast})(\textbf{Jones})(e) \wedge \\ \textbf{in}(\textbf{the-bathroom})(e) \wedge \textbf{with}(\textbf{the-knife})(e) \wedge \\ \textbf{at-midnight}(e) \end{array} \right]$

Because it's framed in terms of conjunction, this instantly explains the diamond entailment pattern:

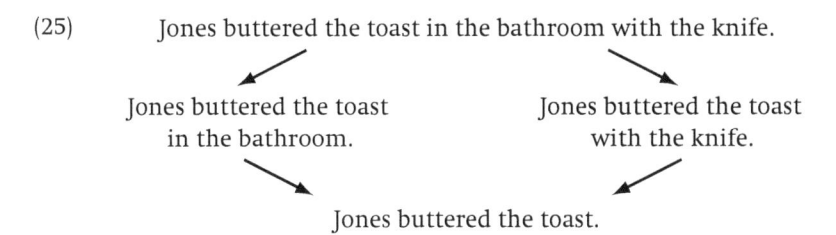

(25)   Jones buttered the toast in the bathroom with the knife.

   Jones buttered the toast   Jones buttered the toast
      in the bathroom.   with the knife.

                  Jones buttered the toast.

Each conjunct in the denotation of the sentence can be dropped without rendering it false, and for this reason the adverbials in (25) are droppable too.

The denotations of the individual adverbials are straightforward ($e, e', \ldots$ are variables over events):

(26) a. $[\![\textit{in the bathroom}]\!] = \lambda e \,.\, \mathbf{in}(\text{the-bathroom})(e)$
      b. $[\![\textit{with the knife}]\!] = \lambda e \,.\, \mathbf{with}(\text{the-knife})(e)$

Manner adverbs can receive the same treatment:

(27) $[\![\textit{quietly}]\!] = \lambda e \,.\, \mathbf{quiet}(e)$

This is strikingly elegant. It's simple, of course, but it also perfectly parallels the denotation of the adjective *quiet*:

(28) $[\![\textit{quiet}]\!] = \lambda x \,.\, \mathbf{quiet}(x)$

That seems as it should be, given the close relation between the two.

Before getting too excited, one should verify that the bits come together compositionally. To achieve this, the verb will need an event argument as well:

(29) $[\![\textit{buttered}]\!] = \lambda x \lambda y \lambda e \,.\, \mathbf{buttered}(x)(y)(e)$

The types fit as in (30), where v is the type of events:[7]

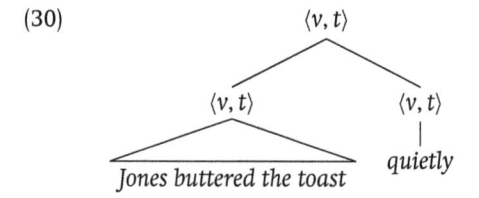

(30)
```
                    ⟨v, t⟩
                   /      \
              ⟨v, t⟩       ⟨v, t⟩
             /      \         |
                            quietly
       Jones buttered the toast
```

At this point, these can combine intersectively by Predicate Modification, which now has to be generalized to include properties of events:

(31) PREDICATE MODIFICATION (GENERALIZED TO EVENTS)

If a branching node α has as its daughters β and γ, and $[\![\beta]\!]$ and $[\![\gamma]\!]$ are either both of type $\langle e, t \rangle$ or both of type $\langle v, t \rangle$, then $[\![\alpha]\!] = \lambda X \,.\, [\![\beta]\!](X) \land [\![\gamma]\!](X)$, where X is an individual or an event (whichever would be defined).

---

[7] The type of events is often – indeed, probably more often – represented as s, but this can be confusing because this is also used as the type of possible worlds.

5.3 The compositional puzzle

Thus:

(32)   a. $[\![quietly]\!] = \lambda e \,.\, \mathbf{quiet}(e)$
         b. $[\![Jones\ buttered\ the\ toast]\!]$
             $= \lambda e \,.\, \mathbf{buttered}(\text{the-toast})(\text{Jones})(e)$
         c. $[\![Jones\ buttered\ the\ toast\ quietly]\!]$
             $= \lambda e \,.\, \mathbf{buttered}(\text{the-toast})(\text{Jones})(e) \wedge \mathbf{quiet}(e)$

The result is a property of events, which doesn't seem a reasonable sentence meaning. What we really want the sentence to say is that there was an event that has this property – that is, we want to introduce existential quantification over events:

(33) $\exists e[\mathbf{buttered}(\text{the-toast})(\text{Jones})(e) \wedge \mathbf{quiet}(e)]$

One way to do this is to assume that there is an existential closure operation (Heim 1982) that automatically quantifies-off any free event arguments. A more sophisticated option, advanced in Kratzer (1998), involves attributing the existential quantifier to a particular node in the tree. She suggests it's the aspect morpheme that's responsible (which in this case is not expressed independently). Either way, the right denotation results.

What about our earlier objections to doing things intersectively? Well, one of them relied on the assumption that *quietly* would denote a property of individuals. If it had, interpreting the sentence intersectively would entail that Jones is quiet, not his buttering. But it doesn't.

The other objection is more complicated. The scenario was one in which everyone who ran juggled and vice versa. The problem was that this would mean *run* and *juggle* mean the same thing, and therefore *ran quickly* and *juggled quickly* should mean the same thing. As it turns out, though, the problem is again about framing denotations only in terms of individuals. An event analysis requires looking at things a different way. It might well be that everyone who ran juggled and vice versa, but this doesn't make the **events** of running and juggling the same. On a Davidsonian view, it would have to be both the runner-jugglers **and** the events that are identical to bring about the problem. In fact, there is now no reason to think that *quickly* is intensional. The worries have been dispelled without requiring an intensional system.

Everything has fallen beautifully into place. The simple Davidsonian move easily resolved the confusion and conflicting evidence that had plagued us in section 5.3.3. It provided an elegant intersective way of interpreting adverbs, assigned them denotations that mirror those of their adjectival counterparts, delivered a simpler semantics overall, and allowed us to avoid having to posit an intensional denotation in the face of evidence against it. Not a bad result for something that began with forbidden toast.

5.4 MANNER AND SUBJECT ORIENTATION

5.4.1 Augmentation and passive-sensitivity

So far, we've encountered a theory of manner adverbs based on events, and a theory of subject-oriented adverbs based on intensionality. One might wonder whether one can be assimilated to the other. It would be challenging, because the two classes of adverbs do seem to differ in nontrivial ways. But the alternative doesn't seem ideal: assuming that subject-oriented and manner adverbs have distinct homophonous lexical entries. This certainly wouldn't be catastrophic – perhaps there is simply a null affixation process that maps from one class to the other – but even so, avoiding having to stipulate an ambiguity would be desirable.

That's the impulse that drove McConnell-Ginet (1982). She observes contrasts like those in (34–36):

(34)   a. *subject-oriented:*   Louisa rudely answered Patricia.
       b. *manner:*   Louisa answered Patricia rudely.

(35)   a. *subject-oriented:*   Louisa rudely departed.
       b. *manner:*   Louisa departed rudely.

(36)   a. *subject-oriented:*   #Josie lavishly has furnished the house.
       b. *manner:*   Josie has furnished the house lavishly.

What these examples show especially starkly is the importance of syntactic position in the contrast. The reading changes with the position of the adverb. The point is made especially clear in (36): (36a) is odd because its sole available interpretation is the pragmatically bizarre one that it was lavish of Josie to furnish her house at all. Given everything that's been said so far, it's not clear what accounts for this.

McConnell-Ginet also homes in on another effect involving subject-oriented adverbials: PASSIVE SENSITIVITY (Ernst 2002 traces the observation itself back to at least Lakoff 1972). This refers to a curious fact about how some subject-oriented adverbs behave in passives:

5.4 Manner and subject orientation

(37) a. $\left\{\begin{array}{l}\text{Reluctantly}\\ \text{Wisely}\\ \text{Unwillingly}\end{array}\right\}$, Joan instructed Mary.

b. $\left\{\begin{array}{l}\text{Reluctantly}\\ \text{Wisely}\\ \text{Unwillingly}\end{array}\right\}$, Mary was instructed by Joan.

Unlike (37a), (37b) is ambiguous. It has a reading on which it's Mary who's reluctant (or wise or unwilling) and another on which it's Joan.

On a straightforward predicate-modifier approach, it's certainly possible to provide an account of this fact (Landman 2000). What's less clear is how to do so in a way that simultaneously satisfies McConnell-Ginet's desire to avoid a lexical ambiguity between subject-oriented and manner adverbs.

Her diagnosis of the situation is that we've been thinking the wrong way about modification itself. On a predicate-modifier approach, adverbs are functions that take arguments. But in her estimation this overlooks the basic fact that adverbs are **additional**. They are essentially grammatical accessories, and to treat them as functions that apply to verbal meanings is to mistake them for something more. It's not entirely clear how this could be an argument against an intersective interpretation, but perhaps there is a way to finesse that point. So the question is how to do justice to the analytical intuition that adverbs should be subordinate to and dependent on verbs. Her answer is that adverbs are really arguments. The fact is easy to miss because they're almost always optional arguments – almost always, but not always. Some verbs do require an adverb:

(38) a. Floyd behaved *(badly).
b. Floyd treated Clyde *(badly).
c. Floyd worded the letter *(badly).
d. New York is situated *(on the Hudson).

This shows that it's possible in principle for verbs to take adverb arguments. If it can happen here, she asks, why not in general? Why not suppose that this is how manner modification generally works?

At least one reason to resist this is that it would require all verbs to have argument positions for adverbs, and surely that would be missing a generalization. It's also not clear how this would accord with the intuition that adverbs are in some way additional. To address this, she suggests that adverbs are arguments of a special kind: they are introduced after a verb has undergone a process of 'augmentation'.

The augmentation process gives verbs additional argument slots, which adverbs can then occupy.

This idea can be expressed rather naturally in an event semantics. This is counter to her wishes, but I'll go down this road in any case. Here's a very rough sketch of how this might work. *Walk*, when modified by *quickly*,[8] is augmented using an AUG-SPEED shift that maps it to a similar predicate that has an argument position for a speed adverb. *Quickly* itself denotes a property of rates of speed, indicated with the variable and type-label r in (39):

(39)   a. Floyd AUG-SPEED walked quickly.
       b. ⟦ AUG-SPEED ⟧
           $= \lambda R_{\langle e, vt \rangle} \lambda P_{\langle r, t \rangle} \lambda x \lambda e . R(x)(e) \wedge P(\mathbf{speed}(e))$
       c. ⟦ *quickly* ⟧ $= \lambda r : \mathbf{is\text{-}a\text{-}speed}(r) . \mathbf{quick}(r)$
       d. ⟦ *Floyd* AUG-SPEED *walked quickly* ⟧
           $=$ ⟦ AUG-SPEED ⟧ (⟦ *walked* ⟧)(⟦ *quickly* ⟧)(⟦ *Floyd* ⟧)
           $= \lambda e . \mathbf{walk}(\mathbf{Floyd})(e) \wedge \mathbf{quick}(\mathbf{speed}(e))$

The result of the particular augmentation illustrated here is that *walked* winds up awaiting an adverb, which it will predicate of the speed of an event, indicated here with a **speed** function that maps an event to its speed. It's an interesting question whether that commits us to enriching the ontology with a new atomic type for objects such as 'speeds' or whether they can be constructed out of other objects. For speeds, degrees seem a natural alternative, but for manners it's less clear (see section 5.4.6). With sufficiently many augmentation relations – and there would in fact have to be many – one can imagine a process like the one in (39) working for adverbs in general. Indeed, on a Cinque (1999)-style view, this has a natural implementation: the augmentation relations might be linked to the functional heads associated with particular modifiers (Morzycki 2004a, 2005a explore something vaguely along these lines). There's certainly no shortage of such heads in a Cinquean theory.

Perhaps the most interesting aspect of this, though, is its groundbreaking treatment of passive-sensitivity. McConnell-Ginet's paraphrase of an ordinary subject-oriented adverb is in (40):

---

[8] Further examination of the lexical semantics of *quickly* can be found in Cresswell (1979) and Rawlins (2010). It turns out to reveal interesting subtleties with broader consequences.

5.4 Manner and subject orientation

(40) Louisa rudely departed.
  'Louisa acted rudely to depart.'

For me, 'acted rudely in departing' is much more natural. Either way, this reflects that the meaning of subject-oriented *rudely* is about deliberate action. If in the middle of a conversation Louisa tripped and fell out an open window, we wouldn't think she had rudely departed, no matter how interesting the conversation she had interrupted had been. McConnell-Ginet suggests that we can reflect that aspect of the meaning of the sentence with a higher abstract ACT verb, with a meaning vaguely along the lines of normal English 'act'. This, of course, just raises the question of what *act* means.

It might be represented using two lexical-semantic ingredients that are useful in a variety of other contexts. The first is a **cause** predicate, which I will treat as a relation between events, so that $\textbf{cause}(e')(e)$ means that e caused e'. The second is the THEMATIC ROLE PREDICATE **agent**, which maps an event to its agent (or, roughly, instigator; more on this in section 5.4.2). Thus:

(41) $[\![\text{ACT}]\!] = \lambda R_{\langle e, vt \rangle} \lambda x \lambda e \,.\, \exists e' \begin{bmatrix} \textbf{cause}(e')(e) \wedge \textbf{agent}(e) = x \wedge \\ R(x)(e') \end{bmatrix}$

This adds into the mix a causing event, of which x is the agent. We have now gone considerably beyond McConnell-Ginet's original proposal, but it helps spell out what *act* might actually mean and places on the table some tools that will prove useful.

If a lower, main verb can be augmented, we should expect that this higher abstract one could as well. That's precisely what she suggests happens with subject-oriented adverbs. The act predicate in (41) is augmented by adding a manner argument. Thus the syntactic representation will be as in (42a). The semantics will be built from an adverb that denotes a property of manners, as in (42b), and ultimately leads to (42c):

(42) a. Louisa rudely AUG-MANNER ACT departed.
  b. $[\![rudely]\!] = \lambda m : \textbf{is-a-manner}(m) \,.\, \textbf{rude}(m)$
  c. $[\![\text{AUG-MANNER}]\!] ([\![\text{ACT}]\!])([\![rudely]\!])([\![departed]\!])([\![Louisa]\!])$
   $= \lambda e \,.\, [\![act]\!] ([\![depart]\!])([\![Louisa]\!])(e) \wedge$
   $\hspace{6em} [\![rudely]\!] (\textbf{manner}(e))$
   $= \lambda e \,.\, \exists e' \begin{bmatrix} \textbf{cause}(e')(e) \wedge \textbf{agent}(e) = \text{Louisa} \wedge \\ \textbf{depart}(\text{Louisa})(e') \end{bmatrix} \wedge$
   $\hspace{12em} \textbf{rude}(\textbf{manner}(e))$

The result is a property of events whose agent is Louisa, whose manner was rude, and which caused an event that was a departing by Louisa.

This provides an alternative theory of subject-oriented readings that doesn't require distinct lexical entries for subject-oriented and manner adverbs, and that correctly makes a connection between how high an adverb is and which reading it gets.

The other challenge was providing an account of passive-sensitivity. It turns out that this can do that, too, provided we are willing to accept a single lexical ambiguity. It's in the passive form of *be*. One of its forms can be semantically vacuous, but the other is a volitional form of passive *be* that is just a way of pronouncing the ACT predicate (a similar proposal was made by Partee 1977). That being the case, two readings are possible, depending on which of passive *be* is used:

(43)   a. Reluctantly, Mary was$_\varnothing$ instructed by Joan.
         b. Reluctantly, Mary was$_{ACT}$ instructed by Joan.

In (43a), *reluctantly* gets its usual interpretation, modifying a verb of which Joan is the underlying subject. In (43b), it is interpreted as modifying a higher form of ACT, of which Mary is the subject. Reluctance is therefore correctly attributed to different people on the two readings.

5.4.2 The Neo-Davidsonian strategy and thematic roles

Adopting Davidsonian events radically changes the picture of how adverbial modification works, and it allows an elegant explanation of manner adverbs. But the only explanations of how subject-oriented adverbs work that we've encountered so far – Thomason and Stalnaker's and McConnell-Ginet's – don't depend on events. It would be nice to have an inherently event-based account of those, too, if only as a point of comparison. Articulating such an account is what Wyner (1998) sets out to do, in a way that builds on the insights of both McConnell-Ginet and Davidson. Before we can consider his proposal, though, we have to make a new tool available.

We've already used an **agent** thematic-role predicate (both in this chapter and in Chapter 2). Thematic roles are often thought to play a major role in the syntax, but using the **agent** predicate suggests they have a semantic role, too. And indeed, it's not clear how they could be understood in any way that's not essentially semantic. What any thematic-role does is group together various ways of being a participant in an event. Being an agent is one way: it typically involves acting volitionally, causing the event, and a variety of other things (Dowty 1991). Being a patient is another: it involves being affected. And so on for thematic roles like experiencer, source, goal, beneficiary, etc.

5.4 Manner and subject orientation

Sometimes semanticists are skeptical about thematic roles because their definitions are a bit vague and they're not actually necessary to relate predicates to their arguments – function application does that just fine. Nevertheless, it means something that we've already resorted to an **agent** predicate twice. It's also striking how easy it was to do. In describing thematic roles, I characterized them with respect to an event. If events are at the core of the semantics, extracting from them information about who played what role seems entirely natural. So in addition to **agent**, we could also treat the other thematic roles as thematic-role predicates that map events to individuals. (Alternatively, we could treat them as relations, so instead of writing **agent**(e) = x we'd write **agent**(e)(x), which would avoid committing to the idea that any event has at most one agent.) The idea that thematic roles could be construed as event predicates is advocated in detail in Parsons (1990), and a semantics that combines thematic roles and events in this way is referred to as NEO-DAVIDSONIAN.[9] Parsons illustrates many ways in which it might be useful. The first application of the idea, though, is in decomposing predicates to allow arguments to be added conjunctively, in much the way intersective modifiers are. Instead of *give* having a denotation like (44), it would be as in (45):

(44) *Davidsonian*:

    a. $[\![give]\!] = \lambda x \lambda y \lambda z \lambda e \,.\, \textbf{give}(x)(y)(z)(e)$

    b. $[\![\textit{Floyd gave cheese to the walrus}]\!]$
       = $\exists e[\textbf{give}(\textbf{cheese})(\textbf{the-walrus})(\textbf{Floyd})(e)]$

(45) *Neo-Davidsonian*:

    a. $[\![give]\!] = \lambda x \lambda y \lambda z \lambda e \,.\, \textbf{give}(e) \wedge \textbf{theme}(e) = x \wedge \textbf{goal}(e) = y \wedge \textbf{agent}(e) = z$

    b. $[\![\textit{Floyd gave cheese to the walrus}]\!]$
       = $\exists e \begin{bmatrix} \textbf{give}(e) \wedge \textbf{theme} = \textbf{cheese} \wedge \\ \textbf{goal}(e) = \textbf{the-walrus} \wedge \textbf{agent}(e) = \textbf{Floyd} \end{bmatrix}$

If nothing else, it's a bit easier to read (though if that were a concern, we should have just written '*e* is an event of *z* giving *x* to *y*').

---

[9] The term is also sometimes used to refer to the idea that all verbs (or perhaps even all predicates) should receive an event or state argument, rather than just predicates in 'action sentences' as Davidson originally intended (Parsons 1990; Higginbotham 1985).

Another nice aspect of this approach is that it has an à la carte quality. One can pick only the thematic-role predicates one cares to believe in, and reject any one finds unappetizingly vague. The leading idea in this vein is to accept only **agent** (Kratzer 1996, 2002 and many others since), a position she calls semi-neo-Davidsonian. What Kratzer actually proposes is that all arguments but the agent are introduced in the conventional way, but that the agent is introduced indirectly. She does this in a separate syntactic node, Voice, that has come to be identified with *v* (pronounced 'little *v*'; Marantz 1996). It heads a functional projection above VP. The idea that the agent is special and separate from other arguments, and introduced at a higher level in the tree, seems ready-made for a theory of subject-orientation. But we don't need to adopt these syntactic assumptions quite yet.

Wyner (1998) uses these neo-Davidsonian tools to build a theory of subject-orientation. The first step is to return to the observation that the subject in sentences with subject-oriented adverbs must be volitional. Wyner illustrates this with sentences like (46):

(46)   #The antibiotic reluctantly killed the infection.

The only way to make sense of this is to suppose that the antibiotic had some choice in the matter. To Wyner, this indicates that the lexical semantics of subject-oriented adverbs involve not an abstract ACT verb, but rather an **agent** predicate built into their lexical semantics.[10] He frames his denotations around paraphrases like (47):

(47)   Floyd reluctantly killed Clyde.
        'Floyd was the agent of an event of killing Clyde, and Floyd was the experiencer of a state of reluctance.'

There is a minor additional variation here on the Davidsonian theme: STATES. States are like events but don't involve anything actually happening. Rather, they're about something just being the case. They're of the same semantic type as events, but of a different SORT. It's conventional to use *s* as the variable for them.

The paraphrase can be cashed out as a denotation directly in terms of thematic-role predicates (I'm adjusting Wyner's denotation nontrivially):[11]

---

[10] The predicate he actually uses is **volition**, which he takes to be part of a family of predicates that collectively constitute the content of **agent**.

[11] I've changed Wyner's denotation slightly to reflect more directly that the reluctance is about the killing rather than something else by giving **reluctant** an additional predicate-of-events argument.

5.4 Manner and subject orientation

(48)   a. $[\![\textit{reluctantly}]\!] = \lambda P_{\langle v, t \rangle} \lambda e . P(e) \wedge$
$\exists s[\textbf{reluctant}(P)(s) \wedge \textbf{experiencer}(s) = \textbf{agent}(e)]$

        b. $[\![\textit{Floyd kill Clyde}]\!] = \lambda e . \textbf{kill}(e) \wedge \textbf{agent}(e) = \text{Floyd} \wedge$
$\textbf{theme}(e) = \text{Clyde}$

        c. $[\![\textit{reluctantly [Floyd killed Clyde]}]\!]$
$= \lambda e. \textbf{kill}(e) \wedge \textbf{agent}(e) = \text{Floyd} \wedge \textbf{theme}(e) = \text{Clyde} \wedge$

$$\exists s \left[\textbf{reluctant} \begin{pmatrix} \lambda e . \textbf{kill}(e) \wedge \\ \textbf{agent}(e) = \text{Floyd} \wedge \\ \textbf{theme}(e) = \text{Clyde} \end{pmatrix}(s) \wedge \\ \textbf{experiencer}(s) = \textbf{agent}(e) \right]$$

This requires that there be a state of reluctance about Floyd killing Clyde, and that the experiencer of that state be the agent of an event of Floyd killing Clyde. To achieve an account of passive-sensitivity, Wyner does something similar to McConnell-Ginet in using a volitional passive *be*.

What's important about this is that it provides a theory of subject-orientation in a Davidsonian – indeed, neo-Davidsonian – event framework. One could of course quibble. If this particular configuration of thematic-role predicates is simply a fact about certain lexical entries, should we also expect lexical entries that combine thematic-role predicates in arbitrary different ways? Why not an adverb that targets the theme, for example, as in (49)?:

(49) $[\![\textit{reluctantliciously}]\!] = \lambda P_{\langle v, t \rangle} \lambda e . P(e) \wedge$
$\exists s[\textbf{reluctant}(P)(s) \wedge \textbf{experiencer}(s) = \textbf{theme}(e)]$

That said, it's possible to write conceivable but apparently linguistically impossible denotations for adverbs for any predicate-modifier type, so it's debatable how much of a concern this should be.

5.4.3 Comparison classes and related tools

There is another insight in Wyner's approach – and the general Davidsonian one – that's worth recognizing: the connection it makes between subject-oriented adverbs and adjectives. Wyner's denotation is actually based on an adjective-like **reluctant** predicate. The connection between adverb orientation and adjectives is made especially clearly by Geuder (2000), who observes that (50a) is actually best paraphrased not with *act* but as in (50b):

(50)   a. Floyd rudely departed.
        b. Floyd was rude to depart.

One reason to prefer this to the *act* paraphrase is that it's not possible to say e.g. *Floyd acted to depart*. The connection to adjectives behind (50) extends to quite a number of subject-oriented adverbs:

(51) a. Floyd $\begin{Bmatrix} \text{stupidly} \\ \text{thoughtlessly} \\ \text{gladly} \end{Bmatrix}$ departed.

b. Floyd was $\begin{Bmatrix} \text{stupid} \\ \text{thoughtless} \\ \text{glad} \end{Bmatrix}$ to depart.

Not all subject-oriented adverbs can be paraphrased this way. The class that includes *intentionally*, *accidentally*, and *deliberately* doesn't support such paraphrases. *Anxious*, *eager*, and *(un)willing* all support them in principle, but the adjectival paraphrase lacks an entailment that its adverb counterpart has:

(52) a. Floyd $\begin{Bmatrix} \text{anxiously} \\ \text{unwillingly} \end{Bmatrix}$ departed.

b. Floyd was $\begin{Bmatrix} \text{anxious} \\ \text{unwilling} \end{Bmatrix}$ to depart.

Only (52a) and not (52b) entails that Floyd actually departed. For Geuder, this is evidence that the theory of adverb orientation has to be built on top of a theory of **adjective** orientation, and that in particular we have to develop an understanding of the infinitival arguments these adjectives take.

I won't pursue this further here, but the connection to adjectives does present another analytical opportunity that a number of researchers have found appealing. In principle, adjective semantics provides many semantic knobs and dials one might want to twiddle, but one especially promising one is comparison classes (see Chapter 3, especially sections 3.4 and 3.5.3). Ernst (2002) noticed that the subject-oriented adverb in (53a) and the manner adverb in (53b) differ in just this respect:

(53) a. Rudely, she left.
    comparison class: things she might have done
b. She left rudely.
    comparison class: ways she might have left

This insight seems so clear that it hardly needs elaborating. Ernst doesn't claim that this is all there is to subject-oriented/manner

5.4 Manner and subject orientation

contrast. He couches his semantic component in a version of Discourse Representation Theory (DRT; Kamp 1981b), which, in its classic form, has construction-specific rules for constructing semantic representations. He leverages this to create an effect in which (53a) winds up meaning that the event 'warrants positing' rudeness in the agent, whereas (53b) winds up with 'manifests' rudeness in the agent. It's the comparison class difference that we should focus on here, though.

Matsui (forthcoming) builds on the comparison class distinction, and Schäfer (2005) pursues an analytical course that is similar in important respects. Discussion of comparison class sensitivity in this connection can also be found in Rawlins (2004/2008). For Matsui, the starting point is the striking observation that in Japanese, the particle *mo* – which famously has a dizzying array of semantically interesting uses, including expressing universal quantification – can be suffixed to a manner adverb to create a subject-oriented one:

(54) a. John-wa orokani odotta.
John-TOP stupidly danced.
'John danced stupidly.' (manner reading only)

b. John-wa orokani-mo odotta.
John-TOP stupidly   danced.
'Stupidly, John danced.' (subject-oriented reading only)

This effect persists irrespective of syntactic position. In (55), the adverb is fronted, and again, the presence or absence of *-mo* unambiguously determines the available reading:

(55) a. Orokani John-wa odotta.
stupidly John-TOP danced.
'John danced stupidly.' (manner reading only)

b. Orokani-mo John-wa odotta.
stupidly   John-TOP danced.
'Stupidly, John danced.' (subject-oriented reading only)

This helps resolve an issue that, from the perspective of English alone, was unclear: should there be a lexical ambiguity between manner and subject-oriented adverbs, or should both have a single denotation whose interpretation is determined by the adverb's position? The Japanese facts would seem to argue for a lexical distinction. But more than that: they suggest that – at least in Japanese – the manner form should be basic, and that the subject-oriented form should be derived from it.

To combine this insight with Ernst's, she relies on an independently motivated way of introducing the subject: namely, via a Kratzerian Voice head (Kratzer 1996; see previous section). A version of such a structure is in (56):[12]

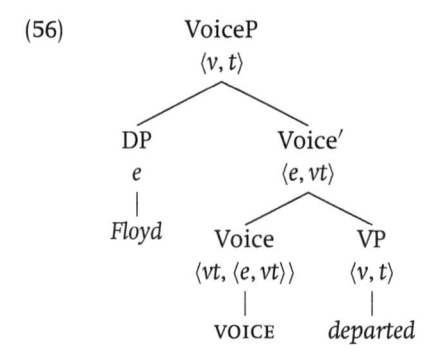

(56)
```
              VoiceP
              ⟨v, t⟩
             /      \
           DP       Voice'
            e       ⟨e, vt⟩
            |       /     \
          Floyd  Voice     VP
                 ⟨vt, ⟨e, vt⟩⟩  ⟨v, t⟩
                    |            |
                  VOICE       departed
```

The voice head simply introduces an agent in the Neo-Davidsonian style:

(57) a. $[\![\text{VOICE}]\!] = \lambda P_{\langle v, t \rangle} \lambda x \lambda e . P(e) \wedge \textbf{agent}(e) = x$
      b. $[\![\text{VOICE}]\!] ([\![\textit{departed}]\!])([\![\textit{Floyd}]\!])$
         $= \lambda e . \textbf{departed}(e) \wedge \textbf{agent}(e) = \text{Floyd}$

The denotation of pure-manner *orokani* 'stupidly' is designed to combine with the VP, below Voice, and to be sensitive to a comparison class. The actual implementation is based on a degree-based semantics for adjectives (see Chapter 3). All that's crucial here is the comparison class, so I will simply write **stupid**$(e)(C)$ to mean e counts as stupid with respect to the comparison class C, which for convenience we can think of as a property of events (that all and only members of the comparison class have):

(58) $[\![\textit{orokani}]\!] = \lambda P_{\langle v, t \rangle} \lambda e . P(e) \wedge \textbf{stupid}(e)(P)$

This could adjoin directly to VP, yielding an interpretation as in (59) (I'll use English words in place of other Japanese ones):

---

[12] Kratzer actually uses a special rule, Event Identification, rather than function application to combine the subject and VP.

5.4 Manner and subject orientation

(59)   a. $[\![\,orokani\ departed\,]\!] = [\![\,orokani\,]\!]\,([\![\,departed\,]\!])$
             $= \lambda e\,.\,\mathbf{departed}(e) \wedge \mathbf{stupid}(e)(\mathbf{departed})$

       b. $[\![\,Floyd\ \textsc{voice}\ orokani\ departed\,]\!]$
             $= [\![\,\textsc{voice}\,]\!]\,([\![\,orokani\ departed\,]\!])([\![\,Floyd\,]\!])$
             $= \lambda e\,.\,\mathbf{departed}(e) \wedge \mathbf{stupid}(e)(\mathbf{departed}) \wedge$
                                            $\mathbf{agent}(e) = \mathbf{Floyd}$

Thus 'Floyd stupidly departed' is a property of events of Floyd departing that are stupid compared to departing events generally.

The subject-oriented version should, of course, occur higher. For our purposes, we can assume it's one node up, at Voice′, and that it has the semantics in (60):

(60) $[\![\,orokani\text{-}mo\,]\!] = \lambda R_{\langle e,vt\rangle}\lambda x\lambda e\,.\,R(e)(x) \wedge \mathbf{stupid}(e)(\lambda e'\,.\,R(e')(x))$

This is very similar to its plain manner counterpart, except that it has access to the subject and it uses a comparison class sensitive to the subject. Things are clearer after the computation:

(61)   a. $[\![\,\textsc{voice}\ departed\,]\!] = [\![\,\textsc{voice}\,]\!]\,([\![\,departed\,]\!])$
             $= \lambda x\lambda e\,.\,\mathbf{departed}(e) \wedge \mathbf{agent}(e) = x\text{'}$

       b. $[\![\,Floyd\ orokani\text{-}mo\ \textsc{voice}\ departed\,]\!]$
             $= [\![\,orokani\text{-}mo\,]\!]\,([\![\,\textsc{voice}\ departed\,]\!])([\![\,Floyd\,]\!])$
             $= \lambda e\,.\,[\![\,\textsc{voice}\ departed\,]\!]\,(e)(\mathbf{Floyd}) \wedge$
                         $\mathbf{stupid}(e)(\lambda e'\,.\,[\![\,\textsc{voice}\ departed\,]\!]\,(e')(\mathbf{Floyd}))$
             $= \lambda e\,.\,\mathbf{departed}(e) \wedge \mathbf{agent}(e) = \mathbf{Floyd} \wedge$
                  $\mathbf{stupid}(e)(\lambda e'\,.\,\mathbf{departed}(e') \wedge \mathbf{agent}(e') = \mathbf{Floyd})$

The result is a property of events of Floyd departing that are stupid compared to (other) events of Floyd departing. So the difference between the two readings is that the manner reading compares against other departures ('stupid as far as departures go'), whereas the subject-oriented reading compares against other departures the subject could have performed ('stupid as far as ways Floyd could have departed'). This isn't precisely Ernst's initial characterization of the difference in terms of comparison classes, but it's certainly similar.

This account also makes possible providing a denotation for the morpheme that turns manner adverbs into subject-oriented ones:

(62) $[\![\,mo\,]\!] = \lambda f_{\langle vt,vt\rangle}\lambda R_{\langle e,vt\rangle}\lambda x\lambda e\,.\,f(\lambda e'\,.\,R(e')(x))(e)$

The computation that leads to the subject-oriented reading is somewhat formally gruesome, so it's in a note.[13] The larger point, though, is the evidence for a lexical distinction between subject-oriented and manner adverbs, and an analysis of the difference driven by the intuition that comparison classes are crucial.

Schäfer (2005) approached a slightly different challenge in this domain with an analysis that has a similar structure, with a twist. He was interested in explaining enigmatic sentences like (63):

(63) a. John painstakingly wrote illegibly.   (Parsons 1990)
      b. Hans skillfully answered the questions stupidly. (Frey 2003)

Focusing on (63b), the odd effect is that *skillfully* and *stupidly*, normally at odds with each other, are perfectly compatible when one has a subject-oriented reading. The solution, Schäfer suggests, lies not in comparison classes but in something similar: an implicit-argument position of *skillful(ly)* that indicates what one is skillful with respect to: surgery, arson, poker, etc (see Chapter 2, especially section 2.3.4). For the adjective, it's actually possible to spell out both this argument and the comparison-class argument with *at* (or *as*) and *for*, respectively:

(64)   Floyd is skillful at surgery for a 90-year-old arthritic.

We can construe the *at*-PP argument as expressing a property of events – to be skillful at surgery, for example, one is skillful with respect to surgery events. Thus a simple sentence with *skillfully* might be interpreted as in (65):

---

[13] Here is the gruesome computation:

(i) ⟦ *mo* ⟧ (⟦ *orokani* ⟧)

$= \lambda R_{\langle e, vt \rangle} \lambda x \lambda e \,.\, ⟦ orokani ⟧ (\lambda e' \,.\, R(e')(x))(e)$

$= \lambda R_{\langle e, vt \rangle} \lambda x \lambda e \,.\, \begin{bmatrix} \lambda P_{\langle v, t \rangle} \lambda e'' \,.\\ P(e'') \wedge \\ \textbf{stupid}(e'')(P) \end{bmatrix} (\lambda e' \,.\, R(e')(x))(e)$

$= \lambda R_{\langle e, vt \rangle} \lambda x \lambda e \,.\, \begin{bmatrix} \lambda e'' \,.\\ [\lambda e' \,.\, R(e')(x)](e'') \wedge \\ \textbf{stupid}(e'')(\lambda e' \,.\, R(e')(x)) \end{bmatrix} (e)$

$= \lambda R_{\langle e, vt \rangle} \lambda x \lambda e \,.\, \begin{bmatrix} \lambda e'' \,.\\ R(e'')(x) \wedge \\ \textbf{stupid}(e'')(\lambda e' \,.\, R(e')(x)) \end{bmatrix} (e)$

$= \lambda R_{\langle e, vt \rangle} \lambda x \lambda e . R(e)(x) \wedge \textbf{stupid}(e)(\lambda e' \,.\, R(e')(x))$

5.4 Manner and subject orientation

(65) a. Hans skillfully answered the questions.

b. $\exists e \begin{bmatrix} \text{skillful}(\text{answer}(\text{the-questions}))(e) \land \\ \text{answer}(\text{the-questions})(e) \land \\ \text{agent}(e) = \text{Hans} \end{bmatrix}$

To skillfully answer the questions, then, is to be the agent of a question-answering event performed in a way that's skillful at question-answering. So (64b) might be rendered as in (66):

(66) a. Hans skillfully answered the questions stupidly.

b. $\exists e \begin{bmatrix} \text{skillful}\begin{pmatrix} \lambda e' \,.\, \text{answer}(\text{the-questions})(e') \land \\ \text{stupid}(e') \end{pmatrix}(e) \land \\ \text{answer}(\text{the-questions})(e) \land \\ \text{agent}(e) = \text{Hans} \land \text{stupid}(e) \end{bmatrix}$

Hans is now the agent of a stupid question-answering event, but that event was performed in a way that's skillful at answering questions stupidly.

The importance of this result is not just in the analysis of subject-orientation, but also in the approach it provides to reconciling the fact that intersective modifiers don't scope with respect to each other with the deeply felt intuition many have that, well, somehow they do. One option is of course to just implement *skillfully* as a predicate modifier. That would be perfectly respectable and might resolve any tension directly. But one might imagine that the implicit argument is provided in another way, perhaps as a contextual default, one more similar to how a *skillful surgeon* behaves, or perhaps – to take a more straightforward comparison-class case – *expensive BMW* (Kennedy 2007). In subsequent work (Schäfer 2008), Schäfer rejected his previous strategy. But these ideas more broadly, including implicit arguments in the analysis of adverbs and their relation in this respect to their adjectival counterparts, bear further investigation.

5.4.4 The bottom-up analytical strategy

There is a common methodological strategy behind all the analyses we've encountered so far: they all begin with an attempt at a general theory of subject-oriented and manner readings. There is an alternative analytical impulse worth highlighting. Rather than beginning top-down with an attempt at identifying a range of properties that extend across many adverbs, one might begin bottom-up with a fine-grained investigation of a few carefully selected ones.

For adverbs in particular, there might be something to recommend the bottom-up strategy. To simply say that a manner adverb is a predicate of events is insightful, but ultimately doesn't delve much deeper into the lexical semantics of the adverb than saying of an adjective that it is a property of individuals. There's much more that should be said about adjectives – and about how they vary and the subclasses they fall into – and we have no reason to think adverbs are any different. Indeed, if they do vary in ways we haven't detected, we may miss important generalizations. Before attempting generalizations about fruit, it may be wise to ensure you can distinguish apples from oranges.

An especially clear example of this research strategy is Rawlins (2004/2008), who begins with a single adverb: *illegally*. It has three uses. The first two can be noncommittally described as 'low' and 'high' (because prematurely assigning adverbs to classes is one of the dangers a bottom-up approach may help avoid), and the third is an adjective-modifying use:

(67)   a. *low:*   White moved illegally.
       b. *high:*   Illegally, White moved.
       c. *adjectival:* an illegally uninsured business

For (67a) and (67b), we should picture a chess game. One might say (67a) to describe violating rules about where a piece can move, and (67b) to describe moving when it's the other player's turn.

Because *illegally* is a deontic modal – it's about what is and isn't permitted – it's tractable with tools that have proven themselves in the analysis of other modals. The question then becomes how those tools need to be adapted to account for the different uses. We'll focus on the non-adjectival ones. The denotation of the high use is something like (68a) (where **permitted**$_w$ is the set of worlds compatible with what is permitted in w), which leads to the sentence denotation in (68b):

(68)   a. $[\![illegally_{\text{HIGH}}]\!] = \lambda p_{\langle s, t \rangle} \lambda w \,.\, p(w) \wedge \neg \exists w' \in \textbf{permitted}_w [p(w')]$

       b. $[\![Illegally_{\text{HIGH}} \text{ VOICE } White \text{ } moved]\!]$

$= \lambda w \,.\, \exists e [\textbf{move}_w(e) \wedge \textbf{agent}_w(e) = \text{White}] \wedge$

$\neg \exists w' \in \textbf{permitted}_w \left[\exists e' \left[\begin{array}{l} \textbf{move}_{w'}(e') \wedge \\ \textbf{agent}_{w'}(e') = \text{White} \end{array} \right] \right]$

I've omitted explicit reference to a Kratzerian conversational background (Kratzer 1981, 1991), which is actually quite important but won't figure in the brief discussion here. This also assumes a Kratzerian

5.4 Manner and subject orientation

Voice head and that the event variable is existentially closed somewhere above it. This results in (68b), which is true iff there was a moving by White, and there is no permitted world in which there is a moving by White. The denotation of the lower use varies mainly in its type, as in (69a), but something interesting happens when it attaches below the Voice head (and therefore below the point where existential closure occurs), as in (69b):

(69)   a. $[\![\textit{illegally}_{\text{LOW}}]\!]$
$= \lambda P_{\langle v, st \rangle} \lambda e \lambda w . P(e)(w) \wedge \neg \exists w' \in \textbf{permitted}_w [P(e)(w')]$
        b. $[\![\textit{White} \text{ VOICE } [\textit{moved illegally}_{\text{LOW}}]]\!]$
$= \lambda w . \exists e \begin{bmatrix} \text{move}_w(e) \wedge \text{agent}_w(e) = \text{White} \wedge \\ \neg \exists w' \in \textbf{permitted}_w [\text{move}_{w'}(e)] \end{bmatrix}$

So (69b) is true iff there was a moving by White and there is no permitted world with such a moving. This seems to accord with the facts. Rawlins then considers ways of unifying the denotations of *illegally* and deriving the difference purely in terms of the adverb's position. One aspect of the difference between these two readings, though, should seem familiar. As in Matsui (forthcoming), a major part of the difference between them arises from whether the agent is present or absent in a crucial part of the denotation.

This provides an elegant theory of a high–low contrast for a single case, but one might think it wouldn't readily generalize because adverbs are only occasionally modal. But, as Rawlins points out, that's not actually so clear. Many adverbs that manifest low–high contrasts might be viewed as quantifying over worlds (or situations). *Rudely*, for example, makes reference to laws of courtesy. *Tactfully* is similar. Many others – he mentions *cleverly, stupidly, wisely, foolishly, graciously* – may be construed as varying worlds quantified over as well, all differing in subtle ways in how those worlds are determined in view of the conversational background. (Anand and Brasaveanu 2010 take some further steps in this general direction.) So, by carefully examining a single case in detail and generalizing outward, one might discover empirical parallels and analytical possibilities that wouldn't be apparent by considering the whole paradigm at once.

5.4.5 Topic-orientation

Analyses of subject-orientation generally agree on at least one thing: it involves something like a subject. In some cases, it is more about thematic roles than subjects as such, but the overall characterization of the facts is not generally in dispute.

Potts (2003) makes a radical departure from this consensus. He argues that subject-orientation is not about the subject at all, or even about the agent, but rather about the DISCOURSE TOPIC. Topichood is a slightly elusive notion and comes in several flavors (Büring 1999), but it means something close to what it sounds like it means, at least in the flavor Potts intends.[14] The idea that topics are relevant comes from Stump (1985)'s analysis of ABSOLUTE CONSTRUCTIONS like those in (70) (see also Portner 1992):

(70) a. After more than a month in jail, my mother posted bond, bless her soul.
b. Signed by Columbia Records in 1999, his first album was never released.

In none of these cases is the underlined absolute construction oriented toward the subject. Indeed, in all of them, that would be pragmatically bizarre.[15]

Potts suggests that subject-oriented adverbs are simply special cases of this phenomenon. He offers these naturally occurring examples of adverbs that seem to be oriented to a non-subject topic:

(71) a. Physically, the keyboard is smaller than I expected, and extremely well built – there's no creaking or flexing. The keys look as if they will last well – including their paint. Thoughtfully, there is a clip-on cover for the connector while not in use.
b. The music, while well constructed, is rather annoying after a while, with a lack of any instantly recognizable tunes apparent. But, thoughtfully, there is an option to turn the sound off at any time during the game, so the rather twee sound effects and jauntily repetitive soundtrack won't annoy the parents ...
c. What is the function of the marking in the highest clause? Tentatively, it signals the left edge of a nominalized relative clause-type syntactic constituent.

---

[14] The term 'discourse topic' stands in only an indirect relation to sentence topics of the sort found in languages with overt topic-marking, such as Japanese.
[15] There is a prescriptive injunction to avoid structures such as these, in which the modifier isn't oriented toward the subject (this is what leads to the morbid dread of 'dangling participles').

5.4 Manner and subject orientation

Unlike for (70), there is some question about whether (71a) and (71b) are actually well-formed,[16] but for the sake of argument let's accept them at face value. It's also not obvious that these are really subject-oriented adverbs. Certainly, one might suspect (71c) of being a speech-act adverb because it can be replaced with *speaking tentatively* (see section 5.5.1). *Thoughtfully* might be an evaluative adverb (see section 5.5.2).[17] But let's set that aside as well, because the hypothesis these might seem to support is interesting – and if it's true, people have spent almost four decades barking up the wrong tree.

One way of introducing a topic in English is with a phrase such as *as for X* or *speaking of X*, so these may provide a way of testing the claim (if we grant that these involve the relevant notion of topichood):

(72) $\begin{Bmatrix} \text{As for Clyde,} \\ \text{Speaking of Clyde,} \end{Bmatrix}$ Floyd $\begin{Bmatrix} \text{cleverly} \\ \text{stupidly} \\ \text{eagerly} \end{Bmatrix}$ built a robot monkey with him.

Even though Clyde is clearly the topic, this doesn't allow construals on which it isn't Floyd that is clever or stupid or eager. The situation is even clearer in (73):

(73) #$\begin{Bmatrix} \text{As for Clyde,} \\ \text{Speaking of Clyde,} \end{Bmatrix}$ there was $\begin{Bmatrix} \text{cleverly} \\ \text{stupidly} \\ \text{eagerly} \end{Bmatrix}$ a robot monkey built with him.

This sentence is trying really hard to let Clyde be the target of orientation. Floyd has been eliminated entirely, so that the sentence involves no conceivable alternative. And yet the result is flagrant ill-formedness. The judgments remain consistent with various other ways

---

[16] They have an acceptable-ungrammaticality or grammatical-illusion quality: one parses them smoothly, but with the sensation that the parser might have smoothed over a grammatical rough spot (as it does in, e.g., ?*More people have been to Russia than I have*, which seems well-formed until one reflects on its meaning; Phillips et al. 2011). I wonder whether their authors would reject these sentences if presented with them. One can't, I suppose, be sure one hasn't just unconsciously internalized the prescriptive injunction, but if so, that shouldn't be disregarded – if it's internalized, it's part of the language, no matter how unsavory its source.

[17] This would make it like the evaluative adverbs *fortunately* and *amazingly* in having paraphrases with the corresponding adjective predicated of a proposition: *It's thoughtful/fortunate/amazing that there is an option to turn the sound off.* If these examples are actually grammatical for their speakers, they might have simply generalized *thoughtfully* to an evaluative adverb use.

of establishing Clyde as a topic, such as *Who did Clyde build a robot monkey with?*. Topichood is a complex and slippery notion, and the term is not always used consistently, so it might be that to defend this theory, we need to pick just the right definition. That would still leave behind the difficult task of finding an alternative explanation of the Thomason and Stalnaker (1973) subject-object opacity asymmetry (section 5.3.2).[18]

All of this is an argument against an exclusively topic-based theory. What it is not is an argument against the broader idea that there might be a connection between orientation in adverbs and in absolute constructions. That's a good topic for further inquiry. More generally, even if subject-orientation and topic-orientation are distinct phenomena in English, their similarity presents the tantalizing possibility that in some other language, they might not be – or that there might simply be a different division of labor between them. There may also be discoveries yet to be made about how adverb(ial) interpretation overall is sensitive to discourse structure.

5.4.6 Is there such a thing as a manner?

The notion of manner has an odd ghostly status in all this, and indeed in most discussions of manner adverbials. When we talk about predicate modifiers, we obviously assume that there are predicates in the model – Likewise for propositional attitude verbs and propositions. Less obviously, when we talk of temporal or locative adverbials, we have in the back of our minds the idea that the model contains times and locations. One could go on in this vein. Yet for all our talk of manner adverbials, we don't normally have in mind a model that includes objects in it called 'manners'. Why not?

One answer is that we don't seem to need to. It's possible to arrive at a perfectly respectable theory of what manner adverbs mean without appeal to the notion of 'manners'. Another answer is that there's something dangerously ontologically precarious about it. One probably shouldn't rush headlong into adding novel abstract objects into the model. But of course, all these things can be said about events (and situations and possible worlds). Whatever metaphysical qualms or methodological reservations one might entertain, the linguist's primary responsibility is to follow the linguistic evidence. So the question we should really ask is this: if adding manners to the model isn't

---

[18] At least some of the opacity facts for at least some adverbs may actually be due to independent contextual factors (Geuder 2000). If so, that might be a good analytical path to take in a topic-based approach.

5.4 Manner and subject orientation

necessary for an account of manner modification, are there other reasons to do so?

There may be. For one thing, there are expressions like *the way he did it*, which would seem to refer to manners. Manners can also be questioned with *how* (*how did he do it?*). Indeed, in providing a semantics for questions, Gutiérrez-Rexach (1997) adopts an ontology with manners in it. Landman and Morzycki (2003) and Anderson and Morzycki (forthcoming) provide further evidence from a systematic connection across several languages among manners, degrees, and kinds. In German, for example, a single word, *so*, is used as a kind anaphor with nouns, as a degree anaphor with adjectives, and as a manner anaphor with verbs:

(74) a. *kind:* so einen Hund
such a dog
'a dog of the same kind'

b. *degree:* Ich bin so groß
I am such tall
'I am this tall.'

c. *manner:* so getanzt
such danced
'danced like that'

All of these have the same *wh*-word counterpart, *wie*. Precisely the same pattern is found in Polish. Even in English, there are traces of these parallels. *As* has exactly the same range of uses:

(75) a. *kind:* such a dog as this
b. *degree:* Clyde is as tall as Floyd.
c. *manner:* Clyde behaved as I did.

The connection between (75b) and (75c) in particular is extremely common across languages (Haspelmath and Buchholz 1998). Rett (2011b) provides an analysis of this connection that relies on the assumption that just as degrees are objects in the model, so too are manners. For similar reasons, the overall paradigm also supports this conclusion. If kinds, degrees, and manners are treated in systematically parallel ways in constructions across many languages, and if kinds and degrees are in the model, it would be odd indeed if manners weren't.

None of this implies that manners must be atomic types. It might be possible to build them out of something else. (That's exactly what Landman and Morzycki 2003 and Anderson and Morzycki forthcoming do.)

But it certainly points to recognizing 'manner' as something more than a descriptive convenience.

Before we leave the topic of manner modification in general, a few suggestions for further exploration in this area: for more on whether manners are objects in the model, see Maienborn and Schäfer (2011) and references therein; for discussion of manner in connection with stative predicates, see Katz (2008); for more on the effect of syntactic position, see Shaer (2000, 2003); Ernst (2004); Morzycki (2004b, 2005a) and Wyner (2008); for cases where subject-oriented readings are conspicuous by their absence, see Schäfer (2002).

5.5 SPEAKER-ORIENTED ADVERBIALS

5.5.1 Speech-act adverbials

In many respects, it's possible to analyze language without taking into consideration that it's actually used by humans. This is one of the central principles and surprising discoveries of generative grammar. There are, however, certain phenomena that go out of their way to preclude this possibility. Surely SPEECH-ACT ADVERBIALS such as *frankly, confidentially*, and *seriously* merit a spot near the top of that list. There is no getting around the fact that they seem to be characterizing the speaking event itself. They are also known as PRAGMATIC, DISCOURSE-ORIENTED, or UTTERANCE-MODIFYING adverbials.

To the semanticist, this isn't terribly alarming. Semantics deals in questions of discourse context routinely, and dynamic semantics (Stalnaker 1979; Kamp 1981b; Heim 1982; Groenendijk and Stokhof 1991) is founded on the idea that meaning is about turning one discourse state into another via speech acts. Yet there's something to be said for setting one's open-mindedness aside and allowing oneself to be momentarily scandalized by it. This is partly an exercise in historical imagination. The analysis of this class of adverbs played an important role in the vicious infighting of the early years of generative syntax (see Newmeyer 1980; or, for a history intended for a general readership, Harris 1993). At issue was whether the deep structure of a sentence could, if only it could be pushed back deep enough by undoing enough syntactic operations, turn out to be its semantic representation too. The school of thought that held that it could was called Generative Semantics.

Speech-act adverbs were important in this debate because they seemed to reveal that the syntactic structure of a sentence directly reflects information about the speech act performed in saying it. This may support an especially expansive view of how much semantic

5.5 Speaker-oriented adverbials

information can be encoded in a syntactic representation. The key fact is that speech-act adverbs support paraphrases involving manner modification of a verb of speaking:[19]

(76) a. $\left\{\begin{array}{l}\text{Frankly,}\\ \text{Confidentially,}\\ \text{Seriously,}\end{array}\right\}$ you really shouldn't talk to Floyd.

b. I hereby say to you $\left\{\begin{array}{l}\text{frankly}\\ \text{confidentially}\\ \text{seriously}\end{array}\right\}$ that you really shouldn't talk to Floyd.

A more natural paraphrase would be of the form 'frankly speaking' (Bellert 1977). Either way, the correspondence might suggest that all sentences involve an underlying verb of speaking that expresses their illocutionary force (saying, asking, ordering, etc.), which seemed strong evidence in favor of the Generative Semantics position. This sense of getting a glimpse into the structure of speech acts is also part of what makes these adverbs especially interesting.

The view that there is an underlying speech-act verb in all sentences is called the PERFORMATIVE HYPOTHESIS (Ross 1970; Lakoff 1972; Sadock 1974), because it renders every utterance a PERFORMATIVE one (Austin 1961) – that is, one that accomplishes something by the very act of its being said. Here are some other examples:

(77) a. I (hereby) christen this ship The Robot Monkey.
b. I (hereby) declare you legally divorced.
c. I (hereby) claim this island for Spain.

From our contemporary perspective, we may have more tools to address the problem, but the facts remain and similar issues arise.

The natural modern rendering of the idea would be to make use of an assertion operator (Ginzburg and Sag 2001; Krifka 2001; Hacquard 2007; Cohen and Krifka 2011). I'll provide rough a sketch of how this might work, which won't be too different from the original proposal and therefore inherits some of its shortcomings (see Boër and Lycan 1980 and Levinson 1983).

Perhaps the most elegant option would be to use the same denotation for speech-act adverbs as for manner adverbs: a property of events.

---

[19] Not all manner modifiers of verbs of speaking have speech-act adverb counterparts, however. *Hesitantly*, *eagerly*, and *insincerely*, for example, all lack speech-act uses.

If these adverbs are to combine with an assertion operator, the node above it must also denote a property of events. This suggests that the assertion operator should apply to a proposition to be asserted, and return a property of an event of having asserted it:

(78) $[\![\text{ASSERT}]\!] = \lambda p_{\langle s, t \rangle} \lambda e \lambda w . \textbf{assert}(p)(e)$

There's a slight twist here: ASSERT collects up a world argument, but doesn't actually use it. There's no need to use it because ASSERT is always interpreted with respect to the actual world. The argument needs to be there only to ensure that it yields the right type to combine with *frankly*. With that in place, it can combine intersectively with a manner adverb (via an intensional variant of a rule of intersective interpretation):

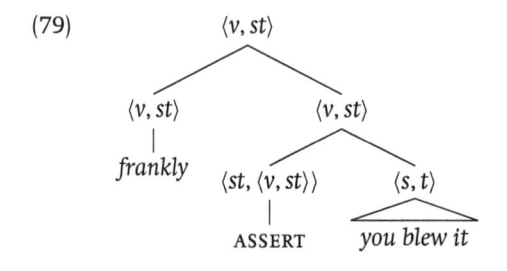

(79)

```
                    ⟨v, st⟩
                   /       \
              ⟨v, st⟩      ⟨v, st⟩
                 |        /       \
             frankly  ⟨st, ⟨v, st⟩⟩  ⟨s, t⟩
                           |          /  \
                        ASSERT    you blew it
```

(80)   a. $[\![frankly]\!] = \lambda e \lambda w . \textbf{frank}_w(e)$
        b. $[\![\text{you blew it}]\!] = \lambda w . \exists e [\textbf{blow-it}_w(\textbf{you})(e)]$
        c. $[\![\text{ASSERT}]\!] ([\![\text{you blew it}]\!])$
             $= \lambda e' \lambda w' . \textbf{assert}(\lambda w . \exists e [\textbf{blow-it}_w(\textbf{you})(e)])(e')$
        d. $[\![\text{Frankly, ASSERT you blew it}]\!]$
             $= \lambda e' \lambda w' . [\![frankly]\!](e')(w') \wedge$
                                          $[\![\text{ASSERT you blew it}]\!](e')(w')$
             $= \lambda e' \lambda w' . \textbf{frank}_{w'}(e') \wedge$
                         $\textbf{assert}(\lambda w . \exists e [\textbf{blow-it}_w(\textbf{you})(e)])(e')$

This asks for an event and a world and is true if the event was a frank one, and it was an event of asserting the proposition that you blew it. For this to function in discourse, a principle like (81) needs to be adopted:

(81)   If a linguistic expression of type $\langle v, st \rangle$ is uttered unembedded, interpret it with respect to the utterance event and the actual world.

5.5 Speaker-oriented adverbials

This means that (80) will be judged true iff the utterance event is a frank one in the actual world, and if it's an event of asserting that you blew it.

This suffers from a classic problem with the Performative Hypothesis: this would always come out true by the very act of it being uttered so long as the utterance is, in fact, frank. This could be corrected by simply adding a conjunct predicating the asserted content of the evaluation world:

(82)   a. $[\![\text{ASSERT}]\!] = \lambda p_{\langle s, t \rangle} \lambda e \lambda w \,.\, \textbf{assert}(p)(e) \wedge p(w)$
      b. $[\![\textit{Frankly}, \text{ASSERT } \textit{you blew it}]\!]$
          $= \lambda e' \lambda w' \,.\, [\![\textit{frankly}]\!](e')(w') \wedge [\![\text{ASSERT } \textit{you blew it}]\!](e')(w')$
          $= \lambda e' \lambda w' \,.\, \textbf{frank}_{w'}(e') \wedge$
                                 $\textbf{assert}(\lambda w \,.\, \exists e[\textbf{blow-it}_w(\textbf{you})(e)])(e') \wedge$
                                 $\exists e[\textbf{blow-it}_{w'}(\textbf{you})(e)]$

Now, in addition to the previous requirements, the sentence will be judged true only if you did, in fact, blow it. There's another problem here, though, which this doesn't address. It's not clear that we would actually judge this sentence merely false if we found its utterance something other than frank. To express disagreement with this sentence, one couldn't felicitously say 'No, that's not true. I blew it, but you weren't being frank.' We'll have to set this problem aside here. One natural approach to it, though, would involve treating the contribution of *frankly* as a distinct kind of meaning: a conventional implicature (Potts 2003; more on this in the following section).

To improve on this rough sketch, one could introduce a more sophisticated ontology. Krifka (2001), for example, introduces speech acts into the model. His assertion operator applies to propositions and yields speech acts. This makes it possible to state rules of how discourse should be structured, but it would not allow speech-act adverbs to be interpreted intersectively because the node above the speech-act operator doesn't denote a property. There may be a way to bring the ideas a bit closer together, though. One might modify Krifka's proposal by treating speech acts as a sort of event, so that the domain of speech acts is a proper subset of the domain of events. This would mean the assertion operator could be as it is above, but Krifka's rules governing how discourse is structured would have to change in a single consistent way. The change wouldn't need to be profound. It might suffice to stipulate that when a property of events is uttered unembedded, a contextually restricted definite description operator is added that maps it to the unique speech-act that satisfies the description and is currently being performed.

Potts (2003) proposes an articulated and formally explicit semantics for speech-act adverbs. His analysis also involves enriching the model, in his case with utterances themselves.[20] This makes it possible to place speech-act adverbials on a separate dimension of meaning from ordinary content. They wind up modifying instead the relation that holds between a speaker and an utterance. This helps capture the sense that speech acts and ordinary semantic content live in different tiers of the semantics. What it doesn't do in his formulation is provide an interpretation for speech-act adverbs that is intersective, or indeed one on which their meaning is identical to their manner counterparts. So there is a trade-off here: one theoretical desideratum for another.

Potts also provides an account of how speech-act adverbs behave in questions:

(83) a. Honestly, are you drunk?
b. Confidentially, which student do you find the most irritating?

In these cases, the adverb seems to be directed at the addressee rather than the speaker. It's not the asking in (83a) that's honest – it's the desired answer. Potts encodes this by treating all speech-act modifiers as systematically ambiguous between related homophonous question- and declarative-modifying meanings.

One important property of speech-act adverbials that this theory, like an assertion-operator theory, captures is their resistance to embedding:

(84) a. ??Clyde suspects that, seriously, you blew it.
b. ??Great wondered whether, confidentially, you blew it.
c. ??Floyd doubts that, frankly, you blew it.

To varying extents, these can be interpreted as though the adverb were parenthetical and interpreted as though it were high (although there is another problem with (84c), as we'll see in section 5.5.4). It is of course also possible to embed these adverbs on the manner reading.

Given how neat the puzzle is, and how old, it's a bit surprising that all this hasn't been further explored from a formal-semantic perspective. The ingredients for a more satisfactory account may be floating about.

---

[20] This isn't quite true. In Potts (2003), these objects appear to be sentences more than utterances: they have a syntax and a semantics, but no phonology. Utterances in a stricter sense are introduced in Potts (2007a).

5.5 Speaker-oriented adverbials

At the moment, they await someone to assemble them in a satisfying and enlightening way.

5.5.2 Evaluative adverbs

Another class of speaker-oriented adverbs express the speaker's evaluation of the proposition expressed by the modified sentence:

(85) $\begin{Bmatrix} \text{Remarkably,} \\ \text{Fortunately,} \\ \text{Oddly,} \end{Bmatrix}$ Floyd can recite the *Iliad* in Basque.

These are EVALUATIVE ADVERBS. They differ fundamentally from speech-act adverbs in that they don't seem to be analogous to manner adverbs. Normally, they support paraphrases in which their adjective counterpart is predicated of a proposition:

(86) It is $\begin{Bmatrix} \text{remarkable} \\ \text{fortunate} \\ \text{odd} \end{Bmatrix}$ that Floyd can recite the *Iliad* in Basque.

These adverbs are impossible before questions (Bonami et al. 2004; Bonami and Godard 2007):

(87) *Fortunately, who rescued you?

In English, they don't easily occur inside questions either, or in the antecedents of conditionals (Ernst 2009):

(88) a. ??Who fortunately rescued you?
b. ?If, remarkably, Floyd can recite all of the *Iliad*, he probably can't do it in Basque.
c. ??If, unfortunately, Floyd went to Flint, he no doubt regretted it.

Bonami and Godard (2007) report that in French, these are both well-formed, but the adverb is interpreted independently of its immediate surroundings:

(89) a. Si Paul va, malheureusement, voir Marie, elle sera
     if Paul goes unfortunately to-see Marie she will-be
     furieuse.
     furious

   'If, unfortunately, Paul goes and sees Marie, she will be furious.'

> *not:* 'If it is unfortunate that Paul met Marie, she will be furious.'
>
> b. Qui Marie a-t-elle malheureusement invité?
> who Marie has-she unfortunately   invited
> *asks:* 'Who did Mary invite?'
> *commits speaker to:* 'Whoever Marie invited, it's unfortunate that she did.'

In (89a), the meaning of the adverb doesn't contribute to the semantics antecedent, and in (89) it doesn't form part of the question.

Along with Potts (2003), they argue that this demonstrates that these expressions should be interpreted on a separate semantic dimension distinct from ordinary truth-conditional content. They articulate this claim in the spirit of Potts' theory of CONVENTIONAL IMPLICATURES (see also section 6.5). These are elements of meaning that Grice (1975) first recognized, but didn't characterize in a way that made them linguistically useful. Potts changed that. In part, the important insight is that conventional implicatures aren't at all like conversational implicatures. Conversational implicatures arise pragmatically as interlocutors work out each other's communicative intentions, and they can be denied without contradiction. Conventional implicatures have neither of these properties, and one makes more progress by focusing on the differences between the two than on their similarities. The 'conventional' thing about conventional implicatures is that they are part of the conventionalized – that is, lexical – semantics of particular morphemes.[21] What makes them different from ordinary meaning is that they don't contribute directly to the at-issue truth-conditional meaning of a sentence, they resist semantic embedding, and they tend to involve the perspective of the speaker in some way (the latter two claims may need significant qualification; Amaral et al. 2007; Schlenker 2007; Harris and Potts 2009). Potts analyzes nominal appositives, such as *a cyclist* in (90), in this way:

(90) a. Lance, a cyclist, wound up disappointing everyone.
      b. It's not true that Lance, a cyclist, wound up disappointing everyone.

The resistance to embedding is reflected in (90b), which denies that Lance wound up disappointing everyone, but not that he was a cyclist.

---

[21] Sometimes, these morphemes are spelled out by prosody alone, like the COMMA morpheme of Potts (2003) (see section 6.5), which licenses nominal appositives.

5.5 Speaker-oriented adverbials

Potts builds conventional implicatures into the semantics by compartmentalizing them. As the semantics gets built up compositionally, conventionally implicated content is set aside in a kind of holding area – a different 'dimension' of meaning – in which it is no longer accessible to elements higher in the tree. Formally, this is implemented by distinguishing expressions that contribute conventional implicatures by assigning them a distinct type. This type triggers the compartmentalization. The type of $[\![\,unfortunately\,]\!]$, for example, would be type $\langle st, t^c \rangle$, where t^c is the conventional-implicature analogue of the ordinary truth value type t. The denotation, then, might be as in (91) (the type must be indicated explicitly because it isn't recoverable from the lambda expression alone):

(91) $[\![\,unfortunately\,]\!] = \lambda p_{\langle s,t \rangle}.\mathbf{unfortunate}(p)$ type: $\langle st, t^c \rangle$

This applies to an ordinary proposition, and places in the conventional-implicature dimension the information that it is unfortunate.

Interestingly, many adverbs of this class have counterparts that occur as degree modifiers of APs (see section 5.7) For discussion of the scope and opacity properties of these adverbs, see Bonami and Godard (2008). For discussion of how such adverbs work in German, see Liu (2009).

5.5.3 Modal adverbs

We have already encountered the MODAL ADVERBS *necessarily* and *possibly* in section 5.3.1. It's conventional to group them with a number of other modal adverbs with a similar syntactic distribution under the label epistemic adverbs. The term isn't optimal because at least a few of them can get other kinds of readings:

(92) In view of the regulations, Floyd will $\begin{Bmatrix} \text{obligatorily} \\ \text{necessarily} \\ \text{inevitably} \end{Bmatrix}$ be shot.

If *hopefully* and *ideally* are placed in this class, this is even clearer. Other members of the class include *probably*, *certainly*, *definitely*, *surely*, and *clearly*.

The standard analysis of modal adverbs is of course to treat them as, well, modal: as quantifiers over possible worlds. We saw that in action for *necessarily*, and it could be extended to other members of the class. In the lexical semantics of modal auxiliaries, fine-grained variation among modals can be achieved by varying the accessibility relation that determines what worlds the modal quantifies over (Kratzer 1981, 1991). The same tools can be put to work in the analysis of these adverbs (Anand and Brasaveanu 2010). Such an analysis gives rise to some analytical challenges too. Some modal adverbs are gradable (*very probably*, *quite possibly*). Providing an analysis of this that does justice to the fact that they are both gradable and modal is not trivial, and is another aspect of the problem gradable modal adjectives raise (see section 3.7.5).

5.5.4 Polarity

It's a surprising characteristic of speaker-oriented adverbs that they are ill-formed in structures like (93b):

(93) a. Floyd $\begin{Bmatrix} \text{(un)fortunately} \\ \text{amazingly} \\ \text{probably} \\ \text{certainly} \end{Bmatrix}$ hasn't died.

b. *Floyd hasn't $\begin{Bmatrix} \text{(un)fortunately} \\ \text{amazingly} \\ \text{probably} \\ \text{certainly} \end{Bmatrix}$ died.

This reflects that speaker-oriented adverbs can't occur in the scope of negation. Speech-act adverbs aren't included in (93) only because they resist embedding in general. Nilsen (2004, 2003) (building on observations in Bellert 1977) observes that the natural way to make sense of this is to suppose that speaker-oriented adverbs are POSITIVE POLARITY ITEMS – expressions that occur in environments in which negative polarity items (NPIs) like *ever* and *any* aren't licensed. These observations aren't limited to English. Nilsen (2004) observes similar effects in Norwegian, Dutch, and Greek, Cinque (1999) in Italian, and Ernst (2009) in French and Mandarin.

This is slightly surprising. Non-adverbial paraphrases of (93b) don't have this property:

(94) It isn't $\begin{Bmatrix} \text{(un)fortunate} \\ \text{amazing} \\ \text{probable} \\ \text{certain} \end{Bmatrix}$ that Floyd has died.

One of the most prominent way of accounting for polarity sensitivity involves ideas that were first articulated in Kadmon and Landman (1993). In a nutshell, NPIs are treated as broadening contextually

5.6 *Locative adverbials* 237

supplied restrictions on the domains of quantifiers. In many sentences, this would have the effect of weakening the truth-conditional claim they make – saying that someone in the world wears glasses is weaker than saying that someone in the room does. The other part of the meaning of NPIs, on this view, is that they require that they have a strengthening, not a weakening effect. The only way this can come about is if domain-widening happens in certain environments, and only these license NPIs. Such environments include the scope of negation: saying that no one in the world wears glasses is stronger than saying no one in the room does. This is the framework Nilsen (2004) adopts. He derives the difference between speaker-oriented adverbs and their non-PPI adjectival counterparts by assigning the adverbs subtly different denotations, ones that have a domain-shrinking effect. Ernst (2009) considers some of the same facts, but provides an analysis built around an alternative theory of polarity sensitivity (associated with Giannakidou 1999).

5.6 LOCATIVE ADVERBIALS

5.6.1 Types and positions of locative adverbials

Maienborn (2001) provides a helpful typology of locative adverbials. There are, in her system, three, distinguished by both their syntactic position and their interpretation. These positions are especially clear in German, the language she focuses on, but the principles apply more broadly. The first is the easiest case, EXTERNAL MODIFIERS (her examples):

(95) a. Eva signed the contract <u>in Argentina</u>.
 b. Paul sang the Marseillaise <u>in front of the Capitol</u>.

These can be analyzed in a straightforward Davidsonian style. For (95a), for example, the denotation might be as in (96):

(96) $\exists e[\mathbf{sign}(\mathbf{the\text{-}contract})(\mathbf{Eva})(e) \wedge \mathbf{in}(\mathbf{Argentina})(e)]$

If one wanted to spell things out a little further, one could add to the model a domain of spatial REGIONS (Link 1998; Bierwisch 1988a, 1996; Wunderlich 1991). A rough representation of how this might be used is in (97), where **region** maps individuals or events to the regions they occupy (a spatial trace function in the sense of Link 1998) and $\sqsubseteq$ is the part-of relation for regions:

(97) $\exists e \begin{bmatrix} \text{sign(the-contract)(Eva)}(e) \land \\ \text{region}(e) \sqsubseteq \text{region(Argentina)} \end{bmatrix}$

Thus the signing event occupies a region that is part of the region Argentina occupies. The other classes of locatives are not so neatly handled, however.

The second type is INTERNAL MODIFIERS:

(98) a. Eva signed the contract <u>on the last page</u>.
b. Paul sang the Marseillaise <u>on his head</u>.

In (98a), it's not really true that Eva's contract-signing took place on the last page of the contract. Likewise for (98b) and Paul's singing. Both are internal in the sense that they don't provide information about the location of an event as a whole, but rather information about the location of a part of the event or spatial information relevant to the manner in which it was carried out. In English, internal modifiers (naturally enough) occur closer to the verb than external ones.

The third type is one we have already encountered, FRAME-SETTING ADVERBIALS:

(99) a. <u>In Argentina</u>, Eva still is very popular.
b. <u>In Bolivia</u>, Britta was blond.

One striking difference between these locative and the others, she notes, is that they're not droppable. One can't conclude from (99a) that Eva is still very popular, or from (99b) that Britta was blond. Maienborn ultimately analyzes these adverbials as topic-like.

5.6.2 Vector Space Semantics

There is an alternative to thinking about locatives simply in terms of regions, and it's especially natural for spatial prepositions. This view, articulated and refined by Zwarts (1997), Zwarts and Winter (2000), and Winter (2005), involves conceptualizing preposition meaning in terms of VECTORS in a VECTOR SPACE. Vectors are simply directed line segments, a contiguous linear set of points. They are introduced directly into the model.

On this view, a PP such as *above the house* is true of vectors that start at the house and point upward (i.e. that end at some point above it), like those in (101):

(100) 〚 *above the house* 〛
 = $\lambda v . \text{start(the-house)}(v) \land \textbf{upward}(v)$

5.6 Locative adverbials

(101) ABOVE THE HOUSE

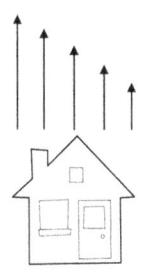

A sentence meaning, then, would be as in (102):

(102) $[\![\text{The bird is above the house}]\!]$
$$= \exists v \begin{bmatrix} \text{start(the-house)}(v) \wedge \text{upward}(v) \\ \text{end(the-bird)}(v) \end{bmatrix}$$

This requires that there be a vector that starts at the house and ends at the bird. In order to get here compositionally, the property of vectors the PP denotes needs to be turned into a property of individuals located at the end of those vectors. This could be accomplished by a type shift (Partee 1987), or by supposing that there is an unpronounced morpheme that does this work. Up to this point, this is relatively intuitive, but nothing special has happened. One place this framework shines, though, is in the interpretation of modifiers of the PPs, which in turn sheds light on the PPs themselves.

Measure phrases, for example, are compatible with *above the house* but not *near the house*:

(103) six feet $\begin{Bmatrix} \text{above} \\ \text{\#near} \end{Bmatrix}$ the house

To make sense of this, a first step is to suppose that measure phrases denote properties of vectors too – specifically, of vectors with a certain length:

(104) $[\![\text{six feet}]\!] = \lambda v \,.\, \text{length}(v) \geq \text{6-feet}$

This can be interpreted intersectively with *above the house*:

(105) $[\![\text{six feet above the house}]\!] = \lambda v.\text{start(the-house)}(v) \wedge$
$\text{upward}(v) \wedge \text{length}(v) \geq \text{6-feet}$

Near the house, on the other hand, imposes a restriction not on the direction of vectors, but on their length:

(106) $[\![\text{near the house}]\!] = \lambda v \,.\, \text{start}(\text{the-house})(v) \wedge \text{short}(v)$

(107) NEAR THE HOUSE

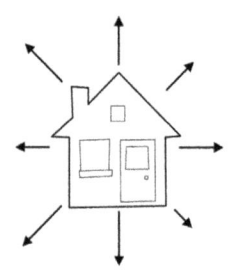

Given all this, *six feet* should be able to combine with *near the house*.

As Zwarts and Winter (2000) and Winter (2005) show, though, there is a crucial distinction to be made. If it rises a bit, it will be at the end of a new vector, but it will still be above the house. It therefore must be the case that $[\![\text{above the house}]\!]$ holds of this new vector. As it rises further, this will continue to be the case: it's still above the house, so $[\![\text{above the house}]\!]$ must hold of each longer vector. By contrast, let's suppose a car is near the house and gradually driving away. Eventually, it will no longer be near the house, so $[\![\text{near the house}]\!]$ can't hold of each longer vector. Zwarts and Winter argue that measure phrases are possible only with modifiers like *above the house* – ones that are upward monotonic in the sense that if it holds of a vector, it holds of all longer ones.[22] *Near the house* lacks this property, and so doesn't allow measure phrases.

A bonus feature of this framework is that it makes it possible to provide natural intersective denotations for ill-understood PP modifiers like *diagonally* in *diagonally across the quad*.

5.7 ADVERBS AS MODIFIERS OF ADJECTIVES

A common thing to say about adverbs is that they are modifiers of verbs, sentences, or adjectives. Sometimes prepositions are thrown in, too. It's rarely remarked that this is actually slightly mysterious: sentences are verbal projections, and so of course are VPs, but if adjectives

---

[22] In fact, they actually require monotonicity in both directions.

5.7 Adverbs as modifiers of adjectives

and prepositions are to be included as well, it behooves us to ask why. Given how freely the term 'adverb' is thrown about, one might suspect that this is simply the result of an age-old analytical error. At some point, words like 'degree morpheme' and certainly 'degree head' and 'Deg' were unavailable, and perhaps someone mistakenly applied the principle that everything is an adverb until proven otherwise. It would be satisfyingly iconoclastic to dismiss all that. But we can't.

One slight indication that we might be dealing with adverbs after all is that some degree words seem to have an -*ly* ending (*really, truly*). But these can – and probably should – be set aside as inconsequential remnants of the history of these expressions. The phenomenon runs deeper, though, as these examples from Castroviejo Miró (2008a) reflect:

(108)   extremely tall, endlessly frustrating, colossally stupid, deeply talented, widely successful, ridiculously expensive

The crucial thing is not just that there is a regular pattern in the distribution of -*ly* here. That too we might be able to handle, at worst by positing two homophonous -*ly* morphemes. It's that many of these expressions remain closely related to their VP-modifying counterparts and are probably more than just phonologically identical to them.

That becomes even clearer when one focuses on particular subclasses of these adverbs. There is, for example, a proper subset of evaluative adverbs that systematically have AP-modifying degree uses (Katz 2005; Nouwen 2005, 2011; Morzycki 2008a):

(109)   a. *evaluative adverbs*

$$\left\{ \begin{array}{l} \text{Amazingly,} \\ \text{Remarkably,} \\ \text{Surprisingly,} \\ \text{Alarmingly,} \\ \text{Disappointingly,} \end{array} \right\} \text{Floyd is tall.}$$

     b. *evaluative degree adverbs*

$$\text{Floyd is} \left\{ \begin{array}{l} \text{amazingly} \\ \text{remarkably} \\ \text{surprisingly} \\ \text{alarmingly} \\ \text{disappointingly} \end{array} \right\} \text{tall.}$$

Part of what's entertaining about this effect is that the degree readings in (109b) are systematically related to the ordinary adverbial ones in (109a). But the connection is not direct. *Floyd is remarkably tall* can't merely be paraphrased as *Remarkably, Floyd is tall*. One might dismiss this lack of synonymy on the grounds that only the latter involves a POS morpheme. Degree *remarkably* and POS, it's reasonable to assume, compete for the same syntactic position and are thus in complementary distribution.[23]

That alone won't suffice, though. The details need to be spelled out, and there are two natural ways of doing so. The meaning of (110a) might be something like (110b), in which **remarkable** is predicated of a degree; or something like (110c), in which it's predicated of a proposition:

(110)   a. Floyd is remarkably tall.
         b. $\exists d[\textbf{tall}(d)(\textbf{Floyd}) \wedge \textbf{remarkable}(d)]$
         c. $\exists d[\textbf{tall}_w(d)(\textbf{Floyd}) \wedge \textbf{remarkable}(\lambda w' . \textbf{tall}_{w'}(d)(\textbf{Floyd}))]$

One difficulty with both of these is that neither reflects that if (110a) is true, it must be the case that Floyd is tall – that is, neither reflects that (110a) doesn't neutralize the adjective. But this isn't the deepest problem. It could be addressed by shoehorning in a conjunct about exceeding a contextually provided standard. The deeper problem in (110b) is that, on the usual understanding of degrees, one can't really predicate remarkableness of them. They're just not rich enough. A degree of height is something like '6 feet', but '6 feet' can't be said to be remarkable on their own. The alternative in (110c) avoids this problem by predicating remarkableness of the proposition that Floyd is d tall. But this won't suffice either. Suppose there has been an eery coincidence, and Floyd was born at 5:09 in 1959, lives at 59 Fifty-ninth Street, and his precise height is 5'9''. In this scenario, it's certainly remarkable that his height is 5'9'', but we still can't truthfully say of him that he's *remarkably tall*. In Morzycki (2008a), I try to account for this by pursuing an analogy to the paraphrase 'It's amazing how tall Floyd is.' But Nouwen (2011) proposes a more elegant solution that combines insights in Katz (2005) to get the result that one is only remarkably tall to a degree if it would be the case that being tall to any higher degree is also remarkable (see also discussion in Castroviejo Miró and Schwager 2008 and Schwager 2009). Interestingly, Nouwen shows this can be

---

[23] Actually, a more subtle way of implementing this is available. POS and *remarkably* can be framed in a way that would ensure that either can combine with the type of a gradable predicate, but neither can combine with the result of combining the other with a gradable predicate.

related to the observation, due to Zwicky (1970), that when evaluative adverbs occur in antonymous pairs, only one member can occur as an AP modifier (#*usually*/#*unremarkably tall*).

Castroviejo Miró (2008a) broadens the picture to include a wider range of adverbial AP modifiers. She shows that at least some of them – members of a class that includes *extremely* – behave as though they contribute secondary, conventionally implicated content in the Potts (2003) style.

Finally, the last nail in the coffin of the idea that AP-modifying adverbs aren't true adverbs: in some cases, it looks like APs host manner adverbs. There is some debate about whether apparent examples of this are misleadingly exceptional (Katz 2003, 2008; Geuder 2006; Mittwoch 2005; Maienborn 2007), but there's certainly no shortage of them (as Ernst 2011 demonstrates in an especially systematic way):

(111) a. Floyd is $\begin{Bmatrix} \text{visibly happy} \\ \text{strangely beautiful} \end{Bmatrix}$.
 b. The talk was $\begin{Bmatrix} \text{oddly unnerving} \\ \text{fatally flawed} \end{Bmatrix}$.
 c. These examples might be misleadingly exceptional.

Some of these also have degree readings, but they all have another reading which would at least seem to be a manner one.

The principal conclusion to draw from all this, I think, is just that much remains yet to be understood about how adverbial modification of AP works.

5.8 PHENOMENA WE WILL MOSTLY SET ASIDE

5.8.1 Temporal adverbials

Temporal adverbials aren't so much a semantic phenomenon as they are a semantic industry. They are one of the principal topics in temporal semantics, itself a vast enterprise. For that reason, I will set them aside here. Their semantics is directly connected to relatively few ideas that are a focus of this book, and depends on too many that aren't.

Nevertheless, at least one point should be made. The best-known fact about temporal adverbials is that they are sensitive to TELICITY – very roughly, whether a predicate characterizes an event as bounded. One common way of understanding the idea is that a VP is ATELIC iff it describes an event in a way that would also describe any part of the event. Otherwise, it is TELIC. Thus *push the cart* is atelic, because every part of an event of pushing the cart is also an event of pushing the cart. On the other hand, *push the cart off a cliff* is telic, because not every part of an event of pushing the cart off the cliff is is also an event of pushing the cart off a cliff.

It's sometimes hard to avoid lapsing into talk of events themselves being telic or atelic. As the characterization above reflects, though, strictly speaking it's event **descriptions** – VPs, essentially – that are telic or atelic, not the events themselves. Indeed, the same event of pushing the cart off a cliff can be described with both the atelic VP *push the cart* and the telic VP *push the cart off the cliff*. This may seem a pedantic point, but something important depends on it – and it's something immediately relevant here.

First, the fact. Setting aside various complications, English temporal *for* PPs are generally compatible only with atelic VPs, and temporal *in* PPs with telic ones (Vendler 1967; Dowty 1979, and many others):

(112) a. Floyd pushed the cart $\begin{Bmatrix} \text{for} \\ \text{\#in} \end{Bmatrix}$ an hour.

b. Floyd pushed the cart off the cliff $\begin{Bmatrix} \text{\#for} \\ \text{in} \end{Bmatrix}$ an hour.

So, compositionally, how would one capture this? There are two obvious possibilities: *for an hour* could denote a property of events or a predicate modifier. If we can get away with a property denotation, we should. Using a needlessly high type is always undesirable, like lighting a cigarette with a blowtorch. But as it turns out, we're not lighting a cigarette. Although it's perfectly reasonable to think of lasting an hour as a property of an event, these adverbs also need to impose the telicity requirement. As we just established, being telic or atelic is **not** a property of an event but rather of an event description. The PP therefore needs to know not just about an event, but also about the whole VP – which means it has to denote a predicate modifier. One way to represent the atelicity requirement, in the spirit of Dowty (1979), is in (113) (τ is a function mapping events to their running times and $\sqsubseteq$ is the subevent relation; Link 1998):

(113) $[\![\text{for an hour}]\!]$
= $\lambda P_{\langle v, t \rangle} \lambda e : \forall e'[e' \sqsubseteq e \to P(e')] . P(e) \land [\![\text{an hour}]\!] (\tau(e))$

This encodes the atelicity requirement as a presupposition (expressed with the colon notation of Heim and Kratzer 1998) that the event

5.8 Phenomena we will mostly set aside

description P also holds of all subevents of e, and treats *an hour* as a property of times. Imposing this requirement requires access to the VP denotation. A property denotation wouldn't provide that access, so it would preclude imposing such a requirement. If, however, events had inherent telicity on their own, a property denotation might have sufficed.

Importantly, the problem here is linguistic, not conceptual. The idea that events might be telic or atelic on their own isn't incoherent. Boundedness in scales works in precisely that way. Open and closed scales can be represented as open and closed intervals. Like degrees, times also involve linearly ordered points, and their analogous notion of boundedness might have been consistent with an account in terms open and closed intervals as well (indeed, Dowty 1979 considers the possibility). As it turns out, it doesn't seem to be.

The importance of this here, then, is threefold. First, it shows that at least some temporal adverbials seem to need to a predicate-modifier type. Second, it highlights an asymmetry between the notion of boundedness in the degree and temporal domains. Third, it's a useful reminder that abstractions like this aren't somehow inevitable consequences of certain formal assumptions, but reflections of particular empirical facts about language that could well have been otherwise.

A good starting point in the literature on temporal semantics is Dowty (1979), and classic references include Vendler (1957, 1967); Partee (1973); Bach (1986); Krifka (1989, 1998); and Kratzer (1998).

5.8.2 Adverbs of quantification

The other major issue we will set aside is adverbs of quantification such as *frequently*, *often*, *always*, and *rarely*, and we will do so for similar reasons. Adverbs of quantification are among the major issues addressed under the rubric of quantification generally. Classic references in the area include Lewis (1975), Kamp (1981b), Heim (1982), and de Swart (1993).

Again, though, there is one small point that bears making. The analysis of these adverbs has taken various forms over the years, but a relatively consistent current is treating them as basically quantifiers. The essential contribution of *always*, for example, is universal quantification, and of *sometimes*, existential. One leading idea has been that they are UNSELECTIVE QUANTIFIERS, ones that bind all free variables in their scope. Such an analysis, like most typical ones, makes them profoundly different from other classes of adverbs – certainly, quite different from all the predicational adverbs we've examined here.

And yet, there's something that such a sharp demarcation leaves unexplained – that some adverbs of quantification are gradable:

(114) a. Floyd $\begin{Bmatrix} \text{very} \\ \text{quite} \end{Bmatrix} \begin{Bmatrix} \text{frequently} \\ \text{often} \\ \text{rarely} \end{Bmatrix}$ explodes.

b. Floyd explodes more $\begin{Bmatrix} \text{often} \\ \text{frequently} \\ \text{rarely} \end{Bmatrix}$.

This suggests that these adverbs have a degree argument, or in any case a type that is compatible with degree modification. It's not trivial to reconcile such a gradable predicate type that with a semantics that introduces a quantifier with scope extending outside the adverbial itself. A similar issue comes up in the semantics of *many* and *few* (see section 6.2.1), but in those cases the standard move is to assume that the quantifier is actually introduced independently.

5.9 ADVERB ORDER REVISITED

We have already encountered several ways in which the position of an adverb can influence its interpretation. Being very high in the clause can cause a manner adverb to be interpreted as a speech-act adverb, perhaps due to the proximity of a speech-act operator. (Or perhaps there is simply an ambiguity between manner and speech-act adverbs, but independent principles ensure that the latter occur high. See section 5.5.1.) Subject-oriented adverbs may need to be above a Voice head to get interpreted in the right way, thereby explaining why they tend to occur higher than manner adverbs. Evaluative adverbs apply to propositions, so they need to be high enough in the clause to find a proposition-denoting expression as their sister.

One can be more or less persuaded by these kinds of explanations, but one definitely shouldn't conclude that they constitute a full account of how adverb position and interpretation correlate. There is an extensive array of interesting generalizations and puzzles in this domain, explored most comprehensively in Cinque (1999) and Ernst (2002). Some of these are purely about the relative order of adverbs, and some involve restrictions on the order of adverbs relative to various other non-adverb syntactic constituents, including most prominently verbal heads.

I'll briefly mention two such puzzles, just to provide a sense of the problems. One is that evaluative adverbs can occur above epistemic ones, but not vice versa:

5.9 Adverb order revisited

(115) a. $\left\{\begin{array}{l}\text{Unfortunately,}\\ \text{Unsurprisingly,}\end{array}\right\}$ the students will $\left\{\begin{array}{l}\text{certainly}\\ \text{probably}\end{array}\right\}$ object.

b. ??$\left\{\begin{array}{l}\text{Certainly,}\\ \text{Probably,}\end{array}\right\}$ the students will $\left\{\begin{array}{l}\text{unfortunately}\\ \text{unsurprisingly}\end{array}\right\}$ object.

Another is that speaker-oriented adverbs must scope over subject-oriented ones (example from Ernst 2009):

(116) a. They obviously have cleverly been siphoning off little bits of cash.
b. *They cleverly have obviously been siphoning off little bits of cash.

One striking aspect of this is that *obviously* is perfectly capable of occupying the lower position in (116b), provided a speaker-oriented adverb doesn't occur above it:

(117) They have obviously been siphoning off little bits of cash.

As for restrictions on the relative order of heads and adverbs, here is another example from Ernst (2009):

(118) a. They will ideally be leaving.
b. *They will be ideally leaving.
c. *They will have been ideally leaving.

Ernst (2002) and Ernst (2009) provide accounts of these sets of facts.

There is a bigger picture here, though. There are two classes of approaches to such problems, and they mesh with the semantics differently. One is a widely held view in syntax that restrictions on adjuncts – on their relative order and on what can adjoin to what – need not be specified in the syntax because they will follow from the semantics. This idea is longstanding, dating back to at least the early 1980s, but it was always a curious one: it's a promissory note issued by syntacticians and payable by semanticists. In the intervening decades, the semantics has been able to provide some explanations of the necessary sort, but certainly not enough to fully deliver on it.

The guiding principle of Ernst (2002) is to pursue semantic explanations that begin to do this. The concrete semantic proposals he makes aren't in a fully compositional framework, and more generally they are intended more as a demonstration of the general proposition that syntactic position can follow from semantics than as a complete and compositional theory of particular constructions. Nevertheless, it provides a firm foundation of observations and analytical insights upon which one might develop more detailed semantic analyses. This makes it an excellent starting point for semantic inquiry in this area.

The alternative option is the one championed by Cinque (1999): to reclaim such facts for syntax, and take responsibility for explaining them syntacticly. Cinque does so with an extensive array of functional heads corresponding to the adverb hierarchy in (3) in section 5.2, whose specifier positions adverbs occupy. This would relieve semantics of the responsibility to account for puzzles it has, to a large extent, neglected in any case.

It's an interesting state of affairs. Adverbs are difficult semantic territory, certainly, but syntactic work in this area highlights how much there remains to be explained of their semantics. Adjectives are fascinating, and there is no shortage of semanticists who have fallen under their spell. Adverbs, by contrast, haven't been able to attract quite the same following. The difference is as understandable as it is unfortunate.

5.10 QUESTIONS FOR FURTHER REFLECTION AND DISCUSSION

- Compare the various explanations provided for subject-orientation. How might one adjudicate among them? What synthesis might be possible? Are there broader insights on which the research may converge?
- What accounts for the syntactic position of adverbs?
- How are adjectives and adverbs related? This questions has some obvious answers, but it's interesting to seek out non-obvious ones – that is, to ask the question at a more fine-grained level of detail. What specific observations or ideas in Chapters 2 and 3 have analogues in this chapter, or might prove analytically useful here? Conversely, might issues in the grammar of adverbs shed light on adjectives?
- Given their diverse distribution, what do adverbs have in common? And what about their semantics makes them so flexible?
- The Davidsonian picture on which event adverbs are simply predicates of events is quite beautiful – but is it sufficient? Is it enough, for example, to simply say that *quietly* requires of an event that it was a quiet one? Is that like predicating *quiet* of an individual, where we feel no great need to probe further into how an individual might be quiet? Or could something further be said?

5.11 SUGGESTIONS FOR FURTHER READING

Good entry points into the literature cited in this chapter include the following:

- For the syntax of adverbs, the standard references are Cinque (1999) and Ernst (2002). Both are books. As the prose above indicates, though, the Ernst book is especially well-positioned to be helpful to the semantically inclined.
- Works such as Thomason and Stalnaker (1973) and McConnell-Ginet (1982) are important in part for the influence they have had, but neither is as readable as it once was in light of changes to the prevailing semantic frameworks. A reader interested in moving in that direction might be well-advised to do so in reverse, by starting with more recent work (Wyner 1998 or Geuder 2000, for example) and moving backwards.
- One should read Davidson (1967). It is both foundational to a huge swath of semantic theory and accessible. To push further into event semantics, Parsons (1990) is a good follow-up.

6 Crosscategorial concerns

6.1 INTRODUCTION

One of the more interesting properties of the grammar of modification is that it can reveal connections across syntactic categories and across semantic types. There remain on our agenda a few issues that provide a taste of this – ones that involve multiple categories or interactions among several of the domains we've already examined.

This chapter takes up these crosscategorial issues. In section 6.2, we confront expressions that measure individuals by their amount, and the comparatives built out of these expressions. This requires combining our standing assumptions about degree semantics with assumptions about DPs and individuals. Section 6.3 examines the issue of crosscategorial gradability more broadly, focusing on verbs and nouns, both of which seem to be gradable in different ways and one of which introduces into the discussion some new parallels between individuals and events. Section 6.4 addresses the problem of crosscategorial modifiers that hedge or reinforce a claim, but can't be readily assimilated to the degree modifiers we've already encountered in other domains. Section 6.5 focuses on an issue we've systematically set aside throughout the book: nonrestrictive interpretations of modifiers, which turn out to extend far beyond relative clauses, their traditional home. Part of that entails struggling with what 'nonrestrictive' actually means. Finally, section 6.6 investigates an aspect of meaning that is inherently subjective in a particular way that can be made precise – and that makes it possible for interlocutors to contradict each other truth-conditionally without being at odds pragmatically.

6.2 AMOUNTS AND CARDINALITY SCALES

6.2.1 Quantity adjectives and number words

The aim of section 6.2 is to provide a sketch of how the assumptions we've made about degrees and degree constructions in Chapters 3 and 4 might scale up to uses such as those in (1):

(1)   a. There were many monkeys.
         b. There were three monkeys.
         c. There were more than three monkeys.
         d. There were more monkeys than ~~there were~~ ferrets.

The important fact about these examples is that they involve evaluating or comparing on a scale of CARDINALITY, the number of individuals that make up a plurality.

In order to get off the ground, we need to make some assumptions about plurals. The standard account is that of Link (1983), who distinguishes between atomic individuals (singular ones) and plural individuals formed by combining atomic individuals. For Link, both singular and plural individuals are of type e. Link's theory of plurals involves far more than just this, but these bare-bones assumptions alone will suffice for our current goals. We will, however, need one additional piece of equipment: a cardinality function, written $|x|$ (an alternative notation is $\#x$), that maps individuals to their cardinalities.[1] The cardinalities themselves are just natural numbers, so they form a scale. We therefore have every reason to regard them as degrees. This makes $|\cdot|$ a measure function, type $\langle e, d \rangle$.

As a first approximation, then, the denotation of *many* could simply be a property of having a cardinality that exceeds some standard:

(2) $[\![\text{many}]\!] = \lambda x \,.\, |x| > \textbf{standard}$

It's unclear what the argument of the **standard** predicate should be here, so I've omitted it. But there is a deeper problem. *Many* is an adjective. It doesn't very naturally occur predicatively in English (*??We are many*), but in attributive positions it happily combines with degree morphemes: *very many*, *as many*, and *too many* are all possible.

---

[1] A true theory of plurals requires, minimally, an explicit definition of the individual-sum operation that combines individuals and an ordering relating individuals to individuals of which they are a part. It also involves a characterization of the difference between plurals like *monkeys* and mass individuals like *water*.

The antonym of *many*, *few*, even has a synthetic comparative *fewer*. Perhaps *many* itself does too, pronounced not *manier* but *more*. In fact, *many*, *few*, *much*, and *little* form a class of QUANTITY ADJECTIVES with a number of interesting properties in common (see Rett 2008b and Solt 2009 for detailed exploration).[2] What is really necessary, then, is an adjective denotation, type $\langle d, et \rangle$, that relates an individual to its cardinality:[3]

(3) $[\![many]\!] = \lambda d \lambda x [|x| = d]$

This could then combine with the POS morpheme to yield (4):

(4)   a. $[\![\text{POS}]\!] = \lambda G_{\langle d, et \rangle} \lambda x . \exists d [G(d)(x) \wedge d > \textbf{standard}(G)]$
       b. $[\![\text{POS } many]\!]$
           $= \lambda x . \exists d [[\![many]\!](d)(x) \wedge d > \textbf{standard}([\![many]\!])]$
           $= \lambda x . \exists d [|x| = d \wedge d > \textbf{standard}(\lambda y \lambda d' . |y| = d')]$

This holds of an individual iff the cardinality of that individual exceeds the standard. The puzzle of the argument of **standard** is now (arguably) solved as well. The standard is simply the standard for having a sufficiently large cardinality, provided by *many* itself.[4] This can combine intersectively with a noun:

(5)   a. $[\![\text{POS } many\ monkeys]\!]$
           $= \lambda x . [\![\text{POS } many]\!](x) \wedge [\![monkeys]\!](x)$
           $= \lambda x . \exists d [|x| = d \wedge d > \textbf{standard}([\![many]\!])] \wedge \textbf{monkeys}(x)$
       b. $[\![there\ were\ \text{POS } many\ monkeys]\!]$
           $= \exists x \exists d [|x| = d \wedge d > \textbf{standard}([\![many]\!])] \wedge \textbf{monkeys}(x)$

Thus POS *many monkeys* will hold of an individual that consists of monkeys and whose cardinality exceeds the standard, as in (5a). The full sentence would then be interpreted as in (5b), with the individual

---

[2] Rett (2008b) calls these *m*-words and Solt (2009), Q-adjectives.
[3] I've forsaken the period notation for brackets only to clarify that = is part of the denotation itself.
[4] One possible qualm about this approach is that it suggests that in the right context, the standard for having a sufficiently large cardinality might be set at 1, thereby making 2 count as many. Indeed, the situation may be worse still: on a theory like that of Kennedy and McNally (2005) and Kennedy (2007), this scale would be lower-closed (it has a minimum value but no maximum), which in turn would **require** the standard to be set at the bottom in precisely this way.

6.2 Amounts and cardinality scales

variable existentially closed – perhaps by the denotation of expletive *there* – yielding a sentence that simply asserts that there is a monkey plurality with a sufficiently large cardinality.

This is fine as far as it goes, but what about NUMBER WORDS or numerals such as *three*? Again, we have a few options. One would be to treat numerals as simply properties, as we considered for *many*:

(6) $[\![three]\!] = \lambda x[|x| = 3]$

This is actually a reasonably well-subscribed view of numeral meaning (Landman 2003; Chierchia 2010; Rothstein 2010). Certainly, *three* isn't gradable, as *more* is, so it seems unlikely to denote a gradable predicate.[5] In the current context, though, this strategy has a major drawback: it doesn't accord how we have treated measure phrases. Numerals can occur as differential measure phrases in comparatives as in (7a) and (7b), and expressions anaphoric to numerals can occur in the measure-phrase position of *many* as in (7c):

(7) a. There were three more monkeys.
       compare to: Floyd was three inches taller

   b. There were more than three monkeys.
       compare to: Floyd seemed taller than six feet.

   c. There were three weasels, and there were also that many monkeys.
       compare to: Floyd was that tall.

Given our standing assumptions, such measure-phrase positions are where we expect a degree-denoting expression.[6]

What all this suggests is that numerals aren't actually adjectives, but like measure phrases, just the names of degrees:

(8) $[\![three]\!] = 3$

But if that's the case, how do these combine compositionally with a noun? What we really need is an adjective like *many*, which would lead us back to the property denotation we originally desired, the one in (9b):

---

[5] This, of course, doesn't mean it can't be analyzed as an adjective, though it's best to set the question of its syntactic category aside.
[6] This may actually be misguided, as Schwarzschild (2005) persuasively argues. It's probably ultimately preferable to assume that measure phrases have property denotations. Such a move has consequences that reverberate widely, beyond our current concerns, so we will set the issue aside.

(9) a. $[\![\,many\,]\!] = \lambda d \lambda x [|x| = d]$
 b. $[\![\,three\ many\,]\!] = [\![\,many\,]\!]([\![\,three\,]\!]) = \lambda x[|x| = [\![\,three\,]\!]]$
    $= \lambda x[|x| = 3]$

Inconveniently, that's not actually the structure we pronounce: *three many monkeys* is ill-formed. Since Bresnan (1973), the standard move at this point has been to suppose that *many* has an unpronounced variant, MANY. This might seem a kludge, but it turns out to be independently motivated. For example, *too many monkeys* is possible while *too monkeys* is not. On the other hand, *many enough monkeys* isn't possible while *enough monkeys* is. Yet *too* and *enough* are otherwise parallel. That suggests that some idiosyncratic morphophonological rules determine when and how the abstract MANY morpheme is pronounced. *Too* MANY is pronounced *too many*, while MANY *enough* is pronounced as simply *enough*. Either way, these morphophonological considerations need not worry us here. With this assumption in place, the denotation of numerals is straightforward.

For both numerals and *many*, a fairly innocent and independently motivated further assumption is required to deal with attributive DPs such as (10a), namely, that in these cases there is a null existential determiner:

(10) a. $\emptyset_D$ three MANY monkeys frowned.
 b. $[\![\,\emptyset_D\,]\!] = \lambda P_{\langle e, t\rangle} \lambda Q_{\langle e, t\rangle} . \exists x [P(x) \wedge Q(x)]$
 c. $[\![\,\emptyset_D\,]\!]([\![\,three\ \text{MANY}\ monkeys\,]\!])([\![\,frowned\,]\!])$
    $= \exists x[|x| = 3 \wedge \textbf{frowned}(x)]$

Assuming a null determiner is perfectly plausible for bare plurals and mass nouns in general (though see Chierchia 1998 for a richly articulated theory of the relation between determiners and mass nouns). It also accords with the possibility of using an overt determiner in this position: *the three monkeys, the many monkeys I saw*. Nevertheless, this could be viewed as a kind of decomposition of the meaning of MANY. Further pursuing a decomposition strategy may reap further rewards (Solt 2009).

These results were possible because of the well-motivated assumption that *many* is an adjective and that numerals are interpreted with its help, but this assumption is not a universal one. In work in Generalized Quantifier Theory like Barwise and Cooper (1981) and Keenan and Faltz (1985), *many*, *more*, and numerals are treated as determiners. Interesting results follow from doing this, but syntactic and compositional considerations point in another direction (see Hackl 2000 for extensive discussion). Another approach to these issues, advanced in

6.2 Amounts and cardinality scales

Cresswell (1976), is to treat not *many* but rather the noun itself as having a degree argument. A noun would thus relate an individual and a degree representing its cardinality. This idea isn't widely adopted, but it may provide a means of avoiding positing the null MANY. There are also other reasons to suppose that nouns may have degree arguments, although in an entirely different way (see section 6.3.2).

On the surface, the denotation for MANY provided here seems to provide an 'exactly' interpretation: *three monkeys* is a property of a plurality with exactly three members and no more. The relation involved is $=$, not $\geq$. Nevertheless, every plurality with more than three members also contains a part with three. If a plurality of exactly four monkeys arrived, there must also be as part of it a plurality of exactly three monkeys that did so too. The issue is worth considering, though, because the question of whether numerals get 'exactly' or 'at least' interpretations is a live one. The longstanding and widely accepted view is that *Floyd has three children* asserts that Floyd has at least three, but gives rise to a Gricean conversational implicature that he has no more than that (Grice 1975; Horn 1972; Levinson 1983). Evidence for the 'exactly' view can be found in Geurts (2006); Breheny (2008); Huang et al. (2013), and counterevidence in Barner et al. (2011).

This all barely scratches the surface of how numerals work, or for that matter *many* and its relatives (*few*, *little*, and *much*). For discussion of measure phrases and amount measurement in nominal domain and its connections to other areas, see Krifka (1989); Schwarzschild (2006); for detailed examination of the lexical semantics of words like *many* and *much*, see Rett (2006, 2008b), Solt (2009, 2011b); for a fine-grained theory of the compositional properties of numerals, see Ionin and Matushansky (2006); for work on these issues that also incorporates scalar modifiers such as *at least* into the picture, a good start is Geurts and Nouwen (2007).

6.2.2 Amount comparatives

We've only accomplished half our task. The other half was to sketch an outline of AMOUNT COMPARATIVES such as those in (11):

(11) a. There were more than three monkeys.
      b. There were more monkeys than there were ferrets.

These are also often called NOMINAL COMPARATIVES.[7]

---

[7] I find this term unfortunate because it suggests that it's the noun that is the gradable predicate. As we'll see, it is individuals and their cardinalities or amounts,

It turns out that we have a version of a standard treatment of these expressions already, if we assemble the existing building blocks just right. First, beginning with the phrasal comparative in (11a), the structure should be analogous to (12a), with the gradable predicate *tall* replaced by the abstract cardinality predicate MANY:

(12)   a. Floyd is [taller than six feet].
       b. There were [MANY-er than three monkeys].

Because *more* is a pronunciation of MANY-*er*, it's customary in these contexts to write the comparative morpheme as -*er*. The structures in (12) are too simple, though. They don't take into account degree movement, the process by which a DegP, which denotes a generalized quantifier over degrees, vacates its base position and leaves behind a degree trace (see Chapter 4). The actual structure for (12b) is in (13b), derived by movement from (13a):

(13)   a. There were [[-er than three] MANY] monkeys.
       b. [-er than three] ∅ λd_1 there were [d_1 MANY] monkeys

We'll return to the assumption from Chapter 4 that phrasal *than* has no interpretation, and to the denotation for the comparative morpheme in (14a). The computation would thus be:

(14)   a. $[\![\text{-}er]\!] = \lambda d \lambda D_{\langle d, t \rangle} . \mathbf{max}(D) > d$
       b. $[\![\text{than three}]\!] = [\![\text{three}]\!] = 3$
       c. $[\![d_1 \text{ MANY}]\!] = [\![\text{MANY}]\!]([\![d_1]\!]) = \lambda x[|x| = d_1]$
       d. $[\![d_1 \text{ MANY monkeys}]\!] = \lambda x[[\![d_1 \text{ MANY}]\!](x) \wedge [\![\text{monkeys}]\!](x)]$
          $= \lambda x[|x| = d_1 \wedge \mathbf{monkeys}(x)]$
       e. $[\![\text{there were } [d_1 \text{ MANY}] \text{ monkeys}]\!]$
          $= \exists x[|x| = d_1 \wedge \mathbf{monkeys}(x)]$
       f. $[\![\emptyset \lambda d_1 \text{ there were } d_1 \text{ MANY monkeys}]\!]$
          $= \lambda d_1 . \exists x[|x| = d_1 \wedge \mathbf{monkeys}(x)]$
       g. $[\![\text{-}er]\!]([\![\text{than three}]\!])([\![\emptyset \lambda d_1 \text{ there were } d_1 \text{ MANY monkeys}]\!])$
          $= \mathbf{max}([\![\emptyset \lambda d_1 \text{ there were } d_1 \text{ MANY monkeys}]\!]) >$
          $ \qquad\qquad\qquad\qquad\qquad\qquad\qquad\qquad [\![\text{than three}]\!]$
          $= \mathbf{max}(\lambda d_1 . \exists x[|x| = d_1 \wedge \mathbf{monkeys}(x)]) > 3$

not nominal predicates, that are the crucial ingredient here – and there are in fact different structures that do indeed seem to grade nouns (see section 6.3.2).

6.3 Gradability and non-adjectival predicates

The result is that the number of monkeys (more precisely, the maximum number that is the cardinality of a monkey plurality) is greater than three, as desired.

What about a full clausal comparative? We need to return to our denotation for clausal *than* in (16a), which contributes a maximality operator, but beyond that it's smooth sailing:

(15) a. There were more monkeys than there were ferrets.
 b. [-er than ∅ λd_2 there were [d_2 MANY] ferrets]
   λd_1 there were [d_1 MANY] monkeys

(16) a. $[\![than]\!] = \lambda D_{\langle d,t \rangle} . \mathbf{max}(D)$
 b. $[\![∅\ \lambda d_2\ there\ were\ [d_2\ \text{MANY}\ ]\ ferrets]\!]$
   = $\lambda d_2 . \exists y[|y| = d_2 \wedge \mathbf{ferrets}(y)]$
 c. $[\![than\ ∅\ \lambda d_2\ there\ were\ [d_2\ \text{MANY}\ ]\ ferrets]\!]$
   = $\mathbf{max}(\lambda d_2 . \exists y[|y| = d_2 \wedge \mathbf{ferrets}(y)])$
 d. $[\![-er]\!]\ ([\![than\ ∅\ \lambda d_2\ there\ were\ [d_2\ \text{MANY}\ ]\ ferrets]\!])$
   $([\![\lambda d_1\ there\ were\ d_1\ \text{MANY}\ monkeys]\!])$
   = $\mathbf{max}(\lambda d_1 . \exists x[|x| = d_1 \wedge \mathbf{monkeys}(x)]) >$
   $\mathbf{max}(\lambda d_2 . \exists y[|y| = d_2 \wedge \mathbf{ferrets}(y)])$

Again, the desired result: the maximum number that is the cardinality of a monkey plurality exceeds the maximum number that is the cardinality of a ferret plurality.

This overall picture is more or less a standard one, following a trajectory from Bresnan (1973) through Hackl (2000) and to more recent work like Solt (2009) and Wellwood et al. (2012).

6.3 GRADABILITY AND NON-ADJECTIVAL PREDICATES

6.3.1 Verbal gradability

The distribution of measure phrases and degree constructions seems to suggest that some verbs are gradable and others aren't:

(17) a. Floyd hates natto $\begin{Bmatrix} \text{a lot} \\ \text{more than Clyde} \\ \text{as much as anyone} \end{Bmatrix}$.

 b. Floyd believes in capitalism $\begin{Bmatrix} \text{a lot} \\ \text{more than Clyde} \\ \text{as much as anyone} \end{Bmatrix}$.

(18) ??Floyd $\begin{Bmatrix} \text{died} \\ \text{arrived} \\ \text{solved this problem} \end{Bmatrix}$ $\begin{Bmatrix} \text{a lot} \\ \text{more than Clyde} \\ \text{as much as anyone} \end{Bmatrix}$.

The natural interpretation of this would be that some verbs have degree arguments and others simply lack them. There is a twist, though:

(19) Floyd $\begin{Bmatrix} \text{talked} \\ \text{slept} \\ \text{smokes} \end{Bmatrix}$ $\begin{Bmatrix} \text{a lot} \\ \text{more than Clyde} \\ \text{as much as anyone} \end{Bmatrix}$.

This seems to be degree modification, but in a very specific sense. It doesn't seem to measure an event along a scale provided lexically by the particular verb, as in 17. Rather, it measures along a scale of amount, like amount comparatives in the nominal domain. These two kinds of gradability might be called LEXICAL and AMOUNT gradability, respectively. (Bolinger 1972 used the terms 'intensity' and 'extensibility'; Caudal and Nicolas 2005 favor 'intensity' and 'quantity'.)

Lexical gradability is the style favored by adjectives, and it can be accommodated in a similar way in verbs: by providing the appropriate verbs with a degree argument (Caudal and Nicolas 2005; Villalta 2007; Piñón 2008; Bochnak 2010; Anderson forthcoming; see Rett 2011b for reasons not to). This has interesting consequences, including the probable need to add a verbal POS morpheme.

For amount gradability, though, a different strategy is needed. The theory appropriate for lexical gradability, based in verbal degree arguments, risks failing to capture an important generalization: all verbs with an appropriate semantics support such amount modification.[8] What seems to be necessary are tools analogous to those used for amount gradability in DP. This is the path pursued in Nakanishi (2004a,b, 2007) and Wellwood et al. (2012). Nakanishi proposes that because events have a part structure analogous to that of nouns (Bach 1986), they can be measured similarly: by their cardinality (for count-noun-like events), by their amount (for mass-noun-like events), and in other ways, including spaciotemporally. This can be represented with a verbal analogue of MANY, which I'll write MUCH:[9]

(20)   〚 MUCH 〛 $= \lambda d \lambda e [\mathbf{amount}(e) = d]$

---

[8] For more on what 'an appropriate semantics' means if not simply having a degree argument, see Nakanishi (2007) and Wellwood et al. (2012).
[9] This departs considerably from her proposal in implementation and abstracts away from numerous additional features.

6.3 Gradability and non-adjectival predicates

This can be interpreted intersectively just like MANY, yielding an interpretation for (21) as in (22):

(21) a. Floyd talked more than Clyde talked.
      b. [-er than ∅ λd_2 Clyde talked [d_2 MUCH]]
          λd_1 Floyd talked [d_1 MUCH]

(22) a. [[than ∅ λd_2 Clyde talked [d_2 MUCH]]]
          = $\max(\lambda d_2 . \exists e[\textbf{talked}(\textbf{Clyde})(e) \wedge \textbf{amount}(e) = d_2])$
      b. [[λd_1 Floyd talked [d_1 MUCH]]]
          = $\lambda d_1 . \exists e'[\textbf{talked}(\textbf{Floyd})(e') \wedge \textbf{amount}(e') = d_1]$
      c. [[-er]] ([[than ∅ λd_2 Clyde talked [d_2 MUCH]]])
                  ([[λd_1 Floyd talked [d_1 MUCH]]])
          = $\max$([[λd_1 Floyd talked [d_1 MUCH]]]) >
              [[than ∅ λd_2 Clyde talked [d_2 MUCH]]]
          = $\max(\lambda d_1 . \exists e'[\textbf{talked}(\textbf{Floyd})(e') \wedge \textbf{amount}(e') = d_1])$ >
              $\max(\lambda d_2 . \exists e[\textbf{talked}(\textbf{Clyde})(e) \wedge \textbf{amount}(e) = d_2])$

This winds up meaning that the amount of a talking by Floyd exceeds the amount of a talking by Clyde.

Interestingly, lexical gradability in verbs can arise not just idiosyncratically for particular lexical items, but systematically for whole classes of them. This can have consequences for their temporal semantics. One such class is DEGREE ACHIEVEMENTS such as *widen, cool, darken,* and *ripen*.[10] Kennedy and Levin (2008) argue that they are built around a core adjective meaning and inherit their gradability from it.

Positing lexical degree arguments for verbs also predicts that there should be verbal counterparts of degree morphemes – and indeed, there are:

(23) The pie cooled $\begin{Bmatrix} \text{halfway} \\ \text{slightly} \\ \text{fully} \\ \text{completely} \end{Bmatrix}$.

This example involves a degree achievement, and in light of Kennedy and Levin's analysis it's what we might expect. Whether a verb has an

---

[10] They're called 'achievements' in view of their place in the aspectual classification of Vendler (1967), Dowty (1979), and others.

adjectival core or not, so long as it has a degree argument it should be associated with a particular scale structure to which degree words are sensitive. The line between these and manner modifiers is not always easy to draw, though:

(24) Floyd $\begin{Bmatrix} \text{loves monkeys} \\ \text{believes in capitalism} \end{Bmatrix}$ $\begin{Bmatrix} \text{intensely} \\ \text{passionately} \\ \text{deeply} \\ \text{fervently} \\ \text{with all his heart} \end{Bmatrix}$.

To some extent, the same issue can arise in AP-modifying contexts (e.g. *passionately/deeply affectionate*), but the issue is especially stark with verbs.

6.3.2 Nominal gradability

If there are two different kinds of gradability in the verbal domain, one might wonder whether there are two kinds in the nominal domain too. We've already seen amount gradability among nominals in section 6.2. What about lexical gradability? Are there nouns that have a degree argument lexically?

This is very much an open question, but some of the facts that bear on it are clear:

(25) a. Floyd is a(n) $\begin{Bmatrix} \text{big} \\ \text{true} \\ \text{total} \\ \text{absolute} \end{Bmatrix}$ $\begin{Bmatrix} \text{idiot} \\ \text{asshole} \end{Bmatrix}$.

b. Floyd is $\begin{Bmatrix} \text{a bigger} \\ \text{more of a(n)} \end{Bmatrix}$ $\begin{Bmatrix} \text{idiot} \\ \text{asshole} \end{Bmatrix}$ than Clyde.

c. Floyd is $\begin{Bmatrix} \text{such} \\ \text{as much} \end{Bmatrix}$ a(n) $\begin{Bmatrix} \text{idiot} \\ \text{asshole} \end{Bmatrix}$.

Pre-theoretically, these certainly seem to be grading the degree to which Floyd is an idiot or an asshole. This general issue, recognized since at least Bolinger (1972), has begun to be examined formally (Morzycki 2005b, 2009b, 2012b; Sassoon 2013b; de Vries 2010; Xie 2010; Bylinina 2011; Constantinescu 2011).

The constructions in (25) are actually quite varied, and probably require distinct analyses, but perhaps the least complicated of them

6.3 Gradability and non-adjectival predicates

involves what I have argued (Morzycki 2005b, 2009b, 2012b) are overt adnominal degree morphemes:

(26) a(n) $\begin{Bmatrix} \text{true} \\ \text{complete} \\ \text{absolute} \\ \text{slight} \\ \text{veritable} \end{Bmatrix}$ idiot

These are, of course, all homophonous with adjectives, so one has to demonstrate their distinctness. Among the defining characteristics of adjectives in English is the ability to occur as the complement to *seem*. None of the expressions in (26) can occur there on a degree reading:

(27) That idiot seems $\begin{Bmatrix} \text{\#real} \\ \text{\#complete} \\ \text{\#absolute} \\ \text{\#slight} \\ \text{\#veritable} \end{Bmatrix}$.

If these were adjectives, one might also expect them to accept degree modification of their own. But they don't:

(28) a. *a(n) $\begin{Bmatrix} \text{more utter} \\ \text{utterer} \end{Bmatrix}$ idiot than Clyde

b. *a $\begin{Bmatrix} \text{quite} \\ \text{rather} \\ \text{somewhat} \\ \text{really} \end{Bmatrix}$ $\begin{Bmatrix} \text{\#real} \\ \text{\#complete} \\ \text{\#absolute} \\ \text{\#slight} \\ \text{\#veritable} \end{Bmatrix}$ idiot

Nor do they nominalize in the adjectival style. One can't refer to *the utterness of the idiot*, for example. Even beyond this, one might suspect that these are distinct from their adjective homophones from meaning alone. A *real idiot*, for example, is not one that isn't artificial; a true one isn't one that's not false; a total one isn't one that isn't incomplete.

These all suggest that there is a distinct degree morpheme position inside the extended NP. That in turn suggests that nouns, like adjectives and verbs, can have degree arguments. That wouldn't entail that **all** nouns have them, though. It might be restricted to the most adjective-like of nouns, like *idiot*. Unlike most nouns, it has an especially simple meaning, involving a single dimension of measurement: idiocy. This contrasts with a more ordinary noun like *chair*: there are many different factors that go into making something a chair. And indeed, *chair* resists degree readings with many of these modifiers:

(29) #a(n) $\begin{Bmatrix} \text{complete} \\ \text{absolute} \\ \text{slight} \\ \text{veritable} \end{Bmatrix}$ chair

That said, there are various ways of dealing with these facts. The description above accords with Morzycki (2005b, 2009b). Constantinescu (2011) and Morzycki (2012b) both move in a different direction, away from providing nouns with degree arguments. Constantinescu suggests that degree-like interpretations may arise via different means entirely. Morzycki (2012b) suggests that degrees are involved, but that nouns and degrees are associated only indirectly, via other conceptual and compositional mechanisms.

As for the other forms of apparent nominal degree modification, they seem to be a mixed bag. Size adjectives are striking in that it is only adjectives of bigness that get degree readings (# here indicates the unavailability of the relevant reading):

(30) $\begin{Bmatrix} \text{big} \\ \text{huge} \\ \text{\#miniscule} \\ \text{\#tiny} \end{Bmatrix}$ idiot

This fact holds true across numerous languages. (An account can be found in Morzycki 2005b, 2009b.)

Constantinescu discusses forms such as *such an idiot*, which she suggests are related to the ordinary use of *such* as an anaphor to kinds (Carlson 1977). The *more of a* construction may perhaps be amenable to an analysis as a form of metalinguistic comparison, which would make it only indirectly a means of grading nouns.

6.4 HEDGING AND REINFORCING ACROSS CATEGORIES

Degree modifiers like *very* and *slightly* are well behaved in the sense that they occur where we would expect expressions with such meanings to occur: in the vicinity of an adjective. There is, however, a much larger class of expressions that do work that – like that of well-behaved degree modifiers – might be characterized as hedging and reinforcing whose distribution is considerably more free. These come in a variety of flavors

6.4 Hedging and reinforcing across categories

and with a variety of names, and don't all form a natural class. Among the examples:

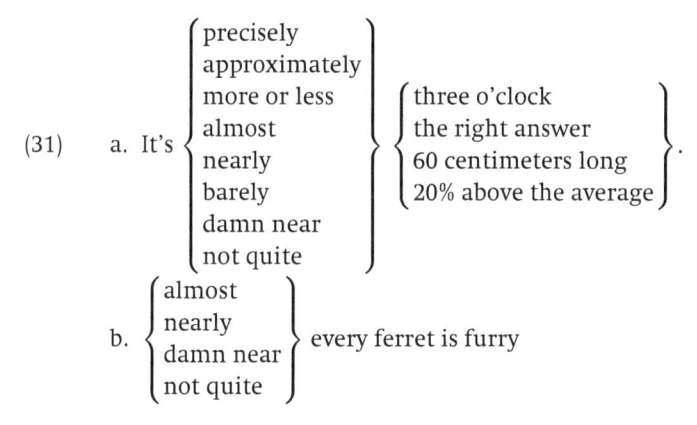

(31) a. It's $\begin{Bmatrix} \text{precisely} \\ \text{approximately} \\ \text{more or less} \\ \text{almost} \\ \text{nearly} \\ \text{barely} \\ \text{damn near} \\ \text{not quite} \end{Bmatrix} \begin{Bmatrix} \text{three o'clock} \\ \text{the right answer} \\ \text{60 centimeters long} \\ \text{20\% above the average} \end{Bmatrix}$.

b. $\begin{Bmatrix} \text{almost} \\ \text{nearly} \\ \text{damn near} \\ \text{not quite} \end{Bmatrix}$ every ferret is furry

Many of these expressions are sometimes referred to as adverbs. Perhaps there's something to that – they have the -*ly* suffix, if nothing else – but ultimately, labeling them adverbs isn't particularly helpful. Neither their distribution nor their meaning is a close match to that of more prototypical adverbs. The morphological fact of the -*ly* suffix might need explaining, though that explanation might turn out to be entirely historical and have no direct bearing on the synchronic grammar. Certainly, many such expressions don't have at all the form of adverbs (*more or less, damn near*), or presumably an adverbial etymology. Moreover, expressions with which many of these do form a semantic natural class can occur in clearly non-adverbial categories. Appalachian English, for example, has a form *liketa* ([lɑktə]) that resembles many uses of *almost* but is clearly verbal (Johnson 2013).

Expressions like *almost* and *barely* are occasionally called PROXIMATIVE or APPROXIMATIVE modifiers. A broader range of such expressions have been called APPROXIMATORS (e.g. Sauerland and Stateva 2007), HEDGES (for the weakening ones; Lakoff 1973), or SLACK REGULATORS (Lasersohn 1999).[11]

Probably the best-studied such expression is *almost* (Adams 1974; Sadock 1981; Atlas 1984; Partee 1986, 1995; Hitzeman 1992; Sevi 1998; Rapp and von Stechow 1999; Morzycki 2001; Horn 2002; Rotstein

---

[11] The nice thing about the term 'slack regulator' is that it clearly includes both weakening modifiers like *approximately* and strengthening ones like *precisely*. Its drawback is that it refers not to a class of expressions pre-theoretically but rather to one defined by the proposal in Lasersohn (1999). It would be nice to have a term like this that's theory-neutral. Perhaps 'modulator' would work.

and Winter 2004; Penka 2005, 2006; Nouwen 2006; Amaral 2007; Amaral and Del Prete 2010; van Gerrevink and de Hoop 2007; Jayez and Tovena 2008; Pozzan and Schweitzer 2008; Horn 1991; Kamoen et al. 2011). It once figured intimately in arguments for lexical decomposition of verbs like *kill* because of a possible ambiguity in (32) (McCawley 1971):

(32) Floyd almost killed Clyde.
  a. Floyd acted to cause Clyde to become <u>almost</u> dead.
  b. Floyd acted to <u>almost</u> cause Clyde to become dead.
  c. Floyd <u>almost</u> acted to cause Clyde to become dead.

In (32a), Floyd might have shot Clyde and injured him almost mortally; in (32b), he might have shot Clyde and missed him only narrowly; in (32c), he might merely not even have done anything like this, but seriously considered the possibility. Independently, *almost* was of interest as a diagnostic for universal quantification (Horn 1972; Carlson 1977; Kadmon and Landman 1993):

(33) almost $\left\{\begin{array}{l} \text{every} \\ \text{all} \\ \text{\#some} \\ \text{\#few} \end{array}\right\}$

Its other important properties include sensitivity to scalar properties of predicates. With telic VPs, *almost* gives rise to an 'almost complete' reading that is absent with atelic VPs, as (34) reflects:

(34) a. Floyd almost $\left\{\begin{array}{l} \text{ran three miles} \\ \text{reached the top} \end{array}\right\}$. (telic)

  b. Floyd almost $\left\{\begin{array}{l} \text{ran around} \\ \text{reached the top} \end{array}\right\}$. (atelic)

The only readings available for (34b) involve scenarios in which Floyd has almost begun an action, not ones in which he has almost completed it. A related restriction is that *almost* is incompatible with adjectives that lack upper-closed scales (or, in slightly different terminology, that don't denote total predicates; Hitzeman 1992):

(35) The swimming pool is almost $\left\{\begin{array}{l} \text{full} \\ \text{complete} \\ \text{\#incomplete} \\ \text{\#long} \end{array}\right\}$.

6.4 Hedging and reinforcing across categories

Barely and *hardly*, unlike *almost*, also license negative polarity items:

(36) Floyd $\begin{Bmatrix} \text{barely} \\ \text{hardly} \\ \text{\#almost} \end{Bmatrix}$ saw anyone at all.

The meaning of *almost* is usually construed as involving two inferences, the status of one of which is controversial:

(37) It's almost the case that it's raining.
 a. *entails:* It's close to being the case that it's raining.
 b. *possibly entails?:* It's not raining.

If (37b) isn't an entailment, it may be a conversational implicature or be in some other way, in Horn's phrase, 'assortorically inert'. See Nouwen (2006) and Horn (1991) for recent discussion of its status.

The ability to modify quantificational determiners seems to be a property of the *almost* class alone. Other expressions that hedge and reinforce lack can't do this:

(38) # $\begin{Bmatrix} \text{Exactly} \\ \text{Approximately} \\ \text{Definitely} \\ \text{Outright} \\ \text{Flat-out} \\ \text{Sorta} \end{Bmatrix}$ $\begin{Bmatrix} \text{every} \\ \text{all the} \end{Bmatrix}$ deer were spotted.

Unsurprisingly, there are more general restrictions of various kinds on the categories different classes of approximator can attach to. *Loosely speaking*, for example, is a speech-act adverbial and, setting aside parenthetical uses, can only occur quite high in the clause (see section 5.5.1).

Another interesting distinction among such expressions is observed in Sauerland and Stateva (2007) (the examples are theirs):

(39) a. What John cooked was $\begin{Bmatrix} \text{exactly} \\ \text{approximately} \end{Bmatrix}$ fifty tapas.
 b. #What John cooked was $\begin{Bmatrix} \text{exactly} \\ \text{approximately} \end{Bmatrix}$ Beef Stroganoff.

Their analysis of this hinges on the idea that *fifty tapas* and *Beef Stroganoff* are vague in different ways. In our terms, one might say that *fifty tapas* is imprecise but essentially not vague,[12] but *Beef Stroganoff* is vague. *Sorta* seems to have the opposite behavior in this respect (Anderson 2013, 2014):

(40)   a.   ??What John cooked was sorta fifty tapas.
           b.   What John cooked was sorta Beef Stroganoff.

Anderson frames an account of this that relies on modulating imprecision.

In various contexts and to varying extents, we have encountered many of the analytical strategies that are employed to account for these expressions. One strategy, prominent in the analysis of *almost*, is intensional. The crucial component of meaning is the proximal 'close to true' one. This can be expressed as requiring that a proposition be true in all worlds that are relevantly similar (i.e., sufficiently close) to the evaluation world (Sadock 1981; Rapp and von Stechow 1999; Morzycki 2001). Zaroukian (2011) shows an intensional strategy may be useful for other approximators, with interesting results.

Another line of attack is some notion of modulating imprecision. There are different ways this can be implemented. Lasersohn (1999)'s halos and operations defined on them are one. Sauerland and Stateva (2007) suggest an alternative approach involving scale granularity.

Yet another option, which we haven't encountered yet and is in fact a bit fuzzy at the margins, is speaker commitment. A proposition expressed with *definitely*, for example, commits the speaker more strongly than one without. To cash this out explicitly, of course, it's necessary to have a well-developed and predictive theory of speaker commitment.

Finally, there is the familiar option of appealing to degrees and treating expressions as degree modifiers. That's the move Morzycki (2012a) makes for *downright* and *flat-out*, for example. On such a strategy, we might expect these expressions to be only as crosscategorial as degree arguments themselves are. This distinguishes it from the other strategies, all of which involve notions – modality, imprecision, and speaker commitment – that are inherently quite crosscategorial. (Though not

---

[12] This isn't quite true. *Tapas* remains a potential source of vagueness. It's also worth pointing out that *exactly* is a bit more flexible than this example alone suggests:

(i)   a.   Beef Stroganoff was exactly what John cooked.
       b.   We expected something like Beef Stroganoff, and indeed, it was exactly Beef Stroganoff that John cooked.

More discussion of these issues can be found in Zaroukian (2011, 2013).

necessarily equally so, and certain theories of each may predict more or less crosscategoriality than others.)

This all leads to a bigger picture that's both interesting and a bit muddled. In part, the muddle is a consequence of discussing different expressions simultaneously, as I have done. But such a bird's-eye view may be useful because there is also something real about the muddle. There are probably several different phenomena jostling with each other here, each in need of explanation and more precise delineation. There are also several different analytical strategies jostling with each other, all of which probably play some role in the grammar and may explain certain of these phenomena. Part of what makes it all interesting is that the bigger picture is likely to come more sharply into view as aspects of the larger problem are explored in further detail.

6.5 NONRESTRICTIVE MODIFIERS

A classic and foundational distinction made in the grammar of modification – particularly for relative clauses – is between RESTRICTIVE and NONRESTRICTIVE modifiers. Alternative terms for 'nonrestrictive modifiers' include SUPPLEMENTS, PARENTHETICALS, and APPOSITIVES. Huddleston and Pullum (2002) also advocate INTEGRATED in place of 'restrictive'.

The basic distinction in relative clauses is found in (41):

(41)   a. All the linguists who live in Michigan have learned to pronounce 'Novi'.
        b. All the linguists, who live in Michigan, have learned to pronounce 'Novi'.

The claim in (41a) is a perfectly plausible one involving a community near Detroit. The claim in (41b) is completely implausible, as it requires that all linguists both live in Michigan and pronounce 'Novi' correctly. This example goes out of its way to make the difference clear – it's apparent prosodically (the commas), truth-conditionally, and in the complementizer *that* – but real life isn't always so tidy. *Who* can and routinely does head restrictive relatives, for example (despite a prescriptive fiction to the contrary). Simply removing the comma intonation in (41b) demonstrates this, by imbuing the sentence with the truth-conditionally weaker meaning of (41a). As Huddleston and Pullum (2002) point out, the truth-conditional effect is not always present: in *the bachelors that are unmarried*, the relative is grammatically restrictive but has no truth-conditional impact.

The most influential theory of the semantics of these expressions is that of Potts (2003), who argues that they contribute CONVENTIONAL IMPLICATURES (see also section 5.5.2), a kind of meaning Grice (1975) originally recognized, but which turns out to be not at all like conversational implicatures. Rather, conventional implicatures make a secondary semantic contribution, one independent of the at-issue truth-conditional meaning of the sentence. For Potts, this is represented as a distinct tier or dimension of meaning, one that the compositional semantics sets aside – as though saving it for later – as it works its way up the tree. Setting it aside in this way reflects that conventional implicatures are always interpreted (as though) with matrix scope, never contribute to the descriptive meaning of higher nodes in the tree, create the sense that the sentence is making more than one assertion at a time, and involve the perspective of the speaker (but see Amaral et al. 2007; Schlenker 2007; Harris and Potts 2009 for qualifications).

This is implemented by distinguishing separate types for expressions that give rise to conventional implicatures, types which end not in t but in t^c. The meaning of a nonrestrictive relative like *who live in Michigan*, for Potts, involves an operator COMMA that shifts a predicate from type $\langle e, t \rangle$ to $\langle e, t^c \rangle$. It can therefore shift the regular property-denoting relative clause in (42a) to the nonrestrictive one in (42b):

(42)   a.   ⟦ *who live in Michigan* ⟧ = **live-in(Michigan)**   type: $\langle e, t \rangle$
        b.   ⟦ COMMA *who live in Michigan* ⟧
            = **comma(live-in(Michigan))**   type: $\langle e, t^c \rangle$

The type has to be indicated explicitly in this system because it can't be read off the lambda expressions (which are identical in (42a) and (42b)).

With appropriate rules in place for manipulating conventional-implicature types, this yields trees like (43):

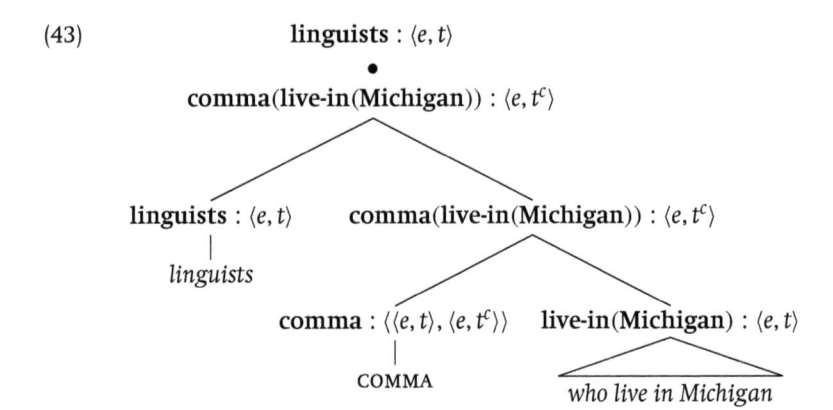

(43)   **linguists** : $\langle e, t \rangle$
                                •
       comma(live-in(Michigan)) : $\langle e, t^c \rangle$

      linguists : $\langle e, t \rangle$ **comma(live-in(Michigan))** : $\langle e, t^c \rangle$
         |
        linguists
                  comma : $\langle \langle e, t \rangle, \langle e, t^c \rangle \rangle$ **live-in(Michigan)** : $\langle e, t \rangle$
                           |
                        COMMA   *who live in Michigan*

6.5 Nonrestrictive modifiers

The material below the bullet is the set-aside conventional implicature.

Relative clauses and nominal appositives aren't the only potentially nonrestrictive modifiers. Another case Potts cites is NOMINAL APPOSITIVES like *Lance, a cyclist*. But there are others. One kind involves expressive modifiers like *fucking* and *damn*, as Potts observes:

(44) Floyd (fucking) lost his $\begin{Bmatrix} \text{fucking} \\ \text{damn} \end{Bmatrix}$ glove again.

These too can be analyzed as contributing conventional implicatures. There might be a distinction worth making between conventional implicatures and EXPRESSIVE MEANING (see also Kratzer 1999 and Potts 2007b; McCready 2010; Gutzmann 2011, 2013), but if so, it's not immediately relevant.

Another kind of nonrestrictive meaning is involved in (45), first observed by Bolinger (1967b) (and further explored in Larson and Marušič 2004, who provide this particular example), which has two readings:

(45) Every unsuitable word was deleted.
    a. *restrictive:* 'Every word that was unsuitable was deleted.'
    b. *nonrestrictive:* 'Every word was deleted. They were unsuitable.'

This reading is unavailable postnominally in English:

(46) Every word unsuitable was deleted.
    a. *restrictive:* 'Every word that was unsuitable was deleted.'
    b. #*nonrestrictive:* 'Every word was deleted. They were unsuitable.'

In Spanish and Italian, the situation is slightly different: prenominal adjectives are obligatorily **non**restrictive, and postnominal ones are ambiguous (Cinque 2003, 2010; Demonte 2008; Katz 2007; examples are Spanish, from Demonte 2008):

(47) La débil voz apenas se oía.
    'The soft voice could hardly be heard.'
    a. #*restrictive:* 'The voice that was soft could hardly be heard.'
    b. *nonrestrictive:* 'The voice could hardly be heard. It was soft.'

Across languages, the nonrestrictiveness of these adjectives is also reflected in their resistance to focus (Umbach 2006).

Adverbs also demonstrate a contrast in nonrestrictiveness, as Shaer (2000, 2003) showed. This is perhaps clearest in embedded contexts (the example is a variation of one in Peterson 1997):

(48) a. It's regrettable that the Titanic slowly sank.
b. It's regrettable that the Titanic sank slowly.

In (48b), only a restrictive reading is available on which the slowness of the sinking figures in the regret.

Morzycki (2008b) argued that all these nonrestrictive modifiers – adjectives and adverbs alike – should be viewed as contributing expressive meaning, like *fucking*, and be represented in Potts' conventional-implicature dimension. Katz (2007) further articulates this sort of approach and provides additional evidence. I also suggested that the crosscategorial and crosslinguistic facts point to another conclusion: that there is a grammatical connection between expressive interpretations and left branches in the syntax. This is further reflected in the behavior of modifiers that are lexically (i.e., inherently) expressive:

(49) a. He fucking ate the whole goddamn thing.
b. #He ate the whole goddamn thing fucking.

(50) a. He'll damn well invade Iran.
b. #He'll invade Iran damn well.

Both *fucking* and *damn well* get their usual expressive meaning on the left. When on the right, as in the (b) sentences, the only possible interpretations are irrelevant non-expressive ones.

Particularly surprising is evidence adduced in Solt (2011a) that even attributive uses of numerals, *few*, and *many* may be nonrestrictive (her examples):

(51) a. The three dogs growled menacingly.
b. The few people we met were friendly.
c. His many friends supported him through his illness.

Solt argues that these further support construing nonrestrictive meaning along a separate dimension of meaning.

6.6 PREDICATES OF PERSONAL TASTE

Some people think roller coasters are fun. Others don't. For the most part, we couldn't possibly be more bored by this fact. It's certainly not grounds for a fight. So in the discourse in (52), Floyd comes off as at least belligerent:

(52)   Floyd: Roller coasters are fun.
         Clyde: No, they're not.
         Floyd: #That's a lie!

But something deeper seems to have gone wrong here. Floyd's response is not just belligerent but outright infelicitous, even though there's no denying that he and Clyde disagree about something. Indeed, if Floyd wanted to **prove** that Clyde had been lying, it's not at all clear what his next step should be. There's something wrong with the very idea of escalating this kind of disagreement into an argument. We're not so casual about all disagreements:

(53)   Floyd: This roller coaster is wooden.
         Clyde: No, it isn't.
         Floyd: That's a lie!

Here, there's belligerence but no infelicity. It's also completely clear how the question should be resolved empirically.

The phenomenon illustrated in (52) – and not in (53) – is FAULTLESS DISAGREEMENT (Kölbel 2002). The crucial fact is that when the interlocutors contradict each other in such scenarios, they are not actually expressing contradictory views about an objective matter of fact. They are certainly disagreeing in some sense, but not in a sense that is easy to characterize precisely.

The locus of the puzzle seems to be what Lasersohn (2005) termed PREDICATES OF PERSONAL TASTE, which include *fun* and *tasty*. These predicates, he observed, need to be understood relative to a particular individual. Whenever something is fun, it is because someone has judged it fun. Lasersohn concluded that the semantics of these predicates makes reference to what he called a JUDGE.

There are a number of ways one might implement this idea, and he considered several. The most straightforward would probably be simply to suppose that these predicates have an implicit argument, a kind of unpronounced PP with a meaning like 'according to' (or 'for' or 'to'):

(54) a. Roller coasters are fun $\begin{Bmatrix} \text{according to} \\ \text{for} \end{Bmatrix}$ me.
b. Cilantro is tasty (according) to me.

We could represent this implicit argument directly in the object language, like the referential index of a pronoun, and assume it's provided by context:

(55) $[\![fun_j]\!] = \lambda x \,.\, \textbf{fun-for}(j)(x)$

This is a property of things that are fun according to the judge j that is provided as an implicit argument. But, as Lasersohn observed, this doesn't quite jibe with our intuitions. If in each utterance, the judge were identical to the speaker, the faultless disagreement scenario would be analyzed along the lines of (56):

(56)   Floyd: Roller coasters are fun for me.
       Clyde: #No, they're not fun for me.

Now something has gone wrong even earlier. This account certainly captures why the disagreement is faultless, since Floyd and Clyde are now asserting different propositions:

(57)   Floyd: **fun-for**(Floyd)(roller-coasters)
       Clyde: ¬**fun-for**(Clyde)(roller-coasters)

What this misses, though, is that faultless disagreement is still disagreement. The discourse in (56) and (57) isn't disagreement at all. That's what makes Clyde's *no* in (56) odd.

If, on the other hand, the judge in each utterance were the same – say, Floyd in both cases – there would be real disagreement, but it would be disagreement over a matter of fact: whether Floyd enjoys roller coasters. It would not be faultless. One of the speakers has said something false.

Lasersohn's suggestion is that judges must be introduced in a different way, one that doesn't resemble the way pronouns work. He suggests that the interpretation function itself is relativized to a judge – but, importantly, indirectly. It's often necessary to relativize the interpretation function to a context, which includes a variety of information about the circumstances of use. The judge is one of those pieces of information, so the denotation of *fun* can be (roughly) as in (58):

(58) $[\![fun]\!]^c = \lambda x \,.\, \textbf{fun-for}(\textbf{judge}(c))(x)$

This says that x is fun according to the judge in c. It's superficially similar to the previous denotation, but there is an important difference: the disagreement is now over the truth of a single proposition: in a context c, **fun-for**(**judge**(c))(**roller-coasters**). So there is real disagreement. If the context is held constant, the interlocutors would indeed be contradicting each other. Yet it's faultless because to arrive at contradiction, the context must be fixed **exactly**. In actual use, it never is – we never know precisely the context against which we're evaluating utterances. The faultlessness, on Lasersohn's account, arises from this indeterminacy.[13]

The notion of judge-dependence has attracted the attention of researchers in a number of areas, among them Nouwen (2007), Stephenson (2007a,b,c), Stojanovic (2007), Lasersohn (2008), Sæbø (2009), Lasersohn (2009), Sassoon (2010c), and Kennedy (2012b). Importantly, there is nothing about judge-dependence that's necessarily about adjectives, or indeed about modifiers. Like vagueness, one can find it anywhere. It's therefore perhaps not surprising that the idea has also found a natural home in the analysis of epistemic modals (Stephenson 2007a,b,c). Verbs might be sensitive to a judge as well, but, more interestingly, they might also be sensitive to whether an expression they've combined with is judge-sensitive. This seems to be the case for *find* (Sæbø 2009):

(59) a. Floyd found this roller coaster fun.
b. #Floyd found this roller coaster wooden.

The precise distribution of judge-dependence across the grammar, and the distribution of sensitivity to it, and even whether it exists as such (Nouwen 2007) is a focus of active inquiry. At a minimum, though, it constitutes a potentially useful analytical tool: the concept itself is a good probe into subtleties of meaning, and the way of thinking about it Lasersohn articulates can be applied more widely.

6.7 QUESTIONS FOR FURTHER REFLECTION AND DISCUSSION

- It may be the case that adjectives generally have degree arguments, and that only certain nouns and verbs do. Is this the right

---

[13] This is reminiscent of the epistemic theory of vagueness (Williamson 1994; see section 3.2.4): the disagreement would be a factual one if only we knew precisely what context we're in. But we can't know, just as on an epistemic theory of vagueness we can't know where the standard lies.

conclusion? If so, why should there be variation in this respect in a single category and what compositional – and therefore syntactically detectable – consequences might that have? Where do prepositions fit into this picture? And why the asymmetry between adjectives and other categories?
- What do various hedging expressions have in common? How do they differ? How much homogeneity or heterogeneity should we **expect** in this class? Do they do fundamentally different sorts of things that add up to a similar overall effect, or similar things by different means, or is it misleading to even think about them collectively? How might they serve as a probe into the semantics of the expressions they modify? What other expressions like this might there be?
- How best can we understand nonrestrictive modification? What should we expect of an account of the difference between *(the) dogs that are mammals* (restrictive) and *(the) dogs, who are mammals* (nonrestrictive)? The most obvious initial observation is that they have the same extension, and that it's identical to that of simply *(the) dogs*. But of course there is more to meaning than this, and they clearly mean different things.
- Can judge-dependency be reduced to some other aspect of lexical semantics, or assimilated to some other phenomenon? How does it relate to vagueness and imprecision? How should it be encoded in the grammar? Does it provide a sufficiently explanatory theory of faultless disagreement?

6.8 SUGGESTIONS FOR FURTHER READING

Good entry points into the literature cited in this chapter include the following:

- For more on amount comparatives, a good next step is Hackl (2000). Solt (2009) is a very readable more recent option in the same family, focusing especially on *many* and its relatives. Both of these are dissertations. Geurts and Nouwen (2007) is a paper that focuses on modifiers such as *at least*.
- Nakanishi (2007) and Kennedy and Levin (2008) are a fitting next step into verbal gradability, and Morzycki (2009b) into nominal gradability.
- Lasersohn (1999)'s seminal work on pragmatic slack modulation addresses some of the big-picture issues concerning hedging and

6.8 Suggestions for further reading

reinforcing. Further steps depend on what class of expressions and style of analysis one is inclined to pursue, but it's worth calling attention to the Rapp and von Stechow (1999) analysis of the German counterpart of *almost* because of the connections it makes to other topics, including lexical decomposition, intensionality, and syntactic issues.
- For more on conventional implicatures and related notions, including their place in a theory of modification, see Potts (2003), which is both influential and very accessibly written.
- Further exploration of predicates of personal taste should begin with Lasersohn (2005).

7 Taking stock

7.1 BACK TO THE BEGINNING

The book began by asking what precisely a modifier is. Inevitably, we must return to the question. As a reminder, the question, in its more articulated form, is this:

- Is it possible to discern in the concept of modification some clear theoretical content, something that can be expressed explicitly with some rigor and precision?
- Does that theoretical content correspond to a natural class of linguistic phenomena, or is it inherently disjunctive?

In Chapter 1, I distinguished between two ways of using descriptive terms for linguistic expressions. One was external, on the basis of the properties an expression has as part of a larger structure. 'Subject', 'complement', 'adjunct' are all examples, as are more semantic-flavored ones like 'purpose clause' or 'resultative'. 'Modifier' has a sense on which it belongs in this group, an external characterization of how one expression relates to another. The other sense of 'modifier' is the internal one. This was the more challenging of the two. If you are handed a linguistic expression, and you don't know where in the syntactic tree it will go, can you in principle tell whether it's a modifier, or at least whether it's the sort of thing that's likely to be one?

Even right at the start, we made some progress toward clarifying the external sense. On the external sense, something is a modifier iff it's interpreted as either a predicate modifier or intersectively. Done. As sharply defined as this is, it too gets hazy at the margins. If we assume a grammar with a fairly free system of type shifts, any intersective modifier could be lifted to a predicate-modifier type. Here's how that might work:

276

7.1 Back to the beginning

(1) Canadian dentist
 a. **shift** $\stackrel{\text{def}}{=} \lambda P_{\langle e, t \rangle} \lambda Q_{\langle e, t \rangle} \lambda x . P(x) \wedge Q(x)$
 b. **shift**([[*Canadian*]]) $= \lambda Q_{\langle e, t \rangle} \lambda x .$ [[*Canadian*]] $(x) \wedge Q(x)$
 c. **shift**([[*Canadian*]])([[*dentist*]])
  $= \lambda x .$ [[*Canadian*]] $(x) \wedge$ [[*dentist*]] (x)

The result is precisely what an intersective interpretation would ultimately deliver. The difficulty with the definition is that we could just as easily have shifted *dentist*:

(2) a. **shift**([[*dentist*]]) $= \lambda Q_{\langle e, t \rangle} \lambda x .$ [[*dentist*]] $(x) \wedge Q(x)$
 b. **shift**([[*dentist*]])([[*Canadian*]])
  $= \lambda x .$ [[*dentist*]] $(x) \wedge$ [[*Canadian*]] (x)

The result is the same. After the shift, *dentist* denotes a predicate modifier. But it seems wrong to say that it therefore **is** a modifier – or, to make this less about the term itself, it seems wrong to claim that the shifted denotation has anything important in common with true modifiers.

If this external definition is to hold up, we have several options. We could put our foot down and insist that there can be no such type shift. That seems unenlightening (and somehow petulant). Alternatively, we could assume that modification is defined in terms of inherent, unshifted characteristics of expressions. Or we could bite the bullet and accept that the shift in (2) does make *dentist* a modifier. Or we could introduce an appeal to both syntax and semantics: perhaps, to be a modifier you also need to be adjoined. That might work, but what of theories like that of Cinque (1999) and others in which modifiers routinely occupy specifier positions? Indeed, even on more off-the-rack syntactic theories, measure phrases – which may or may not be modifiers – often occupy specifier positions. Yet another alternative is the most radical of them: we could assume that only intersective modifiers are **really** modifiers. That has the obvious problem of excommunicating whole classes of apparent modifiers: modal adjectives and adverbs, and possibly many subsective adjectives, subject-oriented adverbs, and adverbs of quantification.

Nevertheless, this option – the excommunication – is actually the most interesting one. Looking back, very few modifiers were inherently, unavoidably quantificational. And for both adjectives and adverbs, there was a historical move away from predicate-modifier interpretations and toward intersective ones. For adjectives, this took the form of intersective analyses of subsective adjectives, and of various qualms and uneasiness expressed about all the adjectives that denote predicate modifiers. The complicated semantics they would otherwise have was instead attributed to how they interact with other elements in the sentence. For adverbs, we focused on the predicational ones, which was in this respect cheating. But that focus reflects that many of the inherently quantificational elements one might call 'adverbs' may actually be mischaracterized that way. Adverbs of quantification such as *(in)frequently*, *often*, and *rarely* are all clearly adverbs, but they are all suspiciously property-like. They are all gradable, for one thing. For another, the 'determiners' they correspond to – *many* and *few* – are actually adjectives, and intersective ones at that. That suggests that strong quantificational adverbs like *always* and *never*, which aren't gradable, are really a different sort of object from *(in)frequently* and the rest. Perhaps they're not even phrasal. Whatever they are, there is something to be said for stigmatizing them the way we stigmatize aberrant adjectives like *alleged*. Indeed, whatever analytical decision we take to cope with either of these, one should inform our decisions about how to cope with the other.

Such reasoning constitutes a kind of progress toward a clearer idea of what modification is, I suppose, though it's progress only insofar as it suggests that the notion must be narrowed considerably to be made theoretically meaningful. If that's right, it hasn't vindicated taking the term 'modifier' particularly seriously – but it **has** vindicated the effort of reflecting on whether one should. It's not completely idle naval-gazing.

About the internal sense of 'modifier', well, that seems harder to judge. In broad strokes, we made some progress beyond just 'adjectives and adverbs', but it's not terribly surprising progress. The principal commonality is gradability. Many things follow from that – sensitivity to comparison classes, compatibility with degree modification, participation in degree constructions, sensitivity to scale structure – but it all falls under the same rubric. In spelling out **how** gradability works across categories, though, subtler and more unexpected insights became possible. There is, for example, a pleasing symmetry in the idea that subsective adjectives might be analyzed with implicit 'role' arguments (section 2.3.4), and that subject-oriented adverbs might need to be too (section 5.4.3). Something similar could be said for the problem posed by gradable modal adjectives and their adverbial counterparts. There might be some additional insights to be gleaned consistent with the old philosophical intuition that nouns like *chair* are complex in a way that adjectives like *red* are not. Modifiers tend to involve a single quality, which may or may not be gradable. Non-modifiers tend to involve more than one. This may be independent of gradability, or it might be that gradability at least in part itself follows from this distinction.

Setting gradability aside, the idea that modifiers can be properties of different types and sorts in the model is an important theme. For adjectives alone, there is the option of being a predicate of an individual, a kind, or an event. Perhaps, with some analytical imagination, finer-grained distinctions could be justified. For adverbs, such variation is largely taken for granted: adverbs can be properties of worlds, situations, or events, and probably of times and spatial regions too – and we may yet have some use for the introductory semantics class treatment of some adverbials as properties of individuals. Varying what something is a property of is an analytical strategy, above all, but it helps characterize on internal grounds what a modifier is, too. A modifier is the sort of expression whose distribution and external characteristics are determined in large measure by the ontology of the objects of which it is predicated.

Beyond these, most of the questions modifiers raise are special cases of more general grammatical ones – they involve imprecision, scope-taking mechanisms, vagueness, metalinguistic phenomena, intensionality, context-sensitivity of various sorts, and the like.

So I think it **is** possible to say something a bit more concrete – or in any case, a bit more elaborated – about modification on both the internal and the external sense. But I don't think that makes modification a unitary concept. It can be useful to reflect on whether it might be, of course, and thinking in terms of crosscategorial connections among modifiers can be especially useful. The imbalance that this brings to light between our understanding of adjectives and adverbs is striking, for example.

In the end, it may be just as well to leave 'modification' as a primarily vague descriptive term. That would leave the notion defined as perhaps many noun meanings ultimately must be: in terms of more or less prototypical exemplars. Perhaps this is an anticlimactic way of answering the overall question. But I think it's probably right.

7.2 WHERE TO FROM HERE?

A few years ago, I found myself in a bleary-eyed conversation at an airport with a colleague who, like me, had just gotten off a transatlantic flight. Somehow we found ourselves talking about whether semantics ever really makes much progress – and even if it does, whether it can live up to the hopes people had for it in its infancy. The latter strikes me as an interesting but essentially historical question, one to which the answer will inevitably be at least partly 'no'.[1] People always have unreasonable expectations and life is mostly bitter disappointment. It's become a cliché to observe that we still don't have the flying cars we were once confidently promised. But that contrasts sharply with the answer to the first question. We **have** made progress, at least in the areas this book covers. Indeed, excitingly and surprisingly, we have made a great deal of it in just the last decade and a half.

We now have a far better understanding of adjectives than we once did. We know a great deal about the classes they fall into, categorizing them on a number of different criteria. We can express rigorously various subtleties of their lexical semantics. We have a much better handle on the facts surrounding issues like adverbial readings of adjectives and on subsectivity, even if we can't say we have a fully refined theoretical understanding of either. Excitingly, though, it feels like we might be on the cusp of one.

The greatest progress has probably been made in areas that touch on degrees. We have a good sense of how gradable predicates vary in their scale structure. We know how that affects degree modification possibilities. We understand degree constructions like comparatives and superlatives much better than we once did. We have a better idea of their scope properties and how they interact with intensional operators – though here, again, the research is in a state of lively ferment. We are examining a variety of languages, many typologically different from English and German, in increasing detail, developing ways of thinking about how their degree constructions and modification strategies more generally vary.

We also have shiny new theoretical tools that have already been proving very useful and leading us to make new observations and, probably more important, to ask new questions. These include a new understanding of conventional implicature and expressive meaning, and new ideas like judge-dependence.

It's not flying cars, I suppose. But we don't have much cause for dissatisfaction. That said, we should probably deliberately **cultivate** some dissatisfaction, if only because, to abuse the expression, it's dissatisfaction – and not necessity – that is the mother of invention.

---

[1] That said, Barbara Partee for one has said publicly that she isn't at all disappointed with what the field has grown into.

7.2 Where to from here?

I'm told it's appropriate to close a book like this by highlighting open issues. That seems a bit bold, inasmuch as it's bound to make the book seem dated virtually instantly and to make the author seem to be pompously issuing marching orders. Nevertheless, I'll mention a few issues that interest me.

One relatively big-picture question is that of the relative order of modifiers. There are well-established syntactic constraints on the relative order of adjectives and adverbs, and these are robust and consistent across the world's languages. For adjectives especially, to a really alarming extent we don't seem to have much of an idea of why. It might be purely a syntactic question, and indeed, there are purely syntactic theories (e.g. Cinque 2010) to account for it. But it seems odd to say that it's a purely syntactic fact that size adjectives occur higher than color adjectives, for example. Surely it should have at least a semantic dimension. And given that at least some such restrictions may follow from the semantics, it would be nice if we could say something more than we currently can about the subject. Part of the problem may be quite foundational: it may be that we're simply wrong to think that there are just two ways of combining modifiers and modified expressions.

Relatedly, we don't have a very good sense of the relationship between adjectives and adverbs, apart from cases in which the theory seems to be just that adjectives are predicates of individuals and adverbs of events. Pursuing parallels between these two domains seems worthwhile. If they turn out to be very similar, this would be interesting and might enable progress on issues such as constraints on their order and questions of lexical semantics. If they turn out to be quite different, again, that would be interesting, and the differences would shed light on both.

Another issue has to do with the two competing approaches to gradability. A great deal of progress has been made in degree-based approaches. But as we examine more facts – across categories and across languages – there might be reason to wonder about the pervasiveness of degree arguments. It seems likely that there are various operations that are degree-like but that don't explicitly manipulate degrees. For some languages, that might be in non-adjectival categories alone; in others, it may be everywhere. Either way, there's something to be said for exploring alternative implementations of degree-based theories, and exploring the middle ground between them and inherent-vagueness theories.

It also remains the case that we don't have a very good grip on what the relationship is between semantics and syntactic category (sections 2.7 and 3.7.6). This relates to another major area that has already been attracting attention, and surely will continue to do so: crosslinguistic variation in how modifiers work. Research of this ilk has so far tended to focus on degrees, perhaps because interesting contrasts in that domain emerge quite readily. But one could just as easily ask such questions about other issues, such as the nature of subject-orientation in adverbs or of adverbial readings of adjectives. Indeed, both of these areas in particular remain a bit foggier than one would like, even in English.

Another issue that we currently don't have a handle on is what constitutes a possible modifier meaning, and what constraints would rule out any impossible ones. There is, for example, no good account of the observation that there apparently can't be an adjective that maps the denotation of noun like *city* to a property of people who live in a city (section 2.3.5). An analogous question could be asked for adverbs: if *intentionally murder* is possible, could there be a VP with precisely the same meaning but a form like *murderously intend*? If predicate-modifier denotations could be ruled out for modifiers entirely, these issues wouldn't arise – but that amounts to saying just that if things were different, they would be different.

Finally, a remark about methodology. Increasingly, laboratory experimentation and corpus research are providing interesting and often novel ways of addressing questions that might otherwise be intractable. This is by any standard an important development, and an exciting one. But we should remember that we're not adopting these techniques because they're the only way to discover new puzzles or to make progress on old ones. We're in no danger of running out of puzzles, or of interesting things to say about them. Indeed, there remain whole language families that no formal semanticist has ever examined, and even in the best-studied languages, large swaths of the grammar we have only begun to understand.

William Blake alluded to seeing the world in a grain of sand. The semanticist, notoriously, can see the world in a single sentence about donkeys.[2] Close and careful scrutiny of a few enlightening facts has proven itself a fruitful research strategy many times over, and we have every reason to continue to prize the ability to see the big consequences

---

[2] For the uninitiated, 'donkey sentence' is a technical term for a sentence with a certain kind of anaphoric dependency. There are many variations, but the two basic ones are *Every farmer who owns a donkey beats it* and *If a farmer owns a donkey, he beats it*. They spawned an industry and led to many of the most important theoretical developments of the 1980s and 1990s (Kamp 1981b; Heim 1982, and countless others).

7.2 Where to from here?

of little facts. Considering a larger range of facts need not – and absolutely should not – change that. But, as I hope this book conveyed, there remain whole barnyards of phenomena to explore. Certainly, for the topics covered here, we have versatile analytical tools at our disposal and mysteries enough to entertain us indefinitely.

Glossary

absolute adjective Used in a variety of senses (see also 'absolute construction' and 'absolute reading (of a superlative)'):
(a) An adjective whose standard is provided by a maximum or a minimum on its scale rather than by context, such as *wet* (anything even slightly wet counts as wet) or *dry* (only things that are fully dry count as dry). Contrasts with the sense of 'relative adjective' that refers to adjectives such as *tall* and *wide*, which have open scales and whose standard is contextually determined. See section 3.7.2 and Kennedy and McNally (2005).
(b) An adjective in its positive form.
(c) An adjective whose meaning isn't relativized to an additional argument, often a nominal it modifies. Used in contrast with (one sense of) 'relative'. In particular, 'absolute' has been used to refer to intersective adjectives in contradistinction to subsective ones with predicate-modifier denotations dependent on the modified noun (Siegel 1976a). See section 2.3.2.
(d) Rarely, simply a nongradable adjective. 'Nongradable' is a preferable term, if only because it is unambiguous.

absolute construction A syntactic adjunct of a clause that is often (but not necessarily) a participle or non-finite clause itself: <u>Having died</u>, *Clyde was ineligible*. See Stump (1985).

absolute reading (of a superlative) In *Floyd climbed the highest mountain*, the absolute reading is 'there is no mountain higher than the one Floyd climbed'. Contrasts with the 'comparative reading', on which there is no one who climbed a higher mountain than Floyd did. See section 4.3.3.

adverbial reading (of an adjective) An interpretation of an adjective that can be paraphrased with a corresponding adverb, as in *An occasional sailor strolled by* 'Occasionally, a sailor strolled by'. Contrasts with 'internal reading' and, for some frequency adjectives, 'generic reading'. See section 2.5.

amount comparative A comparative that compares the number of members in a plural individual or the amount of a mass individual: *more monkeys, less cheese*. Also called a 'nominal comparative'. I find the latter term

Glossary 285

misleading, in that it suggests that comparison is along a dimension lexically determined by a noun.

analytic comparative A comparative construction formed with a free comparative morpheme such as *more* rather than a bound one such as *-er*. Contrasts with 'synthetic comparative'.

antisymmetric (of a relation) A relation is antisymmetric iff the order of its non-identical arguments is never reversible without changing the truth value; that is, R is antisymmetric iff $\forall x \forall y[[R(x,y) \land x \neq y] \to \neg R(y,x)]$ (or equivalently, iff $\forall x \forall y[[R(x,y) \land R(y,x)] \to x = y]$). Compare to 'asymmetric' and 'symmetric'. Example: among calendar years, the 'be no later than' relation.

approximative (or proximative) Characterizes *almost* and similar expressions across languages. See section 6.4.

approximator A word such as *approximately*, *roughly*, and – in a somewhat less natural use – *precisely*, used to hedge or reinforce a claim in a particular way. See section 6.4.

asymmetric (of a relation) A relation is asymmetric iff the order of its arguments is never reversible without changing the truth value; that is, R is asymmetric iff $\forall x \forall y[R(x,y) \to \neg R(y,x)]$. Compare to 'antisymmetric' and 'symmetric'. Example: the mother-of relation.

attributive adjective An adjective embedded in (a projection of) the nominal it modifies. Contrasts with 'predicative adjective'.

big DegP Term proposed here for the view of the syntax of the extended adjectival projection in which AP is embedded inside DegP, typically the complement of Deg. Contrasts with 'small DegP'. See section 4.2.4.

borderline case An object of which a vague predicate is neither clearly true nor clearly false. For example, if it is unclear whether Clyde is tall or not, he is a borderline case for *tall*. See section 3.2.1.

cardinality The number of atomic (i.e., singular) members in a plural individual (or, more generally, the number of elements in a set).

classificatory adjective An adjective such as *religious* in *religious official* or *Indian* in *Indian deserts*. The defining property of these is difficult to characterize clearly, but may involve the subkind relation. A religious official, for example, is a kind of official. See section 2.4.3 for a potentially more helpful (or at least longer) characterization. Also referred to as 'relational adjectives'.

closed (of an interval or scale) Including both a minimal and a maximal element. Intervals and scales that lack only one of these are 'partially closed', and those that lack both are 'open'. See section 3.7.2.

comparative clause A clause introduced by *than* (e.g. *than Floyd is tall*) or its counterparts in other languages.

comparative deletion An ellipsis process in comparative clauses that deletes an adjective identical to one in the matrix clause: *Floyd will seem taller than Clyde will seem tall*. Distinct from VP ellipsis and generally obligatory. See section 4.2.2.

comparative ellipsis The radical ellipsis process at work in *Floyd will seem taller tomorrow than he seemed tall today* (Bresnan 1975; Lechner 1999).

See section 4.2.2 for comparison with other ellipsis processes in comparatives.

comparative reading (of a superlative) In *Floyd climbed the highest mountain*, the comparative reading is the one on which he climbed a mountain higher than any other climber did. Contrasts with the 'absolute reading' on which there is no mountain higher than the one he climbed. See section 4.3.3.

comparative subdeletion The term for the absence of an overt degree expression in comparative clauses. This is no longer generally viewed as deletion or ellipsis per se, but rather as the result of an unpronounced degree morpheme. Intuitively, though, it can be thought of as deletion from a source such as *Floyd knows fewer philosophers than Clyde knows ~~that many~~ linguists*. See section 4.2.2.

comparison class A set of objects with respect to which a vague predicate is evaluated. The interpretation of *tall*, for example, changes depending on whether the comparison class is basketball players or children. It can be expressed in English with a *for* phrase: *tall for a basketball player*. This is a useful descriptive term, but it also has a precise formal definition in some theories of vagueness and gradability.

comparison of deviation The form of comparison in *Floyd is more boring than Clyde is entertaining*, where what is compared seems to be the extent to which Floyd exceeds the standard for being boring and the extent to which Clyde exceeds the standard for being entertaining. See section 4.3.7 and Kennedy (1997).

conjoined comparative A kind of comparative present in many languages, formed via conjunction with one negated conjunct. English lacks a comparative that overtly takes this form, but it would resemble *Floyd is tall and Clyde isn't tall* and mean simply 'Floyd is taller than Clyde'. See section 4.5.2.

conventional implicature A kind of secondary meaning independent of the at-issue truth-conditional meaning of the sentence but distinct from presupposition. It was originally proposed by Grice (1975) to characterize the semantic contribution of words like *but*. Conventional implicatures create a sense of 'double assertion', resist semantic embedding, and are typically tied to the speaker. They are very unlike conversational implicatures, and in that respect the term is unfortunate. See sections 5.5.2 and 6.5.

cross-polar anomaly The anomaly of comparatives formed from antonymous adjectives: *??Floyd is shorter than Clyde is tall*. See section 3.7.1 and Kennedy (2001).

degree An object in the model directly representing a measurement (such as '6 feet' or '2 hours').

degree achievement A verb (or VP) such as *widen, cool, darken*, and *ripen*. These are related to adjectives, are generally compatible with measure phrases, and have related aspectual properties. See section 6.3.1 and Kennedy and Levin (2008).

Glossary

degree construction A comparative or related construction such as a superlative, equative (*as tall as Clyde*), sufficiency construction (*tall enough*), or excessive construction (*too tall*). See Chapter 4.

degree function In the inherent vagueness theory of Klein (1980), a function that applies to a vague predicate (such as an adjective) and manipulates the membership of its positive or negative extensions. See section 3.4.5.

degree modifier A modifier that characterizes a degree associated with a gradable predicate. Prototypical examples include *very*, *mostly*, and *slightly*.

degree morpheme Descriptively, a morpheme that modulates the degree to which an adjective holds and, in English, generally occurs to its left. These include *-er*, *more*, *-est*, *very*, *somewhat*, *slightly*, and *too*. Generally analyzed syntactically as the sole occupant of a head position labeled Deg.

degree relation The ordering relation between degrees supplied by a degree morpheme, such as $>$, $\geq$, or $=$.

degree word A word that is a degree morpheme.

degree-based theories Theories of gradability and vagueness based on the idea that there is a distinguished type in the model directly representing a measurement (such as '6 feet' or '2 hours') and called a 'degree'. Typically, gradable adjectives are treated as taking an argument of this type.

delineation The sharpening of a vague predicate to eliminate borderline cases, a cut-off used in doing so, or a function associated with either. Inherent vagueness theories such as that of Klein (1980, 1982) are sometimes referred to as 'delineation theories', which isn't ideal. The term hardly occurs in work that established the approach – none of van Fraassen (1966), Fine (1975), Kamp (1975), Klein (1980, 1982), Ballweg (1983), Pinkal (1983), Larson (1988), or Kamp and Partee (1995) use it. (The sole exception is McConnell-Ginet 1973.) Worse, delineations are equally compatible with degree-based theories. See section 3.4.1, particularly footnote[8].

dense order, dense scale A relation is a dense order iff for any two elements it orders, there is another ordered between them; that is, $\leq$ is a dense order iff $\leq$ is an order and $\forall x \forall y [x \leq y \rightarrow \exists z [x \leq z \wedge z \leq y]]$. Examples: the $\leq$ relation on real numbers. A scale is dense iff its order is dense.

diamond entailment pattern A pattern of entailments that is characteristic of intersective interpretations, reflecting the fact that intersective modifiers are generally droppable (outside of downward-entailing contexts). See 25 in section 5.3.4.

differential comparative A comparative with a measure phrase that expresses the difference between two degrees, such as *two feet taller*. See section 4.3.1.

dimension The kind of measurement a gradable predicate is associated with: length, weight, intelligence, laziness, etc.

dimensional adjective An adjective such as *tall*, *heavy*, or *hot*, which typically has a single clear antonym and often an associated unit of measurement, and whose domain is 'clearly delimited' and 'systematically structured' (Bierwisch 1988b). Contrasts with 'non-dimensional' or, in Bierwisch's original terminology, 'evaluative'. (I avoid the original term because it is multiply ambiguous.) See section 3.7.3.

direct analysis In phrasal comparatives like *Floyd is taller than Clyde* and their counterparts in other languages, an analysis in which the comparative morpheme takes as arguments only a gradable predicate and two individuals compared (Heim 1985). See section 4.5.3.

direct modification The antonym of 'indirect modification'.

discourse-oriented adverb A speech-act adverb.

domain adverbial An adverbial such as *legally*, *botanically*, or *psychologically* that characterizes the 'domain' (in an intuitive sense of the term) with respect to which a sentence should be evaluated. For example, *Botanically, a tomato is a fruit*.

droppable Characterizes a modifier that, if omitted from a sentence, creates a sentence that is entailed by the original (at least outside of downward-entailing contexts). Intersective modifiers are generally droppable. See section 5.3.4.

epistemic adjectives Subsective adjectives such as *undisclosed* in *Dick is hiding at an undisclosed location*. See section 2.5.7 and Abusch and Rooth (1997).

epistemic adverb An adverb such as *probably*, *certainly*, *definitely*, and *surely*. A kind of speaker-oriented adverb. See sections 5.5.3 and 5.9.

epistemic view of vagueness A view of vagueness associated with Williamson (1994) in which vague predicates are held to have sharp but unknown cut-offs. See section 3.2.4.

equative An English degree construction such as *as tall as Clyde* and its counterparts in other languages. (Sometimes also used in an entirely unrelated sense to characterize certain copular sentences.)

equivalence class A set of elements that stand in the same equivalence relation to each other. Example: everyone with the same height.

equivalence relation A relation that is reflexive, symmetric, and transitive. Examples: 'has the same age as', 'is precisely as tall as'.

evaluative adjective Used in a variety of ways (I suggest avoiding it in any but the first of the following senses, probably the most intuitive and widespread; see also 'evaluative adverb'):

(a) An adjective that simply implies some evaluative judgment, such as *good* or *terrible*. This use is particularly common in discussions of adjective order and of implicational universals about what concepts are lexicalized as adjectives (e.g. Hetzron 1978; Laenzlinger 2000; Scott 2002; Cinque 2010). This sense of the expression is not confined to syntactic and typological literature, though (Kiefer 1978; Geuder 2000; van Rooij 2008).

(b) Bierwisch (1988b, 1989)'s term for non-dimensional adjectives, which are typically also evaluative in the above sense. See 'dimensional adjective' and section 3.7.3.

(c) A subsective adjective of the *skillful* class (Beesley 1982). See section 2.2.2.

Glossary

(d) Used to characterize adjectives in degree constructions that license inferences to the positive form (Neeleman et al. 2004 and Rett 2008a,b). Because 'evaluative' is already multiply ambiguous, I prefer to use another term, 'biased' (an alternative with its own drawbacks is 'norm-related'). See section 4.4 for discussion of the pitfalls of terminology in this area.

evaluative adverb An adverb such as *fortunately*, *amazingly*, or *disappointingly* which expresses a speaker's evaluation of the propositional content of the modified sentence: <u>Fortunately</u>, *it's raining*. A subclass of speaker-oriented adverbs. Related to 'evaluative adjective' on some of its senses. See section 5.5.2.

evaluative (of a degree construction) See 'biased'.

event An object in the model directly representing something that has taken place, such as the killing of Floyd, the eating of a particular sandwich, or the pushing of a particular cart. Contrasts with 'states', which simply hold rather than taking place, such as Floyd being tall or the sandwich being lousy. These are of the same semantic type (but different sorts), a collective term for which is 'eventuality' (Bach 1986). See section 5.3.4.

event adverbial An adverbial that occurs low in the clause and characterizes some essential feature of an event. The class includes manner adverbials (e.g. *softly*, *tightly*), certain temporal and locative adverbials, and perhaps resultative adverbs. See section 5.2.

eventuality A state or event (Bach 1986).

exceed comparative A kind of comparative present in many languages, formed via an expression that means something like 'exceed' (as in *Floyd's height exceeds Clyde's*). In many languages this is the principal way of forming a comparative. See section 4.5.2.

explicit comparison Antonym of 'implicit comparison'.

expressive meaning A variety of non-truth-conditional (or at least non-descriptive) meaning associated with words such as *ouch* or *whoops* (Kratzer 1999), and *damn*, *fucking*, and racial and ethnic epithets (Potts 2007b). Typically, this kind of meaning is linked to the here-and-now and resists semantic embedding. Expressions with this kind of meaning can often be repeated for a stronger effect *that damn, damn toaster oven*. They are closely related to conventional implicatures, and on the analysis of Potts (2003), analyzed almost identically. See section 6.5. For an extended discussion, see Potts (2007b).

extension gap In inherent-vagueness theories, the set containing borderline cases associated with a predicate. The extension gap of *tall*, for example, consists of individuals that are neither clearly tall nor clearly not tall. Contrasts with 'positive extension' (the set of individuals of which a vague predicate definitely holds) and 'negative extension' (the set of individuals of which it definitely doesn't hold). See section 3.4.1.

extreme adjectives Adjectives such as *fantastic*, *magnificent*, or *enormous*. See section 3.7.4.

factor phrase A measure phrase that expresses degree multiplication, as in <u>three times</u> *as tall*. Also known as a 'ratio phrase'. See section 4.3.1.

faultless disagreement A situation in which interlocutors seem to be disagreeing despite not having obviously asserted contrary propositions. See section 6.6.

frame-setting adverbial An adverbial such as the PPs in *In Japan*, *the elderly seem not to be disposable* or *In linguistics, uncertainty is widespread*. See sections 5.2 and 5.6.

frequency adjective An adjective such as *occasional* in *The occasional sailor strolled by*. These often have adverbial readings, as well as some others, all interesting. See sections 2.5.2, 2.5.3, and 2.5.4.

gradable adjective, gradable predicate An adjective or (other) predicate that can support degree constructions or degree modification.

granularity The size of the units from which a non-dense scale is built. A scale measuring in centimeters has a higher granularity than one measuring in meters.

higher-order vagueness Vagueness with respect to the membership of an extension gap.

implicit comparison Comparison without the use of an overt dedicated comparative morpheme: e.g. *Compared to Floyd, Clyde is tall*. See section 4.5.3 and Kennedy (2007, 2011).

imprecision A characteristic of linguistic expressions arguably distinct from ordinary vagueness. *Floyd is six feet tall* isn't vague because we know how tall he must be to count as tall, but it's still potentially imprecise because we can't be sure whether being a tenth of an inch under six feet counts as close enough for the sentence to be judged 'true enough' in the discourse context. See section 3.2.3.

incommensurable Not able to be directly compared; e.g. the adjectives in *??Floyd is taller than Clyde is heavy*. See sections 3.3.2, 3.6, and 4.3.7.

indirect comparison Comparison in a degree construction involving distinct and apparently incommensurable adjectives that are nevertheless grammatical (e.g. *He's angrier than a Smurf is happy*). Indirect comparison appears to differ from comparison of deviation. Also known as 'interadjective comparison' (van Rooij 2011c) and 'relative comparison' (Doetjes et al. 2011). See section 4.3.8 and Bale (2006, 2008).

indirect modification Modification accomplished with the aid of a relative clause or similar structure, or a morpheme specialized for this purpose (Larson and Cho 2003). Some languages appear to rely on this strategy primarily or exclusively in attributive positions. See section 2.6.2.

inherent-vagueness theories A term used in this book for theories of vagueness and gradability in which certain sentences with vague predicates may lack a truth value and there is no direct representation of measurements as objects in the model (i.e. there are no degrees as such). These are sometimes referred to with terms that name some theoretical mechanism these theories tend to use (including supervaluation, delineation, extension gap, comparison class, precisification) or as the 'vague predicate analysis'. See section 3.4.

integrated See 'restrictive'.

Glossary 291

intersective Characterizes a modifier that can be interpreted via conjunction or its set-theoretic counterpart, intersection. *Canadian surgeon*, for example, picks out the intersection of the set of Canadians and the set of surgeons. See sections 2.2.1 and 5.3.4.

intensifier An alternative term for degree word, though one that is rather awkward when used of degree words like *slightly*.

interval A continuous portion of a scale (or other linearly ordered set); that is, the set of all degrees between any two degrees on the scale (inclusively or exclusively, depending on whether the interval is closed or open). See section 3.7.2 for a more explicit characterization.

irreflexive (of a relation) A relation is irreflexive iff no object stands in that relation to itself; that is, R is reflexive iff $\neg \exists x[R(x,x)]$. Example: the older-than relation.

linear order, total order An order is total iff it orders all distinct elements in the set over which it is defined (its field); that is, $\leq$ is a linear order iff $\leq$ is an order and $\forall x \forall y : x \neq y[x \leq y \vee y \leq x]$. Orders – or indeed any relations – with this property are also called 'connected'.

locational comparative Stassen (1984, 1985, 2006)'s term for a kind of comparative present in many languages, formed with the use of a locative adposition (such as 'from', 'out of', or 'to') or case to mark the standard of comparison. In such languages, a comparative might come out as approximately 'Floyd is tall from Clyde'. See section 4.5.2.

lower-closed scale A scale that includes a minimal element. See section 3.7.2.

manner adverb An adverb that characterizes the manner in which an event took place and typically occurs low in the clause: e.g. *loudly*, *roughly*, *tightly*. Some adverbs of this class (or, depending on one's analysis, their homophones) can also receive other readings, including subject-oriented ones (*rudely*, *thoughtfully*) or speech-act ones (*frankly*, *confidentially*).

maximal standard adjective An absolute adjective whose standard is at the top of its scale. *Dry*, for example, has a maximal standard because, to count as *dry*, something must be dry to the maximum degree. Also called a total predicate. See section 3.7.2.

maximality modifier A degree modifier such as *fully* or *completely*, which is only possible with adjectives that have upper-closed scales. See section 3.7.2.

maximality operator An operator that returns the maximum of an ordered set, or of the characteristic function of one. See sections 3.7.2 and 4.2.3.

maximum, maximal element A maximal element of an ordered set has no elements ordered above it. In a totally ordered set, there can be at most one such element, called the 'greatest element' or 'maximum'. (An example of an order with multiple maximal elements is the 'body part of' relation, with respect to which each body is maximal. See also 'minimal element'.)

measure function A function that yields degrees (or analogous objects, such as numbers) that represent a measure of its argument along a particular dimension. Typically of type $\langle e, d \rangle$. See sections 3.5.1 and 4.2.4.

measure phrase A nominal expressing a measurement such as *six feet* or *a few pounds*. Often used in a more specific sense to refer to such nominals when they occur in construction with an adjective, as in *six feet tall* or *a few pounds heavier*.

metalinguistic comparative A comparative such as *more dumb than crazy*, in which it seems to be something about the words themselves that is compared, perhaps having to do with the appropriateness of choosing one over the other. See section 4.3.6.

minimal standard adjective An absolute adjective whose standard is at the bottom of its scale. *Wet*, for example, has a minimal standard because to count as wet an object need only exceed the minimum (zero) degree of wetness. Also called partial predicate. See section 3.7.2 and Kennedy and McNally (2005).

minimum, minimal element A minimal element of an ordered set has no elements ordered below it. In a totally ordered set, there can be at most one such element, called the 'least element' or 'minimum'. (See also 'maximal element'.)

modal adjective An adjective that expresses quantification over possible worlds, such as *alleged* or *potential*. See section 2.2.4.

modal adverb An adverb that expresses quantification over possible worlds, such as *necessarily* or *possibly*. See sections 5.5.3 and 5.3.1.

monotonicity With respect to adjectives, a term for the assumption that if Floyd is tall to a degree, he is also taller to every lower degree.

negative adjective The negative or marked member of an antonym pair: e.g. *short* (vs. *tall*), *narrow* (vs. *wide*). See section 3.7.1.

negative extension The set of objects of which a vague predicate clearly doesn't hold. The negative extension of *tall*, for example, is the set of individuals who aren't tall and aren't even borderline cases. Contrasts with 'extension gap' and 'positive extension'.

neo-Davidsonian Describes a theory of event semantics in which (at least some) arguments of a verb are introduced indirectly with thematic-role predicates like **agent** and, typically, event arguments are generalized beyond just 'action sentences' as Davidson originally proposed. See section 5.4.2.

neutralization The effect on an adjective of blocking entailments to its positive form (see, e.g., Winter 2001). For example, *Floyd is taller than Clyde* neutralizes *tall* because it fails to entail *Floyd is tall*; in contrast, *Floyd is as short as Clyde* doesn't neutralize *short* because it entails *Floyd is short*. See also 'bias', 'evaluative adjective', and 'norm-related', and section 4.4 for general discussion of the pitfalls of terminology in this area.

nongradable adjective, nongradable predicate An adjective or (other) predicate that can't support degree constructions or degree modification. Examples include *triangular*, *wooden*, and *prime* (*??a very wooden table*). These are very easily coerced into gradability, however.

norm-related Bierwisch (1988b, 1989)'s term for adjectives that require that a norm be exceeded. *Floyd is tall*, for example, is norm-related because it requires that Floyd exceed the norm for tallness. *Floyd is as short as Clyde* is also norm-related because it requires that Floyd exceed the norm for

Glossary

shortness. See also 'bias(ed)', 'evaluative adjective', and section 4.4 for more on the pitfalls of terminology in this area.

nominal comparative See 'amount comparative'. The term isn't normally intended to include e.g. *more of an idiot than Clyde*. (See section 6.3.2 for discussion of those cases.)

nonrestrictive Characterizes a modifier, especially a relative clause, that is not restrictive. Precisely what this means is an analytical question, the answer to which may be different for different nonrestrictive modifiers. Classically, though, nonrestrictive modifiers are viewed as secondary comments on the main assertion in which they are embedded. They typically don't make a discernible contribution to the ordinary, descriptive truth conditional meaning of a sentence. Because restrictive modifiers can also on occasion fail to contribute to overall truth conditions (e.g. by virtue of making a redundant contribution), it may be wise to focus on the secondary-assertion part of this characterization instead. For this reason, Huddleston and Pullum (2002) prefer the term 'supplemental' to 'nonrestrictive'. See 'restrictive' and section 6.5 for more.

open (of an interval or scale) Lacking both a minimal and a maximal element. Contrasts with 'closed'. See section 3.7.2.

order(ing relation), partial order A relation that is transitive, antisymmetric, and either reflexive (in a weak order) or irreflexive (in a strict order).

parasitic scope A scope-taking operation in which an expression moves to a position created by earlier movement of another expression, or the analogue of this process in theories without movement (Barker 2007). See section 2.5.5.

partial order See 'order'.

partial predicate A minimal standard adjective, or a predicate of another category with similar properties. Informally, a partial predicate is one that, if it is satisfied to any nonzero degree, counts as having been satisfied (e.g. anything that isn't fully dry counts as wet). Contrasts with 'total predicate'. See section 3.7.2 and Yoon (1996).

partially closed (of an interval or scale) Including a maximal or minimal element, but not both. See section 3.7.2.

passive-sensitive adverb Characterizes subject-oriented adverbs that, in passive sentences, can orient toward either the surface subject or the agent. This ambiguity arises in, for example, *Floyd was willingly abused by Clyde*, where either Floyd or Clyde could be the willing party. See section 5.4.1.

phrasal comparative A comparative in which the phrase expressing the standard of comparison – in English, the *than*-phrase – is structurally smaller than a clause: e.g. *taller than Clyde*. See section 4.2.2.

positive adjective Used in two unrelated ways:
(a) The positive or unmarked adjective in a pair of polar antonyms: e.g. *tall* (vs. *short*), *old* (vs. *young*). See section 3.7.1.
(b) An adjective in its positive form.

positive extension The set of objects of which a vague predicate clearly holds. The positive extension of *tall*, for example, is the set of individuals who are definitely tall and aren't borderline cases. Contrasts with 'extension gap' and 'negative extension'.

positive-entailing (of a degree construction) Licensing entailments to the positive form. For example, *Floyd is as short as Clyde* is positive-entailing because it entails *Floyd is short*; in contrast, *Floyd is as tall as Clyde* isn't because it doesn't entail *Floyd is tall*. The term is cumbersome and easily mistaken as referring to positive adjectives, but it's preferable to alternatives such as 'evaluative' and 'norm-related'. See section 4.4 for discussion.

positive form (of an adjective) The bare, morphologically unmarked form of an adjective; that is, an adjective that is not in a comparative or superlative. Also known as the 'absolute form'.

pragmatic adverb A speech-act adverb. (Sometimes used more broadly to include other speaker-oriented adverbs.)

precisification The sharpening of a vague predicate to eliminate some or all borderline cases, or a particular means of doing so. Used especially (but not exclusively) in inherent vagueness theories, in which precisifications may be quantified over. See section 3.4.

predicate modifier A modifier that takes the modified expression as an argument and yields something of the same semantic type. The term is reserved for modifiers of predicates (rather than, say, individuals or propositions); 'operator' and 'operator type' can occasionally be encountered as more general terms. See sections 1.4, 2.3.1, and 5.3.

predicational adverb An adverb in the class characterized by being related to a gradable predicate, lacking a quantificational denotation, and, in English, ending in *-ly*. These include event adverbs (including manner adverbs), subject-oriented adverbs, and speaker-oriented adverbs. Typically, evaluative adverbs such as *fortunately* and epistemic adverbs such as *probably* are included in this class even though they presumably involve quantification over worlds.

predicative adjective An adjective that isn't attributive. Often the object of a copular verb.

preorder, quasiorder A relation is a preorder or quasiorder iff it is reflexive and transitive but not necessarily antisymmetric. Example: the 'having at least the same age as' relation (because people can have the same age without being identical).

privative adjective An adjective such as *fake*, *pretend*, or *fictitious*, which seems to exclude all members of the extension of the noun from the extension of the adjective–noun combination. See section 2.2.5.

proportional modifier A degree modifier such as *mostly* or *half*, which is only possible with adjectives that have closed scales. See section 3.7.2.

proximative See 'approximative'.

pure manner adverb A manner adverb that lacks any non-manner readings, such as *softly* and *tightly* (Ernst 2002).

ratio phrase See 'factor phrase'.

reflexive (of a relation) A relation is reflexive iff every object stands in that relation to itself (i.e., R is reflexive iff $\forall x[R(x,x)]$). Example: the 'being at least as tall as' relation.

Glossary

relational adjective See 'classificatory adjective', though 'relational adjective' is also used in a broader sense that includes both classificatory adjectives and adjectives that seem to saturate a noun's argument position ('thematic adjectives' as in *the American invasion of Grenada*).

relative adjective Used in a variety of more or less related senses (all distinct from 'relational adjective'):

(a) An adjective such as *tall* or *wide* whose standard is provided by context rather than as a consequence of its scale structure (or some other feature of its lexical entry). Contrasts with the sense of 'absolute adjective' that refers to adjectives such as *wet* and *dry*. See section 3.7.2 and Kennedy and McNally (2005).

(b) An adjective whose meaning is relativized to an argument. In particular, 'relative adjective' has been used to refer to adjectives with predicate-modifier denotations that take a noun as an argument (Siegel 1976a), in contradistinction to one sense of 'absolute adjective'. See section 2.3.2.

(c) Sometimes used to mean simply 'gradable adjective'. This use is best avoided because of the ambiguity.

restrictive Characterizes a modifier, especially a relative clause, that can in principle make a contribution to strengthening the ordinary truth-conditional meaning of a sentence. Nonrestrictive modifiers make a secondary comment about the sentence. See section 6.5. Huddleston and Pullum (2002) prefer the term 'integrated', in part because a restrictive modifier may sometimes fail to strengthen truth conditions (*the dogs that are mammals*).

resultative adverb An adverb that characterizes a result state of an event participant and can often be paraphrased using an adjectival resultative: *chopped it coarsely* (it winds up coarse), *wound him fatally* (he winds up dead). These might be a variety of manner adverb.

scale A linearly ordered set of degrees that represent measurement along a dimension. See section 3.5.1.

sentence adverbial An adverbial that attaches to a clause. See section 5.2.

slack regulator An expression that indicates how much pragmatic slack should be afforded. See sections 3.2.3 and 6.4.

small DegP A term proposed here for the view of the syntax of the extended adjectival projection in which DegP is embedded inside AP and doesn't itself contain the adjective. This view is sometimes referred to as the 'classical' one. Contrasts with 'big DegP'. See section 4.2.5.

sorites paradox, sorites sequence Respectively, the paradox of the heap and a series of objects which give rise to a version of it by differing only in a negligible way. See section 3.2.1.

speaker-oriented adverb A member of the class that consists of speech-act, evaluative, and epistemic adverbs. These characteristically occur higher than other adverbs.

speech-act adverb An adverb that characterizes the speech act being performed: e.g. *Frankly, you blew it*; *Confidentially, there's cyanide in the salsa*. See section 5.5.1.

standard, standard of comparison A degree (or, depending on the analysis, an individual) relative to which an adjectival comparison is made. For example, in *Floyd is taller than Clyde*, the standard is provided by *than Clyde*. In *Floyd is tall*, the standard is a contextually provided cut-off that constitutes the smallest height that counts as tall. When the standard is provided by a syntactically overt expression such as a comparative clause, 'standard' may by extension refer to that expression itself. See section 4.2.1.

standard marker *Than* and its counterparts across languages; that is, morphemes that mark the standard of comparison. See section 4.2.1.

state An object in the model directly representing something that simply is the case rather than taking place, such as Floyd being tall or the sandwich being lousy. Contrasts with 'event'. States and events are of the same semantic type (but different sorts), a collective term for which is 'eventuality' (Bach 1986). See section 5.3.4.

strict order, irreflexive order An order that is irreflexive.

subcomparative A comparative that has undergone comparative subdeletion but not comparative deletion. See section 4.2.2.

subject-oriented adverb An adverb such as *intentionally* or *accidentally* that gives rise to entailments specifically involving the subject or agent, or a manner adverb interpreted in this way. See section 5.3.2.

subsective An adjective such as *skillful* in *skillful surgeon* that can be viewed as mapping the extension of a noun to a subset of it (skillful surgeons are a subset of surgeons). By extension, any modifier with these characteristics. Strictly speaking, all intersective modifiers are also subsective, but the term 'subsective' is usually used more narrowly to include only non-intersective subsective modifiers. *Skillful*, for example, is non-intersective because a skillful surgeon isn't simply someone who is a surgeon and skillful at something. See section 2.2.2.

supervaluation The assignment of a truth value to a sentence with respect to all (total) precisifications. See section 3.4, especially section 3.4.2.

supplement, supplemental See 'nonrestrictive'.

supremum, least upper bound The smallest element of a set that is ordered above (or equal to) all the members of a given subset. The dual of 'supremum' is 'infimum' or 'greatest lower bound'.

symmetric (of a relation) A relation is symmetric iff the order of its arguments is reversible with no change in truth value; that is, R is symmetric iff $\forall x \forall y [R(x,y) \rightarrow R(y,x)]$. Compare to 'antisymmetric' and 'asymmetric'. Example: the sibling or classmate relations.

synthetic comparative A comparative construction formed with a bound comparative morpheme such as *-er* rather than a free one such as *more*. Contrasts with 'analytic comparative'.

total order See 'linear order'.

total predicate A maximal standard adjective, or a predicate of another category with similar properties. Informally, a total predicate is one that doesn't count as having been satisfied unless it is satisfied to the highest possible degree (e.g. to count as dry, an object must be fully dry). Contrasts with 'partial predicate'. See section 3.7.2 and Yoon (1996).

Glossary

transitive (of a relation) A relation is transitive iff whenever it relates one object to a second, and the second to a third, it also relates the first to the third; that is, R is transitive iff $\forall x \forall y \forall z[[R(x,y) \wedge R(y,z)] \rightarrow R(x,z)]$. Example: the taller-than relation among heights.

upper-closed scale A scale that includes a maximal element. See section 3.7.2.

utterance-modifying adverb A speech-act adverb.

weak order, reflexive order, non-strict order An order that is reflexive.

zeugma The use of an expression on two distinct senses simultaneously: e.g., *As the economy worsened, Floyd and his savings both lost interest.* This is a test for ambiguity, in this case demonstrating that *interest* is ambiguous. See section 3.2.2.

References

Abbott, Barbara. 2010. *Reference*. Oxford Surveys in Semantics & Pragmatics. Oxford University Press.

Abney, Steven. 1987. The English noun phrase in its sentential aspect. Ph.D. thesis, MIT.

Abrusán, Márta, and Spector, Benjamin. 2011. A semantics for degree questions based on intervals: negative islands and their obviation, *Journal of Semantics*, **28**(1), 107–147.

Abusch, Dorit, and Rooth, Mats. 1997. Epistemic NP modifiers. In Lawson, A. (ed.), *Proceedings of Semantics and Linguistic Theory (SALT) 7*. Ithaca, NY: CLC Publications.

Adams, Ernest. 1974. The logic of 'almost all', *Journal of Philosophical Logic*, **3**(1–2), 3–17.

Aihara, Masahiko. 2009. The scope of *-est*: evidence from Japanese. *Natural Language Semantics*, **17**(4), 341–367.

Alexiadou, Artemis. 2001. Adjective syntax and noun raising: word order asymmetries in the DP as the result of adjective distribution, *Studia Linguistica*, **55**(3), 217–248.

Alexiadou, Artemis, and Stavrou, Melita. 2011. Ethnic adjectives as pseudo-adjectives: a case study on syntax–morphology interaction and the structure of DP, *Studia Linguistica*, **65**(2), 117–146.

Aljović, Nadira. 2010. Syntactic positions of attributive adjectives. In Cabredo Hofherr and Matushansky (2010).

Alrenga, Peter. 2006. Scalar (non-)identity and similarity. In Baumer, Donald, Montero, David, and Scanlon, Michael (eds.), *Proceedings of the West Coast Conference on Formal Linguistics (WCCFL) 25*. Somerville, MA: Cascadilla Press.

   2007a. Comparisons of similarity and difference. In *Proceedings of the 2005 Workshop on the Formal Analysis of Adjectives (JET Adjectifs)*. University of Paris 7 Jussieu.

   2007b. Tokens, types, and identity. In *Proceedings of the North East Linguistic Society (NELS) 38*. Amherst MA: GLSA Publications.

Alrenga, Peter, Kennedy, Christopher, and Merchant, Jason. 2012. A new standard of comparison. In Arnett, Nathan, and Bennett, Ryan (eds.),

References

Proceedings of the West Coast Conference on Formal Linguistics (WCCFL) 30. Somerville, MA: Cascadilla Press.

Amaral, Patrícia. 2007. The meaning of approximative adverbs: evidence from European Portuguese. Ph.D. thesis, The Ohio State University.

Amaral, Patrícia, and Del Prete, Fabio. 2010. Approximating the limit: the interaction between quasi 'almost'and some temporal connectives in Italian, *Linguistics and Philosophy*, **33**(2), 51–115.

Amaral, Patrícia, Roberts, Craige, and Smith, E. Allyn. 2007. Review of 'The Logic of Conventional Implicatures' by Chris Potts, *Linguistics and Philosophy*, **30**(6), 707–749.

Anand, Pranav, and Brasaveanu, Adrian. 2010. Modal concord as modal modification. In Prinzhorn, Martin, Schmitt, Viola, and Zobel, Sarah (eds.), *Proceedings of the Fourteenth Sinn und Bedeutung Conference*. Berlin: Zentrum fur Allgememe Sprach wissenschaft.

Anderson, Curt. 2013. Gradability in the absence of degree scales. In *Proceedings of Semantics and Linguistic Theory (SALT) 23*. Ithaca, NY: CLC Publications.

2014. A Hamblin semantics for **sorta**. In Kohlberger, Martin, Bellamy, Kate, and Dutton, Eleanor (eds.), *Proceedings of ConSOLE XXI*. Leiden: University centre for linguishes.

Forthcoming. Verbal gradability and degree arguments in verbs. In *Proceedings of Penn Linguistics Colloquium 37*. University of Pennsylvania Working Papers in Linguistics.

Anderson, Curt, and Morzycki, Marcin. Forthcoming Degrees as Kinds. Ms., Michigan State University. To appear in *Natural Language & Linguistic Theory*.

Arsenijević, Boban, Boleda, Gemma, Gehrke, Berit, and McNally, Louise. 2014. Ethnic adjectives are proper adjectives. In *Proceedings of the Chicago Linguistic Society (CLS) 46*. Chicago Linguistic Society.

Atlas, Jay David. 1984. Comparative adjectives and adverbials of degree: an introduction to radically radical pragmatics, *Linguistics and Philosophy*, **7**(4), 347–377.

Austin, J. L. 1961. Performative utterances. Chap. 11 of *Philosophical Papers*. Oxford: Clarendon Press.

Bach, Emmon. 1968. Nouns and noun phrases. In Bach, Emmon, and Harms, Robert (eds.), *Universals in Linguistic Theory*. New York: Holt, Rinehart and Winston.

1986. The algebra of events, *Linguistics and Philosophy*, **9**(1), 5–16.

1989. *Informal Lectures on Formal Semantics*. Stony Brook: State University of New York Press.

Baker, Mark C. 1988. *Incorporation: A Theory of Grammatical Function Changing*. University of Chicago Press.

2003. *Lexical Categories: Verbs, Nouns, and Adjectives*. Cambridge University Press.

Bale, Alan. 2006. The universal scale and the semantics of comparison. Ph.D. thesis, McGill University.

2008. A universal scale of comparison, *Linguistics and Philosophy*, **31**(1), 1–55.

2011. Scales and comparison classes, *Natural Language Semantics*, **19**(2), 169–190.

Ballmer, Thomas T., and Pinkal, Manfred (eds.). 1983. *Approaching Vagueness*. Amsterdam: North-Holland.

Ballweg, Joachim. 1983. Vagueness or context-dependence?: Supervaluation revisited in a semantics based on scales. In Ballmer and Pinkal (1983).

Bally, Charles. 1944. *Linguistique générale et linguistique française*. Berne: A. Francke.

Barker, Chris. 2002. The dynamics of vagueness, *Linguistics and Philosophy*, **25**(1), 1–36.

2007. Parasitic scope, *Linguistics and Philosophy*, **30**(4), 407–444.

Barker, Chris, and Jacobson, Pauline (eds.). 2007. *Direct Compositionality*. Oxford Studies in Theoretical Linguistics, vol. 14. Oxford University Press.

Barner, David, Brooks, Neon, and Bale, Alan. 2011. Accessing the unsaid: the role of scalar alternatives in children's pragmatic inference, *Cognition*, **118**(1), 84 – 93.

Bartsch, Renate, and Vennemann, Theo. 1973. *Semantic Structures: A Study In the Relation Between Semantics and Syntax*. Frankfurt: Athenäum Verlag.

Barwise, Jon, and Cooper, Robin. 1981. Generalized quantifiers and natural language, *Linguistics and Philosophy*, **4**(2), 159–219.

Beck, Sigrid. 2000. The semantics of 'different': comparison operator and relational adjective, *Linguistics and Philosophy*, **23**(2), 101–139.

2009. DegP scope reanalysed. Ms., Universität Tübingen.

2010. Quantifiers in **than**-clauses, *Semantics and Pragmatics*, **3**(1), 1–72.

2011. Comparison constructions. In Maienborn et al. (2011).

2012. DegP scope revisited, *Natural Language Semantics*, **20**(3), 227–272.

2013. Lucinda driving too fast again: the scalar properties of ambiguous **than**-clauses, *Journal of Semantics*, **30**(1), 1–63.

Beck, Sigrid, Oda, Toshiko, and Sugisaki, Koji. 2004. Parametric variation in the semantics of comparison: Japanese vs. English, *Journal of East Asian Linguistics*, **13**(4), 289–344.

Beesley, Kenneth Reid. 1982. Evaluative adjectives as one-place predicates in Montague grammar, *Journal of Semantics*, **1**(3–4), 195–249.

Bellert, Irena. 1977. On semantic and distributional properties of sentential adverbs, *Linguistic Inquiry*, **8**(2), 337–351.

Beltrama, Andrea, and Bochnak, M. Ryan. Forthcoming. *Intensification without degrees cross-linguistically*. Ms., University of Chicago. To appear in *Natural Language & Linguistic Theory*.

Bennett, Michael R. 1974. Some extensions of a Montague fragment of English. Ph.D. thesis, UCLA.

Bhatt, Rajesh, and Pancheva, Roumyana. 2004. Late merger of degree clauses, *Linguistic Inquiry*, **35**(1), 1–45.

2007. Degree quantifiers, position of merger effects with their restrictors, and conservativity. In Barker and Jacobson (2007).
Bhatt, Rajesh, and Takahashi, Shoichi. 2007. Direct comparisons: resurrecting the direct analysis of phrasal comparatives. In *Proceedings of Semantics and Linguistic Theory (SALT) 17*. Ithaca, NY: CLC Publications.
 2011. Reduced and unreduced phrasal comparatives, *Natural Language and Linguistic Theory*, **29**(3), 581–620.
Bierwisch, Manfred. 1988a. On the grammar of local prepositions. In Bierwisch, M., Motsch, W., and Zimmermann, I. (eds.), *Syntax, Semantik und Lexikon*. Berlin: Akademie-Verlag.
 1988b. Tools and explanations of comparison: Part 1, *Journal of Semantics*, **6**(1), 57–93.
 1989. The semantics of gradation. In Bierwisch, Manfred, and Lang, Ewald (eds.), *Dimensional Adjectives*. Berlin: Springer-Verlag.
 1996. How much space gets into language? In Bloom, P. (ed.), *Language and Space*. Cambridge, MA: MIT Press.
Black, Max. 1937. Vagueness: an exercise in logical analysis, *Philosophy of Science*, **4**(4), 427–455.
Bloomfield, Leonard. 1962. *The Menomini Language*, New Haven, CT: Yale University Press.
Blutner, Reinhard. 1998. Lexical pragmatics, *Journal of Semantics*, **15**(2), 115–162.
 2008. Pragmatics and the lexicon. In Horn, Laurence R., and Ward, Gregory (eds.), *The Handbook of Pragmatics*. Oxford: Blackwell Publishing.
Bochnak, M. Ryan. 2010. Quantity and gradability across categories. In Li, Nan, and Lutz, David (eds.), *Proceedings of Semantics and Linguistic Theory (SALT) 20*. Ithaca, NY: CLC Publications.
 2013a. Cross-linguistic variation in the semantics of comparatives. Ph.D. thesis, University of Chicago.
 2013b. The non-universal status of degrees: evidence from Washo. In Keine, Stefan, and Slogget, Shayne (eds.), *Proceedings of the North East Linguistic Society (NELS) 42*. Amherst, MA: GLSA Publications.
Boër, Steven E., and Lycan, William G. 1980. A performadox in truth-conditional semantics, *Linguistics and Philosophy*, **4**(1), 71–100.
Bogusławski, Andrzej. 1975. Measures are measures: in defence of the diversity of comparatives and positives, *Linguistische Berichte*, **36**, 1–9.
Bolinger, Dwight. 1967a. Adjective comparison: a semantic scale, *Journal of English Linguistics*, **1**(1).
 1967b. Adjectives in English: attribution and predication, *Lingua*, **18**, 1–34.
 1972. *Degree Words*. The Hague: Mouton.
Bonami, Olivier, and Cabredo Hofherr, Patricia (eds.). 2008. *Empirical Issues in Syntax and Semantics 7: Proceedings of the Colloque de Syntaxe et Sémantique à Paris*. Paris: CSSP.

Bonami, Olivier, and Godard, Danièle. 2007. Parentheticals in underspecified semantics: the case of evaluative adverbs, *Research on Language & Computation*, 5(4), 391–413.

2008. Lexical semantics and pragmatics of evaluative adverbs. In McNally and Kennedy (2008).

Bonami, Olivier, Godard, Danièle, and Kampers-Manhe, Brigitte. 2004. Adverb classification. In Corblin, Francis, and de Swart, Henriëtte (eds.), *Handbook of French Semantics*. Stanford: CSLI Publications.

Bosque, Ignacio. 1999. El Sintagma Adjetival: modificadores y complementos del adjetivo: Adjetivo y participio. In Bosque, Ignacio, and Demonte, Violeta (eds.), *Gramática Descriptiva de la Lengua Española*, vol. I. Madrid: Espasa Calpe.

Bosque, Ignacio, and Picallo, Carme. 1996. Postnominal adjectives in Spanish DPs, *Journal of Linguistics*, 32, 57–78.

Bouchard, David-Étienne. 2012. Long-distance degree quantification and the grammar of subjectivity. Ph.D. thesis, McGill University.

Bouchard, Denis. 2002. *Adjectives, Number, and Interfaces: Why Languages Vary*. Oxford: Elsevier.

Brasoveanu, Adrian. 2008a. Comparative and equative correlatives as anaphora to differentials. In *Proceedings of Semantics and Linguistic Theory (SALT) 18*. Ithaca, NY: CLC Publications.

2008b. Measure noun polysemy and monotonicity: evidence from Romanian pseudopartitives. In *Proceedings of the North East Linguistic Society (NELS) 38*. Amherst, MA: GLSA Publications.

2011. Sentence-internal *different* as quantifier-internal anaphora, *Linguistics and Philosophy*, 34, 93–168.

Breheny, Richard. 2008. A new look at the semantics and pragmatics of numerically quantified noun phrases, *Journal of Semantics*, 25(2), 93–139.

Bresnan, Joan. 1973. Syntax of the comparative clause construction in English, *Linguistic Inquiry*, 4(3), 275–343.

1975. Comparative deletion and constraints on transformations, *Linguistic Analysis*, 1(1), 25–74.

Büring, Daniel. 1999. Topic. In Bosch, Peter, and van der Sandt, Rob (eds.), *Focus: Linguistic, Cognitive, and Computational Perspectives*. Cambridge University Press.

2007a. Comparative sandwichology. In Colavin, Rebecca, Cooke, Kathryn, Davidson, Kathryn, Fukuda, Shin, and del Giudice, Alex (eds.), *Proceedings of the Western Conference on Linguistics (WECOL) 2007*. University of California, San Diego.

2007b. Cross-polar nomalies. In *Proceedings of Semantics and Linguistic Theory (SALT) 17*. Ithaca, NY: CLC Publications.

2007c. More or less. In *Proceedings of the Chicago Linguistic Society (CLS) 43*. Chicago Linguistics Society.

Bylinina, Lisa. 2011. This is so NP! In Partee, Barbara Hall, Glanzerg, M., and Skilters, J. (eds.), *Formal Semantics and Pragmatics: Discourse, Context and Models*. Riga: New Prairie Press.

Cabredo Hofherr, Patricia, and Matushansky, Ora (eds.). 2010. *Adjectives: Formal Analyses in Syntax and Semantics*. Linguistik Aktuell/Linguistics Today, vol. 153. Amsterdam: John Benjamins Publishing.

Carlson, Greg. 1977. *Reference to Kinds in English*. Ph.D. thesis, University of Massachusetts Amherst. Published in 1980 by Garland, New York.

  1987. *Same* and *different*: some consequences for syntax and semantics, *Linguistics and Philosophy*, **10**(4), 531–565.

Carlson, Greg, and Pelletier, Francis Jeffry. 2002. The average American has 2.3 children, *Journal of Semantics*, **19**(1), 73–104.

  (eds.) 1995. *The Generic Book*. University of Chicago Press.

Castroviejo Miró, Elena. 2007. A degree-based account of *wh*-exclamatives in Catalan. In Puig-Waldmüller (2007).

  2008a. Adverbs in restricted configurations. In Bonami and Cabredo Hofherr (2008).

  2008b. Deconstructing exclamations, *Catalan Journal of Linguistics*, **7**, 41–90.

  2008c. An expressive answer: some considerations on the semantics and pragmatics of wh-exclamatives. In *Proceedings of the Chicago Linguistic Society (CLS) 44*. Chicago Linguistic Society.

  2013. Gradation in Modified AdjPs. In Snider, Todd (ed.), *Proceedings of Semantics and Linguistic Theory (SALT) 23*. eLanguage.

Castroviejo Miró, Elena, and Schwager, Magdalena. 2008. Amazing DPs. In *Proceedings of Semantics and Linguistic Theory (SALT) 18*. Ithaca, NY: CLC Publications.

Caudal, Patrick, and Nicolas, David. 2005. Types of degrees and types of event structures. In Maienborn, Claudia, and Wöllenstein, A. (eds.), *Event Arguments: Foundations and Applications*. Tübingen: Niemeyer.

Centeno-Pulido, Alberto. 2010. Reconciling generativist and functionalist approaches on adjectival position in Spanish. Ph.D. thesis, University of Georgia.

Champollion, Lucas. 2006. A game-theoretic account of adjective ordering restrictions. Ms., University of Pennsylvania.

Chierchia, Gennaro. 1984. Topics in the syntax and semantics of infinitives and gerunds. Ph.D. thesis, University of Massachusetts Amherst.

  1995. Individual-level predicates as inherent generics. In Carlson and Pelletier (1995).

  1998. Reference to kinds across languages, *Natural Language Semantics*, **6**(4), 339–405.

  2010. Mass nouns, vagueness and semantic variation, *Synthese*, **174**(1), 99–149.

Chierchia, Gennaro, and McConnell-Ginet, Sally. 1990. *Meaning and Grammar: An Introduction to Semantics*. Cambridge, MA: MIT Press.

Chomsky, Noam. 1965. *Aspects of the Theory of Syntax*. Cambridge, MA: MIT Press.

  1977. On *wh*-movement. In Culicover, Peter, Wasow, Thomas, and Akmajian, Adrian (eds.), *Formal Syntax*. New York: Academic Press.

Cinque, Guglielmo. 1994. Evidence for partial N-movement in the Romance DP. In Cinque, Guglielmo, Koster, Jan, Pollock, Jean-Yves, Rizzi, Luigi, and Zanuttini, Raffaella (eds.), *Paths Toward Universal Grammar: Essays in Honor of Richard S. Kayne*. Washington, DC: Georgetown University Press.

  1999. *Adverbs and Functional Heads: A Cross-Linguistic Perspective*. New York: Oxford University Press.

  2003. The dual source of adjectives and XP- vs. N-raising in the Romance DP. Paper presented at the North East Linguistic Society (NELS)35, SUNY at Stony Brook, November 7–9, 2003.

  2010. *The Syntax of Adjectives: A Comparative Study*. Linguistic Inquiry Monographs, vol. 57. Cambridge, MA: MIT Press.

Clark, Romane. 1970. Concerning the logic of predicate modifiers, *Noûs*, 4(4), 311–335.

Cohen, Ariel, and Krifka, Manfred. 2011. Superlative quantifiers as modifiers of meta-speech acts, *The Baltic International Yearbook of Cognition, Logic and Communication*, 6, 1–56.

Constantinescu, Camelia. 2011. Gradability in the nominal domain. Ph.D. thesis, Rijksuniversiteit Leiden.

Corver, Norbert. 1990. The syntax of left branch extractions. Ph.D. thesis, Tilburg University.

  1993. A note on subcomparatives, *Linguistic Inquiry*, 24(4), 773–781.

  1997. The internal syntax of the Dutch extended adjectival projection, *Natural Language and Linguistic Theory*, 15(2), 289–368.

Cresswell, Max J. 1973. *Logics and Languages*. London: Methuen.

  1974. Adverbs and events, *Synthese*, 28(3), 455–481.

  1976. The semantics of degree. In Partee, Barbara H. (ed.), *Montague Grammar*. New York: Academic Press.

  1979. Adverbs of space and time. In Guenthner, F., and Schmidt, S. J. (eds.), *Formal Semantics and Pragmatics for Natural Languages*. Dordrecht Reidel. Reprinted in Cresswell (1985).

  1985. *Adverbial Modification: Interval Semantics and Its Rivals*. Dordrecht: Reidel.

Crisma, P. 1993. On adjective placement in Romance and Germanic event nominals, *Rivista Di Grammatica Generativa*, 18, 61–100.

Cruse, D. Allan. 1986. *Lexical Semantics*. Cambridge University Press.

Cummins, Chris, Sauerland, Uli, and Solt, Stephanie. 2012. Granularity and scalar implicature in numerical expressions, *Linguistics and Philosophy*, 35(2), 135–169.

Davidson, Donald. 1967. The Logical Form of action sentences. In Rescher, Nicholas (ed.), *The Logic of Decision and Action*. University of Pittsburgh Press. Republished in 1980, in Donald Davidson, *Essays on Actions and Events*. Oxford University Press.

de Swart, Henriëtte. 1993. *Adverbs of Quantification: A General Quantifier Approach*. New York: Garland.

de Vries, Hanna. 2010. Evaluative degree modification of adjectives and nouns. M.Phil. thesis, Utrecht Institute of Linguistics.
Déchaine, Rose-Marie. 1993. Predicates across categories: Towards a category-neutral syntax. Ph.D. thesis, University of Massachusetts Amherst.
Delfitto, Denis. 2007. Adverb classes and adverb placement. In Everaert, Martin, and van Riemsdijk, Henk (eds.), *The Blackwell Companion to Syntax*. Blackwell Publishing.
Demirdache, Hamida, and Matthewson, Lisa. 1996. On the universality of syntactic categories. In Beckman, Jill (ed.), *Proceedings of the North East Linguistic Society (NELS) 25*. Amherst, MA: GLSA Publications.
Demonte, Violeta. 2008. Meaning–form correlations and adjective position in Spanish. In McNally and Kennedy (2008).
DeVries, Karl. 2010. Frequency adjectives. BA thesis, Michigan State University.
Diesing, Molly. 1990. The syntactic roots of semantic partition. Ph.D. thesis, University of Massachusetts Amherst.
Dixon, R. M. W. 1982. *Where Have All the Adjectives Gone?* Berlin: Mouton.
Dixon, R. M. W., and Aikhenvald, Alexandra Y. 2004. *Adjective Classes: A Cross-Linguistic Typology*. Oxford University Press.
Doetjes, Jenny. 2010. Incommensurability. In Aloni, Maria, Bastiaanse, Harald, de Jager, Tikitu, Schulz, Katrin, and Doetjes, Jenny (eds.), *Logic, Language and Meaning: Lecture Notes in Computer Science*, vol. 6042. Berlin: Springer.
Doetjes, Jenny, Constantinescu, Camelia, and Součková, Kateřina. 2011. A neo-Kleinian approach to comparatives. In Cormany, Ed, Ito, Satoshi, and Lutz, David (eds.), *Proceedings of Semantics and Linguistic Theory (SALT) 19*. Ithaca, NY: eLanguage.
Dowty, David R. 1991. Thematic proto-roles and argument selection, *Language*, **67**(3), 547–619.
  1979. *Word Meaning in Montague Grammar*. Dordrecht: Reidel.
Dowty, David R., Wall, Robert, and Peters, Stanley. 1981. *Introduction to Montague Semantics*. Dordrecht: Reidel.
Égré, Paul, and Klinedinst, Nathan (eds.). 2011. *Vagueness and Language Use*. Palgrave Studies in Pragmatics, Language and Cognition. Houndmills, Hampshire: Palgrave Macmillan.
Enç, Mürvet. 1981. Tense without scope: an analysis of nouns as indexicals. Ph.D. thesis, University of Wisconsin, Madison.
Engdahl, Elisabet. 1986. *Constituent Questions: The Syntax and Semantics of Questions with Special Reference to Swedish*. Dordrecht: Reidel.
Ernst, Thomas. 2002. *The Syntax of Adjuncts*. Cambridge University Press.
  2004. Principles of adverbial distribution in the lower clause, *Lingua*, **114**, 755–777.
  2009. Speaker-oriented adverbs, *Natural Language and Linguistic Theory*, **27**(3), 497–544.

2011. Modification of state predicates. Handout, Workshop on Modification with and without Modifiers, Madrid.

Evans, Gareth. 1978. Can there be vague objects? *Analysis*, **38**, 208.

Farkas, Donka F., and Kiss, Katalin É. 2000. On the comparative and absolute readings of superlatives, *Natural Language and Linguistic Theory*, **18**(3), 417–455.

Fine, Kit. 1975. Vagueness, truth, and logic, *Synthèse*, **30**, 265–300.

Fischer, Olga. 2006. On the position of adjectives in Middle English, *English Language and Linguistics*, **10**, 253–88.

Fleisher, Nicholas. 2008a. Adjectives and infinitives in composition. Ph.D. thesis, University of California Berkeley.

2008b. A crack at a hard nut: attributive-adjective modality and infinitival relatives. In Chang, Charles B., and Haynie, Hannah J. (eds.), *Proceedings of the West Coast Conference on Formal Linguistics (WCCFL) 26*. Somerville, MA: Cascadilla Press.

2011. Attributive adjectives, infinitival relatives, and the semantics of inappropriateness, *Journal of Linguistics*, **47**(02), 341–380.

Fox, Danny. 1999. Reconstruction, binding theory, and the interpretation of chains, *Linguistic Inquiry*, **30**(2), 157–196.

Fox, Danny, and Hackl, Martin. 2006. The universal density of measurement, *Linguistics and Philosophy*, **29**(5), 537–586.

Frey, Werner. 2003. Syntactic conditions on adjunct classes. In Lang et al. (2003).

Gajewski, Jon. 2009. More on quantifiers in comparative clauses. In Friedman, Tova, and Ito, Satoshi (eds.), *Proceedings of Semantics and Linguistic Theory (SALT) 18*. Ithaca, NY: eLanguage.

Gamut, L. T. F. 1991. *Logic, Language and Meaning*. University of Chicago Press.

Gawron, Jean Mark. 1995. Comparatives, superlatives, and resolution, *Linguistics and Philosophy*, **18**(4), 333–380.

Gehrke, Berit. 2011. Stative passives and event kinds. In Reich et al. (2011).

Gehrke, Berit, and McNally, Louise. 2010. Frequency adjectives and assertions about event types. In Cormany, Ed, Ito, Satoshi, and Lutz, David (eds.), *Proceedings of Semantics and Linguistic Theory (SALT) 19*. Ithaca, NY: eLanguage.

Geuder, Wilhelm. 2000. Oriented adverbs: issues in the lexical semantics of event adverbs. Ph.D. thesis, Universität Tübingen.

2006. Manner modification of states. In Ebert, Christian, and Endriss, Cornelia (eds.), *Proceedings of the Tenth Sinn und Bedeutung Conference*. Berlin: Zentrum for Allgemeine Sprach wissenschaft.

Geurts, Bart. 2006. Take 'five': The meaning and use of a number word. In Vogeleer, Svetlana, and Tasmowski, Liliane (eds.), *Non-definiteness and Plurality*. Amsterdam and Philadelphia: John Benjamins Publishing.

Geurts, Bart, and Nouwen, Rick. 2007. *At least* et al.: the semantics of scalar modifiers, *Language*, **83**(3), 533–559.

References

Giannakidou, Anastasia. 1999. Affective dependencies, *Linguistics and Philosophy*, **22**(4), 367–421.
Giannakidou, Anastasia, and Stavrou, Melita. 2008. On metalinguistic comparatives and negation in Greek. In *Proceedings of the Workshop on Greek Syntax and Semantics*. Cambridge, MA: MIT Working Papers in Linguistics.
Giannakidou, Anastasia, and Yoon, Suwon. 2009. Metalinguistic comparatives in Greek and Korean: attitude semantics, expressive content, and negative polarity items. In Riester and Solstad (2009).
  2011. The subjective mode of comparison: Metalinguistic comparatives in Greek and Korean, *Natural Language and Linguistic Theory*, **29**(3), 621–655.
Giegerich, Heinz J. 2005. Associative adjectives in English and the lexicon-syntax interface, *Journal of Linguistics*, **41**, 571–591.
Gillon, Brendan S. 1990. Ambiguity, generality, and indeterminacy: tests and definitions, *Synthèse*, **85**(3), 391–416.
  2004. Ambiguity, indeterminacy, deixis, and vagueness: evidence and theory. In Davis, Steven, and Gillon, Brendan S. (eds.), *Semantics: A Reader*. New York: Oxford University Press.
Ginzburg, Jonathan, and Sag, Ivan A. 2001. *Interrogative Investigations: The Form, Meaning, and Use of English Interrogatives*. Stanford: CSLI Publications.
Giorgi, Alessandra, and Longobardi, Giuseppe. 1991. *The Syntax of Noun Phrases*. Cambridge University Press.
Gobeski, Adam. 2009. 'Twice' versus 'two times' in phrases of comparison. M.Phil. thesis, Michigan State University.
Graff, Delia. 2000. Shifting sands: an interest-relative theory of vagueness, *Philosophical Topics*, **28**(1), 45–81.
Grano, Thomas, and Kennedy, Chris. 2012. Mandarin transitive comparatives and the grammar of measurement, *Journal of East Asian Linguistics*, **21**, 219–266.
Grice, H. Paul. 1975. Logic and conversation. In Cole, Peter, and Morgan, Jerry (eds.), *Syntax and Semantics, vol. III: Speech Acts*. New York: Academic Press.
Grimshaw, Jane. 1991. Extended projection. Ms., Brandeis University.
Groenendijk, Jeroen, and Stokhof, Martin. 1991. Dynamic predicate logic, *Linguistics and Philosophy*, **14**(1), 39–100.
Grosu, Alexander, and Horvath, Julia. 2006. Reply to Bhatt and Pancheva's 'late merger of degree clauses': the irrelevance of (non)conservativity, *Linguistic Inquiry*, **37**(3), 457–483.
Grosu, Alexander, and Landman, Fred. 1998. Strange relatives of the third kind, *Natural Language Semantics*, **6**(2), 125–170.
Gutiérrez-Rexach, Javier. 1997. Questions and generalized quantifiers. In *Ways of Scope Taking*. Dordrecht: Kluwer Academic.
  2010. Characterizing superlative quantifiers. In Cabredo Hofherr and Matushansky (2010).

Gutzmann, Daniel. 2011. Expressive modifiers and mixed expressives. In Cabredo Hofherr, Patricia, and Bonami, Olivier (eds.), *Empirical Issues in Syntax and Semantics 8: Proceedings of the colloque de Syntaxe et Sémantique à Paris*. Paris: CSSP.

2013. Expressives and beyond: an introduction to varieties of conventional non-truth-conditional meaning. In Gutzmann, Daniel, and Gärtner, Hans-Martin (eds.), *Beyond Expressives: Explorations in Use-conditional Meaning*. Brill Academic Publishers.

Hackl, Martin. 2000. Comparative quantifiers. Ph.D. thesis, MIT.

Hacquard, Valentine. 2006. Aspects of *Too* and *Enough* Constructions. In Georgala, Effi, and Howell, Jonathan (eds.), *Proceedings of Semantics and Linguistic Theory (SALT) 15*. Ithaca, NY: CLC Publications.

2007. Speaker-oriented vs. subject-oriented modals: a split in implicative behavior. In Puig-Waldmüller (2007).

Hall, Robert A., Jr. 1973. The transferred epithet in P. G. Wodehouse, *Linguistic Inquiry*, 4(1), 92–94.

Hamann, Cornelia. 1991. Adjectives. In von Stechow and Wunderlich (1991).

Hankamer, Jorge. 1973. Why there are two 'than's in English. In *Proceedings of the Chicago Linguistic Society (CLS) 9*. Chicago Linguistic Society.

Harris, Jesse, and Potts, Christopher. 2009. Perspective-shifting with appositives and expressives, *Linguistics and Philosophy*, 32(6), 523–552.

Harris, Randy Allen. 1993. *The Linguistics Wars*. New York: Oxford University Press.

Haspelmath, Martin, and Buchholz, Oda. 1998. Equative and similative constructions in the languages of Europe. In van der Auwera, Johan, and Ó Baoill, Dónall (eds.), *Adverbial Constructions in the Languages of Europe*. Dordrecht: Mouton de Gruyter.

Haumann, Dagmar. 2010. Adnominal Adjectives in Old English, *English Language and Linguistics*, 14(1), 53–83.

Heim, Irene. 1982. The semantics of definite and indefinite noun phrases. Ph.D. thesis, University of Massachusetts Amherst.

1985. Notes on comparatives and related matters. Ms., University of Texas, Austin.

1995. Notes on superlatives. Ms., MIT.

2000. Degree operators and scope. In Jackson, Brendan, and Matthews, Tanya (eds.), *Proceedings of Semantics and Linguistic Theory (SALT) 10*. Ithaca, NY: CLC Publications.

2006a. Little. In Gibson, M., and Howell, J. (eds.), *Proceedings of Semantics and Linguistic Theory (SALT) 16*. Ithaca, NY: CLC Publications.

2006b. Remarks on comparative clauses as generalized quantifiers. Ms., MIT.

2008. Decomposing antonyms? In Grønn, Atle (ed.), *Proceedings of the Twelfth Sinn und Bedeutung Conference*. Oslo: ILOS.

Heim, Irene, and Kratzer, Angelika. 1998. *Semantics in Generative Grammar*. Oxford: Blackwell Publishing.

References

Hellan, Lars. 1981. *Toward an Integrated Analysis of Comparatives*. Tübingen: Narr.
Hetzron, Robert. 1978. On the relative order of adjectives. In Seiler, H. (ed.), *Language Universals*. Tübingen: Gunter Narr Verlag.
Higginbotham, James. 1985. On semantics, *Linguistic Inquiry*, **16**(4), 547–593.
Hitzeman, Janet. 1992. The selectional properties and entailments of *almost*. In *Proceedings of the Chicago Linguistic Society (CLS) 28*. Chicago Linguistic Society.
Hoeksema, Jack. 1983. Negative polarity and the comparative, *Natural Language and Linguistic Theory*, **1**(3), 403–434.
Hoffman, J. 1903. *Mundari Grammar*. Calcutta: Bengal Secretarial Press.
Hogeweg, Lotte. 2012. Rich lexical representations and conflicting features, *International Review of Pragmatics*, **4**(2), 209–231.
Horn, Laurence R. 1972. On the semantic properties of logical operators in English. Ph.D. thesis, UCLA.
  1985. Metalinguistic negation and pragmatic ambiguity, *Language*, **61**(1), 121–174.
  1991. 'Only' XL: the assertoric asymmetry of exponibles. In Moore, Steven K., and Wyner, Adam Zachary (eds.), *Proceedings of Semantics and Linguistic Theory (SALT) 1*. Ithaca, NY: CLC Publications.
  2002. Assertoric Inertia and NPI Licensing. In Andronis, Mary, Debenport, Erin, Pycha, Anne, and Yoshimura, Keiko (eds.), *Proceedings of the Chicago Linguistic Society (CLS) 38*. Chicago Linguistic Society.
Huang, Yi Ting, Spelke, Elizabeth, and Snedeker, Jesse. 2013. What exactly do number words mean? *Language Learning and Development*, **9**(2), 105–129.
Huddleston, Rodney, and Pullum, Geoffrey K. 2002. *The Cambridge Grammar of the English Language*. Cambridge University Press.
Ionin, Tania, and Matushansky, Ora. 2006. The composition of complex cardinals, *Journal of Semantics*, **23**(4), 315–360.
Jackendoff, Ray. 1972. *Semantic Interpretation in Generative Grammar*. Cambridge, MA: MIT Press.
Jäger, Gerhard. 1999. Stage levels, states, and the semantics of the copula. In *ZAS Papers in Linguistics 14*. Berlin: Zentrum fur Allgemeine Sprachwissenschaft.
Jayez, Jacques, and Tovena, Lucia M. 2008. *Presque* and *almost*: how argumentation derives from comparative meaning. In Bonami and Cabredo Hofherr (2008).
Jelinek, Eloise. 1995. Quantification in Straits Salish. In Bach, Emmon, Jelinek, Eloise, Kratzer, Angelika, and Partee, Barbara (eds.), *Quantification in Natural Languages*. Studies in Linguistics and Philosophy. Dordrecht: Kluwer Academic.
Johnson, Greg. 2013. Liketa is not Almost. In *Proceedings of the 36th Annual Penn. Linguistics Colloquium*. University of Pennsylvania Working Papers in Linguistics, 19(1), Article 10. Philadelphia.

Kadmon, Nirit, and Landman, Fred. 1993. Any, *Linguistics and Philosophy*, **16**(4), 353–422.

Kamoen, Naomi, Holleman, Bregje, Nouwen, Rick, Sanders, Ted, and van den Bergh, Huub. 2011. Absolutely relative or relatively absolute? The linguistic behavior of gradable adjectives and degree modifiers, *Journal of Pragmatics*. **43**(13), 3139–3151.

Kamp, Hans. 1971. To the memory of Arthur Prior: formal properties of 'now', *Theoria*, **37**(3), 227–273.

  1975. Two Theories about Adjectives. In Keenan, Edward L. (ed.), *Formal Semantics of Natural Language*. Cambridge University Press.

  1981a. The paradox of the heap. In Mönnich, U. (ed.), *Aspects of Philosophical Logic*. Dordrecht: Reidel.

  1981b. A theory of truth and semantic representation. In Groenendijk, Jeroen, Janssen, Theo, and Stokhof, Martin (eds.), *Formal Methods in the Study of Language*, Part 1, vol. 135. Amsterdam: Mathematical Centre Tracts. Reprinted in 1984 in Jeroen Groenendijk, Theo Janssen and Martin Stokhof (eds.), *Truth, Interpretation, and Information; Selected Papers from the Third Amsterdam Colloquium*, Dordrecht: Foris, pp. 1–41.

Kamp, Hans, and Partee, Barbara. 1995. Prototype theory and compositionality, *Cognition*, **57**(2), 121–191.

Kaplan, David. 1989. Demonstratives: an essay on the semantics, logic, metaphysics, and epistemology of demonstratives and other indexicals. In Almog, Joseph, Perry, John, and Wettstein, Howard (eds.), *Themes From Kaplan*. Oxford University Press.

Katz, Graham. 2003. Event arguments, adverb selection, and the Stative Adverb Gap. In Lang et al. (2003).

  2005. Attitudes toward degrees. In Maier, Emar, Bary, Corien, and Huitink, Janneke (eds.), *Proceedings of the Ninth Sinn und Bedeutung Conference*. Nijmegen: Radboud Universiteit.

  2008. Manner modification of state verbs. In McNally and Kennedy (2008).

Katz, Jonah. 2007. Romance and restriction. Generals paper, MIT.

Kayne, Richard S. 1994. *The Antisymmetry of Syntax*. Cambridge, MA: MIT Press.

Keenan, Edward L. 1992. Beyond the frege boundary, *Linguistics and Philosophy*, **15**(2), 199–221.

  2002. Some properties of natural language quantifiers: generalized quantifier theory, *Linguistics and Philosophy*, **25**(5), 627–654.

Keenan, Edward L., and Faltz, Leonard M. 1985. *Boolean Semantics for Natural Language*. Dordrecht: Reidel.

Keenan, Edward L., and Stavi, Jonathan. 1986. A semantic characterization of natural language determiners, *Linguistics and Philosophy*, **9**(3), 253–326.

Kennedy, Christopher. 1997. *Projecting the Adjective: The Syntax and Semantics of Gradability and Comparison*. Ph.D. thesis, UC Santa Cruz. Published in 1999 by Garland, New York.

2001. Polar opposition and the ontology of 'degrees', *Linguistics and Philosophy*, **24**(1), 33–70.

2007. Vagueness and grammar: the semantics of relative and absolute gradable adjectives, *Linguistics and Philosophy*, **30**(1), 1–45.

2009. Modes of comparison. In Elliot, Malcolm, Kirby, James, Sawada, Osama, Staraki, Eleni, and Yoon, Suwon (eds.), *Proceedings of the Main Session of the 43rd Annual Meeting of the Chicago Linguistic Society*, **43**(1), Chicago Linguistic Society.

2011. Vagueness and comparison. In Égré and Klinedinst (2011).

2012a. Adjectives. In Russell, G., and Graff Fara, Delia (eds.), *Routledge Companion to Philosophy of Language*. New York: Routledge.

2012b. Two kinds of subjectivity. Ms., University of Chicago.

Kennedy, Christopher, and Levin, Beth. 2008. Measure of change: the adjectival core of degree achievements. In McNally and Kennedy (2008).

Kennedy, Christopher, and McNally, Louise. 2005. Scale structure, degree modification, and the semantics of gradable predicates, *Language*, **81**(2), 345–381.

2010. Color, context, and compositionality, *Synthese*, **174**(1), 79–98.

Kennedy, Christopher, and Stanley, Jason. 2008. What an average semantics needs. In Friedman, T., and Ito, S. (eds.), *Proceedings of Semantics and Linguistic Theory (SALT) 18*. Ithaca, NY: CLC Publications.

2009. On 'average', *Mind*, **118**(471), 583–646.

Keshet, Ezra. 2010. Situation economy, *Natural Language Semantics*, **18**(4), 385–434.

Kiefer, Ferenc. 1978. Adjectives and presuppositions, *Theoretical Linguistics*, **5**(1–3), 135–174.

Kim, Min-Joo. Forthcoming. On the position of adnominal adjectival expressions in Korean. In Huang, C.-T. James, and Liu, Feng-hsi (eds.), *Peaches and Plums*. Taipei: Academia Sinica.

Klecha, Peter. 2012. Positive and conditional semantics for gradable modals. In Aguilar-Guevara, Ana, Chernilovskaya, Anna, and Nouwen, Rick (eds.), *Proceedings of the Sixteenth Sinn und Bedeutung Conference*, vol. II. MIT Working Papers in Linguistics.

2013. Shifting modal domains: an imprecision-based account. Abstract, Linguistic Society of America Annual Meeting.

Klein, Ewan. 1980. A semantics for positive and comparative adjectives, *Linguistics and Philosophy*, **4**(1), 1–45.

1982. The interpretation of adjectival comparatives, *Journal of Linguistics*, **18**(1), 113–136.

Kölbel, Max. 2002. Faultless disagreement. *Proceedings of the Aristotelian Society*, **104**, 55–73.

Koopman, Hilda. 1984. *The Syntax of Verbs*. Dordrecht: Foris.

Krasikova, Sveta. 2008a. Comparison in Chinese. In Bonami and Cabredo Hofherr (2008).

2008b. Quantifiers in comparatives. In Grønn, Atle (ed.), *Proceedings of the Twelfth Sinn und Bedeutung Conference*. Oslo: ILOS.

2009. Norm-relatedness in degree constructions. In Riester and Solstad (2009).

2011. Definiteness in superlatives. In *18th Amsterdam Colloquium Pre-Proceedings*. Amsterdam: ILLC.

Kratzer, Angelika. 1981. The notional category of modality. In Eikmeyer, Hans-Jürgen, and Rieser, Hannes (eds.), *Words, Worlds and Contexts*. Berlin: Walter de Gruyter. Reprinted in Partee and Portner (2002).

1989. An investigation of the lumps of thought, *Linguistics and Philosophy*, **12**(5), 607–653.

1991. Modality. In von Stechow and Wunderlich (1991).

1995. Stage-level and individual-level predicates. In Carlson and Pelletier (1995).

1996. Severing the external argument from its verb. In Rooryck, Johan, and Zaring, Laurie (eds.), *Phrase Structure and the Lexicon*. Dordrecht: Kluwer Academic.

1998. More structural analogies between pronouns and tenses, In *Proceedings of Semantics and Linguistic Theory (SALT) 8*. Ithaca, NY: CLC Publications.

1999. Beyond *ouch* and *oops*: how descriptive and expressive meaning interact. Ms., University of Massachusetts Amherst; presented at the Cornell Conference on Theories of Context Dependency.

2002. The event argument and the semantics of verbs. Book manuscript, University of Massachusetts Amherst.

2008. Situations in natural language semantics. In Zalta, Edward N. (ed.), *The Stanford Encyclopedia of Philosophy*. Stanford: CSLI Publications.

Krifka, Manfred. 1989. Nominal reference, temporal constitution, and quantification in event semantics. In Bartsch, Renate, van Benthem, Johan, and van Emde Boas, Peter (eds.), *Semantics and Contextual Expression*. Dordrecht: Foris.

1998. The origins of Telicity. In Rothstein (1998).

2001. Quantifying into question acts, *Natural Language Semantics*, **9**(1), 1–40.

Krifka, Manfred, Pelletier, Francis Jeffry, Carlson, Gregory, ter Meulen, Alice, Chierchia, Gennaro, and Link, Godehard. 1995. Genericity: an introduction. In Carlson and Pelletier (1995).

Kusumoto, Kiyomi. 1999. Tense in embedded contexts. Ph.D. thesis, University of Massachusetts Amherst.

2005. On the quantification over times in natural language, *Natural Language Semantics*, **13**(4), 317–357.

Ladusaw, William. 1980. *Polarity Sensitivity as Inherent Scope Relations*. Bloomington: Indiana University Linguistics Club.

Laenzlinger, Christopher. 2000. French adjective ordering: perspectives on DP-internal movement types. In *Generative Grammar in Geneva*, vol. I. University of Geneva.
Lakoff, George. 1972. Linguistics and natural logic. In Davidson, Donald, and Harman, Gilbert H. (eds.), *Semantics of Natural Language*. Dordrecht: Reidel.
  1973. Hedges, *Journal of Philosophical Logic*, **2**, 458–508.
Landman, Fred. 2000. *Events and Plurality: The Jerusalem Lectures*. Dordrecht: Kluwer Academic.
  2003. *Indefinites and the Type of Sets*. Malden, MA: Blackwell Publishing.
Landman, Meredith. 2001. Adjectival modification restricted. Ms., University of Massachusetts Amherst.
  2006. Variables in natural language. Ph.D. thesis, University of Massachusetts Amherst.
Landman, Meredith, and Morzycki, Marcin. 2003. Event-kinds and the representation of manner. In Antrim, Nancy Mae, Goodall, Grant, Schulte-Nafeh, Martha, and Samiian, Vida (eds.), *Proceedings of the Western Conference on Linguistics (WECOL) 2002*, vol. 14. Fresno: California State University.
Lang, Ewald, Maienborn, Claudia, and Fabricius-Hansen, Cathrine (eds.). 2003. *Modifying Adjuncts*. Interface Explorations, vol. IV. Berlin: Mouton de Gruyter.
Larson, Richard K. 1988. Scope and comparatives. *Linguistics and Philosophy*, **11**(1), 1–26.
  1998. Events and modification in nominals. In Strolovitch, D., and Lawson, A. (eds.), *Proceedings of Semantics and Linguistic Theory (SALT) 12*. Ithaca, NY: CLC Publications.
  1999. Semantics of adjectival modification. Lecture notes, LOT Winter School, Amsterdam.
  2000. ACD in AP? In Billerey, Roger, and Lillehaugen, Brook Danielle (eds.), *Proceedings of the West Coast Conference on Formal Linguistics (WCCFL) 19*. Somerville, MA: Cascadilla Press.
Larson, Richard K., and Cho, Sungeun. 2003. Temporal adjectives and the structure of possessive DPs, *Natural Language Semantics*, **11**(3), 217–247.
Larson, Richard K., and Marušič, Franc. 2004. On indefinite pronoun structures with APs: reply to Kishimoto, *Linguistic Inquiry*, **35**(2), 268–287.
Larson, Richard K., and Segal, Gabriel. 1995. *Knowledge of Meaning: An Introduction to Semantic Theory*. Cambridge, MA: MIT Press.
Larson, Richard K., and Takahashi, Naoko. 2007. Order and interpretation in prenominal relative clauses. In Kelepir, M., and Öztürk, B. (eds.), *Proceedings of the Second Workshop on Altaic Formal Linguistics*. MIT Working Papers in Linguistics.
Lascarides, Alex, Copestake, Ann, and Briscoe, Ted. 1996. Ambiguity and coherence, *Journal of Semantics*, **13**(1), 41–65.
Lasersohn, Peter. 1999. Pragmatic halos, *Language*, **75**(3), 522–551.

2000. Same, models and representation. In Jackson, B., and Matthews, T. (eds.), *Proceedings of Semantics and Linguistic Theory (SALT) 10*. Ithaca, NY: CLC Publications.

2005. Context dependence, disagreement, and predicates of personal taste, *Linguistics and Philosophy*, **28**(6), 643–686.

2008. Quantification and perspective in relativist semantics, *Philosophical Perspectives*, **22**(1), 305–337.

2009. Relative truth, speaker commitment, and control of implicit arguments, *Synthese*, **166**(2), 359–374.

Lassiter, Daniel. 2010. Gradable epistemic modals, probability, and scale structure. In *Proceedings of Semantics and Linguistic Theory (SALT) 20*. Ithaca, NY: CLC Publications.

2011a. *Measurement and Modality: The Scalar Basis of Modal Semantics*. Ph.D. thesis, New York University. To be published by Oxford University Press.

2011b. Nouwen's puzzle and a scalar semantics for obligations, needs, and desires. In Ashton, Neil, Chereches, Anca, and Lutz, David (eds.), *Proceedings of Semantics and Linguistic Theory (SALT) 21*. Ithaca, NY: eLanguage.

Lechner, Winfried. 1999. Comparatives and DP structure. Ph.D. thesis, University of Massachusetts Amherst.

2001. Reduced and phrasal comparatives, *Natural Language and Linguistic Theory*, **19**(4), 683–735.

Levinson, Stephen. 1983. *Pragmatics*. Cambridge University Press.

Lewis, David. 1970. General semantics, *Synthese*, **22**, 18–67. Reprinted in 1972 in Donald Davidson and Gilbert H. Harman (eds.), *Semantics of Natural Language*. Dordrecht: Reidel.

1972. General semantics. Davidson, Donald, and Harman, Gilbert H. (eds.), *Semantics of Natural Language*. Dordrecht: Reidel. Originally published in 1970 in *Synthèse*.

Lewis, David. 1973. *Counterfactuals*. Oxford: Blackwell Publishing.

1975. Adverbs of quantification. In Keenan, Edward L. (ed.), *Formal Semantics of Natural Language*. Cambridge University Press.

1979. Scorekeeping in a language game, *Journal of Philosophical Logic*, **8**, 339–359. Also in Rainer Bäuerle, Urs Egli and Arnim von Stechow (eds.), 1979, *Semantics from Different Points of View*, Berlin: Springer.

Lin, Jo-Wang. 2007. On the semantics of comparative correlatives in Mandarin Chinese, *Journal of Semantics*, **24**(2), 169–213.

2008. The order of stage-level and individual-level relatives and superiority effects, *Language and Linguistics*, **9**(4), 839–864.

Link, Godehard. 1983. The logical analysis of plurals and mass terms: a lattice-theoretical approach. In Bäuerle, Rainer, Schwarze, Christoph, and von Stechow, Arnim (eds.), *Meaning, Use, and Interpretation of Language*. Berlin: Walter de Gruyter.

1998. *Algebraic Semantics*. Stanford: CSLI Publications.

Liu, Mingya. 2009. Speaker-oriented adverbs of the German -weise Sort. In Riester and Solstad (2009).
Łukasiewicz, Jan. 1920. O logice trójwartościowej (On three-valued logic), *Ruch Filozoficny*, **5**, 170–171. Appeared in English translation in 1970, in Jan Łukasiewicz, *Selected Works*, (ed. Ludwig Borkowski), Amsterdam: North-Holland.
Maienborn, Claudia. 2001. On the position and interpretation of locative modifiers, *Natural Language Semantics*, **9**(2), 191–240.
  2007. On Davidsonian and Kimian States. In Comorovski, Ileana, and von Heusinger, Klaus (eds.), *Existence: Semantics and Syntax*. Dordrecht: Springer.
Maienborn, Claudia, and Schäfer, Martin. 2011. Adverbs and adverbials. In Maienborn et al. (2011).
Maienborn, Claudia, von Heusinger, Klaus, and Portner, Paul (eds.). 2011. *Semantics: An International Handbook of Natural Language Meaning*. Handbooks of Linguistics and Communication Science, vol. 2. Berlin and New York: Mouton de Gruyter.
Majewski, Helen. 2002. The same and different: the same or different? Ms., University of Massachusetts Amherst.
Marantz, Alec. 1996. 'Cat' as a phrasal idiom: consequences of late insertion in distributed morphology. Ms., MIT.
Martin, John N. 1982. Negation, ambiguity, and the identity test, *Journal of Semantics*, **1**(3–4), 251–274.
Matsui, Ai. Forthcoming. *Transforming Manner Adverbs into Subject-Oriented Adverbs: Evidence from Japanese*. Ms., Michigan State University. To appear in a special issue of *Natural Language and Linguistic Theory*.
Matsui, Ai, and Kubota, Yusuke. 2012. Comparatives and contrastiveness: semantics and pragmatics of Japanese *hoo* comparatives. In Tucker, Mathew A., Thompson, Anie, Northrop, Oliver, and Bennett, Ryanthe (eds.), *Proceedings of the Fifth Formal Approaches to Japanese Linguistics Conference* (FAJL5). Cambridge, MA: MIT Working Papers in Linguistics.
Matthewson, Lisa. 1998. On the interpretation of wide-scope indefinites, *Natural Language Semantics*, **7**(1), 79–134.
Matushansky, Ora. 2002. Tipping the scales: the syntax of scalarity in the complement of seem, *Syntax*, **5**(3), 219–276.
  2008. On the attributive nature of superlatives, *Syntax*, **11**(1), 26–90.
McCawley, James D. 1971. Prelexical syntax. In *Report of the 22nd Roundtable Meeting on Linguistics and Language Studies*. Georgetown University Press.
McConnell-Ginet, Sally. 1973. Comparative constructions in English: a syntactic and semantic analysis. Ph.D. thesis, University of Rochester.
  1982. Adverbs and logical form: a linguistically realistic theory, *Language*, **58**(1), 144–184.
McCready, Eric. 2010. Varieties of conventional implicature, *Semantics and Pragmatics*, **3**(8), 1–57.

McCready, Eric, and Ogata, Norry. 2007. Adjectives, stereotypicality, and comparison, *Natural Language Semantics*, **15**(1), 35–63.

McNally, Louise. Forthcoming. Modification. In Aloni, Maria, and Dekker, Paul (eds.), *Cambridge Handbook of Semantics*. Cambridge University Press.

McNally, Louise, and Boleda Torrent, Gemma. 2003. Relational adjectives as properties of kinds. In Bonami, Olivier, and Hofherr, P. Cabredo (eds.), *Empirical Issues in Syntax and Semantics 5: Proceedings of the Colloque de Syntaxe et Sémantique á Paris.*, Paris: CSSP.

McNally, Louise, and Kennedy, Christopher (eds.). 2008. *Adjectives and Adverbs: Syntax, Semantics, and Discourse*. Studies in Theoretical Linguistics. Oxford University Press.

Meier, Cécile. 2003. The meaning of *too, enough,* and *so ... that, Natural Language Semantics*, **11**(1), 69–107.

Merchant, Jason. 2009. Phrasal and clausal comparatives in Greek and the abstractness of syntax, *Journal of Greek Linguistics*, **9**, 134–164.

to appear. The two phrasal comparatives of Greek. *Natural Language and Linguistic Theory*.

Miró, Elena Castroviejo. 2012. Gradation in modified AdjPs. In Chereches, Anca (ed.), *Proceedings of Semantics and Linguistic Theory (SALT) 22*. Ithaca, NY: eLanguage.

Mittwoch, Anita. 2005. Do states have Davidsonian arguments? Some empirical considerations. In Maienborn, Claudia, and Wöllstein, Angelika (eds.), *Event Arguments: Foundations and Applications*. Tübingen: Niemeyer.

Moltmann, Friederike. 1992. Reciprocals and *same/different*: towards a semantic analysis, *Linguistics and Philosophy*, **15**(4), 411–462.

1997. *Parts and Wholes in Semantics*. New York: Oxford University Press.

2005. Part structures in situations: the semantics of *individual* and *whole, Linguistics and Philosophy*, **28**(5), 599–641.

2007. Events, tropes, and truthmaking, *Philosophical Studies*, **134**(3), 363–403.

2009. Degree structure as trope structure: a trope-based analysis of positive and comparative adjectives, *Linguistics and Philosophy*, **32**(1), 51–94.

Montague, Richard. 1970. English as a formal language. In Bruno Visentini (ed.), *Linguaggi nella Societ'a e nella Tecnica*. Milan: Edizioni di Communita. Reprinted in 1974, in *Formal Philosophy*, New Havan, CT: Yale University Press.

1973. The proper treatment of quantification in ordinary English. In Hintikka, Jaakko (ed.), *Approaches to Natural Language: Proceedings of the 1970 Stanford Workshop on Grammar and Semantics*. Dordrecht: Reidel. Reprinted in Partee and Portner (2002). Oxford: (eds.).

Morzycki, Marcin. 2001. *Almost* and its kin, across categories. In Jackson, Brendan, Hastings, Rachel, and Zvolenszky, Zsofia (eds.), *Proceedings of Semantics and Linguistic Theory (SALT) 11*. Ithaca, NY: CLC Publications.

2002. Wholes and their covers. In Jackson, Brendan (ed.), *Proceedings of Semantics and Linguistic Theory (SALT) 12*. Ithaca, NY: CLC Publications.

2004a. Feature bundles, prenominal modifier order, and modes of composition below the word level. Ms., Université du Québec à Montréal.

2004b. Measure DP adverbials: measure-phrase modification in VP. Ms., Université du Québec à Montréal.

2005a. Mediated modification: functional structure and the interpretation of modifier position. Ph.D. thesis, University of Massachusetts Amherst.

2005b. Size adjectives and adnominal degree modification. In Georgala, Effi, and Howell, Jonathan (eds.), *Proceedings of Semantics and Linguistic Theory (SALT) 15*. Ithaca, NY: CLC Publications.

2008a. Adverbial modification in AP: evaluatives and a little beyond. In Dölling, Johannes, and Heyde-Zybatow, Tatjana (eds.), *Event Structures in Linguistic Form and Interpretation*. Berlin: Walter de Gruyter.

2008b. Nonrestrictive modifiers in nonparenthetical positions. In McNally and Kennedy (2008).

2009a. Degree modification of extreme adjectives. In Bochnak, Ryan, Nicola, Nassira, Klecha, Peter, Urban, Jasmin, Lemieux, Alice, and Weaver, Christina (eds.), *Proceedings of the Chicago Linguistic Society (CLS) 45*. Chicago Linguistic Society.

2009b. Degree modification of gradable nouns: size adjectives and adnominal degree morphemes, *Natural Language Semantics*, **17**(2), 175–203.

2009c. Metalinguistic comparison in an alternative semantics for imprecision. In Abdurrahman, Muhammad, Schardl, Anisa, and Walkow, Martin (eds.), *Proceedings of the North East Linguistic Society (NELS) 38*. Amherst: GLSA Publications.

2011. Metalinguistic comparison in an alternative semantics for imprecision, *Natural Language Semantics*, **19**(1), 39–86.

2012a. Adjectival extremeness: degree modification and contextually restricted scales, *Natural Language and Linguistic Theory*, **30**(2), 567–609.

2012b. The several faces of adnominal degree modification. In Choi, Jaehoon, Hogue, E. Alan, Punske, Jeffrey, Tat, Deniz, Schertz, Jessamyn, and Trueman, Alex (eds.), *Proceedings of Proceedings of the West Coast Conference on Formal Linguistics (WCCFL) 29*. Somerville, MA: Cascadilla Press.

Musan, Renate. 1995. *On the Temporal Interpretation of Noun Phrases*. Ph.D. thesis, MIT. Published in 1997 by Garland, New York.

1997. Tense, predicates, and lifetime effects, *Natural Language Semantics*, **5**(3), 271–301.

Nakanishi, Kimiko. 2004a. *Domains of Measurement: Formal Properties of Non-Split/Split Quantifier Constructions*. Ph.D. thesis, University of Pennsylvania.

2004b. On comparative quantification in the verbal domain. In Watanabe, Kazuha, and Young, Robert B. (eds.), *Proceedings of Semantics and Linguistic Theory (SALT)* 14. Ithaca, NY: CLC Publications.

2007. Measurement in the nominal and verbal domains, *Linguistics and Philosophy*, **30**(2), 235–276.

Napoli, Donna Jo. 1983. Comparative ellipsis: a phrase structure analysis, *Linguistic Inquiry*, **14**(4), 675–694.

Neeleman, Ad, van de Koot, Hans, and Doetjes, Jenny. 2004. Degree expressions, *The Linguistic Review*, **21**, 1–66.

Newmeyer, Frederick J. 1980. *Linguistic Theory in America: The First Quarter-Century of Transformational Generative Grammar*. New York: Academic Press.

Nilsen, Øystein. 2003. Eliminating positions: syntax and semantics of sentence modification. Ph.D. thesis, Universiteit Utrecht.

2004. Domains for Adverbs, *Lingua*, **114**, 809–847.

Nouwen, Rick. 2005. Monotone Amazement. In Dekker, P., and Franke, M. (eds.), *Proceedings of the Amsterdam Colloquium 15*. Amsterdam: Institute for Logic, Language, and Computation.

2006. Remarks on the polar orientation of *almost*. In van de Weijer, and Los (eds.), *Linguistics in the Netherlands*. Amsterdam: John Benjamins Publishing.

2007. Predicates of (im)personal taste. Ms., Utrecht Institute for Linguistics OTS.

2008. Upper-bounded *no more*: the exhaustive interpretation of non-strict comparison, *Natural Language Semantics*, **16**(4), 271–295.

2011. Degree modifiers and monotonicity. In Égré and Klinedinst (2011).

Nouwen, Rick, van Rooij, Robert, Sauerland, Uli, and Schmitz, Hans-Christian. 2011a. Introduction. In Nouwen et al. (2011b).

(eds.) 2011b. *Vagueness in communication*. Lecture Notes in Computer Science, vol. 6517. Berlin: Springer.

Nunberg, Geoffrey. 1984. Individuation in context. In M. Cobler (ed.), *Proceedings of the West Coast Conference on Formal Linguistics (WCCFL) 2*. Stanford Linguistics Association.

1995. Transfers of meaning, *Journal of Semantics*, **12**(2), 109–132.

Oda, Toshiko. 2008. Degree constructions in Japanese. Ph.D. thesis, University of Connecticut.

Oliver, Michael. 2012. Interpretation as optimization: constitutive material adjectives. Ms., Johns Hopkins University.

Osherson, Daniel N., and Smith, Edward E. 1981. On the adequacy of prototype theory as a theory of concepts, *Cognition*, **9**(1), 35–58.

1997. On typicality and vagueness, *Cognition*, **64**, 189–206.

Pancheva, Roumyana. 2006. Phrasal and clausal comparatives in Slavic. In *Formal Approaches to Slavic Linguistics 14: The Princeton Meeting*. Ann Arbor.: Michigan Slavic Publications.

2010. More Students Attended FASL than CONSOLE. In Browne, W., Cooper, A., Fisher, A., Kesici, E., Predolac, N., and Zec, D. (eds.), *Formal Approaches to Slavic Linguistics 18: The Cornell Meeting*. Ann Arbor: Michigan Slavic Publications.

Pancheva, Roumyana, and Tomaszewicz, Barbara. 2011. Experimental evidence for the syntax of phrasal comparatives in Polish. In *University of Pennsylvania Working Papers in Linguistics*, vol. 17. 1.

Paradis, Carita. 1997. *Degree Modifiers of Adjectives in Spoken British English*. Lund Studies in English, vol. 92. Lund University Press.

2001. Adjectives and boundedness, *Cognitive Linguistics*, **12**(1), 47–65.

Parsons, Terence. 1972. Some problems concerning the logic of grammatical modifiers. In Davidson, Donald, and Harman, Gilbert (eds.), *Semantics of Natural Language*. Dordrecht: D. Reidel.

1990. *Events in the Semantics of English: A Study in Subatomic Semantics*. Cambridge, MA: MIT Press.

Partee, Barbara. 1973. Some structural analogies between tenses and pronouns in English, *Journal of Philosophy*, **70**(18), 601–609.

1977. John is easy to please. In Zampoli, A. (ed.), *Linguistic Structure Processing*. Amsterdam: North-Holland.

1986. *Any, almost*, and superlatives (The Airport Squib). Ms., University of Massachusetts Amherst. Reprinted in 2004 in *Compositionality in Formal Semantics: Selected Papers* by Barbara H. Partee. Malden, MA: Blackwell.

1987a. Noun phrase interpretation and type-shifting principles. In Groenendijk, Jeroen, de Jongh, Dick, and Stokhof, Martin (eds.), *Studies in Discourse Representation Theory and the Theory of Generalized Quantifiers*. Dordrecht: Foris. Reprinted in Partee and Portner (2002).

1995. Lexical semantics and compositionality. In Gleitman, Lila, and Liberman, Mark (eds.), *An Invitation to Cognitive Science, vol. I: Language*. Cambridge, MA: MIT Press.

2007. Privative adjectives: subsective plus coercion. In Bäuerle, Rainer, Reyle, Uwe, and Zimmermann, Thomas Ede (eds.), *Presuppositions and Discourse*. Amsterdam: Elsevier.

Partee, Barbara H., and Borschev, Vladimir. 2003. Genitives, relational nouns, and argument-modifier ambiguity. In Lang et al. (2003).

Partee, Barbara H., and Portner, Paul (eds.). 2002. *Formal Semantics: The Essential Readings*. Oxford: Blackwell Publishing.

Pelletier, Francis Jeffry. 2000. Review of Petr Hájek *Metamathematics of fuzzy logic*, *The Bulletin of Symbolic Logic*, **6**(3), 342–346.

Penka, Doris. 2005. *Almost*: a test? In Dekker, Paul, and Franke, Michael (eds.), *Proceedings of the 15th Amsterdam Colloquium*. Amsterdam: ILLC.

2006. Almost there: The meaning of *almost*. In Ebert, Christian, and Endriss, Cornelia (eds.), *Proceedings of the Tenth Sinn und Bedeutung Conference*. Berlin: Zentrum fur Allgemeine Sprachwissenschaft (ZAS).

Percus, Orin. 2000. Constraints on some other variables in syntax, *Natural Language Semantics*, **8**(3), 173–229.

Peterson, Philip L. 1997. *Fact, Proposition, Event*. Dordrecht: Kluwer Academic.
Phillips, Colin, Wagers, Matthew W., and Lau, Ellen F. 2011. Grammatical illusions and selective fallibility in real-time language comprehension. In Runner, Jeffrey T. (ed.), *Experiments at the Interfaces. Syntax and Semantics*, vol. 37. Emerald Group Publishing Limited.
Pinkal, Manfred. 1983. Towards a semantics of precization. In Ballmer and Pinkal (1983).
    1995. *Logic and the Lexicon: The Semantics of the Indefinite*. Studies in Linguistics and Philosophy, vol. 56. Dordrecht: Kluwer Academic. Trans. Geoffrey Simmons. Originally published in 1985 as *Logik und Lexikon*.
Piñón, Christopher. 2008. Aspectual composition with degrees. In McNally and Kennedy (2008).
Portner, Paul H. 1992. Situation theory and the semantics of propositional expressions. Ph.D. thesis, University of Massachusetts Amherst.
    2009. *Modality*. Oxford Surveys in Semantics and Pragmatics. Oxford University Press.
Portner, Paul, and Zanuttini, Raffaella. 2005. The semantics of nominal exclamatives. In Stainton, Robert, and Elugardo, Reinaldo (eds.), *Ellipsis and Non-Sentential Speech*. Dordrecht: Springer.
Potts, Christopher. 2003. *The Logic of Conventional Implicatures*. Ph.D. thesis, UC Santa Cruz. Published in 2005 by Oxford University Press.
    2007a. The dimensions of quotation. In Barker and Jacobson (2007).
    2007b. The expressive dimension, *Theoretical Linguistics*, **33**(2), 165–198.
    2008. Interpretive economy, schelling points, and evolutionary stability. Ms., University of Massachusetts Amherst.
Potts, Christopher, and Schwarz, Florian. 2008. Exclamatives and heightened emotion: extracting pragmatic generalizations from large corpora. Ms., University of Massachusetts Amherst.
Pozzan, Lucia, and Schweitzer, Susan. 2008. Not Nearly Synonymous: Similarities and differences between *almost* and *nearly*. In Grønn, Atle (ed.), *Proceedings of the Twelfth Sinn und Bedeutung Conference*. Oslo: ILOS.
Prince, Alan, and Smolensky, Paul. 1993. *Optimality Theory: Constraint Interaction in Generative Grammar*. Tech. rept. Rutgers University and University of Colorado. Published in 2004 by Blackwell.
Puig-Waldmüller, E. (ed.). 2007. *Proceedings of the Eleventh Sinn und Bedeutung Conference*. Barcelona: Universitat Pompeu Fabra.
Pullum, Geoffrey K. 1975. People deletion in English. In *Ohio State University Working Papers in Linguistics 18*. Columbus: The Ohio State University.
Pustejovsky, James. 1995. *The Generative Lexicon*. Cambridge, MA: MIT Press.
Pustejovsky, James, and Bouillon, Pierrette. 1995. Aspectual coercion and logical polysemy, *Journal of Semantics*, **12**(2), 133–162.
Putnam, Hilary. 1975. The meaning of 'meaning'. In *Philosophical Papers, vol. II: Mind, Language, and Reality*. Cambridge: Cambridge University Press.
Rapp, Irene, and von Stechow, Arnim. 1999. Fast 'almost' and the visibility parameter for functional adverbs. *Journal of Semantics*, **16**(2), 149–204.

Rawlins, Kyle. 2004/2008. Unifying 'illegally'. In Dölling, Johannes, and Heyde-Zybatow, Tatjana (eds.), *Event Structures in Linguistic Form and Interpretation*. Berlin: Walter de Gruyter.
  2010. On adverbs of (space and) time. Ms., Johns Hopkins University.
Reich, Ingo, Horch, Eva, and Pauly, Dennis (eds.). 2011. *Proceedings of the Fifteenth Sinn und Bedeutung Conference*. Saarbrücken: Saarland University Press.
Reinhart, Tanya. 1997. Quantifier scope: how labor is divided between QR and choice functions, *Linguistics and Philosophy*, 20(4), 335–397.
Rett, Jessica. 2006. How *many* maximizes in the Balkan Sprachbund. In Gibson, M., and Howell, J. (eds.), *Proceedings of Semantics and Linguistic Theory (SALT) 16*. Ithaca, NY: CLC Publications.
  2008a. Antonymy and evaluativity. In *Proceedings of Semantics and Linguistic Theory (SALT) 17*. Ithaca, NY: CLC Publications.
  2008b. Degree modification in natural language. Ph.D. thesis, Rutgers University.
  2010. Equatives, measure phrases and NPIs. In Aloni, Maria, Bastiaanse, Harald, de Jager, Tikitu, and Schulz, Katrin (eds.), *Logic, Language and Meaning*. Lecture Notes in Computer Science, vol. 6042. Berlin: Springer.
  2011a. Exclamatives, degrees and speech acts, *Linguistics and Philosophy*, 34, 411–442.
  2011b. The semantic significance of similatives. Ms., UCLA.
Rice, Keren. 1989. *A Grammar of Slave*. Berlin: Mouton de Gruyter.
Riester, Arndt, and Solstad, Torgrim (eds.). 2009. *Proceedings of the Thirteenth Sinn und Bedeutung Conference*. Online Publikationsverbund der Universität Stuttgart (OPUS).
Roberts, John R. 1987. *Amele*. London: Croom Helm.
Rooth, Mats. 1992. A theory of focus interpretation, *Natural Language Semantics*, 1(1), 75–116.
  1996. Focus. In Lappin, Shalom (ed.), *The Handbook of Contemporary Semantic Theory*. Oxford: Blackwell Publishing.
Rosch, Eleanor. 1973. On the internal structure of perceptual and semantic categories. In Moore, T. E. (ed.), *Cognitive Development and the Acquisition of Language*. New York: Academic Press.
Ross, John Robert. 1964. A partial grammar of English superlatives. M.Phil. thesis, University of Pennsylvania.
  1967. Constraints on variables in syntax. Ph.D. thesis, MIT.
  1970. On declarative sentences. In Rosenbaum, P. S., and Jacobs, R. A. (eds.), *Readings in English Transformational Grammar*. Waltham, MA: Ginn.
Rothstein, Susan (ed.). 1998. *Events and Grammar*. Dordrecht: Kluwer Academic.
Rothstein, Susan. 2010. Counting, measuring and the semantics of classifiers, *The Baltic International Yearbook of Cognition, Logic and Communication*, 6.

Rotstein, Carmen, and Winter, Yoad. 2004. Total adjectives vs. partial adjectives: scale structure and higher-order modifiers, *Natural Language Semantics*, **12**(3), 259–288.

Rullmann, Hotze. 1995. Maximality in the semantics of *wh*-constructions. Ph.D. thesis, University of Massachusetts Amherst.

Russell, Bertrand. 1905. On denoting, *Mind*, **14**, 479–493.

1923. Vagueness, *Australasian Journal of Philosophy and Psychology*, **1**, 84–92.

Rutkowski, Paweł, and Progovac, Ljiljana. 2005. Classification projection in Polish and Serbian: the position and shape of classifying adjectives. In Franks, Steven, Gladney, Frank Y., and Tasseva-Kurktchieva, Mila (eds.), *Formal Approaches to Slavic Linguistics 13: The South Carolina Meeting*. Ann Arbor: Michigan Slavic Publications.

Sadock, Jerrold M. 1974. *Toward a Linguistic Theory of Speech Acts*. New York: Academic Press.

1981. Almost. In Cole, Peter (ed.), *Radical Pragmatics*. New York: Academic Press.

Sæbø, Kjell Johan. 2009. Judgment ascriptions, *Linguistics and Philosophy*, **32**(4), 327–352.

2010. On the semantics of 'embedded exclamatives', *Studia Linguistica*, **64**(1), 116–140.

Sapir, Edward. 1944. Grading: a study in semantics, *Philosophy of Science*, **11**(2), 93–116.

Sassoon, Galit. 2007. The logic of typicality judgments. In Puig-Waldmüller (2007).

2010a. The degree functions of negative adjectives, *Natural Language Semantics*, **18**(2), 141–181.

2010b. Measurement theory in linguistics, *Synthese*, **174**(1), 151–180.

2010c. Restricted quantification over tastes. In Aloni, Maria, Bastiaanse, Harald, de Jager, Tikitu, and Schulz, Katrin (eds.), *Logic, Language and Meaning*. Lecture Notes in Computer Science, vol. 6042. Berlin: Springer.

2013a. A typology of multidimensional adjectives, *Journal of Semantics*, **30**(3), 335–380.

2013b. *Vagueness, Gradability, and Typicality: The Interpretation of Adjectives and Nouns*. Leiden: Brill.

Sauerland, Uli. 1998. The meaning of chains. Ph.D. thesis, MIT, Cambridge, MA.

Sauerland, Uli, and Stateva, Penka. 2007. Scalar vs. epistemic vagueness: evidence from approximators. In Gibson, Masayuki, and Friedman, Tova (eds), *Proceedings of Semantics and Linguistic Theory (SALT) 17*. Ithaca, NY: CLC Publications.

2011. Two types of vagueness. In Égré and Klinedinst (2011).

Sawada, Osamu. 2007. Pragmatic properties of the Japanese scalar reversal adverbs. Talk. Midwest Workshop on Semantics.

2010. Pragmatic aspects of scalar modifiers. Ph.D. thesis, University of Chicago.

2011. Comparison with indeterminateness: a multidimensional approach. In Lima, Suzi, Mullin, Kevin, and Smith, Brian (eds.), *Proceedings of the North East Linguistic Society (NELS) 39*. Amherst: GLSA Publications.

Sawada, Osamu, and Grano, Thomas. 2011. Scale structure, coercion, and the interpretation of measure phrases in Japanese, *Natural Language Semantics*, **19**(2), 191–226.

Schäfer, Martin. 2002. Pure manner adverbs revisited. In Katz, Graham, Reinhard, Sabine, and Reuter, Philip (eds.), *Proceedings of Sinn und Bedeutung 6*. University of Osnabrück, for Gesellschaft für Semantik.

2004. Manner adverbs and scope. In Steube, A. (ed.), *Grammatik und Kontext: Zur Interaktion von Syntax, Semantik und Prosodie bei der Informationsstrukturierung*. Linguistische Arbeitsberichte, vol. 81. Universität Leipzig.

2005. German adverbial adjectives: syntactic position and semantic interpretation. Ph.D. thesis, Universität Leipzig.

2008. Resolving scope in manner modification. In Bonami and Cabredo Hofherr (2008).

2007. On frequency adjectives. In Puig-Waldmüller (2007).

Schlenker, Philippe. 2003. A plea for monsters, *Linguistics and Philosophy*, **26**(1), 29–120.

2007. Expressive presuppositions, *Theoretical Linguistics*, **33**(2), 237–245.

Schwager, Magdalena. 2009. What is amazement all about? In Riester and Solstad (2009).

Schwarz, Bernhard. 2005. Modal superlatives. In Georgala, Effi, and Howell, Jonathan (eds.), *Proceedings of Semantics and Linguistic Theory (SALT) 15*. Ithaca, NY: CLC Publications.

2006. Attributive wrong. In Donald Baumer, David Montero, and Scanlon, Michael (eds.), *Proceedings of the West Coast Conference on Formal Linguistics (WCCFL) 25*. Somerville, MA: Cascadilla Press.

2007. Reciprocal equatives. In Puig-Waldmüller (2007).

Schwarzschild, Roger. 2005. Measure phrases as modifiers of adjectives. In *L'adjectif*. Recherches Linguistiques de Vincennes, vol. 34. Paris: Presses universitaires de Vincennes.

2006. The role of dimensions in the syntax of noun phrases, *Syntax*, **9**(1), 67–110.

2008. The semantics of comparatives and other degree constructions, *Language and Linguistics Compass*, **2**(2), 308–331.

Schwarzschild, Roger, and Wilkinson, Karina. 2002. Quantifiers in comparatives: a semantics of degree based on intervals. *Natural Language Semantics*, **10**(1), 1–41.

Scott, Gary-John. 2002. Stacked adjectival modification and the structure of nominal phrases. In Cinque, Guglielmo (ed.), *Functional Structure in the DP and IP: The Cartography of Syntactic Structures*. Oxford University Press.

Seuren, Pieter A. M. 1973. The Comparative. In Kiefer, Ferenc, and Ruwet, Nicolas (eds.), *Generative Grammar in Europe*. Dordrecht: Reidel.

1978. The Structure and Selection of Positive and Negative Gradable Adjectives. In Farkas, P., Jarobsen, W. J., and Todrys, K. (eds.), *Proceedings of the Chicago Linguistics Society (CLS) 14 (Parasession on the Lexicon)*.

Sevi, Aldo. 1998. A semantics for *almost* and *barely*. M.Phil. thesis, Tel-Aviv University.

Shaer, Benjamin. 2000. Syntactic position and the readings of 'manner' adverbs. In Lang, E., Holsinger, D., Schwabe, K., and Teuber, O. (eds.), *ZAS Papers in Linguistics 17*. Berlin: Zentrum fur Allgemeine Sprachwissenschaft.

2003. 'Manner' adverbs and the association theory: some problems and solutions. In Lang et al. (2003).

Sharvit, Yael, and Stateva, Penka. 2000. Against 'long' movement of the superlative operator. In Jackson, Brendan, and Matthews, Tanya (eds.), *Proceedings of Semantics and Linguistic Theory (SALT) 10*. Ithaca, NY: CLC Publications.

2002. Superlative expressions, context, and focus, *Linguistics and Philosophy*, **25**(4), 453–504.

Shimoyama, Junko. 2011a. Clausal comparatives and cross-linguistic variation. In Lima, Suzi, Mullin, Kevin, and Smith, Brian (eds.), *Proceedings of the North East Linguistic Society (NELS) 39*. Amherst: GLSA Publications.

2011b. Degree quantification and the size of noun modifiers. In McClure, William, and den Dikken, Marcel (eds.), *Japanese/Korean Linguistics 18*. Stanford: CSLI Publications.

2012. Reassessing crosslinguistic variation in clausal comparatives. *Natural Language Semantics*, **20**(1), 83–113.

Siegel, Muffy A. 1976a. Capturing the adjective. Ph.D. thesis, University of Massachusetts Amherst.

1976b. Capturing the Russian adjective. In Partee, Barbara H. (ed.), *Montague Grammar*. New York: Academic Press.

Sleeman, Petra. 2010. Superlative adjectives and the licensing of non-modal infinitival subject relatives. In Cabredo Hofherr and Matushansky (2010).

Smith, Carlota S. 1961. A class of complex modifiers in English, *Language*, **37**(3), 342–365.

1964. Determiners and relative clauses in a generative grammar of English, *Language*, **40**, 37–52. Reprinted in 1969, in *Modern Studies in English*, ed. D. A. Reibel and S. A. Schane, Englewood Cliffs, NJ: Prentice-Hall.

Snyder, William, Wexler, Ken, and Das, Dolon. 1995. The syntactic representation of degree and quantity: Perspectives from Japanese and child English. In Aranovich, Raúl, Byrne, William, Preuss, Suscurne, and Sentoria, Martha (eds.), *Proceedings of the West Coast Conference on Formal Linguistics (WCCFL) 13*. Stanford: CSLI Publications.

References

Solt, Stephanie. 2009. The semantics of adjectives of quantity. Ph.D. thesis, The City University of New York.
  2011a. Attributive quantity words as nonrestrictive modifiers. In Lima, Suzi, Mullin, Kevin, and Smith, Brian (eds.), *Proceedings of the North East Linguistic Society (NELS) 39*. Amherst: GLSA Publications.
  2011b. How many *mosts*? In Reich et al. (2011).
  2011c. Notes on the comparison class. In Nouwen et al. (2011b).
Sorensen, Roy. 2012. Vagueness. In Zalta, Edward N. (ed.), *The Stanford Encyclopedia of Philosophy*. Stanford: CSLI Publications.
Sportiche, Dominique. 1988. A theory of floating quantifiers and its corollaries for constituent structure, *Linguistic Inquiry*, **19**, 425–449.
Sproat, Richard, and Shih, Chilin. 1988. Prenominal adjectival ordering in English and Mandarin. In Blevins, J., and Carter, J. (eds.), *Proceedings of the North East Linguistic Society (NELS) 18*. Amherst: GLSA Publications.
Stalnaker, Robert. 1979. Assertion. In Cole, Peter (ed.), *Syntax and Semantics*, vol. 9. London: Academic Press.
Stanley, Jason. 2003. Context, interest relativity, and the sorites, *Analysis*, **63**(4), 269–280.
Stassen, Leon. 1984. The comparative compared, *Journal of Semantics*, **3**(1–2), 143–182.
  1985. *Comparison and Universal Grammar*. Oxford: Blackwell Publishing.
  2006. Comparative constructions. In Brown, Keith (ed.), *Encyclopedia of Language and Linguistics*, 2nd edn. Oxford: Elsevier.
Stephenson, Tamina. 2007a. Judge dependence, epistemic modals, and predicates of personal taste, *Linguistics and Philosophy*, **30**, 487–525.
  2007b. A parallel account of epistemic modals and predicates of personal taste. In Puig-Waldmüller (2007).
  2007c. Toward a theory of subjective meaning. Ph.D. thesis, MIT.
Stojanovic, Isidora. 2007. Talking about taste: disagreement, implicit arguments, and relative truth, *Linguistics and Philosophy*, **30**(6), 691–706.
Stump, Gregory T. 1981. The interpretation of frequency adjectives, *Linguistics and Philosophy*, **4**(2), 221–257.
  1985. *The Semantic Variability of Absolute Constructions*. Dordrecht: D. Reidel.
Svenonius, Peter. 1994. On the structural location of the attributive adjective. In Erin Duncan, Donka Farkas, and Spaelti, Philip (eds.), *Proceedings of the West Coast Conference on Formal Linguistics (WCCFL) 12*. Stanford: CSLI Publications.
  2008a. Complex predicates and the functional sequence. In *Tromsø Working Papers on Language & Linguistics: Nordlyd*, vol. 35. CASTL, Tromsø. Special issue on complex predication.
  2008b. The position of adjectives and other phrasal modifiers in the decomposition of DP. In McNally and Kennedy (2008).
Swanson, Eric. 2006. Interactions with context. Ph.D. thesis, MIT.
Szabolcsi, Anna. 1986. Comparative superlatives. *MIT Working Papers in Linguistics*, **8**, 245–265.

Tanaka, Takuro. 2006. Lexical decomposition and comparative structures for Japanese determiners. In Gibson, M., and Howell, J. (eds.), *Proceedings of Semantics and Linguistic Theory (SALT) 16*. Ithaca, NY: CLC Publications.

Teodorescu, Alexandra. 2006. Adjective ordering restrictions revisited. In Baumer, Donald, Montero, David, and Scanlon, Michael (eds.), *Proceedings of the West Coast Conference on Formal Linguistics (WCCFL) 25*. Somerville, MA: Cascadilla Press.

Thomason, Richmond, and Stalnaker, Robert C. 1973. A semantic theory of adverbs, *Linguistic Inquiry*, 4, 195–220.

Tonhauser, Judith. 2002. A dynamic semantic account of the temporal interpretation of noun phrases. In Jackson, Brendan (ed.), *Proceedings of Semantics and Linguistic Theory (SALT) 12*. Ithaca, NY: CLC Publications.

2005a. Towards an understanding of the meaning of nominal tense. In Maier, Emar, Bary, Corien, and Huitink, Janneke (eds.), *Proceedings of the Ninth Sinn und Bedeutung Conference*. Nijmegen centre for Semantics.

2005b. What is Nominal Tense? A case study of Paraguayan Guaraní. In Becker, Michael, and McKenzie, Andrew (eds.), *Proceedings of Semantics of Under-Represented Languages in the Americas (SULA) III*. University of Massachusetts Occasional Papers in Linguistics (UMOP). GLSA Publications.

2006. The temporal semantics of noun phrases: evidence from Guaraní. Ph.D. thesis, Stanford University.

Travis, Lisa. 1984. Parameters and effects of word order variation. Ph.D. thesis, MIT.

Truswell, Robert. 2004. Attributive adjectives and the nominals they modify. M.Phil. thesis, University of Oxford.

2005. Non-restrictive adjective interpretation and association with focus. In Ashdowne, Richard, and Finbow, Thomas (eds.), *Oxford Working Papers in Linguistics, Phonetics and Philology*, vol. 9. Oxford: Clarendon Press.

Truswell, Robert. 2009. Attributive adjectives and nominal templates, *Linguistic Inquiry*, 40(3), 525–533.

Tucker, A. N. and Tompo ole Mpaayi, J. 1955. *A Massai Grammar with Vocabulary*. London: Longrans.

Umbach, Carla. 2006. Non-restrictive modification and backgrounding. In Gyuris, Beáta, Kálmán, László, Piñón, Chris, and Varasdi, Károly (eds.), *Proceedings of the Ninth Symposium on Logic and Language*. Budapest: Research Institute for Linguistics, Hungarian Academy of Sciences Theoretical Linguistics Programme, Eötvös Loránd University.

Valois, Daniel. 2007. Adjectives: order within DP and attributive APs. In Everaert, Martin, and van Riemsdijk, Henk (eds.), *The Blackwell Companion to Syntax*. Malden, MA: Blackwell Publishing.

van Fraassen, Bas C. 1966. Singular terms, truth-value gaps, and free logic: A Handbook of Syntactic Case Studies. Oxford: *Journal of Philosophy*, **63**, 481–495.

van Gerrevink, Richard, and de Hoop, Helen. 2007. On the optimal use of *almost* and *barely* in argumentation. In Maria Aloni, Paul Dekker, and Roelofsen, Floris (eds.), *Proceedings of the Sixteenth Amsterdam Colloquium*. ILLC, University of Amsterdam.
van Rooij, Robert. 2008. Comparatives and quantifiers. In Bonami and Cabredo Hofherr (2008).
  2011a. Implicit versus explicit comparatives. In Égré and Klinedinst (2011).
  2011b. Vagueness and linguistics. In Ronzitti, Giuseppina (ed.), *Vagueness: A Guide*, vol. 19. Berlin: Springer.
  2011c. Measurement and interadjective comparisons. *Journal of Semantics*, 28(3), 335–358.
Vander Klok, Jozina. 2009. Adjectival Modification in Javanese. In Bochnak, Ryan, Nicola, Nassira, Klecha, Peter, Urban, Jasmin, Lemieux, Alice, and Weaver, Christina (eds.), *Proceedings of the Chicago Linguistic Society (CLS) 45*. Chicago Linguistics Society.
Vendler, Zeno. 1957. Verbs and times, *The Philosophical Review*, 66(2), 143–160.
  1967. *Linguistics in Philosophy*. Ithaca, NY: Cornell University Press.
Villalta, Elisabeth. 2007. Context dependence in the interpretation of questions and subjunctives. Ph.D. thesis, Universität Tübingen.
von Fintel, Kai. 1994. Restrictions on quantifier domains. Ph.D. thesis, University of Massachusetts Amherst.
von Fintel, Kai, and Heim, Irene. 1999. More on lousy teachers and beautiful dancers. Lecture notes, MIT.
von Stechow, Arnim. 1984. Comparing semantic theories of comparison, *Journal of Semantics*, 3, 1–77.
  2005. *Temporal comparatives: früher 'earlier'/später 'later'*. Handout for a talk presented at the workshops 'Tense and Mood' in Stuttgart and 'QP structure, nominalizations , and the role of DP' in Saarbrücken.
von Stechow, Arnim, and Wunderlich, Dieter (eds.). 1991. *Semantik: Ein internationales handbuch der zeitgenössischen forschung (Semantics: An International Handbook of Contemporary Research)*. Berlin: Walter de Gruyter.
Warotamasikkhadhik, U. 1972. *Thai Syntax*: The Hague: Mouton.
Wellwood, Alexis, Hacquard, Valentine, and Pancheva, Roumyana. 2012. Measuring and comparing individuals and events, *Journal of Semantics*, 29(2), 207–228.
Westerståhl, Dag. 1985. Determiners and context sets. In van Bentham, Johan, and ter Meulen, Alice (eds.), *Generalized Quantifiers in Natural Language*. Dordrecht: Foris.
Wheeler, Samuel C. 1972. Attributives and their modifiers, *Noûs*, 6(4), 310–334.
Williamson, Timothy. 1994. *Vagueness*. London: Routledge.
Winter, Yoad. 1997. Choice functions and the scopal semantics of indefinites. *linguistics and philosophy*, 20(4), 399–467.

2001. Measure phrase modification in vector space semantics. In Megerdoomian, Karine, and Bar-el, Leora A. (eds.), *Proceedings of the West Coast Conference on Formal Linguistics (WCCFL) 20*. Somerville, MA: Cascadilla Press.

2005. Cross-categorial restrictions on measure phrase modification, *Linguistics and Philosophy*, **28**(2), 233–267.

Wunderlich, Dieter. 1991. How do prepositional phrases fit into compositional syntax and semantics? *Linguistics*, 29, 591–621.

Wyner, Adam. 1994. Boolean event lattices and thematic roles in the syntax and semantics of adverbial modification. Ph.D. thesis, Cornell University.

1998. Subject-oriented adverbs are thematically dependent. In Rothstein (1998).

2008. Toward flexible types with constraints for manner and factive adverbs. In McNally and Kennedy (2008).

Xiang, Ming. 2003. A phrasal analysis of Chinese comparatives. In *Proceedings of the Chicago Linguistics Society (CLS) 39*. Chicago Linguistic Society.

2005. Some topics in comparative constructions. Ph.D. thesis, Michigan State University.

Xie, Zhiguo. 2010. The other pole of degree modification of gradable nouns by size adjectives: a Mandarin Chinese perspective. In *Proceedings of the 12th International Symposium on Chinese Languages and Linguistics*. Taipei: Academia Sinica.

Yalcin, Seth. 2007. Epistemic modals, *Mind*, **116**(464), 983–1026.

Yoon, Suwon. 2011. Rhetorical comparatives: polarity items, expletive negation, and subjunctive mood, *Journal of Pragmatics*, **43**(7), 2012–2033.

Yoon, Youngeun. 1996. Total and partial predicates and the weak and strong interpretations, *Natural Language Semantics*, 4(3), 217–236.

Zadeh, L. A. 1965. Fuzzy sets, *Information and Control*, 8, 338–353.

1983. A fuzzy-set-theoretic approach to the compositionality of meaning: propositions, dispositions and canonical forms, *Journal of Semantics*, 2(3-4), 253–272.

Zamparelli, Roberto. 1995. Layers in the determiner phrase. Ph.D. thesis, University of Rochester. (As revised in 2000.)

Zanuttini, Raffaella, and Portner, Paul. 2003. Exclamative clauses: at the syntax–semantics interface, *Language*, **79**(1), 39–81.

Zaroukian, Erin. 2011. Divergent approximators. In Reich et al. (2011).

2013. Quantification and (un)certainty. Ph.D. thesis, Johns Hopkins University, Baltimore.

Zimmermann, Malte. 2000. Pluractional quantifiers: The *occasional* construction in English and German. In Jackson, Brendan, and Matthews, Tanya (eds.), *Proceedings of Semantics and Linguistic Theory (SALT) 10*. Ithaca, NY: CLC Publications.

References

2003. Pluractionality and complex quantifier formation, *Natural Language Semantics*, **11**(3), 249–287.

Zwarts, Joost. 1997. Vectors as relative positions: a compositional semantics of modified PPs, *Journal of Semantics*, **14**(1), 57–86.

Zwarts, Joost, and Winter, Yoad. 2000. Vector space semantics: a model-theoretic analysis of locative prepositions, *Journal of Logic, Language and Information*, **9**, 171–213.

Zwicky, Arnold M. 1970. Usually and unusually. *Linguistic Inquiry*, **1**(1).

Zwicky, Arnold, and Sadock, Jerrold. 1975. Ambiguity tests and how to fail them. In Kimball, John P. (ed.), *Syntax and Semantics*, vol. IV. New York: Academic Press.

1984. A reply to Martin on ambiguity, *Journal of Semantics*, **3**(3), 249–256.

Index

absolute, 174
absolute adjectives, 136
absolute constructions, 224
Adjective Type Heterogeneity Hypothesis, 37, 38, 41, 42
Adjective Type Homogeneity Hypothesis, 27, 41, 51, 51
adnominal degree modifiers, 18, 57
adverbial readings of adjectives, 59–79
adverbs, manner, 36
ambiguity, 91
amount, 258
amount comparatives, 255
analytic, 178
antisymmetric, 111
antonymy, 124
appositives, 267
approximative, 263
approximators, 263
as-phrases, 22
associative adjectives, 49
atelic, 243
Athabaskan languages, 81
attributive adjective, 14
attributive-with-infinitive construction, 56
average, 68

Bach, Emmon, 45
Barker, Chris, 74
beautiful dancer, 18
Beck, Sigrid, 74
big DegP view, 157
big idiot, 18, 57
big mouse, 20
Boleda Torrent, Gemma, 49
borderline cases, 90

cardinality, 251
Catalan, 49
Chomsky, Noam, 68
classificatory adjectives, 18, 49
closed scale, 132
coercion, 55
comparative, 174
comparative clause, 150
comparative deletion, 151
comparative ellipsis, 151
comparative subdeletion, 151
comparison class, 21–22, 102
comparison of deviation, 181
conflicting-intensity anomaly, 142
conjoined comparative, 187
contextual extreme adjectives, 142
contextualism, 101
conventional implicatures, 234, 268
cross-polar anomaly, 126

DE DICTO, 199
DE RE, 199
Degree Abstraction Parameter, 190
degree achievements, 259
degree arguments, 109
degree constructions, 118, 150
degree functions, 108
degree modifiers, 119
degree morphemes, 150
degree words, 119, 150
degree-based theories, 97
degrees, 109
dense, 111
diamond entailment pattern, 203
different, 74
differential comparatives, 171
dimension, 111

Index 331

dimensional, 138
direct analysis, 190
direct modification, 82
discourse anaphoric reading, 74
discourse topic, 224
Discourse Representation Theory, 78, 217
discourse-oriented adverbials, 228
Doublet Theory, 30
downward-entailing environments, 169
droppable, 203

ellipsis, 152
entailment-based, 44
entire, 77
epistemic adjectives, 78
epistemic adverbs, 196
epistemic view, 96
equatives, 150
evaluative, 138, 183
evaluative adverbs, 196, 233
event adverbials, 195
Event Identification, 218 n12
events, 37, 205
exceed comparative, 188
excessive construction, 150
expressive meaning, 269
extension gap, 100
external modifiers, 237
extreme adjectives, 141
extreme degree modifiers, 141

factor phrases, 173
fake gun, 24
faultless disagreement, 271
floated quantifiers, 171
focus, 84, 152
former, 45
for-phrases, 22
frame-setting adverbials, 196, 238
framing, 196
frequency adjectives, 46, 60
future, 45
fuzzy logic, 98
Fuzzy-logic theories, 97

generalized Quantifier Theory, 254
generalizing to the worst case, 28

generic reading, 61
genericity, 37
genitives, 47
gradable adjectives, 90

hedges, 263
Higgins, Roger, 17
higher-order, 27
higher-order vagueness, 121
homophony, 30

imprecise, 94
imprecision, 179
incommensurability, 100, 122, 180
indirect comparison, 181
indirect modification, 82
individual-level, 83
inherent-vagueness theories, 97
integrated, 267
intensional adjectives, 22
internal modifiers, 238
internal reading, 60
intersective, 197
intersective adjectives, 14–15, 20–22
intersective modification, 10, 14–15
intervals, 158

Japanese, 152
judge, 271

Kamp, Hans, 45
Kennedy, Chris, 69
Kusumoto, Kiyomi, 45

Landman, Meredith, 41
Larson, Richard, 45
lexical, 258
lexical extreme adjectives, 142
linear, 111
locational comparatives, 188
long-form adjective (Russian), 30
Louise McNally, 48

manner adverbials, 195
manner adverbs, 36
Mapping Hypothesis, 41
maximality modifiers, 134
measure functions, 110
measure phrase, 94
metalinguistic comparatives, 178

metalinguistic negation, 178
metaphysics, 68
modal adjectives, 22
modal adverbs, 235
modality, 22, 165, 236
monotonicity, 115
Montague, Richard, 28

natural language metaphysics, 68
necessity, 165
negative adjective, 124
negative extension, 100
negative polarity items (NPIs), 236
neo-Davidsonian, 213
neutralization, 184
Niger-Congo languages, 81
nominal appositives, 269
nominal comparatives, 255
non-dimensional, 138
non-local reading, 60
non-subsective adjective, 22
Non-vacuity Principle, 54
nonrestrictive, 267
norm-related, 183
notionally-based, 44
NP-dependent reading, 74
number words, 253

old friend, 18
ontological vagueness, 96
ontology, 68
open scale, 132
Optimality Theory, 55
ordering relation, 110
ordering source, 144

parasitic scope, 72–77
parentheticals, 267
Partee, Barbara, 25, 45
partial, 136
particle comparatives, 187
passive sensitivity, 208
performative, 229
Performative Hypothesis, 229, 231
permission, 165
perspective scale, 143
philosophy of language, 68
phrasal comparatives, 151
polarity phenomena, 236
polysemy, 93

positive, 124
positive extension, 100
positive form, 105, 150
positive polarity items (PPIs), 236
positive-entailing, 184
possessives, 47
pragmatic adverbials, 228
pragmatic halo, 95, 180
pragmatic slack, 94
precisification, 103
Predicate Abstraction Rule, 7n1
Predicate Modification Rule, 15
  in terms of sets, 15
predicate modifier, 10, 26, 197
predicates of personal taste, 271
predicational adverbs, 195
predicative, 14
predicative adjective, 24
privative adjectives, 24–26
proportional modifiers, 132
proximative, 263
pseudo-adjectives, 49
psycholinguistics, 55

Quantifier Raising, 59, 76, 161
quantity adjectives, 252

ratio phrases, 173
reciprocal reading, 74
reference, 68
referential opacity, 200
reflexive, 111
regions, 237
relational adjectives, 18, 49
relative adjectives, 136
resource domain variable, 175
restrictive, 267
resultative adverbs, 195
Russian, 30

same, 74
scale, 110
sentence adverbials, 196
short-form adjective (Russian), 30
Siegel, Muffy, 30
size adjectives, 18
skillful surgeon, 17
slack regulators, 263
Slave language (Athabaskan), 81
small DegP view, 157

Index

small elephant, 20
sorites paradox, 89
sorites sequence, 90
sort, 214
Spanish, 49
speaker-oriented adverbials, 196
speech-act adverbs, 196
speech-act adverbials, 228
stage-level, 83
standard, 113
standard marker, 150
standard of comparison, 150
standards, 21–22
Stanley, Jason, 69
states, 214
subcomparatives, 151
subject-oriented adverbs, 195
subsective, 17
subsective adjectives, 16–22
sufficiency construction, 150
superfalse, 103
supertrue, 103
supervaluation, 103
supplements, 267
synthetic, 178

telic, 244
telicity, 243
temporal-ordering adjectives, 46
thematic-role predicate, 211
tolerance, 90
Tonhauser, Judith, 45
total, 136
totally ordered, 111
transitive, 111
truth-value gap, 100

undisclosed, 78
unselective quantifiers, 245
unknown, 78
utterance-modifying adverbials, 228

vagueness, 21–22, 89–124
Vata language (Niger-Congo), 81
vector space, 238
vectors, 238
very, 119

whole, 77
Wilkinson, Karina, 18

zeugma, 92

Lightning Source UK Ltd.
Milton Keynes UK
UKHW020444240719
346718UK00018B/298/P

9 780521 264167